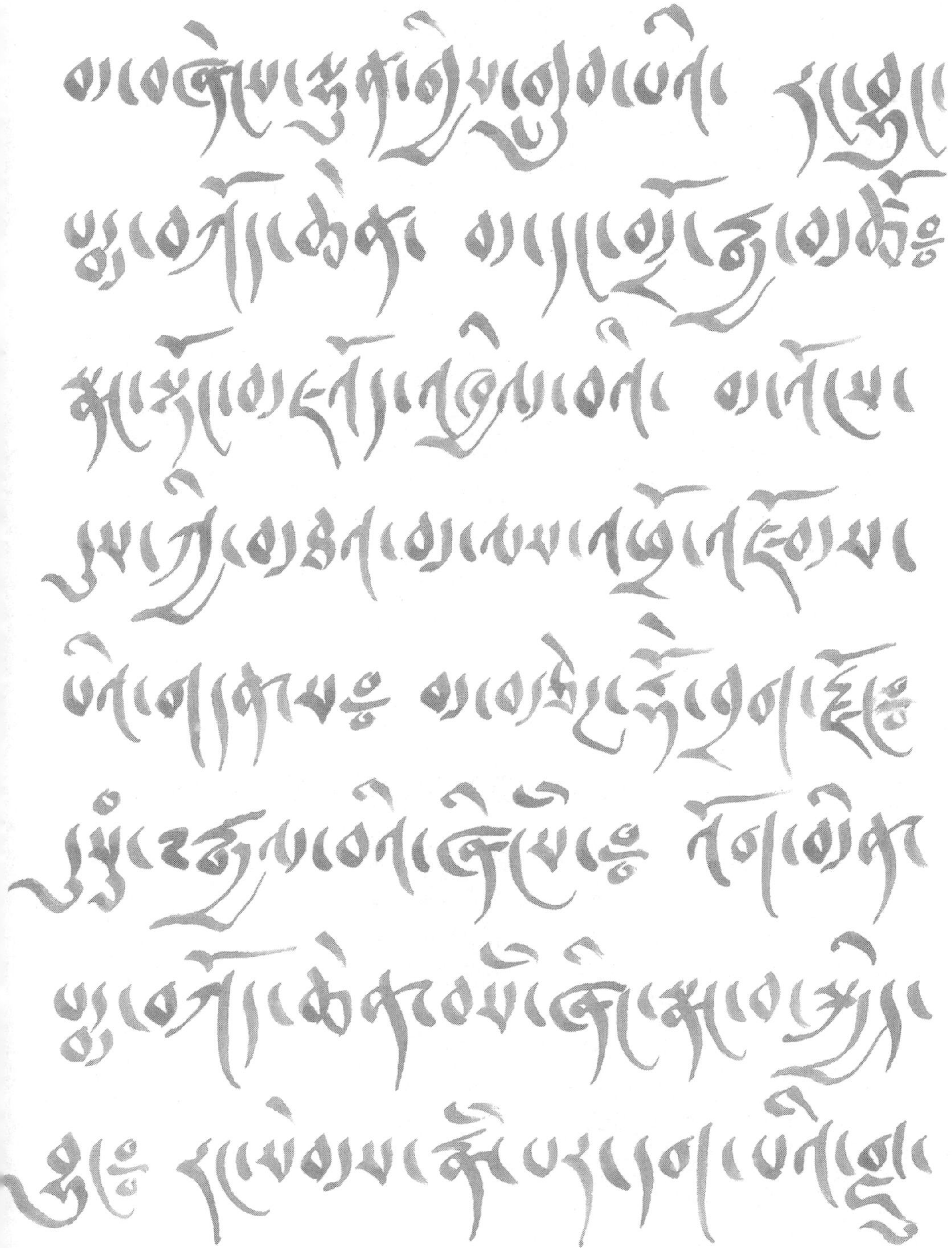

As far as the western world was concerned, [we] were exploring country of which nothing was known, but much was speculated; one of the last remaining secret places of the earth, which might conceal a fall rivaling the Niagra or Victoria Falls in grandeur.

LIEUTENANT-COLONEL F. M. BAILEY, 1913[1]

THE

HEART

OF

THE

WORLD

Mountains lie all about, with many difficult turns leading here and there. The trails run up and down; we are martyred with obstructing rocks. No matter how well we keep the path, if we miss one single step, we shall never know safe return. But whoever has the good fortune to penetrate that wilderness, for his labors will gain a beatific reward, for he shall find there his heart's delight. The wilderness abounds in whatsoever the ears desire to hear, whatsoever would please the eye: so that no one could possibly wish to be anywhere else. And this I well know; for I have been there.

GOTTFRIED VON STRASSBURG, *Tristan and Isolde*

The hagiographic myth of a spiritual journey through material difficulties to the attainment of divine grace would become a paradigm of travel to haunt posterity . . . by promising the ideal as the ultimate goal . . . it served as that purely mythic and always unachievable paradigm located in our historical memory, by contrast with which all human traveling—whatever its achievements and successes—can never transcend the abysm of futility.

JAS ELSNER AND JOAN-PAU RUBIES,
Voyages & Visions

There have always been two kinds of arcadia: shaggy and smooth; dark and light; a place of bucolic leisure and a place of primitive panic . . . the idyllic as well as the wild.

SIMON SCHAMA, *Landscape and Memory*

The Heart of the World

A Journey to the Last Secret Place

IAN BAKER

Introduction by His Holiness the Dalai Lama

THE PENGUIN PRESS ❀ NEW YORK 2004

THE PENGUIN PRESS
Published by the Penguin Group * Penguin Group (USA) Inc., 375 Hudson Street, New York, New York 10014,
U.S.A. * Penguin Group (Canada), 10 Alcorn Avenue, Toronto, Ontario, Canada M4V 3B2 (a division of Pearson
Penguin Canada Inc.) * Penguin Books Ltd, 80 Strand, London WC2R 0RL, England * Penguin Ireland, 25 St.
Stephen's Green, Dublin 2, Ireland (a division of Penguin Books Ltd) * Penguin Books Australia, 250 Camberwell
Road, Camberwell, Victoria 3124, Australia (a division of Pearson Australia Group Pty Ltd) * Penguin Books
India Pvt Ltd, 11 Community Centre, Panchsheel Park, New Delhi – 110 017, India * Penguin Group (NZ), Cnr
Airborne and Rosedale Roads, Albany, Auckland, New Zealand (a division of Pearson New Zealand Ltd)
* Penguin Books (South Africa) (Pty) Ltd, 24 Sturdee Avenue, Rosebank, Johannesburg 2196, South Africa

Penguin Books Ltd, Registered Offices:
80 Strand, London WC2R 0RL, England

First published 2004 by The Penguin Press,
a member of Penguin Group (USA) Inc.

1   3   5   7   9   10   8   6   4   2

Photograph credits appear on page 512

LIBRARY OF CONGRESS CATALOGING IN PUBLICATION DATA
Baker, Ian, 1957–
The heart of the world : a journey to the last secret place / Iaan Baaker ; introduction by His
Holiness the Dalai Lama.
p   cm.
Includes bibliographical references and index.
ISBN 1-59420-027-0
1. Tsango Gorges (China)—Discovery and exploration.   2. Tsangpo Gorges Region
(China)—Description and travel.   I. Title.
DS786.B255 2004
915.1'5—dc22   2004053476

This book is printed on acid-free paper. ∞

Printed in the United States of America

Designed by Marysarah Quinn

For the Unbound . . .

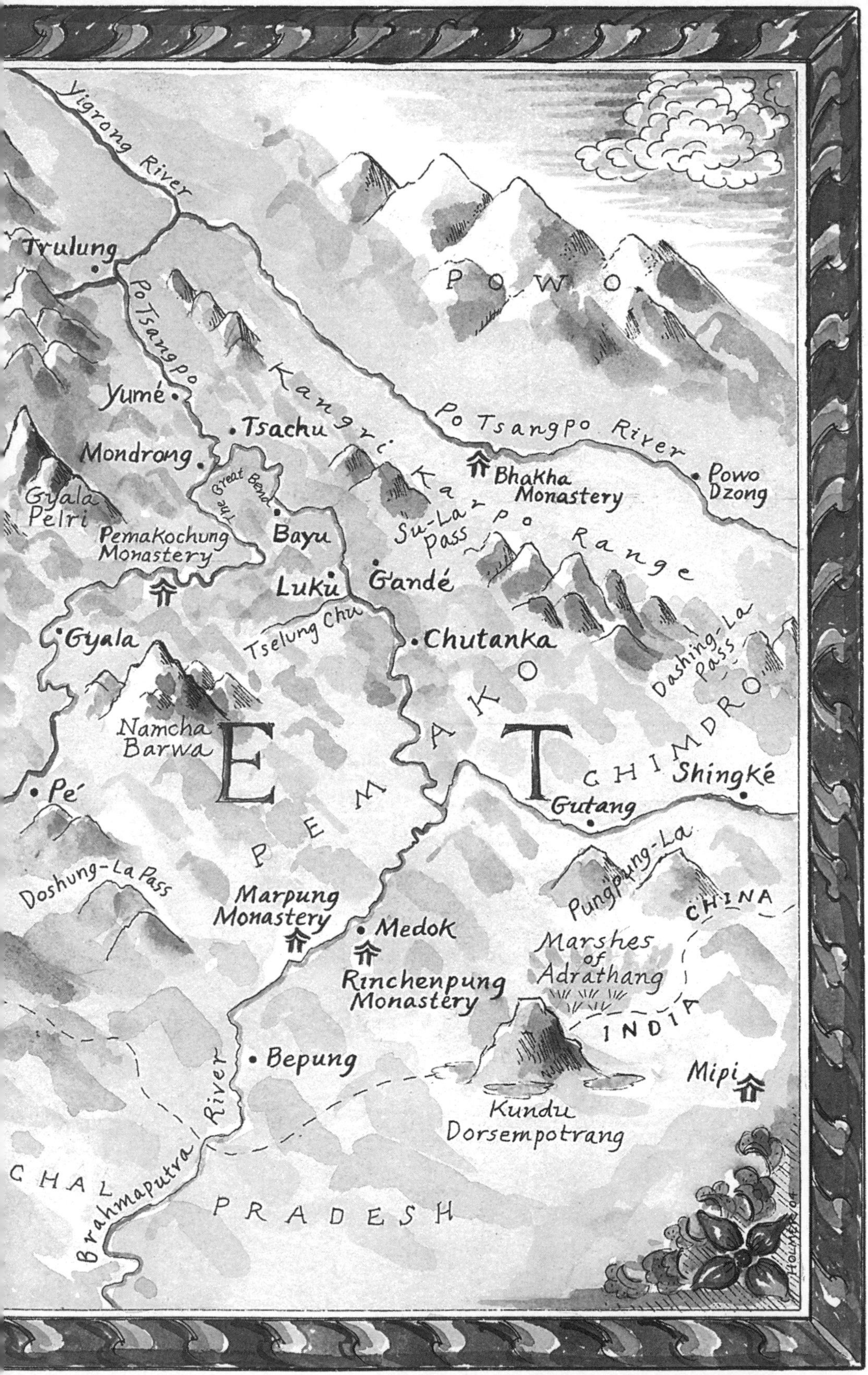

Yigrong River
Trulung
Po Tsangpo
Yumé
Tsachu
Mondrong
The Great Bend
Gyala Pelri
Pemakochung Monastery
Bayu
Luku
Gandé
Gyala
Tselung Chu
Chutanka
Namcha Barwa
Pé
Doshung-La Pass
Marpung Monastery
Medok
Rinchenpung Monastery
Bepung
Brahmaputra River
CHAL
PRADESH
POWO
Kangri Karpo Range
Po Tsangpo River
Bhakha Monastery
Powo Dzong
Su-La pass
Dashing-La Pass
CHIMDRO
PEMAKO
ET
Shingké
Gutang
Pungpung-La
CHINA
Marshes of Adrathang
INDIA
Kundu Dorsempotrang
Mipi

In the borderlands between Tibet and India, in the land of savages, lies Pemako, the supreme of all hidden-lands. This lotus realm is described as the body of Dorje Pagmo with five chakras . . . the cloud and ocean like gathering places of dakas and dakinis. There is a constant menace here from poisonous snakes, leeches, flies, clawed and long-snouted animals with fangs, dangerous wildmen, and vicious savages. One can easily succumb to fever and gout, while blisters, abscesses, ulcers, and sores add to the physical obstacles. The land is full of mischievous spirits [that] . . . constantly display magic and miracles. Those without courage; or those with lingering doubts, too many mental conceptions, or who are strongly attached to the appearances of this life or who . . . out of ignorance, fall into accepting and rejecting . . . such people will have difficulty reaching this land and getting through unscathed. When observed in their essential nature, all the mountains, rocks, trees, and rivers [here] appear as magical realms or deities. . . . Those obstructed by spiritual transgressions can never enter this great mandala.

LELUNG SHEPE DORJE
The Delightful True Stories of the Supreme Land of Pemako, 1729

Not only is Pemako extraordinarily difficult to reach from any direction, it is still more difficult to penetrate and explore when reached. Surrounded on three sides by the gorges of the Tsangpo, the fourth is blocked by mighty ranges of snow mountains, whose passes are only open for a few months in the year. Beyond these immediate barriers to east and west and south, are dense trackless forests, inhabited by wild unfriendly tribes. . . . Add to this . . . a climate which varies from the sub-tropical to arctic, the only thing common to the whole region being perpetual rain, snakes and wild animals, giant stinging nettles and myriads of biting and blood-sucking ticks, hornets, flies and leeches, and you have some idea of what the traveler has to contend with.

FRANK KINGDON WARD
The Riddle of the Tsangpo Gorges, 1925

Although we are accustomed to separate nature and human perception
into two realms, they are, in fact indivisible . . . landscape is the work

of the mind. Its scenery is built as much from strata of memory as from layers of rock.
SIMON SCHAMA, *Landscape and Memory*

Preface

IN A HISTORY OF EXPLORATION along the Tibetan frontier, a British field officer wrote of the futile quest for the Falls of the Tsangpo, a colossal water-fall long dreamed of by Victorian geographers. The author invoked a menacing deity that appears to pilgrims from behind a veil of water at the entrance to Tibet's Tsangpo gorge. This shape-shifting cascade, the author wrote, had lured generations of explorers into a quixotic—and often fatal—search for a numinous waterfall in the depths of the earth's deepest chasm. As the author concluded, Shinje Chogyal—the Lord of Death—"had not yet finished his sport with those disposed to listen to his siren-song." Had they been listening, he maintained, "they might have heard . . . demon laughter borne to them on the wind."[1] This book is a tribute to that ambiguous laughter, an exploration of the forces, internal and external, that led me and others to attend to the hidden voices of the Tsangpo gorge; the perennial call of unknown, secret places.

From ill-fated forays in the early nineteenth century through a final gambit in 1924, British explorers sought doggedly for a "spectacular cataract" to account for the tremendous drop in altitude from where the Tsangpo—one of Asia's greatest and least known rivers—disappeared into an impenetrable chasm in Tibet and where it reemerged 11,000 feet lower as the Brahmaputra in the jungles of Assam. Lured by the prospect of a geographical grail to claim for their expanding empire, turn-of-the-century explorers envisioned the fabled Falls of the Tsangpo as a rival to Victoria Falls, a symbol of imperial power in the deepest heart of Africa.

Long before the legendary waterfall was even imagined, Tibetans followed mystical prophecies into the labyrinth of the Tsangpo gorge—three times the depth of the Grand Canyon—in search of the heart of an earthly paradise called Beyul Pemako, the Secret Land Shaped Like a Lotus.

FROM APRIL 1993 TO NOVEMBER 1998 I made eight journeys into the mist-wreathed gorges of the Tsangpo, following the accounts of early British explorers as well as the visionary narratives of Tibetan lamas who had entered the region centuries earlier. This book chronicles my first and last expeditions as well as a pilgrimage in August 1995 to a mountain thought to conceal the key to Pemako's still undiscovered sanctum sanctorum. As I navigated between wild topography and dizzying myth, each journey opened the door to the next and revealed realms beyond the coordinates of conventional geography. Through historical digressions and extensive endnotes, I have tried to place in context the experiences that ultimately led me and my companions to the lost Falls of the Tsangpo, a place historians of exploration had previously dismissed as a "romance of geography" and "one of the most obsessive wild goose chases of modern times."

Tibetans still search the Tsangpo gorges for the elusive sanctuary that their texts describe as "a celestial realm on earth." The Falls of the Tsangpo, one of several portals into this mysterious domain, was not a goal in itself, but a place of passage, a doorway—whether literal or figurative—to a hidden realm of mind and spirit. For the pilgrim, Pemako's elusive center is not some lost and unattainable Eden, but an eminent paradise veiled more by habits of perception than by features of the landscape.

Lying along a suture between continents that collided more than forty million years ago, Pemako is far more than a source of the legend of Shangri-La.

The Tsangpo gorges present an ecosystem of astounding diversity, from ice falls and subtropical jungles to rare medicinal plants. Like the visionary scrolls that urge their readers into this beautiful terrain, Pemako's orchid-drenched cloud forests and moss-covered cliffs offer doorways for pilgrims into spaces of mysterious promise, to a world unfallen, where some of the deepest dreams of the earth and our species are still vibrantly alive.

As I followed the accounts of Tibetan pilgrims, as well as those of Victorian and Edwardian explorers, Pemako became for me a realm of unbounded possibility, a place where geographical exploration merged with discoveries of the spirit. This book celebrates those who have journeyed into the gorges, not to extract trophies or make dubious claims, but in the deepest spirit of adventure, attentive to the hidden voices of this mythic world. In 1925 the intrepid plant collector Frank Kingdon Ward wrote of his own journey that: "I am fully conscious that a complete presentation of the regions visited is a task beyond my power. All I can strive to do is convey an illusion—my own illusion, if you like—which nothing short of a visit to the great gorge of the Tsangpo can dispel . . ."

MANY TIBETAN LAMAS, SCHOLARS, and artists inspired the journeys that comprise this book. In 1977 Kappa Kalden introduced me through his paintings to other ways of experiencing mountains and rivers. In Sikkim in 1982, Sonam Denjongpa enthralled me with stories of Tibet's hidden-lands and, several years later, the scholar Tashi Tsering plied me with obscure and poetical texts that described them in surreal detail. Chatral Sangye Dorje Rinpoche encouraged me to discover the qualities of beyul firsthand by spending months in remote Himalayan caves, while Bhakha Tulku Rinpoche regaled me with accounts of his own journeys through Pemako, the least accessible and most renowned of these hidden-lands. In 1987 Khamtrul Rinpoche described to me his own journey through the Tsangpo gorges and his visions in the dark cataract of Shinje Chogyal, the "demon falls" responsible for the legend of a monumental cascade in the depths of the Tsangpo gorge. Tulku Pema Wangyal later recounted how his father, Kanjur Rinpoche, had passed through an uncharted waterfall during his search for Chimé Yangsang Né, Pemako's innermost sanctuary. This book is dedicated to the long and propitious lives of these great beings.

On my first journey to Pemako thanks are due especially to Rick Fisher for organizing the expedition and to the Chinese geologists of Mountains & Rivers Special Tours for allowing us to proceed beyond the limits of our permits. On subsequent expeditions special mention is due to Robert Parenteau, a lapsed Taoist and climbing partner from college days, and his intrepid fiancée, Karen Kung, who charmed potential obstructers with her knowledge of Mandarin; Laura Ide for preparing beds of Tibetan sheepskins when our sleeping bags were stolen by Khampa brigands; Gil and Troy Gillenwater for accounts of menacing serpents and eye-adhering leeches; Dr. Oy Kanjanavanit, authority on rainforest ecology, for her knowledge of edible mushrooms, wild ginger, and banana flowers when we were running out of food; Kawa Tulku who, while searching for a vision-inducing plant called *tsakuntuzangpo*, convinced some of us to eat purple flowers growing in a high-altitude marsh; Christian Kuypers for miraculously surviving a headlong plunge into boulders and sheared bamboo when a rain-drenched trail collapsed from under him; Pemba Sherpa for fashioning a bivouac in a leech-infested jungle when rain and night descended while we were far from camp; Ralph Rynning who, while recording a fire-tailed sunbird, nearly stepped on a nest of pit vipers, yet had the presence of mind to take a photograph; "Lama" of Solu Khumbu—who preferred to walk barefoot—for performing *riwosangchod* and other Buddhist rites when successful passage required more than satellite maps and good boots; Ani Rigsang, yogini of Terdrom, for her companionship and insight into the essence of pilgrimage; Ken Storm for sharing an enduring passion for the earth's wildest places; and Hamid Sardar for being convinced, as I am, that Yangsang is more than a myth.

Immeasurable thanks also to Namkha Drimed Rinpoche for his visionary account of his journey through Pemako in the wake of Tibet's Communist invasion; Jigme Rinpoche, the reincarnation of a revered Pemako lama, for his insight into the nature of Pemako's secret topography; as well as Lama Rinchen, Dugu Choegyal Rinpoche, Peko Jedrung Rinpoche, Lama Dawa, Khetsun

Sangpo Rinpoche, and Lama Ugyen for their perspectives regarding the key to Pemako's still undiscovered realms. Special thanks also to Palmo, Sonam, Pede, and Tseyang for their mystic *lingdro* dances and guidance into the living spirit of Pemako's exile community in Jeerong, Orissa; Father Giles of Pluscarden Abbey in Scotland and the Dowager Countess Cawdor of Cawdor Castle for reflections on the Western quest for an earthly paradise while perusing the journals which the late Earl of Cawdor had kept during his journey through the Tsangpo gorge; Peter Miller, Rebecca Martin, and others at National Geographic's Expeditions Council, for taking an interest in a then little-known part of the world and sponsoring our final expedition, and Barbara Moffet, Maryanne Culpepper, Bryan Harvey, Caryn Davidson, and others at National Geographic for ensuring that the region no longer remained unknown; and, not least, to the Chinese Academy of Sciences and Tibet's Forestry Department for their efforts to protect Pemako's unique environment from the ravages of tourism and hydroelectric development. Incalculable gratitude also goes to Scott Moyers, friend and editor at The Penguin Press for his vision, encouragement, and patience, and to Francis L. Kellogg—cousin and ambassador-at-large—for allowing me to complete the draft manuscript at his eighteenth-century Mill House that overlooks a small waterfall tumbling over a rock ledge. Thanks to Ulrich and Heidi von Schroeder for making available images of Tibetan deities still resident in Tibet, to Phuntsok Dhumkhang for his fluent calligraphy, and Erik Pema Kunsang for his contributions to the glossary. Thanks also to my loving and supportive parents and, in diverse ways, to Yeshe Dorje, Victor Chan, Charles Ramble, Jeff Greenwald, Steve Currey, William McGowan, Ann Godoff, Kate Condax, Robert Youdelman, Owen Laster, Robin Needham, Ken Cox, Brian Gregg, George Schaller, Shelley and Donald Rubin, Richard Pegg, Carroll Dunham, Kate Armstrong, Peter Matthiessen, Jamuna Devi, and innumerable others.

Greatest thanks of all goes to the lamas, villagers, and hunters of the Tsangpo gorges—some of whose names I have changed in the narrative to protect their identity—who led the way through pathless jungles and across rusted cables and rotten logs, entrusting us with knowledge of their secret, uncharted places. And to the visionary lamas of earlier centuries who entered Pemako's forbidding wilderness without fear, hope, or hesitation and saw beyond the veils of common vision. These *terton*, or treasure revealers, discovered in the Tsangpo gorges a place of transformation and inspired others to travel beyond conventional limits—to imagine worlds, and selves, without boundaries or walls.

All incidents and occurrences throughout the book are strictly factual; any resemblance to fiction is purely coincidental. The one exception is the timing and precise content of conversations that occurred between team members. These have been reconstructed to the best of my recollection and verified with the concerned individuals. In certain instances, names have been changed to protect privacy. For ease of pronunciation, Tibetan words have been transliterated phonetically, rather than in accordance with scholarly convention. Thus *sbas-yul* becomes beyul, *Pema-bkod* becomes Pemako, *gnas* becomes né, etc. Diacritical marks for Sanskrit words have been similarly omitted. A glossary and key to the illustrations are provided at the back of the book.

IAN BAKER
Norbu Dzong
Kathmandu
March 2004
Year of the Wood Monkey

Padmasambhava, revealer of Tibet's hidden-lands

Contents

Introduction

Centuries ago, texts were discovered in Tibet describing beyul, hidden-lands where the essence of the Buddhist Tantras is said to be preserved for future generations. These revered scriptures are attributed to Padmasambhava, the eighth-century Buddhist adept celebrated as Guru Rinpoche, who helped to establish Buddhism in Tibet. They describe valleys reminiscent of paradise that can only be reached with enormous hardship. Pilgrims who travel to these wild and distant places often recount extraordinary experiences similar to those encountered by spiritual practitioners on the Buddhist path to Liberation.

One of the most renowned of these hidden-lands lies in the region of the Tsangpo gorges in southeastern Tibet. It is called Beyul Pemako, "the hidden land shaped like a lotus." Many pilgrims have journeyed there in search of its innermost sanctuary. From a Buddhist perspective, sacred environments such as Pemako are not places to escape the world, but to enter it more deeply. The qualities inherent in such places reveal the interconnectedness of all life and deepen awareness of hidden regions of the mind and spirit. Visiting such places with a good motivation and appropriate merit, the pilgrim can learn to see the world differently from the way it commonly appears, developing and enhancing the Buddhist virtues of wisdom and compassion.

Whether this mysterious sanctuary hidden amid Pemako's mist-shrouded mountains can ever be located geographically is of secondary importance to the journey itself. In the Buddhist tradition, the goal of pilgrimage is not so much to

reach a particular destination as to awaken within oneself the qualities and energies of the sacred site, which ultimately lie within our own minds.

Ian Baker has made repeated journeys into Pemako, following the accounts
of Tibetan texts describing these places of pilgrimage. These works reveal the
Tsangpo gorge as the life-current of the female deity Vajravarahi (Tibetan: Dorje
Pagmo), whose form is identified with Pemako's inner topography. In the deepest part of the gorge he descended to a waterfall that British explorers had sought
for more than a century. Some Tibetans maintain that these falls are an entrance
to Pemako's hidden center. Whether this waterfall is literally the gateway to Yangsang, as legend maintains, I cannot say, but waterfalls serve an important role
in Buddhist practice as symbols of impermanence and supports for certain kinds
of meditation. Such places often have a power that we cannot easily describe or
explain. When approached with an awareness of the emptiness and luminosity
underlying all appearances, they can encourage us to expand our vision not only
of ourselves, but of reality itself. I hope that Ian Baker's book about his journeys
into one of the least explored regions of Tibet will inspire others not only to venture into unknown lands on a geographical level, but also to discover the inner
realms within which our own deepest nature lies hidden.

TENZIN GYATSO
The XIV Dalai Lama of Tibet

PART ONE

THE CALL
OF
HIDDEN-LANDS

Most races have their promised land, and such legendary places must necessarily be somewhat inaccessible, hidden behind misty barriers where ordinary men do not go . . .

FRANK KINGDON WARD
The Riddle of the Tsangpo Gorges

At the commencement as at the end of the religious history of humanity, we find again the same nostalgia for Paradise. . . . The myths by which this ideology is constituted are among the most beautiful and profound in existence: They are the myths of Paradise and the Fall, of the immortality of primordial man and his conversation with God, of the origin of death and the discovery of the spirit.

MIRCEA ELIADE
Myths, Dreams and Mysteries

People make mistakes in life through believing too much, but they have a damned dull time if they believe too little.

JAMES HILTON
Lost Horizon

I FIRST LEARNED of Tibet's hidden-lands in 1977 in Kathmandu, where I had traveled at nineteen on a college semester abroad program to study Buddhist scroll painting. One day, my teacher told me of places in the Himalayas where the physical and the spiritual worlds overlap. "They are called *beyul*," he said, "and they aren't on any map."

His words lingered in my mind, and three years later, I applied for a grant from New York's Explorers Club to learn more about Tibet's sacred geography. Tibet itself was then a closed country, and I traveled to Sikkim, a once independent Buddhist kingdom wedged between Nepal, Tibet, and Bhutan. At a small mountain hamlet, I unloaded my backpack from the roof of a bus and began climbing toward a monastery called Pemayangtse, Life Essence of the Lotus. I had arranged to base my research there, having corresponded with a resident scholar named Sonam Denjongpa, who'd earned a degree in anthropology at Brown University.

Sonam soon appeared out of the mists at the wheel of a lumbering jeep. He lurched to a halt and stepped out to greet me in knee-high Tibetan felt boots; a long black pigtail hung down the back of his blood-red robe. He stowed my gear in the backseat and we drove the remaining miles to the monastery through moss-strung forests and drifting clouds.

When we reached the timber-framed temple, Sonam swung open the doors on heavy iron hinges. As light flooded onto the walls, he pointed out the sixteenth-century murals of *shingkam*, or Buddhist paradises, painted on the clay surface. I commented that the realms painted with plant pigments, crushed gems, and the ash of cremated bones seemed like manifestations of inner states. Sonam replied, "They're not just imaginary realms; there are places here on earth called beyul, hidden or secret lands, described in texts dating back more than a thousand years. Many lamas have searched for these places in the remotest parts of the Himalayas. Some died trying to find them; others never returned."

Pointing north through a window toward the ice-covered peaks of Kanchen-junga, the world's third-highest mountain, Sonam said, "One of the beyul is hidden there beneath the glaciers. The scrolls describing it were unearthed from a cave in Tibet more than five hundred years ago."

That evening, jackals howled in the surrounding forests as I sat with Sonam and his family around a hearth of blazing rhododendrons. As his wife filled a smoke-blackened pot with rice and water and placed it on the fire, Sonam told me that the beyul were first revealed in the eighth century by Padmasambhava, the lotus-born saint, sorcerer, and sage who helped establish Tibet's Vajrayana,

or Tantric form of Buddhism as well as its tradition of hidden-lands. "He described their secret coordinates to his principal consort, who preserved the locations in cryptic, yellow scrolls that she hid in caves and walls of rock, to be discovered in future generations."

The first scrolls were discovered in 1366, Sonam told me. A wild-haired Tibetan yogi who had spent years meditating in mountain caves received a vision that led him to their hiding place, and he dug them out from the earth.[1] The cryptic texts contained accounts of remote Himalayan valleys where plants and animals have miraculous powers, where aging is halted and enlightenment can be quickly attained. "The beyul are something like Shangri-La," Sonam said. He paused to blow on the coals through a hollow length of bamboo.

Cradling his nine-month-old daughter while his wife lifted the pot from the fire and doled out rice and mustard greens onto brass plates, Sonam told me stories of Tantric yogis who had made pilgrimages in quest of the beyul, among them an itinerant lama named Lhatsun Namkha Jikme—"Fearless Sky"—who crossed the Himalayas from Tibet in the Year of the Fire Dog (1646), guided by a *dakini*, or female spirit, in the form of a white vulture. Leaving his followers behind, Namkha Jikme passed across the face of a cliff and descended into a maze of mist-shrouded ravines beneath Kanchenjunga, searching for the door to the beyul's innermost realm. As the weeks passed and avalanches rumbled down the glaciers, Namkha Jikme's disciples assumed that he had perished and began constructing a memorial cairn to honor his passage. Suddenly they heard the shrill blasts of his *kangling*, or thigh-bone trumpet, echoing from distant cliffs. After another week, the wide-eyed yogi emerged from banks of fog and related his experiences in the heart of the beyul. But he was unable to return there with his disciples, and the hidden realms remain sealed from the outer world not only by towering mountains, dense jungles, and glacier-covered passes, Sonam explained, but by protective veils placed there by Padmasambhava. Only those with the karma to do so can enter the depths of the hidden-lands.[2]

According to Sonam, Namkha Jikme had used his Tantric powers to reverse avalanches and rockfalls. I could only wish I had similar resources. Before leaving for Sikkim, I had been climbing in a glacier-scoured valley in Norway and had fallen from a precipice with a volley of rocks that shattered limbs, fractured my skull, and delayed my journey east for a full two years. I was still limping from the accident.

Over the next several weeks, I recorded Sonam's stories of the hidden-lands. He spoke in a sonorous English he'd learned in part from Hope Cooke, a New York socialite made famous by her marriage to Sikkim's last reigning maharajah. Sonam had tutored the foreign queen in the local dialect of the Tibetan language during her residence at the hilltop palace in Gangtok, which the American press had glamorized as a real-life Shangri-La. Concerned by growing political unrest in the tiny kingdom, Hope Cooke left with her children before India annexed it in a palace coup in 1975, but before she did, she arranged a scholarship at Brown for her precocious tutor.

Sonam told me that in the centuries following Namkha Jikme's arrival in Sikkim, his lineage holders established remote monasteries—including Pemayangtse—where they perfected their meditations, practiced Tantric rites, and staged noble, if quixotic, quests into the heart of the Himalayas in search of the beyul's elusive coordinates. The outer regions of Sikkim and other hidden-lands provided refuge to Tibetans in times of political and social turmoil, Sonam told me, but their innermost realms have yet to be discovered. Written in an obscure "twilight" language that is decipherable only by accomplished lamas, the manuscripts that describe the beyul are not only narrative maps of hidden worlds, Sonam maintained, but treatises that can alter the way we see our surroundings, transforming waterfalls, cliffs, and other natural features of the landscape into doorways to exalted perception. Over the centuries, many Tibetans have sold all their possessions to go off in search of these fabled lands, but only those with faith and merit actually experience the beyul's spiritual qualities. They are hidden not only by their extreme remoteness, he said, but by barriers formed by our habitual ways of perceiving our surroundings.

According to Sonam, as recently as the 1950s, when Chinese Communist forces invaded Tibet, a lama named Kanjur Rinpoche had followed Padmasambhava's prophecies into the gorges of the Tsangpo River in southeastern Tibet, a region known to Tibetans as Beyul Pemako, Hidden-Land Arrayed like a Lotus. According to Padmasambhava's revelations, Pemako is the most dangerous as well as the greatest of all the hidden-lands, "a celestial realm on earth." Fording treacherous rivers and living on wildflowers and powdered bark, the lama eventually passed through a waterfall into an astonishing valley laced with rainbows. The lama's journals, now kept at a Buddhist monastery in the south of France, are silent about the waterfall's specific coordinates, but they proclaim the reality of a place that many Tibetans hold to be an earthly paradise.

As I wandered through the mist-wreathed forests surrounding the monastery, I looked north toward the fluted ice walls of Kanchenjunga and pondered the stories of the hidden waterfall in the gorges of the Tsangpo, 200 miles to the east. I was still convalescing from my mountaineering accident, and with my knee swollen under a poultice offered by a local shaman, my investigation of beyuls was confined to recording Sonam's stories. They offered an alluring mystery that I felt increasingly drawn to explore.

A Curriculum of Caves

TWO YEARS AFTER MY JOURNEY to Sikkim I postponed work toward a master's degree at Oxford and settled in Kathmandu, Nepal, as director of an American college study abroad program. One afternoon, during monsoon season, I took refuge from a downpour in an antique gallery not far from Nepal's Royal Palace. While browsing through a labyrinth of masks, leopard-skin chests, and tribal artifacts, my gaze came to rest on a *thangka*, a Tibetan scroll painting, hanging in a dark corner of the room. The painting depicted a wrathful manifestation of the Tantric sage Padmasambhava. Painted in lapis lazuli and burnished gold, the three-eyed figure wore a tiger skin wrapped around his waist and held a scorpion in one hand and a *vajra*—a Tantric symbol of the mind's innermost nature—in the other. Black snakes coiled around his wrists and ankles. Sinuous waterfalls painted from powdered conch shells streamed from jagged peaks.

WHILE CONTEMPLATING THE THANGKA, I overheard fragments of conversation between the Tibetan shop owner and a maroon-robed monk. The monk was relating the experiences of his teacher, who, while on a meditation retreat in the Tibetan borderlands north of Kathmandu, had dreamed of a beyul hemmed in by vaulting cliffs. After confirming his vision with yak herders who knew the territory, the lama had left his retreat on a quest for the hidden valley that he had seen in his dreams. Trailed by a goat, a dog, and thirty retainers, he cut through thick forest and forded icy streams until he arrived at a flowering meadow nestled beneath the very same white cliffs and glacier-covered

peaks that had appeared in his visions. As the lama performed rituals to appease local spirits, rainbows hovered in the surrounding mists.

I approached the gallery owner after the monk had left and asked him more
about the hidden valley. "Beyul are places where everything we need can be
found and where meditation and Tantric practices are more effective," the gallery owner said, pouring us glasses of tea flavored with cardamom and cloves.
"Only great lamas can find them. We might be right in the middle of one and
still not see it."

AFTER WEEKS OF LECTURES and excursions amid Kathmandu's ancient
markets, palaces, and intricately carved temples, the students in my charge dis-
banded for a month of independent study. On the pretext of exploring locations for future study tours, I packed my rucksack and hired a dilapidated taxi
to take me to the eastern edge of the Kathmandu valley, where I began the six-
day trek that would bring me to the mountain retreat of the lama who had discovered the remote sanctuary I'd heard about in the antique shop.

The path climbed steeply through a breach in the valley wall, following a
chalk-white river that cascaded through dark forests of hemlock and pine. On
the first night I slept on a mud-floored porch in a small village, but as I walked
deeper into the mountains I took smaller side trails that led me through increasingly uninhabited terrain.

On the fourth day, the cobalt-blue flash of a monal pheasant lured me down
a steep track that soon dissipated into dense forest. Garlands of moss swayed
sensuously from ancient oaks and broad-leafed rhododendrons. Fern-covered
cliffs and black-faced monkeys dropped below me into the mist. Enchanted, I
pressed on through the lush forest, putting aside concerns about being off route.

As twilight descended through the canopy of trees, I took off my boots to
cross a stream and began looking for a rock outcrop where I could shelter for
the night. As the light faded, I caught a scent of burning logs and came across
a small clearing and a primitive shelter made from bamboo matting stretched

over saplings. A lone Tamang woodcutter, dressed in a matted wool tunic, sat by a fire stirring leaves in a soot-blackened pot.

Two days later I finally arrived at Neyding, a small collection of retreat cabins that the followers of the lama Chatral Sangye Dorje, the Adamantine Buddha, had hewn from the forest. I was now in the outer reaches of Beyul Yolmo Kangra, Hidden-Land Screened by Snow Mountains, where a maze of cliffs and forested ravines run southward from the main Himalayan range that borders Tibet. As early as the eleventh century, the celebrated Tibetan yogi Milarepa was said to have meditated here to deepen his realization.[3]

Chatral Rinpoche—as he was more commonly known—was already in his seventies when he founded this retreat community not far from Milarepa's cave and instructed his beguiling daughter Saraswati and other disciples to undertake retreats of three years, three months, and three days—a powerful formula in the Tibetan tradition for advancing along the Buddhist path.

I entered Chatral Rinpoche's cabin and found him seated cross-legged on the floor on the skin of a long-haired Tibetan goat. At first glance he looked like some Himalayan avatar of Merlin. His long white beard and undyed cotton robes distinguished him as a master of Tibet's Tantric lineages. A bell and vajra sat on the table, the paired ritual implements symbolizing wisdom and compassion. Thangka paintings hung from rough-hewn wooden rafters.

Speaking in faltering Tibetan, which I had only recently begun studying in Kathmandu, I told Chatral Rinpoche that I had heard of the hidden sanctuary he had discovered and requested directions to get there. For a long moment, the lama was quiet. Then, in a deep, resonant voice, he told me that beyul are not places for the idly curious, but places for meditation. As the mind opens through spiritual practice, Chatral Rinpoche said, so too do new dimensions of the environment. If I really wanted to know the qualities of a beyul, I wouldn't find out by spending one or two nights in one, taking pictures and leaving. Nor would I find out simply by asking questions about them or reading about them in a text.

I tried to steer the conversation toward the exact location of the hidden valley, but Chatral Rinpoche remained adamant. If I was truly serious about understanding beyul, he said, I should come back when I had enough time to stay alone there for at least a month. That way, he said, I wouldn't have to ask what a beyul is; I would experience it for myself. I agreed that I would come back to Yolmo the following summer.

My commitment to completing my degree at Oxford delayed me for another year, but I returned to Neyding in July of 1986, following a path along the Malemchi Khola River. As I climbed through torrential monsoon rains, I passed through Buddhist villages marked by sodden prayer flags and long rows of moss-covered rocks carved with mantras. The villages lay mostly deserted, their surrounding fields fallow and overgrown. The inhabitants of Yolmo had traded goods between Nepal and Tibet until 1959, when Chinese Communist soldiers blocked the passes. Forced to abandon their cross-Himalayan trade, many left their small farms and resettled in Kathmandu. Higher up in leech-infested forests, local herders still tended yak-cow hybrids called *dzo* (*dzomo* if female), shifting their camps according to the season.

When I reached Chatral Rinpoche's encampment it was dark and pouring rain. Saraswati led me to a loosely shingled storage shed piled high with sacks of barley and rice. In the surrounding huts, the Lama's students engaged in esoteric forms of meditation. I faded off to sleep to the piercing blasts of their kanglings, ritual instruments carved from human thigh bones that are used in Tibetan Buddhist rites for severing attachment to the physical body and outmoded forms of thought.

In Kathmandu, Saraswati had told me more about Chatral Rinpoche's earlier life. He had lived for years as a vagabond ascetic, wandering through remote regions of Tibet while perfecting his practice of Tantric yogas, which unveil the body's inner energy currents and illuminate deeper levels of the psyche. In the 1940s, under the direction of his teacher, he served as tutor to the regent of the current Dalai Lama. When mounting Chinese influence and palace intrigue threatened his life he returned from Lhasa to eastern Tibet, but left soon afterward for Bhutan and India, several years before the mass Tibetan exodus in 1959. He eventually settled at a hermitage outside of Darjeeling and married the daughter of Dulshuk Lingpa, a renowned *terton*, or revealer of Buddhist treasures. He later built a small monastery in the hills outside Kathmandu, by the

cave where Padmasambhava, practicing with his consort Sakyadevi, is said to have attained full enlightenment.

Chatral Rinpoche is revered as one of the greatest living masters of Dzogchen, the culmination of Buddhist practice in which the mind sees beyond the threshold of thought directly into its essence: "like mind gazing into mind." Tibetan tradition considers Dzogchen, which translates as the Great Perfection, to be the joyous realization of humankind's highest potential. An early Dzogchen text entitled *Culmination of the Supreme Path* refers to this undivided awareness as "the hidden essence of one's own mind . . . the inner radiance of reality itself."

THE DAY FOLLOWING MY ARRIVAL, Chatral Rinpoche spoke to me about hidden-lands. He pointed to a mandala, a circular icon of expanded consciousness, on one of the thangkas hanging from the roof beam, and said that beyul become increasingly subtle as one approaches their innermost realms. In a voice like softly rumbling thunder, he said that beyul have outer, inner, secret, and ultimately secret levels (*chi, nang, sang, yangsang*) that correspond to advancing stages of spiritual development.[4]

Without offering any further explanation, he told me of a cave several hours away where I should stay for the next month. In firm calligraphic strokes, he painted Tibetan syllables on a silk *khata,* a traditional Tibetan offering scarf, and fixed gold-colored threads at three points along its length. When I reached the cave, he told me, I should fix this banner to a pole as a gesture of sealing the doors to *samsara,* the world of everyday thought and experience. He handed me a sack of *tsampa,* freshly ground roasted barley, which is the staple of Tibetan diets, and told me to return from the cave after a month and tell him of my experience. He had already asked a local herdsman named Pema Rigdzin to take me to the cave; he and his twelve-year-old son were waiting for me outside the hut.

I followed Pema Rigdzin into the forests high above the Malemchi Khola, the roar of the river billowing up in waves from the ravines below. We gradually veered away from the main track up the valley, climbing up steep slopes of bamboo and hemlock and across narrow ledges of fragile shale. When we finally arrived at a shallow cave perched on a steep slope far above Neyding, Pema Rigzin announced that this was the place to which Chatral Rinpoche had told him to take me. We cleared out piles of pungent, matted grass from the cave floor; Pema Rigdzin laughed and said that Chatral Rinpoche had hoped that the bear we were now evicting would not return.

I WAS DISAPPOINTED AT FIRST that we had not crossed over the high passes leading to the more remote cave that I had first heard about in the shop in Kathmandu, but I surrendered to my circumstances. I busied myself at first cutting firewood in the rain and carrying water from a nearby spring. I built a crude hearth from broken rocks and made a rack above it to dry out the soaked logs. Besides Rinpoche's tsampa, which I mixed with local dzomo butter and dried cheese, I had brought a month's supply of mung beans and brown rice, as well as carrots, onions, and spinach, which I had dried weeks earlier on my roof in Kathmandu. To fortify my diet, I'd bought a bag of *yartsagunbu* (*cordyceps sinensis*), a high-altitude caterpillar fungus favored by the Chinese olympic team, from a Tibetan trader in Kathmandu. I evened out the surface of the cave floor with rocks and pine boughs and tied the calligraphied banner to a length of bamboo that I planted in the slope above the cave. I settled into a month of solitude.

I scheduled my day around four three-hour periods of meditation, but before long the persistent dampness caused my watch to stop, and I adopted a less rigid routine. I woke each morning before dawn and began the first in a sequence of practices designed to free the mind from customary patterns of perception.

On most days rain fell like a curtain from a still sky, but when the wind blew I had to cover the fire pit with my poncho and press myself against the inner wall of the shallow cave to keep from getting drenched. To avoid traversing out over sloping ledges to my sole water source, I set out two stainless steel pots to collect water dripping from the cave roof. With neither paper on which to write nor books to distract me, meditation became my only refuge. I found inspiration in the verses that the Buddhist sage Milarepa had composed in a cave farther down the valley nearly a thousand years earlier:

The nature of Mind is Emptiness and Luminosity
Inseparably conjoined . . .
Spontaneously merging with that original state
I am indifferent to experiences of good and bad.
With mind free and effortless, I rest in happiness and joy.

Where subject and object are realized as a single sphere
Happiness and sorrow mingle as one . . .
Whatever circumstances I encounter,
I am free in the blissful realm of self-awakening Wisdom.[5]

I thought back to my previous summer, which I had spent writing essays on Shakespeare at Oxford University. From my vantage point in the cave, the hidden wisdom that King Lear attains as an "unaccommodated man" in a hovel on the heath did not seem unrelated to what the Buddha, Prince Siddhartha, awakened to beneath a flowering *Figus religiosia*. Years earlier, I'd met an Englishman who had played the part of Lear for a theater company that traveled through villages in rural India. One day taking his role to heart, he simply walked off the stage and into the jungle, only emerging five years later. When I met him he'd become the director of Oxfam in the Indian city of Ahmedabad, but was still dreaming of returning to the forest.

Initially my mind mingled happily with the rain shimmering on green leaves and the display of clouds and mists that formed and dissipated in the surrounding ravines. But as the days progressed my mind rushed toward feeble distractions. I found myself reading fragments of Nepal's national newspaper, *The Rising Nepal*, that enclosed the bundles of egg noodles I had brought from Kathmandu. I burned them in the fire to remove the temptation, the words transforming in flames and air. I took short scrambles up the surrounding slopes, but the treacherous terrain and the leeches seemingly on every leaf urged me back to my narrow ledge. On the rare occasions when the sun emerged through banks of mist, bees swarmed on my unwashed body. A crow regularly alighted on the branch of a dead tree below the cave, eyeing me with sideways glances that seemed to mirror my own uncertainties.

In Sanskrit the word *Tantra* refers to the connective principle underlying all existence. Its Tibetan translation, *gyud*, means thread, string, or that which joins together, and its practices encompass all that overcomes the sense of separation stemming from belief in an autonomous self. Rather than renouncing the ephemeral thoughts and emotions that bolster self-identity, Tantra, or Vajrayana, seeks to transform them into potent catalysts for entering deeper, less restricted strata of consciousness, and unveiling the enlightened mind of wisdom and compassion said to be inherent within all beings.

Apart from urging me to spend a month in solitude in a beyul, Chatral Rinpoche had inspired a loftier goal. Padmasambhava's revealed scrolls speak as much about the mind as they do about hidden-lands. "In its true state the mind is naked, immaculate, transparent, empty, timeless, uncreated, unimpeded; not realizable as a separate entity, but as the unity of all things, yet not composed of them; undifferentiated, radiant, indivisible . . . to know whether this is true or not, look inside your own mind." A later seventeenth-century Buddhist master had written: "Do you not weary of the mind's endless convolutions? Cut to the source and rest in the essence, the undivided union of emptiness and spontaneous presence." But the mind's habits do not yield easily. I immersed myself in ancient practices of mantra and visualization. At times waves of doubt and perceived futility opened into edgeless rapture. At other times, thoughts rose up like an impenetrable wall.

As day followed day, I tallied mantras on a string of 108 sandalwood beads, but my mind was often clouded by frustrations that neither conjured deities nor half-remembered Buddhist poetry could dispel. While reciting a lengthy invocation over a brass mandala plate piled with rice, I reached a moment of total exasperation and hurled it off the ledge. It spiraled downward through layers of air and disappeared into the glittering, impenetrable forest.

I gazed blankly down the cliff.

The Buddha proclaimed *sunyata*, or Emptiness, to be the underlying nature

of all phenomena, a web of causal relationships that the philosopher-poet Octavio Paz referred to as a "fathomless abyss above which metaphysical thought flaps its wings." In the Buddhist Tantras, this "truth that does not itself exist" and the concurrent freedom from self-identity is celebrated as the birth of a radiant, compassionate awareness, symbolized by luminous multiarmed deities.

My prescribed month in the cave had come to a close, but as my meditation deepened I resolved to stay on for another week. My food supplies had dwindled, and I lived on little more than lemon water and sautéed yartsagunbu. The monsoon had ended and the small stream where I had once washed my clothes had turned to a trickle. I sat naked in the sun as the cave walls behind me slowly began to dry. Vivid dreams filled my nights and I awoke on one occasion to the sight of strange lights circling down the pathless slopes on the far side of the ravine. I imagined that Chatral Rinpoche might have sent men with torches to check on me, but the luminous spheres began to circle upward in erratic patterns before dissipating into night.

With the leeches now gone, I crawled through the steep and shimmering forests searching fruitlessly for edible mushrooms and for communion with terrain that Tibetan Buddhist texts eulogize as a "tray of gems." The distinction between beyul and so-called ordinary geography absorbed me like a Zen koan. Were the texts describing hidden-lands really evidence of some heightened perception, I wondered, or merely poetic attempts to invest nature with qualities that belonged more properly to the mind? Were they challenges to discover what lies ultimately within ourselves? As I moved through tangles of green-leafed bamboo, my thoughts served only to estrange me from the environment. The crow continued to eye me suspiciously from its perch below the cave.

I finally left my stone aerie, thin from my meager diet, gliding with a light pack through forests of drifting lichen. The weeks in the cave had been richly rewarding, but now I looked forward to seeing the beyul texts that Chatral Rinpoche said he would share with me on my return. Without his oral commentary, their metaphors and symbols—written in *sandhabhasa*, the Tantric "twilight language" in which truths are revealed only indirectly—would be largely unintelligible; I'd be like someone new to English trying to decipher *Finnegans Wake*.

I reached Neyding at nightfall. The prayer flags that circled the clearing hung motionless in the evening air. A long-haired retreatant in a sheepskin jacket was chopping wood at the edge of the compound. He paused to tell me that Chatral Rinpoche and his daughter had left a week earlier for Kathmandu.

I RETURNED TO MY DIRECTORSHIP of the American college program in Kathmandu. The city's rich artistic traditions and often byzantine customs offered a wealth of revelations, but my primary interest remained the enigma of the beyul.

That following spring, in 1987, I arranged an audience with the Dalai Lama for myself and nine American college students who had come to Nepal to study Tibetan language and culture. We traveled by train through northern India and finally arrived in Dharamsala, the seat of the Tibetan government-in-exile on a cloud-wrapped ridge at the base of 18,000-foot mountains. I had arranged to meet with His Holiness privately following our group session.

With disarming warmth the Dalai Lama drew me toward a plush beige couch in his reception room, which was dominated by a gilded statue of Avalokiteshvara, the multiarmed Buddhist divinity representing universal compassion. The supreme leader of the Tibetan people waited patiently as I read through a list of questions, mostly concerning the nature of beyul and *né*—hidden-lands and sacred sites—and their place in Buddhist practice. After a bemused reminder that meditation is not dependent on place, His Holiness conceded that spiritually advanced beings leave imprints on the physical environment. "The fact that many holy beings stay and practice in a certain place changes the atmosphere of that place," His Holiness said. He cited the example of Bodhgaya,

the site where the Buddha attained enlightenment more than 2,500 years ago. "When other beings with less experience or spiritual development practice at such a place they can obtain certain special kinds of experience." The Dalai Lama also spoke at length about subtle beings such as dakas and dakinis[6] who, according to the Tantric teachings, congregate at such sanctified places, bestowing powers on those who meditate there. He then told a story of his previous incarnation, the 13th Dalai Lama, who had traveled to the sacred mountain Wu Tai Shan on the frontiers of Tibet, where he had crossed an invisible threshold and visited a temple that no others could see. Through the power of meditation, His Holiness said, great practitioners are able to enter hidden realms which, though part of this world, are beyond the range of common perception. "It's a bit like quantum physics," he reflected, "which recognizes parallel dimensions and multiple universes."

As our conversation progressed, I told His Holiness about the month that I had stayed in Beyul Yolmo Kangra. I told him that I had requested leave from my work to return there the following summer and fall. As we spoke about

meditation, I confessed my frustration with the lengthy invocations and sup-
plications of Tibetan ritual texts. What practice could I do, I asked, that would
most powerfully reveal the hidden dimensions of mind and landscape? His
Holiness laughed and said, "Buddhism is not about faith in a transcendent deity or higher being, but about thoroughly investigating the nature of our minds
and emotions . . . and discovering the way things truly exist." In Dzogchen, he
said, nothing needs to be abandoned or rejected. The mind's innermost essence—
and its interconnectedness with all things—can be discovered in every moment,
in the flow of every experience. He told me then of a Dzogchen practice that
should be undertaken in total seclusion, remote from human habitation. "If
others see you," he said laughingly, "they will think that you've gone mad." He
demonstrated how one must act out an innumerable range of existences from
heavens to hells. Bringing his hand to his chin and closing the thumb and palm
rapidly together, he said: "At times you'll have to run through the woods howling like a wolf!" He took me by the hand and led me into a back room, where
he took a small gold-plated Buddha from a shelf. After holding it at the top of
his head and reciting an inaudible prayer, he placed it in my hands. When I
walked out onto the lawn a female security guard brandishing an AK-47 smiled
angelically as bougainvillea flooded from the roof like purple light.

THREE MONTHS LATER I trekked to Yolmo during a break in the summer
rains. When I arrived in Neyding, I found Chatral Rinpoche sitting on the
grass outside his hermitage feeding a consecrated elixir to a flock of crows. I
told him of the teachings that I had received from the Dalai Lama and that I
hoped to practice them in Yolmo over the next several months. Releasing one
of the birds into the sky, Chatral Rinpoche said that specific né in Yolmo are
conducive to particular kinds of practice. Places with waterfalls inspire reflection on impermanence. Places with steep cliffs where the rocks are dark and
jagged are good for meditating on wrathful deities. Places with rolling hills and
flowering meadows support meditation on peaceful deities. For the practices I
had received, Chatral Rinpoche said, all elements should be present and the

best place was a valley called Pemthang, the Sandy Plains, at the headwaters of the Malemchi Khola. According to Chatral Rinpoche, Padmasambhava himself had meditated in this remote sanctuary.

Padmasambhava is commonly referred to in Tibet as the second Buddha, and his miracle-filled life and multiple manifestations serve as parables of the Tantric path. In the eighth century, the Tibetan emperor invited him to help establish Tibet's first Buddhist monastery. Legends relate how Padmasambhava converted the Tibetan people to Buddhism by subduing their most belligerent local deities, and performing magical feats, such as driving wooden daggers through solid rock and flying on the rays of the sun.

During an evening meal of buckwheat bread and wild mushrooms, Chatral Rinpoche clarified that the beyul that Padmasambhava established in Tibet are not literal arcadias, but paradises for Buddhist practice, with multiple dimensions corresponding to increasingly subtle levels of perception. Beyond Yolmo's visible terrain of mountains, streams, and forests, he said, lies an inner level, corresponding to the flow of intangible energies in the physical body. Deeper still, the subtle elements animating the environment merge with the elements present within the practitioner—the secret level. Finally, at the beyul's innermost level—yangsang—lies a paradisiacal, or unitary dimension revealed through an auspicious conjunction of person, place, and time. Like other lamas I had spoken with, Chatral Rinpoche contended that yangsang is not merely a metaphor for the enlightened state, but an ever-present, if hidden, reality.

THE VALLEY OF PEMTHANG to which Chatral Rinpoche had directed me lies cradled between towering walls of rock and ice at the headwaters of the Malemchi Khola. To reach it I climbed through forests of rhododendron and oak with Pema Rigdzin, my guide once again. The directions in the Yolmo *neyigs*, the traditional accounts of the hidden-lands' sacred places, were vague and surreal. "Follow the dragon's tongue to the horse's saddle," reads one passage, until you see before you a mountain "like the billowing skirts of a queen." The stocky herder led us up a sinuous stream bed and across shifting landslides toward a high, mist-shrouded pass beyond the reach of the heat-seeking leeches that had plagued our steps. Scree and stones scattered beneath our feet into the dense fog curling up from the ravines below.

We crossed the pass and veered north, skirting the rock wall of Dawajati, the Moon Bird. According to local legend, Padmasambhava stood on the summit of this lofty peak to subdue Yolmo's malevolent spirits and transform them into guardians of the Buddhist path. Near the base of the peak we passed a small lake nestled between mossy spires. Rigdzin told me that local shamans traveled here on the August full moon to draw power from the clear black water. As we moved farther toward what had seemed an impenetrable line of cliffs, a narrow break appeared, and I saw a steep, snow-choked gully leading northward into the mists below. This was the door to Pemthang, Rigdzin said. At that moment the mists parted, revealing walls of blue-gray rock and shimmering ice. Below the clouds lay a green valley laced with streams.

As we descended, the snow and scree gave way to slopes of fragrant bushes of *Rhododendron anthropogen*. Rigdzin collected their tiny pearl-colored flowers to bring back to Chatral Rinpoche. We crossed a series of milky glacier-fed streams where I collected water. Unsure of its purity, I added five drops of iodine solution to my water bottle, and as I shook the mixture, Rigdzin asked me what it was I had added. Jokingly, I told him it was blood of a *dremo*, a Himalayan brown bear, and that like the small flowers that he had collected on the slopes above, it was good medicine. On the valley floor we entered a forest of rhododendrons and boulders wreathed in thick layers of moss. Tendrils of saxifrage swept our faces as we forged our way through. Where the braided streams winding across the valley floor converged into a single torrent, a tree had fallen across the river. A few meters below us the river swept into a seething cataract and dropped into a deep gorge. With his heavily laden bamboo basket Rigdzin walked barefoot across the narrow wet trunk, and I followed him in my sodden leather boots.

A narrow track through a stand of birch and fir led to a gigantic boulder that we had seen from far above. Built into a cave on its southern end was a *tsamkhang*, a hermit's shelter with a crude wooden door. Gray cliffs soared above into a rainy sky. To the north the high, snow-covered range of the Ganja Himal spread out, as the neyig had indicated, "like the silken robes of a queen."

Rigdzin stayed one night to help cut firewood and stack it on a drying rack that we made above the hearth. As I paid him for his services the next morning he asked if he could have a bit of the bear's blood for the journey back.

PEMTHANG LIES in the heart of Yolmo. During monsoon, the surrounding walls of rock are laced with waterfalls. Two streams falling from glaciers to the north join at the headwall and, at the valley's center, wind through marshes teeming with primulas and tall-stemmed turquoise-blue poppies. The snow-covered peaks at the head of the valley lay draped in cloud.[7]

Like the hidden-lands themselves, the Dzogchen rites that I had come here to practice are divided into outer, inner, secret, and yangsang, or ultimately secret, levels. By acting out conjured existences from heavens to hells, the practitioner recognizes how intention shapes reality and connects to an open, heart-centered consciousness in which all experience, emotions, thoughts, and sensations are perceived as the mind's natural state of self-manifesting wisdom, an energetic field empty of inherent existence. As Padmasambhava stated in an ancient text called *Liberation Through Seeing with Naked Awareness:*

> Samsara and Nirvana have no other difference than that between the moment
> of being unaware and aware. . . . Since we are not deluded by perception but by
> fixation, Liberation naturally occurs when we recognize that fixated thoughts
> are only mind grasping at its own empty reflections.[8]

During my months in Pemthang, I followed the trajectory of unbound thoughts and ran through wet forests and rolled in dark streams, seeking the source from which I was never apart. My mind drifted through shadows and vivid absences as leaves glittered in the saturated air and rainwater carved channels down the cave walls. I sometimes heard what I thought were voices and woke from dreams into further dreams. Much of the time, however, I spent simply tending the fire, rigging up tarps to keep the rain from dripping from the granite walls, warding off predatory frogs, and thinking of Chatral Rinpoche's daughter.

By mid October I ran out of food and I began the journey back to Neyding.

I left at first light under a liquid sky. Wet ferns brushed against my legs as I made my way to the river. The stream had widened with recent rains, and I cut birch saplings to use as poles to cross the slippery log above the waterfall. On the other side the entire landscape had rearranged itself since my journey in. Landslides had cut new ravines into the steep slopes, silvery streams fell through vertical jungle, clouds streamed against white cliffs, and the heady scent of sinpati and balushukpa filled the air. I found the narrow break between the cliffs and crossed the pass in heavy rain, the slopes below carpeted in small blue and yellow flowers. Far below the pass, yak and dzo grazed like apparitions in the mist while a lone herder standing beneath a cairn strung with sodden prayerflags buried his head beneath the plastic covering of his pack basket. He offered no reply to my greeting. Lower still, the cries of unseen shepherdesses called home their herds. For perhaps an hour we kept up a dialogue of resonant cries—empty sounds echoing in the mist. I descended lower through stands of wavering bamboo and labyrinths of rhododendrons, the ground soft like wet velvet beneath the interwoven limbs of the trees. I reached Pema Rigdzin's hut and saw that he had piled fresh dzomo butter outside in wooden buckets. I stopped in for tea and tsampa. Lower still, I forded rushing streams, their banks carpeted in thick moss, and finally arrived in twilight at the split-rail fence encompassing Neyding.

I plucked bloated leeches from my hair and limbs; the fallen slugs wallowed on the ground, intoxicated with blood. As I climbed over the wooden gate, dark birds passed above my head, sweeping the earth with their shadows. I took off my sodden boots and entered Saraswati's hut. She sat in a sea of white lambswool, black hair tumbling across her shoulders and her eyes like sonnets. I warmed myself by her fire until the wood turned to glowing coals and then retired to the storage shed. Rain fell in blissful waves against the roof.

The next morning, Saraswati introduced me to a lama named Bhakha Tulku Pema Tenzing, who had arrived in Neyding from his monastery in Powo, a once independent kingdom in southern Tibet. Bhakha Tulku spent his days in a wooden retreat cabin, but he came to Saraswati's hut for his evening meals. Bhakha Tulku had learned fluent English soon after escaping from Tibet in 1959, and in the evenings by the fire, our muddy shoes and umbrellas laid out on

Saraswati's porch, I listened to his stories of Pemako, the place revered in Tibetan tradition as the greatest of all hidden-lands.

In a remote corner of southeastern Tibet, one of Asia's largest rivers, the Tsangpo, descends into a dark and precipitous gorge, circles around the easternmost summit of the Himalayan range, Namcha Barwa, and flows into the jungles of India as the Brahmaputra River. Tibetans refer to this region of soaring glaciers and lush, subtropical rainforests as Beyul Pemako, the Hidden-Land Shaped Like a Lotus. For centuries, Bhakha Tulku told me, the maharajahs of Powo, who ruled the valleys to the north, had laid claim to these territories, which were connected to their kingdom by the Tsangpo's primary tributary (the Po Tsangpo or Po Yigrong River) and by several high snow-covered passes. Primitive tribes that the Tibetans called Lopas inhabited these remote jungles. They climbed half-naked over the mountains to leave pelts of clouded leopard and medicinal plants on the threshold of Powo's monasteries and at the Showa palace, the seat of Powo's kings, in exchange for woven cloth, copper cookware, and iron swords that they carried back over the passes. The wild and remote regions where the Lopa lived were spoken of in Padmasambhava's prophecies as the outer reaches of the most dangerous and sacred of all hidden-lands.

IN THE LATER HALF of the fourteenth century, Bhakha Tulku told me, a renowned Tibetan yogi named Sangye Lingpa discovered texts on Tantric alchemy in a cave on Namcha Barwa and found additional scrolls in a rock wall behind a waterfall near the entrance to the Tsangpo gorge. Two hundred years later, when Tibet was invaded by Mongols headed by Gushri Khan, a scholar and meditation master named Rainbow Heart (Jatsun Nyingpo, 1585–1656), unearthed the first of Padmasambhava's prophecies concerning the remote and unknown lands farther down the gorge. As Bhakha Tulku related, the scrolls proclaimed Pemako as the ultimate place of pilgrimage. Even taking seven steps toward this mysterious realm, stated one of Jatsun's rediscovered scrolls, ensures rebirth in Pemako's innermost sanctum—Chimé Yangsang Né, "the innermost secret place of immortality." According to popular legend, if one could actually find this place one would live to be a thousand years old, and, at the time of death, dissolve into rainbow light. Hoping to establish a refuge from invading Mongol hordes and the resultant civil wars within Tibet, Jatsun Nyingpo encouraged one of his disciples to journey to the region of the Tsangpo gorges and to open a route to the prophesized sanctuary.

Jatsun's disciple, Rigdzin Dudrul Dorje, the Vajra Demon Tamer (1615–72),[9] crossed high blizzard-wracked passes from the valley of Powo and, with a retinue of followers, descended into the tangled forests of Pemako. Following the directives in Padmasambhava's scrolls, the group made shelters from wild banana trees and subsisted on foods from the jungle. They built primitive *stupas*—reliquary shrines symbolizing the body and mind of the Buddha—to pacify the spirits of the land and performed Tantric rites to turn back the Mongol armies that had invaded Tibet. They penetrated deeper and deeper into the wilderness, but hostile tribes, unfamiliar diseases, and plagues of insects prevented them from reaching Chimé Yangsang Né.

Dudrul Dorje passed on his mantle of explorer-yogi to Taksham Nuden Dorje, Powerful Tiger-skirted Vajra, (1655–1708), a revered Buddhist master from eastern Tibet who had settled in the temperate forests of Powo and revealed numerous treasure-texts with detailed descriptions of Pemako's innermost realms. Bhakha Tulku related how Taksham's visionary texts describe Pemako's mountains, valleys, and streams as geographical emanations of a Tantric goddess named Dorje Pagmo, the queen of all dakinis. Taksham's texts invoke the Tsangpo as her spine and the regions through which the river flows as her chakras, or lotus-centers of psychic energy. Bhakha Tulku emphasized that

ཨོཾ། །ཆེདུནཆུདལདོམདོཁམསྐྱེདངེརསྐྱལ། །ཆབསྐྱུགསུནཱུངསུནངཐེགསོགས། །
གནསགཏེརརྒྱུཆེནམདནབདགསནཚུནདནར། །དངདངུནསྐྱིངབེནནསསྐྱུགཚེལ།

these topographical regions ultimately correspond to the pilgrim's own mystical anatomy as visualized during meditation, the ritual journey through Pemako's sanctified landscape and the search for its innermost center paralleling an inner journey toward enlightenment.

AS WE SAT ON GOATSKINS laid out by Saraswati's hearth, Bhakha Tulku described a journey he had made in 1956 to a sacred mountain said to hold the key to Chimé Yangsang Né. Crossing over a high mountain pass from his monastery in Powo, he passed into dense, moss-thick forests abounding with musk deer, tigers, and leopards. At the mountain proclaimed to be the gateway to Pemako's innermost realm, a white musk deer guided him in his quest. But, like those before him, he too had been unable to continue on to Pemako's innermost secret realm.

"Has anyone ever reached it?" I asked. Bhakha Tulku told me of the lama Kanjur Rinpoche, whom I had first heard about in Sikkim; how he had entered through a passage behind a waterfall into a mystical valley surrounded by glittering snow peaks. "The way is lost now," Bhakha Tulku said wistfully. "Even Kanjur Rinpoche could not find the route again." As Bhakha Tulku spoke, the haunting wails of ritual thigh-bone trumpets sounded from the surrounding huts.

A burly Tibetan named Tsampten had recently completed his three-year retreat, but had stayed on at Neyding to manage the transport of supplies. One afternoon he invited me to his house for lunch. As he diced potatoes with a silver-handled dagger, Tsampten looked over his shoulder with a mischievous smile and told me that Bhakha Tulku wasn't the only one in Neyding who had been to Pemako. In 1962 he'd been there himself on a covert surveillance operation for America's Central Intelligence Agency.

Hailing from a fierce warrior tribe in eastern Tibet, Tsampten and nearly three hundred other Khampa freedom fighters had been trained in guerilla warfare at a secret, high-altitude camp in the Rocky Mountains of Colorado, supported by the U.S. government in a futile campaign against the Communist forces that had invaded Tibet. By the early 1960s a ragged battalion of the People's Liberation Army had followed the Tsangpo River into the valleys of Pemako, destroying monasteries and laying claim to all regions north of the Brahmaputra River in the Indian state of Assam. Outfitted with a shortwave radio, pistol, machine gun, and a bracelet containing a vial of cyanide to be swallowed on capture, Tsampten parachuted into the subtropical jungles on the Tibetan border to assess the strength of the Chinese forces. He found a primeval realm, he told me, with foliage so dense that the enemy could be a few feet away and still not be seen. Cobras and deadly vipers abounded, Tsampten said, along with primitive tribes that ate monkeys and dressed in their skins.

Tsampten's interest in this disputed wilderness extended far beyond the shifting line of control that separated India and China. Like most Tibetans he knew of the lost paradise hidden in Pemako's interior. "The Chinese will never find that place," Tsampten told me. "It's not on any map. It will remain hidden until the time is right for it to be revealed." Later Tsampten had been stationed as a sniper with a 55-mm recoilless rifle on a ridge above the Tsangpo River. He slept in a cave where local villagers kept him supplied with meat and tsampa. From his hidden vantage he sabotaged convoys of Chinese supply trucks as they plied the torturous newly constructed road between Lhasa and Beijing.

The survival rate of the Khampas who parachuted into Tibet was extremely low. The only living member of the first mission, a man named Bapa Lekshey, described the operation as "like throwing meat into the mouth of a tiger." When the U.S. government dropped its support for the Tibetan resistance movement after Henry Kissinger's secret visit to Beijing in 1971, Tsampten traded in his commando gear for maroon-colored robes and entered a three-year meditation retreat in Yolmo.

As Tsampten spoke, the daughter of a local herder came up the log ladder carrying fresh butter and a pail of dzomo milk. Pouring the contents into a wooden churn filled with an infusion of salt and boiled tea leaves, she pulled hard on the wooden plunger to make the dubious buttered tea consumed throughout the Tibetan world. "Why are you so interested in beyul?" she asked me teasingly. "Do you think they're places where you won't have to work?"

The Search for Scrolls

BACK IN KATHMANDU, I searched monasteries and private collections for Tibetan texts describing Pemako and other beyul. I also applied repeatedly to the Chinese authorities for permission to visit the Tsangpo gorges, but the same answer came back every time: it was a military zone and completely off limits. For the time being, I contented myself with tracking down and studying block-printed manuscripts based on Padmasambhava's prophecies of the hidden-lands. Padmasambhava's consort, Yeshe Tsogyal—Lake of Gnosis—had written down these accounts on amber parchment and concealed them in temple pillars, lakes, and walls of rock. Throughout the centuries, lamas and yogis were led to these yellow scrolls (*sghog-ser*) in dreams and visions. Those who discovered them were called *terton*, or treasure-revealers, and what were often no more than fragmentary texts written on yellow parchment were called *terma*, or more simply *ter*—concealed treasures that also included ritual objects that inspired the quest for enlightenment. Like the papyrus scrolls of the Christian gnostics, the original manuscripts were often found in earthen jars hidden in caves and cliffs. Unique hazards are said to attend their discovery; a story is told, for example, of a terton who pulled a yellow scroll from an urn found in the opening of a cliff, only to have the rock close on his hand and chop off one of his fingers when he reached back in for more.[10]

Some of the original revealed texts were reputedly written with invisible ink that appeared only when the paper was slowly heated over a flame. Others were coded in a runic alphabet called *khandro dayig*, or secret script of dakinis, which the terton could decipher and interpret only after months of meditation, often embellishing them with his own insights. The decoded yellow scrolls—full of ambiguous terms and cryptic allusions and almost entirely devoid of case

particles—were later transcribed onto insect-resistant paper made by boiling and pressing the inner bark of a Himalayan shrub called yubok (*Daphne papyyracea*).

The scrolls elucidated subtle teachings on the nature of mind and phenomena. Those that described routes to the hidden-lands were known as *neyig*, or guides to sacred places. Most of the neyigs I examined had been reprinted during the last century in loose folios stacked between wooden covers and wrapped in yellow and red silk. They typically opened with apocalyptic prophecies of war and devastation, but shifted into what read at times like a Fodor's Guide to a parallel universe, with outer, inner, and secret descriptions of isolated regions of the Himalayas. Like a Tibetan *Pilgrims' Progress*, the texts refer to the journey's inevitable hazards as inner obstacles that, once surmounted, lead to greater merit and spiritual realization until, ultimately—in the innermost heart of the hidden-land—"the eyes can see and the ears can hear that which elsewhere is obscured." Whatever the reality or coded metaphors behind such claims, the neyigs had reshaped Tibetans' relationship to the natural world and revealed it as a place of continual revelation.

Some collections of the neyigs had been preserved on microfilm at the National Archives in Kathmandu. Sadly, though, the duty manager informed me, the card catalogue was incomplete, as a "high-ranking officer" had stacked the bundles in a corner, where they had been eaten by moths. The greatest surviving collection of these esoteric manuscripts, he assured me, could be found in the Library of Tibetan Works and Archives in Dharamsala, India. In February 1989 I went there to meet the head of the research department, Tashi Tsering.

I FOUND TASHI in his book-lined office chasing flies with a plastic swatter. Tashi was known both for being one of the most knowledgeable of Tibetan scholars and for his refreshing irreverence. He smiled when I told him I was interested in finding Tibetan texts about beyul, and Pemako in particular. "Ah," he said, "you mean the Bermuda Triangle of Tibet."

Tashi's own scholarly research had covered many aspects of Tibetan civilization, but he too had a personal interest in beyul and he waxed eloquent on their role throughout Tibet's volatile history of invasions and civil wars.[11]

He told me of the many lamas and pilgrims who had disappeared over the centuries while searching for Pemako's innermost sanctuary, such as the treasure-revealer Rigdzin Choeje Lingpa (1682–1725), visions of whom Lopa hunters still claim to see, surrounded by retinues of dakinis. He then introduced me to a monk who served as one of the librarians. Climbing up the wooden stacks in his heavy wine-colored robes, the monk returned with armfuls of dusty tomes containing accounts of hidden-lands and biographies of those who had revealed them.

In text after text, Pemako was invoked as an earthly paradise:

There is a secret place known as Pemako. It is shaped like a womb. All the trees are perfumed like akaru, sandalwood, and jasmine. Saffron grows like grass. Wheat, barley and rice grow wild and honey is found in abundance. The animals of Pemako provide endless milk. The rivers flow with amrita the color of milk. When you drink it, you will never feel thirsty. All fruit and water is medicinal. Everyone will become joyful and prosperous. Old men will become youthful. With perfume in the air, a rain of flowers falls and rainbows spread

out everywhere. Food, drink, clothing—all needs are magically satisfied, whatever one wishes for . . .

The happiness and enjoyments here are equal to a god-realm. Even without meditating, anyone who reaches here can attain the state of a Buddha.

I soon had stacks of photocopies to take back to Kathmandu.

When I returned to Tashi's office, I asked him whether Western scholars had ever written about the sacred texts describing Pemako. The first account of Pemako to reach Europe was brought back by a French explorer named Jacques Bacot, Tashi told me. Bacot traveled through eastern Tibet between 1907 and 1910. Traveling toward the semi-independent kingdom of Powo, north of the great bend of the Tsangpo, Bacot learned of Pemako from Tibetan nomads who were fleeing there from the depredations of Chinese warlords in their homeland in eastern Tibet. Bacot was not able to follow the Khampa pilgrims, but he hand-copied the thirty-six folios of their guidebook, which likened Pemako to the terrestrial body of the goddess Dorje Pagmo—the same deity that, in the guise of a vulture, had guided Namkha Jikme into the depths of Sikkim.

A LARGE ROOM IN THE TIBETAN LIBRARY and archives was devoted to works in English. During my stay in Dharamsala, I combed through glassed-in cases in the rare book section and came across several turn-of-the-century works that deepened my perspective on the region of the Tsangpo gorges. Although I had learned a fair amount about what Pemako meant to Tibetans, I discovered how significant a pull the area had also exerted in the West. I spent several days poring over these Victorian-era accounts. A medical officer attached to the British military campaign which had forced a trade treaty on the Tibetans in 1904 had written of efforts by the British Raj "to get a trustworthy map of the great unknown territory of the Land of Lamas which for so many hundreds of miles marched with the frontiers of India." During the nineteenth century very little was known about the forbidden lands north of the

Himalayas; as the eminent Victorian surgeon general L. Austine Waddell wrote, one of the "greatest geographical problems of the day" was the fate of the Tsangpo River after it disappeared into a "*terra incognita* [that] has never yet been penetrated even by the Tibetans."[12]

I learned that geographers in the Great Trigonometrical Survey of India offices in the Northern Indian hill station of Dehra Dun had long speculated that Tibet's Tsangpo River cut through the easternmost Himalayas to join the Brahmaputra River, in the jungles of Assam, but they had no direct evidence of the link between the two rivers. Rival theories, popular in Europe, speculated that the Tsangpo flowed instead into the Irrawaddy in Burma. Some, even more improbably, traced the Brahmaputra to the mythical Lake Chiamay that maps, based more on rumor than fact, situated north of present-day Thailand. As Waddell wrote: "This problem had baffled all attempts at direct solution; for not even the Tibetans themselves know what becomes of their river after it turns southward . . . and enters a tract of country absolutely unexplored, a no-

man's land, peopled by fierce savage tribes who have successfully resisted all entry of strangers into their country, indeed they kill Tibetans on principle."[13]

In 1824, the chief goal assigned to the Assamese branch of the Survey of India was to establish the source of the Brahmaputra River. Its officer-in-charge, Captain James Bedford, was ordered to "unravel the mystery regarding its fountainhead" and to make his way as far upstream as possible. Bedford forged his way through mountains and dense rainforests until his progress up the Dihang—the chief feeder of the Brahmaputra—was halted by hostile warriors dressed in cane helmets fringed with bear skin and brandishing spears; wide, sharp-edged swords called *daos;* and crossbows with arrows dipped in aconite and deadly nightshade. Bedford returned from this encounter unscathed, but his successor was not so lucky: he was hacked to death on a later expedition.

The various clans of Abors—an Assamese word meaning "one who does not submit"—continued to harass villages under British administration until the Raj resolved to restore its lost prestige by "inflicting such chastisement as will teach these savages to respect its power." The punitive expeditions included elephant-drawn howitzers, but the British were still no match for the Abor warriors, who ambushed them with volleys of poison arrows. A climactic military campaign in 1862 ended in political victory for the Abor clans. In exchange for annual subsidies of salt, iron, and cloth and the British government's promise to desist from any further mapping or encroachment into tribal territories, the Adis (as they called themselves) agreed to stop their raids and depredations of Assam's villages and emerging tea estates. The riddle of the link between the Tsangpo, the Dihang, and the Brahmaputra remained unresolved. Cartographers realized that because of the impenetrable barrier of the hostile tribes, any further progress would have to come from the other side of the Himalayas, in Tibet.

The Quest for a Waterfall

DURING THE NINETEENTH CENTURY Tibet itself was a sealed and secret land. Tibet's ruling powers had become deeply suspicious of British expan-
sionism and had forbidden all but a few well-known merchants from Nepal
and Ladakh from entering the country. Hungry for geographical information
about the territory beyond its borders, the British Survey of India began training a class of surveyor-spies to work undercover in Tibet disguised as traders
and Buddhist pilgrims.[14] The first Pundits, as they came to be called, began
training in 1863 at the Great Trigonometrical Survey of India offices in Dehra
Dun. Ethnic Tibetans from the British-ruled territories of Sikkim and Ku-
maon, the Pundits (Sanskrit for learned men) learned to use sextants and pris-
matic compasses and to determine altitudes by measuring the temperature of
boiling tea water with a hypsometer. (In order to obtain measurements accurate to within ten feet, the boiling point had to be calculated to 1/100th of a
degree.)

In the manner immortalized in Rudyard Kipling's classic novel *Kim*, the
Pundits concealed their notes and surveying gear within their Buddhist
prayer wheels and used rosaries of one hundred rather than the conventional 108 beads to count off their steps and measure distances (two thousand paces to the mile). Adopting code names by reversing the first and
last letters of their names, these explorer-spies set out to secretly map the
forbidden frontiers, mountain ranges, lakes, and river systems of Tibet. The
Pundits' first order was to chart the long-debated course of the Tsangpo and,
if possible, to follow it through its innermost chasms to the borders with
India.

ONE OF THE MOST INTREPID of the explorer-spies in the employ of the
British government was an illiterate Sikkimese named Kinthup, code-named
K.P., first dispatched in 1878 as the assistant to a spy named Nem Singh, an am-
ateur Pundit ill-versed in clandestine surveying. Traveling as pilgrims, the two
were ordered to follow the Tsangpo downstream from central Tibet. Two hundred miles from their starting point, they reached a small village called Gyala
where the Tsangpo was seen to disappear into "a gigantic cleft in the Himalayan wall." Unable to proceed farther they retraced their steps and returned to
Darjeeling.

Disappointed with Nem Singh's performance, the officer who commissioned
the expedition replaced him with an even less experienced Chinese lama. With
Kinthup acting as guide, the two were to proceed as far as possible beyond where
Kinthup and Nem Singh had turned back. At the farthest point, the two agents
were instructed to insert metal tubes into 500-foot-long logs and, over a pre-
arranged period, throw them into the river at the rate of fifty per day while Captain Henry Harman's men kept watch at the junction of the Dihang and
Brahmaputra. If the logs appeared, Harman would secure incontrovertible evidence that the Tsangpo and the Brahmaputra were one and the same river.[15]

Kinthup and the Chinese lama reached Gyala in March of 1881 after a journey of seven months, over the course of which the lama managed to lose all of
the expedition funds gambling, and Kinthup was forced to use his own modest
resources to buy the lama out of an entanglement "owing to the Lama falling in
love with his host's wife." The explorers marched for several days below Gyala,
ascending and descending "many steep rocks through jungles and obstructions"
until they arrived at a small monastery called Pemako chung, deep in the Tsangpo
gorge. At this point, towering cliffs barred further progress. After three days of
searching unsuccessfully for a route downriver, they retraced their steps and
looked for a way around the impenetrable chasm. North of the gorge, near a village called Tongyuk Dzong, the lama left on an errand, telling Kinthup that he
would soon return. He failed to reappear, and Kinthup soon learned that the

lama had sold him to the local *dzongpon,* or district administrator, in exchange for a horse and sufficient funds to make it back to his homeland.

AFTER NINE MONTHS in captivity Kinthup managed to escape. Instead of returning to Darjeeling as might have been expected, he rejoined the Tsangpo River below its innermost gorges in a valiant attempt to complete his mission and close the "missing link." Crossing back and forth across the lower Tsangpo on ropes of woven bamboo and "almost perishing from hunger and cold," Kinthup eventually reached a small *gompa,* or monastery, in Pemako where "fifteen nuns and thirty priests were allowed to live together." A search party sent by the dzongpon from whom Kinthup had escaped discovered him at Marpung Gompa, but the abbot took pity on him and after ten days of negotiation, bought him for 50 rupees. Kinthup stayed at the gompa for nearly two years, requesting periodic leave to go on religious

pilgrimages. During the first of these excursions he descended to the banks of the Tsangpo and, to complete the original goal of the expedition, assembled five hundred marked logs that he concealed in a cave. Two months later, Kinthup requested a second leave to go on pilgrimage to Lhasa, from where he dictated a letter to Captain Harman informing him of the date he would launch the logs into the river:

> Sir: the Lama who was sent with me sold me to a Jongpen [headman] as a slave and himself fled away with the Government things that were in his charge. On account of which, the journey proved to be a bad one; however I, Kinthup, have prepared the 500 logs according to the order of . . . Captain Harman, and am prepared to throw 50 logs per day into the Tsangpo from Bepung in Pemako, from the 5th to the 15th of the tenth Tibetan month of the year called Chhu-luk [the water sheep] of the Tibetan calculation.[16]

He sent the letter to Darjeeling with the wife of a fellow Sikkimese whom he had met in the Lhasa bazaar.

Kinthup returned to the *gompa* and served the abbot for another nine months before requesting leave to go on pilgrimage to Kundu Dorsempotrang, a sacred mountain in the heart of Pemako and the gateway to its innermost realms. Impressed by Kinthup's devotion, the abbot reputedly told him, "I am glad to see you visiting the sacred places, so from to-day I have given you leave to go anywhere you like." Freed from slavery, Kinthup set out to release his cache of five hundred logs. For ten days in a row, he set himself a daily regime of throwing fifty logs into the river, after which he attempted to follow the Tsangpo south into India. Confronting hostile Adi (Abor) warriors, he retraced his steps to Lhasa and continued on from there to Darjeeling, which he reached on November 17, 1884, four years after he had set out with the rogue lama. The letter that he had traveled hundreds of miles to dispatch from Lhasa had never reached its destination, and the man to whom it was addressed, Captain Harman, had died in the interim from frost-bitten lungs after a map-making expedition on the slopes of Kanchenjunga. The marked logs that Kinthup had so painstakingly launched either floated unnoticed into the Bay of Bengal, or had been lost in the depths of the gorge in the Tsangpo's fearsome rapids. In Darjeeling, Kinthup dictated an account of his journey to the office of the Trigonometrical Survey through an Indian scribe. His oral report was regarded with suspicion until it was noted that the information he provided largely tallied with the accounts of a Mongolian lama, Serap Gyatso, who had supplied the office with details of his residence in Pemako from 1856 to 1868. Combining Kinthup's account with the "list of monasteries, sacred places and villages" provided by the Mongolian lama, the Survey Department compiled a sketch map of the course of the lower Tsangpo, furnishing what the deputy surveyor general described as "the first contribution to the geography of that unknown tract."

British geographers compared the apparently "genial terrain" of the lower Tsangpo to the vales of Kashmir, and considered it "the probable highway of the future" into Tibet. Even more interesting to the Survey Department was mention in Kinthup's account of a monumental waterfall deeper in the gorge than he himself had been able to reach. As stated in the report published by the Trigonometrical Branch of the Survey of India in 1889: "Two miles off [from a remote monastery called Pemakochung, the Tsangpo] falls over a cliff called Sinji-Chogyal from a height of about 150 feet. There is a big lake at the foot of the falls where rainbows are always observable." Years later, a British field officer would write that this description "translated from the oral report of [Kinthup's] Tibetan travels . . . was responsible for one of the most obsessive wild goose chases of modern times."[17]

FOLLOWING KINTHUP'S RETURN from the Tsangpo gorges, "The Falls of the Sangpo" was placed on the Survey map. One British officer estimated the waterfall "to lie in about 29 degrees 36' N. latitude and 94 degrees 47' E. longitude" and commissioned a Tibetan artist, "a native of the place," to make a drawing of them, which he published in 1895 in the *Journal of the Royal Geographical Society of London.*

FALLS OF THE TSANGPO RIVER.
(*From a Tibetan drawing.*)

Despite the fact that no European had come remotely close to setting eyes on the "spectacular cataract" in the Tsangpo's innermost gorge, the president of the Royal Geographical Society, Sir Thomas Hungerford Holdich, wrote that one "can well imagine the wild magnificence where the river rounds the Himalayas on the east. A dense subtropical jungle, rich with every variety of tree fern and bamboo, stretches up the hillsides.... Towering above all are the eternal snows and the everlasting silence of the ice-fields.... The falls are very sacred, and the bourne of many a devout pilgrimage. Clouds of misty spray rise into the clear atmosphere above them, and it is said that a rainbow ever spans the valley."[18]

IN 1893, THE LURE OF THE IMAGINED WATERFALL prompted another Englishman, Jack Needham, assistant political officer in Sadiya, Assam, to journey into the tribal territories bordering Tibet on the pretext of subduing the Padam Abors, the tribe of "cannibals" who had prevented Kinthup from following the Tsangpo south into British-held territory. In his telegram to Assam's chief commissioner, Needham requested permission to travel north along the Dihang into the "unknown tract" of lower Pemako.

While hacking their way through dense jungle toward the Padam village of Damroh, Needham's rear guard was ambushed by Abors, who had entered the camp pretending to be porters. After killing all but a wounded washerman who had leapt into the river, the half-naked warriors made off with fourteen rifles and crates of reserve ammunition, effectively ending the campaign as well as

Needham's chances for further exploration in the mysterious regions to the north of the Indian-Tibetan frontier.

It was due in part to the unrelenting savagery of the Assamese hill tribes that the British eventually forced their way into Tibet along the trade route between Darjeeling and Lhasa. By 1903, Lord Curzon, India's viceroy, had become increasingly concerned about Russian influence in Tibet and central Asia and, in a culminating gambit of what Rudyard Kipling called the Great Game, launched a full-scale military expedition replete with a caravan of camels, yaks, and mules, led by the illustrious Sir Francis Younghusband, who later planned and organized the first of several British attempts to climb Mount Everest.[19]

Besides forcing an exclusive trade treaty with the isolated Land of the Lamas, the British were eager to continue the mapping of their frontiers. As the Tsangpo-Brahmaputra had already been envisioned as the probable "highway of the future" between British India and the forcibly opened Tibet, a branch of Younghusband's expedition led by a British officer named Captain C.H.D. Ryder was commissioned to push on beyond where Kinthup had turned back and to follow the Tsangpo and Dihang all the way to Assam. (This was the same year, 1904, in which the British brought a railroad to Victoria Falls as part of a projected Cape to Cairo Railway Line that was to traverse the entire African continent through territory held by the United Kingdom.) Like all earlier attempts to penetrate the Tsangpo gorges, however, Ryder's expedition was thwarted, in his case after a mule train carrying essential equipment and supplies was ambushed en route to Lhasa.

Nonetheless, the hook was set. It became conventional wisdom that it was in the commercial and imperial interests of the British Raj to open a route to Tibet along the Tsangpo-Brahmaputra River. In 1906, the president of the Royal Geographical Society wrote:

> The one great natural highway into Tibet is indicated by the valley of the Brahmaputra, which may possibly not only lead by easy grades to the plateau, but directly taps such wealthy valleys as may exist in Zayul and Poyul [Powo]. . . . Approaching the great bend the valley obviously closes to something in the nature of a gorge, and the stupendous falls . . . can only be outflanked by a turning road in-

volving a considerable detour. . . . There is nothing so far which can be reckoned as a formidable obstacle to the engineering of a road unless it be the falls . . . but a further and more detailed exploration of the valley is urgently required.[20]

In 1911, Noel Williamson, Jack Needham's successor as assistant political Officer in Sadiya, made a further push "to get up to the falls" from Assam. On the pretext of arranging for a poll-tax from the local tribes and "to ascertain the extent of Tibetan and Chinese influence in Abor country," Williamson and his Tibetan-speaking companion Dr. Gregorson ventured into territory that the British had circumspectly avoided for decades. The expedition was soon massacred by an Abor war party. The majority of Williamson and Gregarson's Naga, Miri, and Gurkha retainers were speared as they attempted to escape from the Abor *morang*, or long house, where they had lodged, and the two British-ers were hacked to death with *daos.* The few who got away were tracked down by Abor hunting dogs and slaughtered by the banks of the Dihang.

The British government sent out a "miniature army" to avenge the murders. It confronted stockades, rock-chutes, and concealed pits lined with poisoned stakes, but the relentless advance of more than 7,000 fighting troops and 3,500 spear-wielding coolies from the Naga Hills eventually forced the Abor *gams*, or chieftains, to concede victory to the Raj. They heralded their surrender by sending a courier with a double-bent sword and spearhead, signifying their pledge of future peace.

The hostile tribes guarding the frontiers with Tibet had now been subju-gated, offering the British an unprecedented opportunity to explore their long-coveted passageway to Tibet. The major survey column of the Abor Field Force headed north up the Dihang with the express mission "to explore and survey as much of the country as possible, if practicable the Pemakoi [Pemako] falls and incidentally settling the question of the identity of the Tsangpo and the Dihang rivers."[21] Two columns explored surrounding watersheds while the main party, led by Assam's district commissioner with an escort of three hundred rifles un-der a Captain Trenchard, advanced 24 marches up the Dihang to the last of the Abor villages. Supplies had begun to run out and lacking resolute leadership, the

column was unable to penetrate into the region that Kinthup himself had explored nearly three decades earlier. One commanding officer wrote:

> I loathe walking day after day for miles . . . and climbing up and down hills over impossible paths. One is bored with sleeping on the ground and getting wet for the sake of geographical additions to the map.[22]

Confronting a range of jagged snow-covered peaks, the expedition leader, Captain Bentnick, began to doubt the value of their mission, referring to Kinthup's report as "one of the romances of the Survey of India." "It may be said in a word," he continued, "that the nearer we got to where the falls ought to be the less there was to be known of them." Their Abor guides offered to continue but demanded that at least three British officers go with them. "One of you," they said, "will probably die because the country is so bad, and then you will blame us, whereas if three go two may die, but there will still be one to come back and say that it was not our fault."[23] Soon enough, thick fog, torrential

rains, deep snows, and the sheer weight of the unknown brought the expedition to an ignominious halt.

THE MORE IMPREGNABLE THE TSANGPO'S inner gorges seemed, the more the British speculated about what they might conceal. The vast drop in altitude between where the Tsangpo mysteriously disappeared and where it reemerged in Assam as the Brahmaputra supported the notion of a giant waterfall, but the region had thwarted the best efforts of the British Raj to penetrate its depths.

At the turn of the century the unexplored gorges of the Tsangpo were as talked about as Everest, the existence of "the stupendous falls" in their innermost depths calculated through a formula of hope and statistical estimation.[24] Fifty years earlier, on November 16, 1855, David Livingstone had spied the billowing mists of Mosi-oa-Tunya, The Smoke That Thunders, on the Zambezi River and dutifully renamed the 355-foot cataract after the Empress of the British Empire. Victoria Falls became an enduring symbol of imperial power in the heart of the Dark Continent. Now the imagined waterfall in the deepest reaches of the Tsangpo gorge promised to be an analogous geographical trophy, a jewel in the crown of the British Raj.[25] As the president of the Royal Geographical Society put it:

In those good times when the last relics of savage barbarism shall give place to that interchange of commercial rights which is, after all, the best guarantee of international peace (a guarantee founded on mutual interest), it will be realized that the Tsangpo-Brahmaputra is the natural highway from India to Tibet . . . and we shall have a Tibetan branch of the Assam railway, and a spacious hotel for sightseers and sportsmen at the falls. This prospect is not more visionary than twenty-five years was that of a modern hotel at the Victoria Falls of the Zambesi; or the splendid establishments which will soon overlook the falls of Iguazu on the Parana', in South America.[26]

Although it was known only through the unverified report of an unlettered agent of the British government, the Falls of the Tsangpo had transformed in popular imagination into a topographical holy grail.

MY EFFORTS TO SECURE PERMISSION from Chinese authorities to visit the Tsangpo gorge had all been routinely denied. I determined to follow the example of the Pundits and to travel there without official sanction. In June 1986, I arrived in Lhasa with detailed notes on how to proceed surreptitiously along the restricted road paralleling the Tsangpo River. The notes—gathered from Tibetans who had traveled in the region in recent years—revealed the location of Chinese military check posts, bridges that could be circumvented at night by yak-skin coracles, and, when the road ended, unguarded passes by which I could enter into Pemako. To cover the 300 miles between Lhasa and the region of the Tsangpo gorges, I had counted on hiding in the back of a Tibetan logging truck—an established means of transport when traveling beyond the range of permits. But penalties for drivers had become harsh and, after numerous unsuccessful attempts to secure a ride, my covert operation ended at a dismal truck stop east of Lhasa. Frustrated, I returned to Kathmandu.

Long before me, a British field lieutenant named Frederick Marsham Bailey had also tried to reach the Tsangpo gorges without the formality of a permit or passport. A twenty-one-year-old officer on the 1904 Younghusband mission, Bailey was profoundly affected by the failure of Captain Ryder's expedition. As he wrote: "Was there somewhere in the no-man's land which lay between Assam and the terra incognita of Tibet a waterfall which would rival or even surpass Niagara? . . . It became one of my ambitions to solve the mystery of the Tsangpo gorges and I did everything in my power to equip myself for the task . . . [making] plans for attempting alone and as a private individual what the party under Ryder . . . had failed to achieve."[27]

As travel through central Tibet was still restricted, he set out from Peking in January 1911 with a sixteen-year-old Tibetan servant named Putambu, resolved to establish whether the Falls of the Tsangpo were real and to make a rough topographical survey of the lands through which he traveled. Tibetan officials blocked his passage, but he remained undaunted, and in 1912 he secured a place for himself as intelligence officer on a mission into tribal regions east of the Dihang, the name given to the Tsangpo after it crosses the Tibetan border and flows into Assam. While the expedition surveyed a major tributary, Bailey learned of a remote settlement called Mipi that was inhabited by Tibetans. Bailey took a small party to investigate, and after an eight-day march through dense jungle, they reached a collection of huts surrounded by fields of barley. The Tibetans had no warning of the British advance, and when Bailey arrived at the village with his armed escort the Tibetans fled, believing them to be Chinese soldiers sent there to kill them.

After allaying the Tibetans' suspicions, Bailey befriended the local headman, who told him that, ten years earlier, one hundred Khampas in flight from mounting Chinese oppression had journeyed to this remote valley, where they built a temple—Karmoling—from timber and bamboo and set up a base from which to search for Chimé Yangsang Né, the paradisiacal sanctuary described in Padmasambhava's prophecies.

Bailey learned that their quest for the lost paradise had been headed by a lama named Jedrung Rinpoche who had unearthed a neyig called *Clear Light* from a cave in eastern Tibet. The scroll described a crystal mountain in the heart of Pemako with multiple valleys spreading out around it "like the leaves of a thousand-petalled lotus." The hidden sanctuary promised refuge from famine, disease, and war and offered caves for "attaining supreme spiritual accomplishments." Healing springs and medicinal plants assured longevity and miraculous powers. The texts described a "secret path" through dense forests and enumerated the many dangers such as tigers, leopards, and venomous snakes that seekers would face en route, but they failed to indicate what would turn out to be the pilgrims' greatest obstacle: the hostile tribes that confounded their every effort to journey farther up the valley.[28]

The following year, 1903, two thousand more Tibetans had set out from eastern Tibet to join the remote colony of pilgrims. Many died while crossing high snow-covered passes and many more starved when the valleys near Mipi proved unable to support such large numbers. Many of the new arrivals attempted to return to Tibet but perished on the way. The Tibetan settlers who stayed were increasingly harassed by the Chulikata Mishmis. As quarrels escalated, the tribesmen began burning the Tibetans' crops and houses, setting traps along jungle paths, and shooting at them with poisoned arrows. The savagery of the natives, coupled with the ceaseless rainfall and blood-sucking flies, caused many of the pilgrims to lose faith that they were on the threshold of an earthly paradise, and in 1909, when Jedrung Rinpoche returned to Tibet, the majority of pilgrims returned with him. The ninety Tibetans who remained in Mipi were for the most part too old or feeble to attempt the journey, Bailey noted, let alone continue the search for Yangsang. The Mishmi attacks continued unabated. Two of the Khampa men who stayed back to protect the remaining colony were wounded in an ambush the day before Bailey's arrival and were treated by the expedition doctor.

BAILEY LEARNED THAT THE TIBETANS had better relations with the Mishmis of the Emra valley to the west. The tribesmen sold them bamboo baskets, musk, rice, and silks, which the Tibetans carried over high mountain passes into Tibet and bartered for salt, wool, swords, and cooking pots, all of which were highly valued by the local tribes. Bailey quickly realized that this trade route into Tibet was the opportunity he had been waiting for.

Bailey proposed a journey north along the trade route to Captain Henry Morshead, a surveyor attached to the expedition who had impressed him with his "keenness, efficiency and his extraordinary powers of physical endurance." During their journey through Mishmi territory, Morshead often made daily climbs of several thousand feet, waiting on ridge tops for hours in mist and rain for a fleeting break in the weather to triangulate on a distant snow-covered peak across the border in Tibet. He leapt at the opportunity.

Bailey and Morshead set out with ten porters and three Tibetan guides on the astrologically determined date of May 16, 1913 (10th day of the 4th moon of the Water Ox Year). They carried meager rations of barley meal, tea, sugar, and powdered rice that Bailey hoped to supplement with wild pheasants that "were there in great numbers." Cutting their way through dense bamboo that "grew so close together that it was impossible to push or squeeze between them and we had to hack our way through," they proceeded toward the first of the passes. Sinking up to their waists in snow, they crossed the pass in pouring rain that they would soon learn was a near constant presence in the lands of Pemako. On the far side they descended avalanching slopes into thick fir forests, passing the "fleshless skeletons" of past pilgrims who had perished in this no-man's land of mist, rain, and swamp.

Days later they surmounted the pass that would lead them to Chimdro, the first settlement in Tibet. Gazing down from the top of the 14,395-foot pass Bailey described "what looked like an inferno." As he wrote: "We could not see the bottom of the valley. Clouds of dark mist came billowing up obliterating the view. All we saw were steep cliffs in every direction down which, without any firing of gunshots, great masses of snow would break off and avalanche into the mist below." Descending the precipitous slope through waist-deep snow, the mists parted and "there was a gasp of horror as we saw that the slope ended in a sheer drop." Caught in an avalanche, Bailey saved himself with the handle of his butterfly net while his Tibetan guide, Sonam Chumbi, swept past him, calling out for salvation to Padmasambhava before coming to rest safely at the edge of the cliff. That night, their guides chanted prayers and gave thanks for their successful passage.

Once in Chimdro, Bailey dispatched one of the Tibetans to announce their arrival. "Since we had no authority to be where we were," Bailey wrote, "our best tactic was to behave as if we had." The headman in Mipi had written them letters of introduction, and Bailey had brought photographs of the Panchen and Dalai Lamas; with these they managed to allay suspicions and secure food and transport for their journey down the Chimdro River to its confluence with the Tsangpo. Descending three days "through thick forests and climbing over ladders," they reached the river and began heading north up the east bank.

Thirty years earlier, Kinthup had traveled through the same terrain. Bailey wrote: "The villages on the opposite bank which we passed fitted in well with Kinthup's report. If he remembered these so well four years after he had visited them, we told ourselves that he could hardly have been mistaken about the Great Falls."

As they traveled upriver, Bailey asked continuously about the waterfall farther up the gorge, but the information he received was sketchy and vague.[29] Villagers became increasingly hostile. A representative of the Powo court—fearing they were in league with the Chinese—forced the two explorers to change direction and escorted them to Showa over a high snow-covered pass. Powo's remaining court officials kept them there as virtual prisoners until they proved their status as British subjects.[30]

Once cleared, Bailey and Morshead resumed their journey, traveling westward down the Po Tsangpo River in hopes of following it to its confluence with the Tsangpo. Morshead continued his surveying work while Bailey kept notes on the fiefdom's system of taxation and political relations with Lhasa. When time permitted, he netted butterflies and combed the fir and cypress forests for rare pheasants.

Farther down the valley, a flash flood had washed away the bridges leading southward toward the great horseshoe bend of the Tsangpo, and Bailey and Morshead veered west for ten days until they could cross the Tsangpo well above the gorge.

Bailey and Morshead arrived in the village of Gyala on July 17 and continued downriver to the small monastery of Pemakochung, where three decades earlier Kinthup and the Chinese lama had searched fruitlessly for a route deeper into the gorge. "The river here is an extraordinary sight," Bailey wrote, "falling in one roaring rapid over which hangs a mist of spray. In places the water is dashed up in waves twenty feet high."

Huge mountains, mostly obscured by clouds, towered on both sides of the river. Their Tibetan guides referred to the peaks as the head and breasts of the Tantric meditational deity Dorje Pagmo, Pemako's *anima mundi*. Although Bailey noted these ethnographical facts in his journal, he and Morshead were more concerned with the mountains' heights. Triangulating from 100 miles to the south and taking into account the curvature of the earth, atmospheric refractions, and plumb-line deflections, surveyors on the Abor expedition of 1912 had already determined the glacier-covered peak of Namcha Barwa on the south side of the gorge to be 25,445 feet above sea level. Morshead and Bailey had both seen the unmapped peak called Gyala Pelri on the northern side of the gorge during the survey of the upper Dibang and Morshead had already fixed its altitude at 23,460 feet. (This measurement was later adjusted to 23,891). Both peaks were known, but no one had realized that the Tsangpo flowed between them. Clearly this was one of the earth's deepest gorges.

Bailey searched below the Pemakochung monastery for the waterfall described in Kinthup's report but, after lowering himself by roots and vines through a tunnel in the rock, he discovered only a thirty-foot drop where the Tsangpo narrowed to a width of fifty yards and sent up plumes of spray. Beneath the falls, the passageway formed a subterranean grotto where pilgrims had lit butter-lamps and gazed out from a ledge at the rainbows that form above the thundering waters.

With dwindling supplies, Morshead and Bailey returned upriver to the village of Gyala. Across from the small collection of houses, a waterfall poured over a 150-foot limestone cliff and disgorged into the Tsangpo. Bailey learned that this sinuous cataract was also an important place of pilgrimage and reachable by a primitive ferry that crossed the Tsangpo where it widened beneath the falls into the semblance of a lake. The falls were named after Shinje Chogyal, the Tibetan Lord of Death that Waddell's artist had depicted behind the curtain of falling water in the sketch in the *Journal of the Royal Geographical Society of London.* Bailey surmised that this tributary cascade had been conflated in the Survey of India's official report with the thirty-foot falls below Pemakochung—whether due to some fault in Kinthup's memory or an error on the part of the scribe.

Bailey's discovery of the mistake in the Survey's report did not dispel the myth of a colossal waterfall on Tibet's greatest river; it simply suggested that the falls must lie farther downriver in the Tsangpo's unexplored chasms. Bailey had tried to push on alone below Pemakochung, but mutinous porters had thrown down his load and abandoned him at the base of a cliff. "The question of whether or not there were a falls on the Tsangpo was still of great interest," Bailey wrote. "There now remains a gap between the lowest point I was able to reach below Pemakochung (7,480 feet) and Gompo Né (5,700 feet). There is no track of any kind on this stretch of the river, and it was difficult to obtain any information, but, from what I was able to find out from the Monpas who deserted me at the cliff . . . the distance must be about twenty miles."

BAILEY AND MORSHEAD RETURNED to British territory in November of 1913, traveling to Calcutta by train and reporting soon after in Simla, the newly established summer capital of the British Raj. Several months later, Kinthup was found in Darjeeling, where he was working as a tailor, a skill he had learned during his captivity in Tibet. Summoned to the government offices in Simla, he arrived barefoot and dressed in his deep crimson woolen *chuba*, a mala of 108 beads strung around his neck. Kinthup looked less a retired secret agent than the pilgrim he perhaps always was. As he related his journey through Pemako, it emerged that Kinthup had never mentioned a great waterfall on the Tsangpo. Being illiterate, he had dictated his account to an Indian scribe, describing the 150-foot cascade at Gyala which conceals an image of Shinje Chogyal, the Tibetan Lord of Death, and reported the thirty-foot drop on the Tsangpo at Pemakochung. As Bailey had suspected, the error was due to a misunderstanding or mistranslation of Kinthup's words. Either the scribe or the clerk who had translated the document into English had conflated the two waterfalls. Kinthup, not being able to read the report, had never been aware of the mistake.

Bailey requested that the British government of India grant Kinthup a small pension "in recognition of his service to Tibetan exploration," but fearing an "indefinite financial commitment" the government offered him only a thousand rupee bonus. Either way, Kinthup did not need the money. He returned to Darjeeling and died a few months later. Although they never reached the Tsangpo's innermost gorge to confirm or dispel the possibility of a falls deeper in the chasm, Bailey and Morshead's journey brought the mystery of the link between the Tsangpo and Brahmaputra rivers to a definitive end. They established that, after flowing for nearly a thousand miles across southern Tibet, the Tsangpo enters a narrow chasm between the towering summits of Namcha Barwa and Gyala Pelri, cutting through the Himalayan range in one of the deepest, longest, and most spectacular gorges on the planet. Although the section of the gorge that Bailey and Morshead had been unable to enter remained totally unknown, they had narrowed the blank space on the map to less than fifty miles.

Although they themselves lost faith in the possibility of a colossal waterfall in the heart of the Tsangpo gorge, others were not so ready to concede defeat. Shortly after their return, a reporter for London's *Morning Post* interviewed Sir Thomas Holdich, the former president of the Royal Geographical Society. On

November 18, 1913, Londoners read: "While paying a tribute to Captain Bailey's intrepidity and entire credibility as a witness, [Sir Thomas] expressed the gravest doubt whether he could possibly have acquired such evidence as would justify him in saying that the Brahmaputra Falls did not exist." Sir Thomas was quoted as saying that: "The evidence as to their non-existence is imperfect . . . The question of the falls must remain still in the air."

BRITISH EXPLORERS OF THE VICTORIAN and Edwardian age were not all merely agents of empire armed with theodolites, plane tables, and dreams of conquest. Most were as committed to getting off the map as to charting the frontiers of colonized territories. Departing from Bombay for the coast of Africa in 1856, Sir Richard Burton wrote in his journal: "Of the gladdest moments in human life, methinks, is the departure upon a distant journey into unknown lands. Shaking off with one mighty effort the fetters of Habit, the leaden weight of Routine, the cloak of many Cares and the slavery of Civilization, man feels once more happy."[31] A generation later Sir Henry Morton Stanley wrote of his "perfect independence" of mind in Africa. "It is not repressed by fear, nor depressed by ridicule and insults . . . but now preens itself, and soars free and unrestrained; which liberty to a vivid mind, imperceptibly changes the whole man."[32] In 1871 David Livingstone—the first white man to have seen Victoria Falls—explained his wanderings through the Dark Continent as "God's doing . . . I am away from the perpetual hurry of civilization, and I think I see far and clear into what is to come . . ."[33]

Colonel Francis Younghusband, the legendary imperialist who led the British forces into Lhasa in 1904, returned from Tibet with a bronze Buddha given to him by the Dalai Lama's reigning regent. In response to a mystical vision during his campaign, he devoted the better part of his remaining years to exploring "the supreme spiritual ideal," founding the World Congress of Faiths and numerous other religious societies. His Mountain Sanctuaries Association sought to offer pilgrims "the full impress of the mountains" and "that ineffable bliss which springs from deepening union with the spirit."[34] Lieutenant-Colonel Waddell,

who accompanied Younghusband's mission as medical officer, was averse to Tibet's "priestcraft and superstition," but he admitted to hearing "echoes of the
Theosophist belief that somewhere beyond the mighty Kanchenjunga there
would be found a key which should unlock the [ancient] mysteries . . ." Such
turn-of-the-century murmurings later found fuller expression in the novel *Lost
Horizon,* which introduced the word *Shangri-La* into the English language. Sir
Thomas Holdich of the Royal Geographical Society seemed to be referring to
more than Tibetans when he described the Falls of the Tsangpo as "the bourne
of many a devout pilgrimage." Bailey returned from his journey through the
Tsangpo gorges to write of his "annoyance with myself for rushing to conform
again after those splendid months in which none of that mattered; months when
the falls, the map, the flora and the fauna, the lie of the frontier . . . were the only
concerns." In Tibet, he and Morshead had wandered "where and when we could,
happy in the knowledge that every place was unknown."[35]

BY SYSTEMATICALLY CHARTING THEIR FRONTIERS, the British sought
to secure their empire, yet the riddle of the still-undiscovered falls transformed

imperial dreams of geographical conquest into a yearning for what lay beyond the horizons of empirical knowledge. At the end of the nineteenth century, what Joseph Conrad had called the last remaining "blank spots of delightful mystery" represented not only unexplored portions of the Earth but gateways to new orders of experience. Like a distant mirror, the long-imagined Falls of the Tsangpo reflected the era's twinned, if seemingly contrary, spirits of science and romanticism. The waterfall became a symbol of the unattainable for both East and West, Bailey's "last secret place" conflating with the Tibetan vision of an unmappable paradise—a place long imagined but never reached. Like Yangsang—the ultimate goal of Tibetan pilgrims—the lost falls filled a blank spot not only on the map of the world but in the human spirit. In an audience, the Dalai Lama likened Pemako to Shambhala, a mythical kingdom described in the Buddhist Tantras, a place both of the earth but beyond it, a place, His Holiness said, one could actually visit but not by conventional means.

IN THE LATE 1980S TRAVEL RESTRICTIONS tightened in Tibet in response to demonstrations in Lhasa for independence from Chinese rule. I contemplated ever more elaborate ways to reach the Tsangpo gorges. One day while discussing the matter with Tashi Tsering in a Dharamsala teahouse, I learned of a young Tibetan woman named Ayang Lhamo, whose grandfather had been a lama in Pemako. Ayang had lived for several years in Italy but had recently returned to her parents' home in a Tibetan resettlement camp not far from Dharamsala, Tashi told me. "Ayang is spirited and pretty and speaks the local Pemako dialect. She has relatives there who will be able to help you. You should ask her to go with you."

On the day I left Dharamsala, Tashi handed me a stack of thick worm-eaten folios wrapped in a silk khata, or offering scarf. The densely marked pages comprised one of the earliest surviving manuscripts concerning Pemako, Tashi told me, and contained rituals and invocations to open the doors to the hidden-lands.[36] At each cardinal direction are gates with so-called curtains, obstructions that must be overcome before the beyul can be entered. But more important than any ritual, Tashi said, was to go with what Tibetans call *danang*, or pure vision—something, I suppose, like what William Blake meant when he wrote of seeing "not with the eyes but through them."

I hired a vintage Ambassador taxi to drive me to the resettlement camp and sought out the house of Ayang Lhamo. Her grandfather had been the head lama of a monastery only an hour's walk from the one where Kinthup had sought refuge after escaping from slavery. Between bowls of home-brewed *chang*, a potent beverage made from fermented barley, Ayang's mother regaled me with stories of life in this remote land. "When people die there," she told me, "rainbows touch the bodies of the dead." "Have you seen this yourself?" I asked. "Not just me," she said, "everyone sees these things in Pemako."

Ayang took me to meet two *togdens*, dreadlocked yogis, who had escaped from Tibet in 1959 following a route through the Tsangpo gorges. In the middle of winter, they had traveled for weeks through the wilds of Pemako, living on the bark of trees and boiled shoe leather, their dreams deepening and guiding them toward Yangsang. They kept warm practicing *tummo*, the yoga of inner heat. Without the appropriate texts, they had been unable to locate Pemako's innermost realms, and with Chinese soldiers in close pursuit, they had crossed the border into India.

Ayang asked one of the togdens to perform a divination as to whether she should go with me to Pemako. It came out favorably and, with her parents' approval, we made immediate plans to leave for Tibet. Using Ayang's connections, we planned to hire a truck to transport us clandestinely to where we could cross over the mountains into Pemako. As Ayang had relatives in one of the first villages we would reach after crossing the Doshung-La pass, we felt confident that we would be aided in our journey onward toward the heart of the beyul.

In Kathmandu, Ayang and I scoured local trekking shops to outfit her with hiking boots and other essential gear. Bhakha Tulku had come down from Yolmo and began translating the Pemako neyigs which I had brought back from Dharamsala, annotating them with his own insights and experience.

Plans changed abruptly, however, a week before our intended departure. Due to proindependence demonstrations in Lhasa on March 10—the thirtieth anniversary of the day in 1959 when Chinese troops trained their guns on the Dalai Lama's summer palace and massacred thousands of Tibetans—the Chi-

nese government declared martial law and cancelled all travel permits to Tibet. I went to see Chatral Rinpoche, who said, "Go to Beyul Kyimolung instead and meditate."

The hidden-land of Kyimolung lies in the Tibetan borderlands, north of the Himalayas and beyond the headwaters of one of Nepal's greatest rivers, the Buri Gandaki. Milarepa, Tibet's revered poet-sage, had visited the area in the eleventh century and described it as a demon-infested land with an incomprehensible language. Kyimolung's inner valleys were opened only in the seventeenth century, when an itinerant yogi followed a red mountain goat to the base of a sheer cliff. He found three scrolls hidden in the rock, one of which, "The Heart Mirror of Vajrasattva," designates places for meditation where one can reputedly accomplish in a single day what elsewhere takes years to attain.

With Tibet closed and a new agenda of solitary retreat, Ayang returned to India while I prepared for the journey up the Buri Gandaki with Hamid Sardar, a recent graduate of Tufts University who had first come to Nepal two years earlier on a semester abroad program which I had been directing.

Hamid was born in Iran and had lived in Tehran before the revolution, in a house surrounded by gardens and towering walls. He summered with his family at an estate on the Caspian Sea, where his father took him to fish for sturgeon and to hunt bear. When he was ten, his father made a difficult shot over his shoulder to fell a large brown bear that had reared up out of the underbrush and was poised to attack him. As Hamid told the story, he saw a wildness when looking into the eyes of the bear that he had sought to rediscover ever since. In 1978, when street riots calling for the overthrow of the shah erupted, Hamid's family left for Greece, where his uncle was ambassador. Soon thereafter the Ayatollah Khomeini seized power and plunged the country into a decade of war with Iraq. Hamid then moved with his parents and two younger brothers to a château outside of Paris where his father began to breed Arabian horses.

Years later, while attending college in the United States, Hamid learned of Bon, Tibet's pre-Buddhist shamanic religion, which traces its origins to Tazig in ancient Persia. A growing interest in Eastern mysticism led to his college semester abroad in Nepal in 1987 and to our shared interest in Tibet's hidden-lands. I had told Hamid about the remote sanctuary that I had heard about in Kathmandu and, during his independent study period, he had traveled to Yolmo and met with Chatral Rinpoche. Hamid found his way to the hidden cave and spent several weeks alone there, producing a series of haikulike poems called "Naked Mist," which he submitted in lieu of a final report. When he left the valley, he forged a trail through a previously untrammeled gorge. Impressed by his boldness, Chatral Rinpoche initiated him into the practices of Vajrayana Buddhism and conferred on him the name Lekdrup Dorje, Adamantine Accom-plishment. The following summer—while I stayed in the cave in Pemthang—Hamid also returned to Yolmo and began another protracted meditation retreat. Although Pemako and the Tsangpo gorges had become a dream for both of us, we were eager to deepen our Buddhist practice with further moun-tain retreats. Kyimolung, the hidden-land in the Tibetan borderlands, seemed the next best thing to Pemako.

After a ten-day trek Hamid and I passed through a series of stone portals, crossed a plank bridge over a narrow gorge hundreds of feet deep, and entered Beyul Kyimolung. By chance, we arrived on the tenth day of the third Tibetan month, the beginning of an annual festival when herders and shamans from the surrounding mountains gather to perform religious cere-monies and sacred dances at an isolated gompa circled by glaciers and towering peaks. When we reached the monastery, the head lama was performing a ceremony at the valley's "soul tree," an ancient cedar rising above the temple walls. Seated be-side him was a row of rough-clad village *ngakpas,* or lay lamas, visibly drunk and banging on large double-headed ritual

drums. A pretty nun, equally intoxicated, was brewing a batch of potent grain alcohol in an iron cauldron as pilgrims arrived bearing alpine flowers.

Chatral Rinpoche had written us a letter of introduction and, after the conclusion of the three-day festival—during which monastic vows had been resolutely suspended—the head lama, Chokyi Nima, Sun of the Dharma, led Hamid and me through steep forests to two caves—several hours apart—where we would spend the next month in solitary meditation. Hamid's cave, Fortress of the Vajra, was built into a cliff overlooking glaciers; mine, several miles away through fir and bamboo forests, was perched above a waterfall looking across at walls of ice and rock that form the border with Tibet. The lama referred to the cave as Sangwa Dechen Puk, the Secret Cave of Bliss, and told me that it had been used for centuries for the Tantric practices of *korde rushen* and *tsalung.*

During the month that I stayed at the cave wild Himalayan tahr, a species of mountain goat with short curving horns and flowing hair, grazed nearby, entirely unconcerned by my presence. Between sessions of meditation, I made journeys to the waterfall to collect water. The Tibetan saint Milarepa had meditated in the same valley, writing ecstatic verse such as:

The wilderness cave is an open market
    where Samsara can be bartered for Nirvana.
In the monastery of your heart and body
    lies a temple where all the Buddhas unite.

After a month, I traversed along moss-laden cliffs and found Hamid perched on his ledge, gazing out at glaciers hanging from the valley wall.

With our retreats finished, Hamid and I continued up the Buri Gandaki on an ancient trade and pilgrimage route toward Tibet. In 1990, the area was completely closed to foreigners, and to circumvent a police check post guarding the upper valley we camouflaged our packs with pine boughs and traveled after sunset, sleeping in caves to avoid detection. In one of the odd ironies common on pilgrimage, we were assisted on our mission by two young women of Tibetan descent who had seduced and robbed us on our journey up the Buri Gandaki six weeks before.

Once in the upper valley, we visited hermitages where Milarepa had meditated nearly a thousand years ago. The most important site, we learned, lay across the Himalayas in Tibet. Closer to the border we took refuge in a village of retired Khampa guerillas, one of whom offered to send his son to take us into Tibet over an obscure pass that did not appear on our map. Traveling as lightly as possible, we crossed high glaciers and descended snowfields into a village where children announced our arrival by shouting, "The Chinese have come! The Chinese have come!"

To our knowledge, no Westerners had ever visited this remote settlement and there was no precedent for our appearance, still less for our being allowed to continue deeper into Tibet without passports. At our guide's insistence, we attempted to pass ourselves off, not as Chinese, but as a Nepalese doctor and schoolteacher on pilgrimage. Whether or not the headman believed this improbable story, he said he had no authority to let us continue but that if we waited three days, he would send a runner to the nearest Chinese headquarters and request permission for us to continue our journey. Until the runner returned we could stay as his guests. The plan suited us well for, in any event, Hamid was snowblind from our trip over the pass. Expecting a Chinese police patrol to come and arrest us, Hamid and I sat with our packs by an abandoned Chinese bunker above the village. From our lofty vantage point I could watch the trail by which the messenger, and anyone accompanying him, would have to return.

Two days later, we watched the runner descending the steep escarpment leading into the valley with no more than his single companion. He bore surprising news. In the absence of any Chinese officials, the local Tibetan authorities had sent a letter to the headman requesting him to escort us to the region's primary pilgrimage site, a cave complex called Dorje Trakdzong, where Milarepa had perfected the practice of *powa*, or transference of consciousness. Re-

lieved at not being reprimanded for having allowed us to stay the few days that we already had, the headman sent us with horses for the journey to the caves. Accompanying us were his son and daughter. Dressed in a faux leopard-skin jacket, his daughter served us tea beside the trail on colorful Tibetan carpets. After our return to the village the following day, they escorted us up toward the pass. Never sure just who they thought we were—Westerners or Nepalese—we crossed the snow-covered divide with our Khampa guide and descended back into Nepal.

Weeks later, when we were back in Kathmandu, we heard that during our illicit sojourn in Tibet, Chinese students and ordinary citizens had protested in Beijing's Tiananmen Square. Unnerved by their demands for democracy, the eighty-three-year-old Communist party patriarch, Deng Xiaoping, had sent tanks and PLA soldiers to quash the "counter revolutionary rebellion." On June 4, the day we had crossed the pass, hundreds, if not thousands, of Chinese had been killed. Fearing further uprisings beyond Beijing, martial law had been declared throughout Tibet.

Measuring Darkness

I HAD BEEN LIVING in Kathmandu for more than six years now, from 1984 to 1990. Like Paul Bowles's Tangiers or Lawrence Durrell's Alexandria, Kathmandu, with its vital mingling of ethnic groups and cultural traditions, offered a rich curriculum in which lines sometimes blurred between formal study and experiences beyond what Richard Burton had once called "the deadly shade of respectability." Since Nepal opened its borders in the 1950s, many Americans and Europeans had found their way to this crossroads between south and central Asia. Many felt they had come of age here, and the kingdom, ever accommodating, referred to the growing expatriate community as Nepal's "forty-forth tribe." Some found their calling as artists, writers, or photographers. Others dealt in antiques or more nefarious commodities. Many became Buddhist practitioners, supporting themselves by diverse means as their visas, passports, and connections to the West slowly expired.

Unlike foreign communities in other Asian capitals, Kathmandu's expatriates were rarely motivated by economic or career considerations. They were more impelled by an ill-defined sense that this cash-poor mountain kingdom with its wealth of ancient traditions could provide a more fulfilling existence than their cultures of origin. An important aspect of the Kathmandu experience for many of us was the presence of the Tibetan lamas who had settled there after the Communist invasion of their homeland during the 1950s. Their teachings of Tantric Buddhism offered an inspiring vision of a human potential which had resonated deeply and assuaged a spiritual restlessness that more orthodox religions had failed to address.

Despite Kathmandu's legendary enticements I felt an increasing pull to return to graduate school in the West; not to prepare myself for a job in aca-

demia, but to frame what often felt like an excess of experience in some larger perspective. I worried sometimes that, like the narrator in one of Henry James's novels, "I had spent too long in foreign parts."

On trips to America and Europe, I met with professors in anthropology departments at Berkeley and Oxford, but never felt sufficiently inspired to commit myself to the doctoral programs that they headed. In the end, I applied to Columbia's Graduate School of Religion; it offered a Buddhist studies program chaired by Robert Thurman who had recently appointed an erudite Nyingma scholar whom I hoped would prove a sympathetic mentor. Although I sub-

mitted essays, transcripts, and letters of recommendation, I never completed all elements of the application. The Graduate Record Examinations, central to the process, were offered in Kathmandu at a time when my work required me to accompany students on a village stay in the mountains. I accepted then that my fate did not lie in academia and that my interest in Buddhism and sacred landscapes would remain primarily experiential. As I settled deeper into my life in Kathmandu I soon forgot all about the abandoned application.

Months later, in April 1990, I was woken up at two in the morning by a telephone call from the review board at Columbia University. "We're looking over applications," a male voice said, "and we see that yours is not complete." Before I could mumble any response, the voice continued over the static, "You're still interested in coming aren't you?" I replied that I was interested, but that as I wasn't able to take the Graduate Record Exams, I didn't see how it would be possible. "We'll see what we can do," he said, and hung up the phone. The next night I was woken again by a second call. It was the same unknown voice. "We're ready to offer you a full scholarship and stipend," he said, "but you'll have to let us know by the end of the week." The call was as brief as before. I put back the receiver and fell back into troubled dreams.

The offer presented me with a dilemma. I had already planned on leaving my position with the School for International Training at the end of the spring semester. From the summer onward, I intended on making an extended journey to India's *shaktipiths*, the preeminent places of Tantric pilgrimage and primary influences on the Tibetan texts describing hidden-lands.[37] Long before the Tantras were ever written down, practitioners congregated at remote sanctuaries in Assam, Orissa, and other regions of the Indian subcontinent where anatomical parts of a cosmic goddess were said to have fallen to Earth. I planned to keep a journal of a pilgrimage to some of the twenty-four primary *shaktipiths* that Tibetans also hold as sacred, exploring the ways in which the Tantric tradition transformed in its journey north across the Himalayas. If I could later find a sympathetic publisher, I hoped to turn the journey into a book, but the primary motivation was personal; an immersion in places where the physical and spiritual worlds are said to overlap. Now, rather than journeying through the limbs, eyes, and womb of a terrestrialized goddess, I was confronted with the alternative prospect of years in lower Harlem: paper deadlines, sleepless nights, and perambulations through the catacomb-like depths of Columbia's world-renowned library.

I consulted a lama who was famous for his divinations: "It's not the worst thing that could happen," he said. Although far from reassured, I had definite concerns about staying on in Nepal. A complex relationship with a Nepali woman who claimed to be intermittently possessed by the same goddess whose sites I hoped to visit in India had exposed me to energies well over my head and the prospects of cool, academic halls had a sudden if still ambiguous appeal. In addition, the National Merit Fellowship that I had been offered would be hard to turn down. I called back that night and said yes, I would come.

I SHIPPED BACK BOOKS, CLOTHES, OLD MASKS, and Tibetan carpets, but kept my lease, lending the apartment I had been living in to a renegade white-robed Tantrika visiting from India. I arrived in New York on the last day of registration, and to explore my new surroundings got off the train at 125th Street on the east side of Manhattan and walked west through Harlem. With a daypack filled with notebooks and registration materials, I followed 125th Street to Morningside Park and entered a canopy of tall elms. I soon realized that the park was empty except for two ominous-looking men rapidly converging on me from opposite directions. I moved from the grass onto an asphalt walkway, eyeing a staircase leading to a street above. As they quickened their pace, I bolted for the steps with my pursuers close behind.

When I walked through the campus gates—the Goddess Columbia holding up the torch of illumination on the steps of Lowe Library and a bronze owl peering from a fold in her robes—I felt an immediate sense of sanctuary. I met with the head of the department, Professor Robert Thurman, in his office and told him of the route I had taken. "Needle Park! No one in their right mind goes through there," he said. After discussing course options, he asked me whether I had any ideas regarding my dissertation. In this at least I felt no ambivalence. I wanted to write on beyul, the hidden-lands.

AT THE SAME TIME, Hamid entered a doctoral program at Harvard's Department of Sanskrit and Tibetan Studies. We often talked by phone. Hamid shared a small house in Cambridge with a former classmate from Tufts who had recently returned from the Peace Corps in Africa. Because of my fellowship, I was given a tiny studio at the New York Theological Union on 121st Street with a wayward elevator on one side and a subway surfacing from underground on the other. A neurotic neighbor who was studying for the priesthood talked to himself quite audibly on the far side of a thin wall. When I went out to buy textbooks for my courses, I saw a title by Bruce Chatwin that I couldn't resist adding to the ominously large pile: *What Am I Doing Here?*

I registered in the gymnasium for courses in Tibetan language, Indian civilization, and theories and methods in the study of religion. The highlights, however, were the courses I could only audit: Thurman's discourses on Buddhism, and a seminar on the influence of Eastern thought on nineteenth-century American literature. As heady as the subject matter was, the courses lacked the intimacy between student and don that I had experienced at Oxford. The closest approximations were discussions with a professor in the art history department on her fieldwork in northeastern India studying Tantric pilgrimage sites and breakfasts at a local diner with a discontented department head who discoursed jadedly on Claude Lévi-Strauss, structural anthropology, and the soulessness of American universities.

From Columbia's vast library I sought out texts only peripherally related to my class subjects: studies of pilgrimage in medieval Europe (barefoot journeys of atonement—six, ten, or twelve years in duration—often substituted for terms in dungeons) and ethnographies of obscure tribes in northeastern India. Along with staid papers on methodology in the study of religion, I filled pages with arcane speculations on Tantra's assimilation of tribal rites and explored connections between Celtic sea voyages in search of mythical islands, Taoist quests for the Land of the Immortals, and the Tibetans' own search for hidden-lands. As much as I enjoyed these journeys into the archives, I soon realized that the dissertation I had imagined on Tibet's sacred geography would be less than fulfilling. As early as the eighth century a Tantric sage named Saraha had warned of the futility of exclusively intellectual approaches to knowledge, comparing them metaphorically to trying to measure darkness. Although I was grateful for the opportunity to deepen my studies, I worried that the pursuit of a doctorate would restrict me to a world of classrooms and dim-lit libraries.

I skipped classes to visit a Tibetan lama living on West End Avenue and to attend auctions at Sotheby's, where a Japanese collector had enlisted me to purchase thangkas for his collection of Tibetan art. I began to suspect I was no longer cut out for university life. Overt discontent proliferated throughout the graduate school of religion, and New York as a whole began to seem the epitome of samsara, the world of thwarted hopes and unfulfilled, if unacknowledged, desires that Henry Miller had called "the air-conditioned nightmare."

The final turning point in my stay at Columbia was a lecture by Professor Thurman on the origins of Tantric Buddhism. I sat in the auditorium with an alluring woman of Japanese descent whom I had met a month earlier at a Halloween party (and who four years later joined me on my second trip to Pemako). Thurman began the lecture by invoking the life of an eleventh-century Mahasiddha named Naropa, narrating how this great scholar at the Buddhist university of Nalanda had been inspired to renounce his academic studies and pursue a more primary path toward enlightenment. While reading in his cell, a cronelike cleaning lady peered over his shoulder and asked, "Do you understand the meaning or just the words?" When the erudite logician replied that he most definitively understood the meaning, the old woman reprimanded him for lying and encouraged him to leave his cloistered existence and seek out more authentic knowledge in the jungle. With a peal of enigmatic laughter, she dissolved into a rainbow and flew out the window, revealing her true identity as a *dakini*—a tantric muse who urges adepts beyond logic, reason, and abstract

theory and guides them toward the unwalled sanctuaries of the illuminated heart. Reflecting on his encounter, Naropa realized that life as it is commonly experienced is "like a deer chasing a mirage . . . fleeting mist and rippling water . . . a flame flickering in the wind . . . delusion, dreams, and bewilderment, the waterfall of old age and death."[38]

Like other adepts before him Naropa ultimately abandoned dry intellectual pursuits and entered tribal regions beyond the pale of Brahmanical society. Through a series of trials, rich in symbolic meaning, he realized the ultimate nature of mind and phenomena, beyond all divisions and rationally constrained perceptions. As his guru Tilopa instructed him:

Watch without watching for something.
Look from the invisible at what cannot be grasped.
To see and yet to see no things
Is to find freedom in and through yourself . . .
Dwell in the unity of Samsara and Nirvana.
Look into the mirror of your mind, which is radiant delight,
The mysterious home of the dakini.[39]

When I left the auditorium it was already dark. Police sirens and cold November winds swept across Broadway. I realized then that it was time to head for less administered terrain. A week later I wrote a letter to my academic adviser and another to Thurman explaining why I would be leaving the program after the fall semester. By the end of December, I was back in Nepal plotting a journey to Tibet.

WHAT COULD HAVE BEEN an existential crisis was averted by an offer to collaborate on a book on the Tibetan life cycle. I would travel with two close friends through eastern and central Tibet and contribute chapters on Tibetan approaches to pilgrimage, death, and spiritual liberation. Bhakha Tulku's daughter, whose name was Yeshe Choden and who would be studying at Middlebury College the following fall, came with us as a research assistant in areas of Tibet where local dialects bear little resemblance to the classical Tibetan that I had studied in Nepal. If possible, we would visit her father's monastery and ancestral seat in the region of Powo. High, snow-covered passes lead from there into Pemako, and I packed in hopes of possibly following the route which Bhakha Tulku had taken over the Dashing-La pass to the sacred mountain Kundu Dorsempotrang. Although I was officially only on leave from Columbia, I felt freed from the dichotomies presented by Buddhist scholasticism and eager to reenter more vital streams of experience.

After waiting for travel permits in Chengdu in western Szechuan, we were told, somewhat predictably, that the valley of Powo was still out of bounds, as it had been when Bailey had first tried to travel there in 1911. Our month-long journey was restricted to those regions in Kham which lay east of the border with the more politically sensitive Tibetan Autonomous Region.

On our return to Chengdu in August, I gave my name to a prominent Chinese travel agency in hopes that they would contact me if permits were ever granted for the Powo and Pemako regions. The director had told me of a Doctor Fisher who was supposedly organizing a scientific expedition into the Namcha Barwa Grand Canyon. He would give my name to him, he said, but as I immersed myself in the writing of the book I thought little about it.

The Invitation

IN APRIL 1993, after submittiing my contributions to the book on Tibetan life cycles but before its publication, I was awakened in the middle of the night by a call from a night clerk in Kathmandu's telecommunications office. A telegram had come for me, he said, marked urgent. I sat up groggily on my mattress. The heady scent of night jasmine streamed through open shutters. Calling the telephone number at the end of the message, I talked with Richard D. Fisher of Wilderness Research in Tucson, Arizona, who claimed to have been issued the first permits for the Great Bend region of the Tsangpo gorge. This would be a historic journey, he claimed, the first attempt to raft "the Mount Everest of rivers."

Fisher claimed to have a state-of-the-art self-bailing boat and told me that he had applied for permits to raft down the Tsangpo River as far as the Indian border. He asked me what experience I had had on white water. Some, I said, but confessed that I would prefer to travel through the region on land. The prospect of rafting through what Morshead had described as "a boiling, seething mass" was far from appealing. But it was impossible to resist the possibility of a sanctioned journey through the restricted and uncharted regions which I had been reading about for years in Tibetan texts and hearing about from Tibetan lamas, pilgrims, and refugees. Fisher's voice sounded high-strung and the telephone line was plagued by echoes. I wasn't sure whether I was being recruited or discouraged. "If you're not in Lhasa by April 21," he said, "we're leaving without you."

THE DAY BEFORE MY FLIGHT to Lhasa I went to see Chatral Rinpoche at his hermitage at the edges of the Kathmandu Valley. He was sitting outside on

the skin of a clouded leopard, pressing gold leaf into a ceramic bowl to make *mendrup*, a consecrated elixir originally used as a support in the practice of Tibetan Buddhist yogas. He cut up a musk pod and added it to the mortar. You'll see many of these in Pemako, he said. The strong aroma drifted through my nostrils, blending with the scents of sandalwood, saffron, and cloves that provide an aromatic base for various secret ingredients. As Chatral Rinpoche added a bear's gallbladder to the dubious concoction, I sat down with Saraswati and two monks to help add the gold. Each leaf was infinitesimally thin; when touched, it instantly adhered to the skin. As we sat by the bowl, Saraswati told me that one of Rinpoche's students—Daku Sherpa—the wife of Tenzing Norgay, Hillary's companion in 1953 on the first ascent of Everest, had recently died from an illness that she had contracted while on pilgrimage to Pemako. Traveling through villages in Pemako's more accessible regions across the Tibetan border in the Indian state of Arunachal Pradesh, her body had become blue and swollen. Word had been sent that she had been poisoned by a practitioner of a cult in which a mixture of snake venom, toxic plants, and pulverized toads is administered to the unwary. She had eventually died in a town below Darjeeling, claiming that because she had reached the sacred land of Pemako she now had nothing to fear from death. Chatral Rinpoche had performed ceremonies during her cremation, directing her spirit toward the *shingkam*, celestial Buddha Realms of which Pemako is held to be an earthly emanation.

When the mendrup was placed on the fire, Chatral Rinpoche took out a *songdu*, a protection cord spun from the wool of a black yak. He tied nine knots along its length and, over the next hour, as he continued with the preparations of the elixir, he recited mantras over it and rubbed it between his hands. Then, as darkness claimed the limestone cliffs above the monastery, he tied it around my neck. "Don't lose this," he said, speaking in Tibetan, "Pemako can be dangerous." When I asked for parting advice on how to move through the landscape, he replied pragmatically, "It rains a lot and the trails are rough: bring an umbrella and good boots."

As I walked back toward the road with the sachet of mendrup that Chatral Rinpoche had given me on leaving, Saraswati related how, decades earlier, her grandfather Dulshuk Lingpa had perished in an avalanche while searching for a beyul called Pemathang, the Lotus Fields, to the east of Kanchenjunga. Bush-whacking through the dense Himalayan jungles, the lama had told his follow-ers not to remove the leeches that feasted on their blood and to maintain a vision of their goal beyond the ice walls of the 28,208-foot mountain. While crossing a high pass, collapsing cornices had swept Dulshuk Lingpa and his fel-low pilgrims down the glacier, burying them in the snow. The lama perished and those who survived were forced to amputate fingers and toes. After recov-ering, some resumed their journey and were never heard from again.

PART TWO

THE
GORGE

The pious will lack the means to open the way to the hidden-lands. . . . Those who contemplate going will often fall prey to their fears and will lack the requisite courage. Those who do go will often be slandered by [others] who are envious of their good fortune. . . . For all who lack the auspicious circumstances to journey to these hidden-lands. . . . the beyul will remain no more than imagined paradises of enlightened beings; they will not manifest simply through contemplation and idle talk.

PADMASAMBHAVA, *The Outer Passkey to the Hidden-Lands*

With every step the way [into Pemako] seemed to become more difficult; the ground was again rougher and the mountains steeper; the trees here grew much taller. In places we had to negotiate great rocks, only able to be crossed by narrow foot-holds. . . . Our journey now took us through yet stranger country; there were all sorts of trees forming a dense jungle with no level spaces; a tangle of mountains with continual rain and mist. . . .

CHOGYAM TRUNGPA, *Born in Tibet*

Every day the scene grew more savage; the mountains higher and steeper. . . . The great river was plunging down, down, boring ever more deeply into the bowels of the earth. The snow-peaks enclosed us in a ring of ice. Dense jungle surged over the cliffs . . .

FRANK KINGDON WARD, *The Riddle of the Tsangpo Gorges*

There is an unaccountable solace that fierce landscapes offer to the soul.

BELDON LANE, *The Solace of Fierce Landscapes*

April 1993
The Year of the Water Bird

FLYING NORTHEAST from Kathmandu toward Tibet's single commercial airport, our pilot navigated through banks of clouds between Everest and Kanchenjunga, the earth's highest and third-highest mountains. Windswept summits and vast fields of ice and light passed like apparitions beneath the wings of the Boeing 747.

As we continued northward, the skies opened and shimmering glaciers turned into barren high-altitude plains. The Tsangpo River appeared suddenly on the horizon, a glittering swath of water that flows for nearly 1,000 miles across the roof of the world.

We landed at an airstrip built along the braided channels of this legendary river, which has served for millennia as the central artery of Tibetan civilization. Tibetan myths correspond with the geological record and describe the Tsangpo as the remnants of a vast, primeval sea that once covered the Tibetan plateau. Forty to fifty million years ago, the Indian subcontinent began to collide with the Asian landmass, forcing the earth upward into collosal mountains and reducing the ancient Sea of Tethys to scattered lakes and the great river that now flowed before us along the tectonic fault line.

From its source near Mount Kailas in far western Tibet, the Tsangpo—which means the Great Purifier—descends from glaciers and flows eastward through an arid landscape of rock outcrops, wind-blasted dunes, and scrub juniper. As it drops in altitude into warmer, forested regions east of Lhasa, it forms an ever-narrowing chasm, gradually transforming into seething rapids as it bores its way through a still-uplifting wall of jagged, glacier-covered peaks at the eastern end of the Himalayan range. Plunging between two of the world's highest mountains, Namcha Barwa (the Blazing Meteorite) and Gyala Pelri (the Glorious Peak), the river forms a gorge three times as deep as the Grand Canyon and hailed by Chinese geologists as the world's deepest.[1]

A CHINESE GEOLOGIST from the Institute of Mineral Sciences in Chengdu met me at the airstrip. Introducing himself as the guide and liaison officer attached to Richard Fisher's "Namcha Barwa Grand Canyon Rafting Expedition," Geng Quanru—or "Mr. Gunn," as he called himself—told me that Fisher had left with the group at 5 A.M. that morning as they were becoming "scattered" in Lhasa. If we drove all night, Gunn said, we could catch up with them the next morning.

The road to Lhasa runs west along the southern banks of the Tsangpo. The river was more than a mile across here, its gray-green currents punctuated by shifting sandbars, hazards for the yak-hide coracles and primitive barges that ply these placid midsections of the river. Green fields of barley and lines of poplar and dwarf willow fringed the opposite bank, beneath gray cliffs and

barren shale-strewn peaks. We turned north over a bridge guarded by Chinese soldiers and, in another hour, drove into Tibet's capital.

While Gunn and the Chinese driver filled reserve tanks with gasoline, I made a quick visit to the Jokhang, Tibet's most revered temple. Built more than 1,800 years ago, the Jokhang draws pilgrims from all corners of the plateau. Nomads in yak-hide chubas and Khampas from eastern Tibet sporting high fox fur hats and mirrored sunglasses poured crushed juniper into stone censers outside the main gates. Fragrant smoke curled into the sky as offerings to ancient spirits as pilgrims wound their way into the Jokhang's interior.

The temple's innermost sanctum harbors a golden, jewel-encrusted Buddha, but the building's original purpose was to stake down the heart of a malevolent demoness, the Srinmo, whose limbs and energies were said to spread throughout the Tibetan landscape. Tibet's earliest chronicles narrate how the Srinmo's various body parts were pinned down with multitiered Buddhist temples, allowing the Buddhist doctrine to flourish. Two hundred and fifty miles to the east of Lhasa, near the entrance to the Tsangpo gorge, a gilt-roofed temple immobilizes the Srinmo's right elbow. Another seventh-century structure in Powo, the Dungchu Lhakhang, is said to decommission her left palm. Many of the scrolls describing Pemako were discovered in these ancient temples.[2]

All food on the expedition was to be provided by our Chinese host agency, and before setting out from Lhasa, Gunn brought me to a lavish Szechuan-style restaurant with round windows and a red velvet ceiling. The pig's intestines that constituted our main course were not a personal favorite, nor were the tins of sweetened black fish I saw the driver loading into the back of the Land Cruiser. In the markets surrounding the Jokhang, I stocked up on dried yak meat, tsampa, and apricot kernels. Apart from desiring more palatable fare, I wanted to be sure that I could head out on my own. I was not optimistic about the proposed rafting trip, and my major incentive for joining Fisher's expedition was to get through the series of armed check posts on the three-day drive to the gorge leading into Pemako.

My sense of antipiciation was mounting. Aside from the gorge's sacred significance to Tibetans, it was a naturalist's wonderland. Surging through a mountain wall only slightly lower than Mount Everest, the Tsangpo carves its way downward between towering cliffs as warm, moisture-laden air funnels up the gorge from the Bay of Bengal. The clouds collide with the cold, dry air of the Himalayas and create a unique ecosystem that ranges from arctic to subtropical. Glaciers spill into cloud forests, and jungles and ravines teem with rare and unknown plants. Endangered species, including Tibet's last remaining tigers, thrive in the old-growth forests of bamboo, rhododendron, and towering cypress.

Much of Pemako lies in disputed territory between India and China. The only recent map I was able to find—a 1:250,000 projection compiled in 1954 by the Army Map Service in Washington, D.C.—was full of cautionary provisions. Some areas were simply left blank and labeled as "unexplored." Others indicated "indefinite" borders and "approximate alignments." Current Chinese maps show their sovereignty extending as far as the Brahmaputra valley in Assam, but they offer little topographical detail. Although China opened Tibet to tourism in the early 1980s, Pemako was designated a "special military region" and remained resolutely out of bounds. No permits had ever before been issued. Over lunch, Gunn showed me the sheaves of documents from China's Bureau of Foreign Affairs, the Military High Command in Beijing, and Lhasa's Public Security Bureau that he would have to show at checkpoints along the road leading toward the gorge. I kept the translations of the treasure scrolls that I had brought with me from Kathmandu well hidden.

WE DROVE EASTWARD OUT OF LHASA along roads like dry riverbeds. Plumes of dust streamed behind us across the treeless plains. We climbed higher, over snow-covered passes where our tires lurched through slush and half-frozen mud, dangerously close to precipitous drops. Gunn sat in the front of the Toyota Land Cruiser conversing with the driver and recycling the same cassette tape of what sounded like Chinese opera hour after hour. Jostled in the backseat, I brooded about the forthcoming rafting expedition over perhaps the most treacherous stretch of river in the world. My own desire was to wander on foot through Pemako's mist-shrouded valleys, following a very different itinerary. The fact that I had twice nearly drowned, once on a rafting expedition in Nepal, didn't add to my enthusiasm.

I thought of my great grandfather, who had nearly drowned while surveying for the Canadian Pacific Railway during the same years—1881–83—that Kinthup had performed his covert mission for the British Survey of India. Charged with mapping a route through the Rocky Mountains and the lesser-known "snow-clad desolation" of the Selkirk Range, William Edgar Baker (1856–1921) had kept a journal that I'd read as a teenager. I was enthralled by his tales of encounters with roving bands of Blackfoot, Shushwap, and Piegan Indians and, as he ventured deeper into the wilderness, with beaver swamps and moss-carpeted forests where he was "more apt to see bears than anyone else in the party." His wife, my great grandmother, called him the Ruffian, and my father once had a photograph of him looking the part, with a thick black beard and piercing eyes and brandishing a cutlass.

I thought of another long-dead relative, my great-great grandfather, Captain George Knight Griffin, who had journeyed to the Klondike at the age of seventy-six and had been the only member of his party not to drown in the Yukon. A line from his 1904 obituary had stayed with me: "He did not know what it was to fear either man or beast and his reckless courage often placed him in dangerous situations." If I was being foolhardy, perhaps it was in the blood.

Bounding along the muddy, rutted road into the small hours of the night, I thought of the ten Americans crammed into the two Land Cruisers somewhere ahead of us and felt grateful for the time alone. Darkness and frost on the windows of the Land Cruiser veiled the landscape that passed beyond us. Sometime after midnight, we stopped at a derelict roadside hostelry. The dormitory-style rooms were filled with Chinese and Tibetan truck drivers plying the route between Lhasa and eastern Tibet. The proprietor gave me a bed next to a Khampa trader whose wide-brimmed felt hat shielded his eyes from the glare of a bare security light that hung from the ceiling.

We started out again at dawn and we caught up with the rest of the group before noon in the town of Bayi, a colonial outpost built by Chinese soldiers on land reclaimed from a tributary of the Tsangpo. The town's broad avenues, lined with chandeliered street lights, passed between garish buildings built from blue glass and porcelain tile. As we turned a corner near the center of town, we saw Fisher and his group assembled in front of their two mud-splattered Land Cruisers. Bayi was officially closed to foreigners, and three members of Fisher's group who had strayed from a small noodle shop where they had stopped for lunch had been brought in for questioning by plainclothed officials of the local Public Security Bureau, China's secret police. As we drove up, Fisher was reprimanding his wayward charges—now released—for endangering the expedition.

DURING HIS DRAWN-OUT MONOLOGUE I met another member of the group, Ken Storm, Jr., partner in a family enterprise called Aladdin Distributors in Minneapolis, Minnesota. As Fisher continued his tirade, Ken and I drifted away from the main group and sought refuge behind one of the Toyotas. Behind his wire-rimmed glasses, Ken wore the determined air of a missionary bound for far horizons. Ken had traveled extensively in the western Himalayas and had trekked solo through Mexico's Copper Canyon; he had also rafted and kayaked throughout the United States. Richard Fisher (Rick) had recruited him because of his extensive white-water experience, though Ken shared my own doubts about the expedition. He confided that in Lhasa, Rick had forbidden them even to leave their hotel, a Chinese-built edifice with an artificial waterfall and plastic storks suspended from the ceiling. They should conserve their energy for the expedition, Rick had told them, not wander into the bazaars and temples of downtown Lhasa.

Ken had secured a 1:500,000 aeronautical chart of southeastern Tibet from the Defense Mapping Agency Aerospace Center in St. Louis, Missouri. He had photocopied additional maps from a book called *Riddle of the Tsangpo Gorges*, written by the intrepid Britsh plant collector Frank Kingdon Ward, who had entered the Tsangpo gorge in 1924, ten years after Captain F. M. Bailey and Henry Morshead's own efforts to locate the waterfall. Calculating from the boiling points made by Kingdon Ward and his companion, a twenty-four-year old Scottish lord, Ken was convinced even before leaving the States that the river's

rate of descent and enormous volume would make the gorge unrunnable. Where Rick claimed to have scouted near the entrance to the gorge, the gradient was already 50 feet per mile. Deeper into the canyon it dropped between 150 and 200 feet per mile.[3] In comparison, Ken pointed out, the Colorado River descends through the Grand Canyon at an average of only 8 feet per mile and with a much lesser volume. Comparing the figures, Ken concluded that, although kayakers might have some chance, to attempt the Tsangpo in a raft would be suicidal. Ken had shared his calculations with Rick more than a month earlier in the United States, but Rick would not be dissuaded from his ambition to be the first down the gorge in a boat.

IN 1924, THE SAME YEAR that George Leigh Mallory disappeared into mist near the summit of Mount Everest, Captain Frank Kingdon Ward and his companion, the Fifth Earl of Cawdor, had attempted to push beyond where Bailey and Morshead had been forced to retreat. "There remained a gap of 50 miles," Kingdon Ward wrote, "about which nothing was known; indeed, for half that distance there was said to be no track of any sort near the river, which was hemmed in by bare rock walls several thousand feet high. Was it possible that hidden away in the depths of this unknown gorge there was a great water-fall? Such a thing was quite possible, and it was this question that we were re-solved to answer. We would, if possible, go right through the gorge, and tear this last secret from its heart.... Here if anywhere were the 'Falls of the Brahmaputra' which had been a geographical mystery for more than a century; and the solution—falls? or no falls?—was now within our grasp."[4]

Kingdon Ward persevered beyond where Bailey had been able to reach but, confronted by "a howling river . . . boring ever more deeply into the bowels of the earth . . . ," was eventually forced to climb out of the yawning chasm up a rock face which he later described as the most harrowing episode in his several decades of Himalayan exploration. Forging their way through what Lord Jack Cawdor de-scribed as "particularly pestilential jungle," the two explorers penetrated all but a five-to-ten-mile section of the Tsangpo's innermost chasm. They documented several waterfalls on the river, estimating their height to be no more than thirty to forty feet. Kingdon Ward returned to England, and in his lecture at the Royal Ge-ographical Society he concluded that the fabled Falls of the Tsangpo—a "water-fall of a hundred feet or more"—was probably no more than a "romance of geography" and a "religious myth." For his efforts, Kingdon Ward was awarded the society's coveted Gold Medal of Exploration. Since his well-publicized ac-count, no further attempt had been made to penetrate the still-unknown section of the Tsangpo gorge. Ken was as enchanted by the idea of this "blank spot of delightful mystery" as I was, if for somewhat different reasons, and equally con-vinced that it was mad to attempt to reach it in a raft.[5] We began to discuss how we might break away from the group and enter the gorge on foot.

As we climbed back into the overcrowded Land Cruisers, Rick squinted at Ken and me from beneath his red bandana, as if aware of impending insurrection in the ranks. Squeezed in between fellow passengers, we drove southward along the Gyamda Chu, a tributary river that flows into the Tsangpo from the north.

YEARS EARLIER IN DHARAMSALA, the Dalai Lama had directed me to a white-haired lama named Khamtrul Jamyang Dondrup Rinpoche who had es-caped the Communist invasion by following the Tsangpo River into Pemako.

While traveling through the Tsangpo gorges in the late 1950s, Khamtrul Rinpoche had dreamed of being swallowed by an emanation of Pemako's guardian goddess, Dorje Pagmo, and was guided through her anatomy toward the innermost sanctum of the hidden-land. He had kept a journal of his odyssey. It began with ominous prophecies regarding Tibet's future and ended with visionary accounts of Pemako's paradisiacal center and its wealth of magical plants:

> Of all obscure and mystic places, Pemako is supreme—resplendent like an immaculate lotus flower. . . . To enter the hidden-land we travelled after dark upon perilous and slippery rocks through pounding dark rain. . . . We took shelter in caves where Padmasambhava had left imprints of his feet in solid rock and where mantric seed syllables had manifested on the walls. . . . [At the heart chakra of Dorje Pagmo] lie meadows arrayed like a mandala and surrounded by a ring of mountains. Growing here are the five supreme magical plants . . . which confer immortality . . . and the experience of emptiness and bliss. This innermost heart of the sublime holy land is identical to a terrestrial pure land of lotus light. In this place, all obscurations of mind and emotions can be released . . . and the three bodies of the Buddha spontaneously realized . . .[6]

Khamtrul Rinpoche had followed the same route into the gorges as Kingdon Ward, and he too had been unable to penetrate the hidden sections of the gorge on foot, nor locate the "five supreme magical plants." As I took notes, he described the caves and rocks where he had camped and the visions and dreams that had guided him deeper into the hidden-land.

TWO HOURS BEYOND BAYI, we reached the northern bank of the Tsangpo. Green-uniformed Chinese soldiers with AK-47s stood guard over a bridge leading across to the southern shore. Gunn deferentially gave them packs of Wufeng cigarettes and brought out his stack of permits. While the humorless officers made a cursory inspection of our belongings, I watched a small yak-skin coracle float by on the river, its lone boatman losing himself to view as he

drifted down on swift currents. Crowded into the Land Cruiser with acciden-
tal companions, I regretted momentarily that I had not come as I had originally
planned; without a permit, surrendering to the currents of circumstance. The
river here was broad and silted after having flowed for nearly 1,000 miles across
southern Tibet. The glacier-covered slopes of Namcha Barwa, the eastern terminus of the Himalayas, glistened above us behind dark clouds. Beyond the
horizon, the Tsangpo began its circuit around this sacred mountain, transforming into seething rapids and losing itself in the three-mile deep chasm that
had long been the Ultima Thule of Tibetan civilization. In past centuries crim-
inals and deposed kings were bound and thrown into this intractable river in a
rite of capital punishment called *chaplasorwa.*[7]

After crossing the bridge we drove several hours through streambeds and
small slate-roofed hamlets along the southern banks of the Tsangpo. Hemlock,
pine, spruce, and larch grew thickly on the slopes above us. When the road
abruptly ended, we set up camp amid flowering peach trees at a small village
called Kyikar. The supply truck had arrived hours earlier and our Chinese cook,
sheltered in the lee of the truck's oversized tires, was preparing a meal on what
appeared to be a welding torch. We were still at high altitude—nearly 10,000
feet—and, as Gunn explained, the blowtorch could cook rice faster than a fire.
After dinner Rick gathered his recruits around a bonfire made with driftwood
carried up from the Tsangpo. The air was cold and I put on a Khampa fox fur
hat that I'd picked up in Bayi. Rick seemed eager to determine who he had assembled for this improbable journey. He went around the circle offering what
he presumed to be each person's motivations for coming.

Besides Rick there were eleven of us; seven "ecotourists," as Rick referred to
them, and four, myself included, on the rafting team. We were an odd assortment, each drawn here for different reasons. A retired Disney cinematographer
from Alaska had cashed in a life insurance policy to finance what he called "a
mission to reconnect with 'the goddess.'" Others included a lawyer from Tucson,
a real estate broker with a reconsructed knee, a retired brothel owner from
Minneapolis and her twelve-year-old son, a physiotherapist named Jill Bielowski,
and an itinerant biker/electrician named Eric Manthey who wore Levi's jeans
and a Hells Angels sweatshirt throughout the trip. Ken intrigued me most. A

graduate in anthropology, he had traveled widely through Ladakh in the western Himalayas, collaborating on a book entitled *Between Earth and Heaven*. He
had a passion for the works of the eighteenth- and nineteenth-century Romantic poets and owned many first editions. He told the group he was drawn to the
Tsangpo gorges in search of the "sublime," the "paradoxical union of delight
and terror" that had seized Wordsworth on the slopes of Snowdon and
Thoreau on Mount Katadyn in Maine.[8] The bard of Walden Pond had cried
out for "a nature no civilization can endure," and Ken hoped to surpass his
hopes in this hidden corner of Tibet.

Rick spoke of his own life as a "canyoneer" and of his obsession with this
last unexplored gorge. "You know what obsession is?" Rick said. "It's halfway
between love and madness." Standing by the fire, he recounted his journeys to
Tiger Leaping Gorge on the Yangtse River and Colca Canyon in Peru, which,
he claimed, the National Geographic Society had wrongly identified as the
world's deepest gorge. He concluded his soliloquy by stating that "the Tsangpo
is the mother of all gorges" and that he was committed to it "to the point of
insanity." Somewhat incongruously then, he concluded the evening session by
announcing that if the the rapids proved unrunnable, we would pack up the
Land Cruisers and drive approximately eighty miles north and east, circumventing the gorge entirely. A three-day trek down the Po Tsangpo River would
bring us to its confluence with the Tsangpo, from where we could set up a base
to scout the river after it emerged from its innermost chasms.

Rick had torn a ligament in his right knee while training for the expedition
and it was flaring up badly. He limped around the fire using a stick for support.
Bypassing the Tsangpo's innermost gorge, the fabled missing link, seemed out
of character. Ken and I imagined that Rick was so territorial about the area that
he was unwilling to let others on his own team attempt what he himself was
unable to do. When we proposed that the river team retrace Kingdon Ward's
route through the gorge on foot and meet up with the others at the
Tsangpo–Po Tsangpo confluence, Rick claimed that we only had permission to
attempt it in rafts. Having imagined just such a scenerio after his phone conversations with Rick before departure, Ken told me he had brought with him
boxes of salted pilot bread and freeze-dried food, enough to survive on for a

week or more. I had my stores of tsampa, almonds, and apricot kernels and spoke the local language. The two of us resolved that if the next day's reconnaisance confirmed our belief that the river was unraftable, we would head out on our own, permits or no permits.

WE HIKED THE NEXT MORNING through groves of walnut and apple trees and after two hours reached the rapids where the Tsangpo begins its ever more rapid descent toward the gorge. Gray lizards sunned themselves on rocks. Below us, the river pounded between massive boulders in a frenzy of white foam. Kingdon Ward had described this point in the river in 1924: "It is the glacial boulders which cause such a turmoil in the river-bed, where at high water, waves are thrown 20 feet into the air, and the river looks like an angry sea, racing madly down the steep slope into the gorge."[9]

This was the farthest point that Rick and Eric had reached on their scouting expedition the previous October, and they were both visibly distressed that the rapid was now clearly unrunnable—even for Rick, who had been described to me in Kathmandu as a "kamakazi rafter," relying more on bravado than technique. The volume and force of the river was tremendous. Shouting above the Tsangpo's surging drone, Rick estimated it to be flowing at more than 40,000 cubic feet per second. By comparison, the Colorado River flows through the Grand Canyon at an average rate of 10,000 cubic feet per second. Here, before the entrance to the gorge, the Tsangpo was dropping extremely steeply and jagged boulders, massive hydraulics and swirling whirlpools made the route impossible for a raft. Even if one were to emerge unscathed, vertical walls of rock in the deeper and steeper sections of the gorge would prevent escape in case of trouble. Rick stood immobilized on a large boulder, gazing down into the Tsangpo's seething whiteness and its surging waves. Ken likened him to Captain Ahab and the river to his Moby Dick.

The previous night, Rick had referred to his obsession with proving that the Tsangpo was the world's deepest gorge as his "personal Holy Grail." Maps show the Tsangpo descending into a narrow chasm framed between the 23,891-foot summit of Gyala Pelri and the glacial massif of Namcha Barwa whose highest peak rises to 25,436 feet above sea level. Based on measurements by Bailey and Morshead that were confirmed by Kingdon Ward, the altitude at river level between these two peaks is only 8,800 feet and the distance between them a mere fourteen miles. Calculating from maps alone, the gorge is more than 16,000 feet deep. The Grand Canyon, in contrast, is only 4,682 feet deep and more than eighteen miles across. Rick claimed that he had brought this information to the attention of the National Geographic Society as well as the *Guinness Book of World Records,* but that so far it had not been reflected in any of their literature. (Three years later, in its 1996 revised edition, Guinness listed the Tsangpo as the world's deepest *valley.* In the 2002 edition, the average depth of the gorge was given as 16,405 feet and its deepest point 17,658.

After the river team had scouted the rapids leading into the gorge, the plan was for the entire group to assemble for lunch at a thermal spring a half hour's climb above the river. Following a streambed, we reached a grove of trees where steaming waters poured over granite rocks carved with Buddhist mantras. A Tibetan porter told me that the springs were revered locally as a né, or holy place of Vajrapani, a wrathful Tantric deity. Members of the group were washing clothes and resting on the dark and streaming rocks. Avoiding the sulfurous fumes and heeding the Tibetan's words, I sat down under a tree visited by a flock of rose finches and asked my Tibetan companion about the route into the gorge. He pointed to a trail contouring downstream along eroded cliffs. After two days you reach a village called Gyala, he said. Beyond that he had never been.

Gunn was standing nearby and seemed nervous that I was conversing with a local in a language he couldn't understand. To deflect suspicion I asked Gunn about the local geology. Eager to share his knowledge, he elaborated on theories of continental drift and explained how the Tsangpo threads its course along the suture between the ancient continents of Laurasia and Gondwanaland that had begun colliding in the middle Eocene, roughly forty to fifty million years ago. The persistent northward drift of the Indian subcontinent had given birth to the Himalayas and formed a shallow prehistoric sea to the north of the emerging mountains. As the Sea of Tethys subsided, its sediments decayed and metamorphosed into mixed ophiolites. Gunn speculated that he would find these slices of the oceanic crust throughout the gorge, hard evidence that the entire region had once been under water.[10]

Gunn drifted away to speak with Rick, who had hobbled up the streambed. As I finished my packed lunch of yak cheese and apricots I pointed out to Ken the trail the villager had indicated. Ken had also spotted it. While others bathed in the fuming waters, we scrambled up a steep slope and set off down the narrow, dusty track.

Less than an hour later, we spied two figures approaching us with packs towering over their heads and Patagonia stretch pullovers clinging tightly to their emaciated bodies. In this remote corner of Tibet it was the last thing we expected. With hollowed eyes, the two men told a strange tale of their failed attempt to penetrate the inner recesses of the gorge. They'd traversed slick, vegetated cliffs and hacked their way through hanging jungles of towering nettles and tangled rhododendrons. They had trudged, they said, through snow up to their waists and through streams swollen by nearly perpetual rain. Clouds of gnats had plagued their steps, and when they rested they were feasted on by hordes of leeches. They had camped on small ledges or, when these were absent, had built platforms out from the sides of the gorge. David Breashears— as the man in front introduced himself—compared it in difficulty to his several ascents of Everest, claiming that it was the most arduous and unpleasant of any Himalayan expedition he had ever undertaken. Gordon Wiltsie, an intrepid National Geographic photographer, said it was worse than any of his climbs in Antarctica.

Ten days into the gorge, after failing to find a way around a precipitous headwall, six of their nine porters had deserted them, taking with them the majority of Breashears and Wiltsie's food. Breashears described how on their trek out they'd been forced to eat a monkey that a leopard had killed only minutes before. Its fur was slicked back, he said, and its red eyes had not yet misted over.

Breashears and Wiltsie were eager to avail themselves of the hot springs, and we accompanied them back to where the group was still bathing. When they appeared at the sulfur-colored rocks, Rick grew visibly agitated. He tried to prevent them from interacting with his group, invoking a boulder as the dividing line beyond which they could not cross. What followed in the next hours was almost comical. Rick was furious to find that Breashears had beaten him to the gorge and he accused him of appropriating information that he had provided to the National Geographic Society and of intentionally trying to sabotage his expedition. While returning toward camp from the hot springs, Rick rode a small, brown pony to rest his bad knee, and from his high perch he provoked Breashears into a raging dialogue as they passed through orchards of walnuts and flowering peach trees. With the north face of Namcha Barwa glittering above them in the evening sun, Rick shouted that Breashears's presence in Tibet had destroyed his "Zen moment." There was no mistaking the jealousy he felt for the National Geographic–sponsored team. Ken and I trailed some distance behind. "Geez, the way they're going at it," Ken said, "you'd think it was the source of the Nile." Later that evening as Rick limped through camp in his Teva sandals, I kept my distance, resolved to head out the next morning—as much to escape the maniacal atmosphere as to enter the long-dreamed of land of Pemako.

Ken and I withdrew to a nearby juniper grove to discuss our options. If we headed directly downriver we would inevitably be pursued and forced to return. I proposed an alternative route over a 17,000-foot pass called the Nam-La, the Sky Pass, that had once served as a pilgrimage route to a remote hermitage south of Namcha Barwa. No one would expect us to follow this route and Gunn would be unlikely to even know about it. I pointed out on the map how we could circle north again and rejoin the Tsangpo below where Breashears and Wiltsie had turned back and above the farthest point that Kingdon Ward had been able to reach in 1924. We would be poised at the opening of the legendary gap, the last area in the gorge where the Falls of the Tsangpo might still lie. Furthermore, the route would pass through the area that Khamtrul Rinpoche had described in his journals as the gateway to Yangsang, the lost paradise he had reached only in dream. But our hopes were dashed when I asked a local villager about the route over the Nam-La. The pass would lie buried deep in snow for at least another month.

The next morning, Rick hobbled over on his gimp leg. Fueled by his competitiveness with Breashears, he proposed that Ken and I form a team with Eric Manthey, his right-hand man, and Jill Bielowski. Abandoning the raft, we would try to push on beyond the headwall where Breashears and Wiltsie had been forced to turn back and, if possible, beyond where Kingdon Ward and Lord Cawdor had abandoned their mission seventy years earlier. Rick would take the rest of the group and follow the well-established trail down the Po Tsangpo to its confluence with the Tsangpo and meet us, weeks later, where the river emerges from the uncharted section of the gorge.

Elated by this turn of events, I began talking with the group of Tibetans who had been loitering around our camp in hope of work. One of them, wearing a matted tunic and red nylon gaiters, had carried supplies during an ill-fated assualt on Namcha Barwa a year before. Another, a hunter named Dawa Tsering, had just returned with Breashears and Wiltsie. He had been with them when they tried to forge a route around the granite headwall below the ruins of the monastery at Pemakochung and had stayed with them after the rest of the porters had taken off with their food. Although he and other locals had been repeatedly to Pemakochung to hunt or on pilgrimage, neither he nor anyone else had ever attempted to force a route farther downriver through the wall of granite cliffs that bar access to the Tsangpo's inner gorge.

Sherab, the Tibetan in the red gaiters, told me of an elderly lama named Mingyur who was living in retreat at a small hermitage two hours' climb above where we were camped. Forty years earlier Lama Mingyur had lived as a monk at Pemakochung, Sherab told me. Perhaps he might know of a route deeper into the gorge. As Ken, Jill, Eric, and I sorted through mountains of gear for our departure the next morning, Sherab, Dawa Tsering, and another local whom we had promised to hire climbed up the forested slopes to the lama's retreat hut. When Dawa told him of our plans to follow the course of the gorge beyond Pemakochung, the lama allegedly laughed and said, "Do you want to die?" He was the only one, he claimed, who knew the route. When a massive earthquake coinciding with the Chinese invasion in 1950 destroyed the monastery, he had followed the river into Pemako along precipitous paths that not even Chinese soldiers could follow. After staying in Pemako for more than two decades, he returned to Kyikar when political tensions eased and Tibetans were again allowed to practice their faith. Sherab pleaded with him, and he finally offered sketchy descriptions of the route. No one has passed that way in decades, he said. There are no trails. Even if there were trails, and one could navigate them, it would be at least a twenty-day journey to the confluence with the Po Tsangpo. The hunters looked abject and dispirited when they returned to camp, but with promises of high wages they agreed to go.

On the following morning, April 24, a horde of prospective porters grappled for loads and, once they had secured them, proceeded to lighten them of their own accord. The way was difficult, they said. They'd have to bring three weeks' worth of provisions and they'd carry no more than a total of twenty kilos or forty-four pounds in their bamboo baskets. Without a scale, the determination of the stipulated weight remained a highly subjective affair, leading to arguments between Gunn—who would be footing the bill from money we had already paid to his agency—and the band of opportunistic porters. In the end we were forced to hire twelve of them, far more than we had anticipated, as we would be carrying heavy loads ourselves. In addition we hired three horses to carry gear as far as the last known village, where we hoped to recruit hunters who might know of the route which Lama Mingyur had followed into Pemako. Gunn was near despair. "I won't have money to pay for all this," he said. Ken tried to put things in perspective by telling him that when Kingdon Ward and Lord Cawdor headed into the gorge they had hired twenty-three porters, thirteen of them local women. Gunn was hardly mollified. He resolved to carry more of his own food, adding canned fish and army surplus survival bars to his overstuffed haversack.

A short distance beyond our camp, one of the three horses fell through the planks of a log bridge that spanned a torrent cascading down from the glaciers of Namcha Barwa. The horse remained calm, however, and after being unloaded climbed back onto the logs and up the steep slope above the bridge. In less than two hours we reached the hot springs and proceeded along the eroded cliffs where we had first run into Breashears and Wiltsie. After another hour the trail opened into meadows where horses and pigs grazed amid stands of holly and pine trees. Stone walls of long-abandoned dwellings emerged from thick undergrowth.

The porters had been lagging behind, and when they finally caught up with us it was only to put down their loads. They gave no indication that they planned to go any farther. Gunn fretted and, as they spoke little Chinese, asked me to translate for him. Not only did the porters want a higher daily wage than what we had negotiated at the trailhead, but they wanted to be paid for a minimum of sixteen days for the round trip to Pemakochung. They seemed to have little faith that we would make it farther.

I was used to such negotiations, for porter strikes are common throughout the Himalayas, where transport of supplies depends upon human labor. For years I'd organized treks in remote parts of Nepal for American college students and knew the delicate charades that must be played on both sides. But I had no interest in jeopardizing our journey. Gunn said he couldn't pay the porters more than he had already promised, so I was compelled to assure them that we would pay them ourselves, even though our funds were barely sufficient. If need be we could take them to Lhasa at the end of the trip and pay them there.

With our new agreement the porters' attitude changed completely and they became helpful and conciliatory. Even the proud hunters who, acting as guides, had carried nothing but their guns slung over the backs of their black felt tunics, took up some of the loads. Gunn was wary of their new enthusiasm. "What did you promise them?" he asked. I gave him a brief account of the proceedings. With a furrowed brow he slung his army haversack over his shoulder. Loaded down with tins of black fish, he trudged forward in his white Chinese tennis shoes.

The Tsangpo surged below us as we followed the trail through a forest of evergreen oaks strung with wispy moss. Despite my initial concerns about restive porters and the composition of our group, the journey had begun, and I accepted the situation as containing its own hidden logic. Tibetan tradition speaks of *Kha sher lamkhyer*—"whatever arises, carry it to the path"—a Buddhist injunction to abandon preferences and integrate all experience beyond accepting and rejecting. Without that dynamic openness to adventure (from the Latin *ad venio*, "whatever comes"), Tibetans say, pilgrimage devolves into ordinary travel and the hidden-lands—both physical and metaphysical—will never open.

WE CAMPED THAT NIGHT ALONG THE TRAIL. The porters boiled water for the black tea that they mixed with their tsampa and chiles. We cooked rice and lentils. The Kongpopas were amused when they saw me eat from a burl

wood bowl that a Tibetan friend had given to me in Kathmandu. Pemako is renowned for its poisoning cults, and if I ate out of this bowl, my friend maintained, the toxins would be absorbed and I would come to no harm. Several of the porters had similar ones, and they compared the swirling, knotted grains to establish their respective worth. The most valuable bowls, they claimed, were those with patterns like owls' eyes. When the fire grew low, they stretched out on their black wool tunics and curled around the embers for warmth.

The next morning we proceeded through oak and bamboo forests into an area where small streams circled through glades of pine. A primitive stupa surrounded by prayer flags strung from bamboo poles stood on top of an enormous rock overhanging the Tsangpo. An hour later we crossed a steep cliff said by the porters to be a residence of Dorje Traktsen, Vajra Rock Warrior, a fierce protector spirit who lords over Pemako from various rock citadels. The porters placed small quartzite stones and sprigs of juniper on a wayside shrine erected against the wall of rock, mumbling prayers before continuing over narrow logs set against the cliff. With the roar of the Tsangpo reverberating off the metamorphic rocks, I followed suit and looked back to see Ken placing his own stone on the primitive altar. We ate lunch on a sandy beach at the base of the cliffs, as long-tailed parakeets flitted through the pines. The vast glaciers of Namcha Barwa seemed to hang suspended in the sky behind us. Gunn declared that the mountain had begun rising from the ocean floor in a major uplift between eight and eleven million years ago, and that it was still rising more than an inch every year.

Until 1992 Namcha Barwa was the highest unclimbed peak in the world. For Tibetans, and the people of Kongpo in particular, the mountain is the abode of deities as well as the repository of sacred scriptures said to have been concealed there by Padmasambhava. Sherab, our head porter, had carried loads for the joint Chinese-Japanese expedition that had climbed the mountain for the first time. He confided that it wasn't good to climb these sacred peaks; it angered the local spirits. It was for this reason, Sherab maintained, that one of the climbers' lives had been taken in an avalanche. The fatality occurred on October 16, 1991, when one of the Japanese climbers, Hiroshi Onishi, was swept off the mountain en route to camp IV at 20,450 feet. Despite the death, the team remained on the mountain for another eight days, but failed to reach the summit due to extreme weather and avalanches. Together with a team of Chinese climbers, they had returned the following year and succeeded.

In the Buddhist tradition sacred mountains and other holy places are circumambulated, not climbed, one's clockwise orbits linking one's energies with the site's. From Sherab's perspective, all ventures into such hallowed terrain must seek benediction from the unseen spirits of earth and air. Failure to acknowledge them is to invite disaster.

In Yolmo, Bhakha Tulku had spoken of the role of *suma*, or local protector deities, in keeping away those whose intentions are not in harmony with the spirit of the beyul. First they send bad dreams or through other means of psychic intervention attempt to turn one back, Bhakha Tulku said. If this fails they may cause illness or infirmity or other forms of physical distress. If one still persists, they may unleash rock falls, avalanches, or other calamities to obstruct one's passage. Bhakha Tulku had told me how an entire regiment of People's Liberation Army soldiers had been obliterated in a sudden blizzard while attempting to cross the Doshung-La pass into Pemako in 1959. Local Tibetans had credited the weather to the actions of Dorje Traktsen, Pemako's fiercest protector, a wrathful entity described in texts as a warrior figure riding on a snarling brown bear, holding in his right hand a blazing sword and in his left a lasso and a club surmounted by a human skull (in other manifestations he rides on a serpent). The main *dzong*, or fortress, of Dorje Traktsen in lower Powo is a looming precipice guarding Pemako's northern door. Bhakha Tulku related how in 1991 a convoy of seventy-eight trucks and Land Cruisers skirting this rock citadel en route to Lhasa, carrying goods to celebrate the fortieth anniversery of Tibet's "peaceful liberation" by the People's Republic of China, had all been engulfed by a wall of mud and water that descended from above the road. Many of the passengers were able to clamber to safety, but the head officials as well as all of the trucks and their cargo were submerged beneath the Po Tsangpo River. For Tibetans this was no tragedy but a testimony to the power of their local protectors to sabotage the initiatives of outside invaders.

The Falls of Shinje Chogyal

TOWARD DUSK WE ARRIVED IN GYALA, the last outpost of human habitation before the narrowing walls of the gorge make settlement impossible. A cluster of a dozen or so stone and wood houses, Gyala was dark and sunless and our reception by the villagers made us long for the uninhabited spaces deeper in the gorge. Below the village, the Tsangpo widens and pilgrims cross to the opposite bank to visit a revered waterfall called Shinje Badong that tumbles through limestone caves and overhanging rocks, ultimately spilling over a cliff into the Tsangpo. A temple above the waterfall is dedicated to Shinje Chogyal, the Tibetan Lord of the Underworld. An image of this wrathful entity, crowned in skulls and holding at his heart a *melong*, an all-reflecting mirror, is said to appear spontaneously to pilgrims from the rock behind the falls.

I wandered down the banks of the river, where two hollowed-out pine trees lay lashed together on a sandy beach. Gyala's headman had told me that a month earlier a woman had been swept to her death while crossing to the waterfall. Since then no one had been to the other side. Judging by the condition of the makeshift ferry and the labyrinth of swirling eddies between me and the cascade I easily understood why.

IN THE VAJRAYANA, OR TANTRIC, TRADITION of Tibetan Buddhism, the contemplation of archetypal deities such as Shinje Chogyal is not a morbid meditation on death and dissolution, but the fearless embrace of energies which are commonly disowned. In Kathmandu, Khamtrul Rinpoche had explained to me that Shinje Chogyal, an icon of impermanence, lords over the

gates of Pemako. Whether one perceives him as the judge of the dead or the be-
stower of a richer sense of existence—a potent ally in the deeper reaches of
mind and landscape, beyond hope and fear—determines one's experience in the
wilderness downstream.[11] The white-haired lama had held out his palm and
repeated a Tibetan saying: "Heaven and hell are closer than the two sides of a
hand."

I focused my Zeiss binoculars on the pale stream that poured down through
what Kingdon Ward had described as "a collection of poor little temples
clapped against the face of the cliff." I panned downward through rain-streaked
lenses to the ledge where pilgrims invited visions by offering small lamps filled
with melted butter. I saw the line of bells hanging from a heavy chain whose
sounds one account had described as "the tinkle of goblin laughter."

THE SUN HAD SET OVER THE CLIFFS above and gray mists drifted down
the Tsangpo like a wash of ink. As I sat gazing across the Tsangpo at the falls,
I recalled my own near-death experience in a river in the Green Mountains of
Vermont. I'd descended alone into a gorge on the East Middlebury River and
jumped off the top of a waterfall into a deep pool where I knew that a professor had drowned the year before. The river's vertical currents had drawn me
into a whirlpool beneath the falls, and only when—in desperation—I dove
downward rather than struggling toward the surface did I break free. The experience had released me from suicidal impulses that had shadowed me for almost
a year as I despaired of recovering fully from my climbing accident in Norway.
As the Buddha said: "He who knows that this body is but the foam of a wave,
the shadow of a mirage . . . proceeds on his path, undisturbed by the Lord of
Death."

From 100 yards away the sound of the falls mingled indistinguishably with
the surging drone of the Tsangpo, its waves—dark jade striated with foam—
washing up against rock walls that in the twilight seemed almost porous. With
rain spilling down my neck, I gazed into the veil of falling water until failing
light and incessant drizzle urged me back toward the village.

RARELY DID ANYONE FROM GYALA head downriver toward Pemako. Even in Kingdon Ward's day the village headman had told him there was no route into the gorge. Only when a group of Monpa traders ambled into the village did the headman admit there was a path, at least as far as Pemakochung. As Ward wrote: "The *Depa* . . . swore that there was no path, and that no one ever came up through the gorge. . . . Why he was so anxious to conceal from us the fact . . . that a path through the gorge did exist we could not understand." A massive earthquake on August 15, 1950—the strongest ever recorded—had changed the topography of the gorge. The route along the cliffs beyond the abandoned monastery of Pemakochung had collapsed into the Tsangpo and tenuous pilgrim tracks had disintegrated beneath landslides of mud, rock, and shale.

Breashears and Wiltsie had failed to push more than a mile beyond the ruins of the old temple at Pemakochung—a five-day journey downriver—and because only a single hunter had been even that far, our porters were hesitant. I made inquiries. Only a single living person in Gyala had gone through the gorge into Pemako, a toothless eighty-year-old woman half-blind with cataracts who had made the journey more than fifty years earlier. Her name was Olmula. I met her with Sherab and several other porters in the courtyard outside her house. At one time, Olmula said, many people used to travel through the gorge on pilgrimages and trading expeditions. Even then the way was dangerous, she said, but the earthquake in 1950—the year of the Chinese invasion—had altered the course of the Tsangpo and the jungle had reclaimed the trails. Few since then had attempted the journey, Olmula said, except to escape the Chinese army and those had never returned to report on conditions. There were innumerable passes to be crossed, Olmula said, as well as cliffs to be skirted. We could make it to Pemakochung in five days, she said. From there to Luku, the first village in Pemako (where she had an older sister), had taken her five or six days when there was a trail. How long it would take us now she wouldn't even estimate.

I handed Sherab my notebook and as Olmula recounted her memories of the route, he made strange markings resembling the graph of a wildly fluctuating stock market. The same earthquake that had destroyed the monastery, Ol-mula said, had also destroyed the series of ledges and log ladders that skirted the buttress which Breashears and Wiltsie had tried to traverse. Olmula de-scribed an alternative route called the Khandro Sang-La (the Secret Pass of the Dakinis) that ascends through a gap between precipitous crags leading into Shekarlungpa (the Valley of the White Crystal) the region before the Tsangpo turns abruptly north in a great 180-degree arc around a spur of Namcha Barwa. Soon thereafter, Olmula said, we would have to climb out of the gorge over a high snow-covered pass. If the snow was too deep or unstable we would have to return the way we had come. When we asked if there was a route deeper into the gorge without having to cross over the spur, she shook her head adamantly. No one has been into that area, she said. There are only cliffs and swirling, pounding rapids. Olmula's explanation was conveyed in a dialect that I could barely understand, but Sherab seemed confident of the hierogylphic marks that he had made in my notebook.

Gunn had fidgeted nervously during our interview with the old woman. When he spoke he seemed unusually preoccupied by the seismological insta-bility of the region ahead. The continued pressure of the Indian subcontinent against the Asian plate causes frequent slips along the fault line far beneath the mountains, Gunn stated. Tremors here are frequent, he said, pointing out that the epicenter of the 1950 earthquake was directly beneath the Tsangpo. It had measured 8.5 on the Richter scale, Gunn said, the strongest earthquake ever recorded. We must think of safety first. We should be prepared to travel no far-ther than Pemakochung.

During our talk in Olmula's courtyard, a uniformed police officer arrived on horseback. He hailed Gunn and went off with him toward the headman's residence. Ken, Jill, Eric, and I arrived later to find the hatchet-faced official waiting in the headman's log house along with Gunn and most of our porters. Half of the village seemed to be gathered there as well. According to Gunn, the officer was under orders to escort us back to the county seat in Menling, a town halfway to Lhasa. Officials in Menling, he stated, would have to approve our permits before we would be allowed to proceed. The police officer was a Ti-betan cadre of a distinctive type: power hungry and unsympathetic in equal measure. Although Gunn had told him that we hadn't driven by that route, but had come via Bayi where our permits were shown to be in order, the policeman was adamant. He refused even to look at our papers and could give no coherent reason why we were being recalled. Gunn suspected it had something to do with Breashears and Wiltsie; perhaps their guide had told officials in Menling of our intention to trek through the gorge.

Our rations had been strictly calculated. I pointed out to the officer that if we went to Menling it would delay our departure from Gyala by at least five days. We would then not have enough food to make it through the gorge and the onus would be on the officer. Gunn's lips quivered as he translated my words into Chinese. Flickering light from pitch pine torches transformed the wood-framed room into a purgatorial chamber from which it seemed we would never escape. It soon became clear that Gunn was modifying my statements, so I switched and spoke to the officer directly in Tibetan. "Police in our country," I told him, "are supposed to offer help, not obstruction." He sneered at me and said, "Okay. You go, but if any villagers try to go with you I'll put them in jail." As the district's chief of police, the officer had power and influence over all those who had come with us. The porters were thoroughly frightened and, glum faced, had already agreed to go back with him the following morning.

The police official sat beside me on a rough-hewn bench, chain-smoking Chinese cigarettes. The smoke circled around his head like a sinister fog. In a final bid to turn events around, I asked for his name so we could report him to his superiors for obstructing our journey. His reaction was so dismissive that without thinking I ripped the cigarette from his mouth and threw it onto the ground. Most of Gyala's villagers had gathered into the small house and they looked on agape as the enraged officer rose shakily off the bench and fumbled for his revolver. "If you weren't a foreigner," he said, "I'd shoot you." Illumined by sticks of pitch pine burning on a small tray over the cooking fire, he spat on the floor at my feet and in a torrent of Chinese explicatives cursed me to all manner of atheist hells. I smiled back at him. I may not have gotten across the river to the waterfall of Shinje Chogyal, I reflected, but an icon of death had projected across to me. And as Tibet's Tantric tradition maintains, without first encountering the depths of hell, the gates of heaven will never open.

The next morning we had no choice but to store most of our loads with the village headman and return to Kyikar with our police escort. Before leaving, the headman's savage mastiff came bounding out of the house and across the compound, heading directly for me with snarling jowls. A short sledgehammer lay on a workbench next to where I was standing and I hurled it toward the charging dog. By extraordinary luck, the hammer bounced once off the ground and caught the dog under its massive chest, sending it hurtling backward. I looked over at the police officer, whom I suspected of unleashing the dog from its chain, and said I looked forward to reporting these incidents to his superiors. As we left the village, the officer went out of his way to walk counterclockwise around the entry chortens and walls of carved mani stones, not leaving them to his right as is the Buddhist custom. He rode ahead on his horse, his two porters jogging behind him in an effort to keep up. As he passed Gunn, he told him he would have to pay for his porters. "I hate this man," Gunn said, after the police officer had passed out of earshot.

I could only surrender to the changing circumstances; this was a trial that we would not only have to endure but embrace. I thought of something Chatral Rinpoche had told me before I left: "In Pemako, don't try to avoid suffering, but accept whatever comes."

Traveling with a minimum of gear we reached the roadhead in Kyikar in a single day. The police official had lied shamelessly in telling us that there would be jeeps waiting to take us to Menling. The next morning we were forced to hire the only vehicle for miles around, a derelict flatbed truck parked in the mud on the far side of the village. The driver wanted more than $200 for the trip, an exorbitant rate by local standards and money we had set aside to help pay the porters.

Ten miles into our journey the police officer had the driver turn off the road into a walled compound with barbed wire and broken bottles cemented to the tops of the walls. What now? I wondered. We climbed out of the truck and were forced to wait in a small barrackslike room with peeling cement walls and bare desks. It was the head office of the local police headquarters. A forgotten portrait of Chairman Mao, the man who had destroyed much of Chinese civilization and invited famine and destruction in Tibet and China during the Great Proletariat Cultural Revolution, stared from the wall amid propaganda posters of glittering Tibetan peasants rejoicing in their "liberation." The officer sent out two of his men. They returned almost immediately with two cases of Pabst Blue Ribbon, one of China's most popular beers, and placed them on the empty desk.

In a surreal ritual aimed at dissolving whatever lingering animosity might reflect badly on his future career, the Tibetan turncoat urged us to toast the eternal goodwill and friendship between America and China. Without glasses, we drank directly from the oversized bottles. The officer's teeth were as rotten as Mao's, and I wondered if he too had cultivated the habit of cleaning his teeth by chewing tea leaves. With each toast the officer smiled garishly. As he became increasingly intoxicated, he tilted back the bottoms of our bottles until beer foamed down our chins and chests. The Great Helmsman stared impassively from the poster on the wall as empty bottles accumulated on the cement floor.

The strangeness of the proceedings eroded our deep-seated resentment at having been thwarted in our journey. Should all turn out to be in order in Menling, the officer assured us, he would help us on our return. Completely drunk, we climbed back into the open-air truck and the driver headed off under the morning sun, picking up passengers until the vehicle was overflowing with local villagers, nomads, and the two undercover policemen deputied to keep their eyes on us until we reached Menling.

The driver stopped in a streambed to pick up two Khampa pilgrims whom we had met earlier on their way back from Gyala. With black tassles wrapped around their heads, high leather boots and leather jackets, they looked more like pirates than pilgrims. They asked me where we were going and I told him of our intended journey through Pemako. One of the Khampas grinned at me with his gold tooth and ran his fingers along the edge of his sword. Comparing its razor edge to the paths through Pemako's precipitous mountains, he said, "Pemako's like this, one wrong step and you fall."

ALL ACCOUNTS OF PEMAKO seemed to contain this strange mixture of wonder and dread. On one hand it was an earthly paradise and on the other a veritable hell of nearly incessant rain, eroding trails, and insect-infested jungles.

I thought back to the wife of Tenzing Norgay who had made her pilgrimage into Pemako despite Chatral Rinpoche's warnings and unfavorable divinations. She had returned swollen and feverish and died soon afterward in a state of rapture.

For the pilgrim, dying in Pemako is considered oddly fortuitous. Tradition maintains that those who perish there will not pass through the *bardo*—a harrowing interim between one life and the next—but be liberated into a realm of celestial light. Before I left Nepal, Chatral Rinpoche told me that many people had died in Pemako. Conventional Tibetan wisdom decrees that if you drown in one of Pemako's rivers or are bitten by one of the beyul's numerous species of poisonous snakes, there's no need to worry. If pure vision is maintained, powa—the transference of consciousness from the physical body—occurs spontaneously. Believing this, many pilgrims have pushed beyond their physical limits and never returned. After sharing these perspectives with a female friend in Kathmandu, she promised she wouldn't mourn if I didn't come back, but rejoice in my good fortune.

Toward dusk we finally arrived in Menling, utterly exhausted after standing in the back of the truck for seven hours, as sitting was too jarring on the spine. Like us, the town was somewhat worse for wear. A characterless Chinese outpost bordered by steep, thickly forested hills, Menling lies close to the Indian LOC, or political line of control. We pulled in to the district police headquarters where Gunn went in to talk with the authorities. He returned within minutes. No problem, he said, we could proceed as planned. When we asked why we had been brought back after the same authorities had already inspected our permits in Kyikar several days earlier, we received no comprehensible response. Gunn, personally, suspected Breashears and Wiltsie of trying to sabotage Rick's expedition after their own failure to make it through the gorge. While competitiveness has plagued exploration since before Burton and Speke's quarrel over the headwaters of the Nile or Scott and Amundsen's race for the South Pole, Ken's and my own suspicions lay firmly with a display of power by the local Chinese administration.

The following morning we stocked up on additional provisions—tinned pork, glass jars of mandarin oranges, and army surplus survival food, with a main ingredient that turned out to be pig's fat—and then reboarded the truck for the long drive back to Kyikar. This time the truck was overloaded with a group of Kongpo women with thickly swaddled infants who appeared from under stacks of what we had taken to be their luggage. The ride was boisterous, as the women laughed and drank chang from their Mao caps while their babies remained disturbingly still. At the roadhead, we regrouped with Sherab, our head porter, who seemed both surprised and pleased to see us. The police official was nowhere to be seen.

We broke camp early the next morning, stopping at the hot springs to divest ourselves of accumulated grime and then proceeding past the first rapids into the broad valley which four days earlier had been filled with grazing horses. Namcha Barwa stood out majestically above the forested slopes before being enveloped again in clouds.[12]

ANOTHER HOUR DOWN THE TRAIL, Sherab and our other porters put down their loads and again demanded more pay. Gunn left it to me to negotiate. In my rudimentary Tibetan, I told the porters that we would pay them much more than Gunn had offered if they could take us through the gorge. I promised more money than we had, calculating that we could deal with this once we had reached our destination. Pacified by the promise of exorbitant wages, they picked up the pace and we covered the fifteen miles to Gyala in a single day. We walked into the village at dusk, armed with rocks against the savage mastiffs that guarded the village's periphery and startling Gyala's headman, whose own dog was now securely chained.

Four days had been lost, and Gunn was morose: "We will never reach it in time," he said. I was concerned too, but tried to look at it more philosophically. In the Buddhist sense, *né-khor*, or pilgrimage, implies—in part—a journey beyond the human impulse to control one's experience and an openness to serendipity. We ended the day drinking butter tea at the headman's house while his daughter baked us bread over an open hearth. Ken immersed himself in a paperback edition of Wordsworth's *The Prelude*.

IN THE LIGHT OF A pitch pine lantern that turned a blackened prayer wheel suspended from the rafters, I pored over the Pemako neyigs that I had brought with me from Nepal. The headman's wife told me that the villagers had been forced at gunpoint to throw all their block-printed Buddhist texts into the Tsangpo during the Cultural Revolution, and I regretted that I had not brought copies of the Tibetan originals to give to them. Tibet in the 1960s had been much like what Padmasambhava had prophesized in his termas: a period of brutal betrayals and mass destruction. The neyigs all began with accounts of these apocalyptic times and invoked the hidden-lands as places of refuge and spiritual renewal.

Before leaving Nepal, Chatral Rinpoche had told me that the neyigs reveal the underlying nature of the hidden-lands, but that the qualities of the beyul are by no means restricted to what is written. The most essential teachings in Tibetan

Buddhism, Chatral Rinpoche said, have never been written down. The revealed-texts I was reading equate the flow of the Tsangpo through the gorge with the life current of Dorje Pagmo, the Tantric goddess whose body forms an esoteric map of Pemako as a whole. The peak of Gyala Pelri, which looms above Gyala "like a pig gazing into the sky," is invoked as her head while the massif of Namcha Barwa—"like an eight-petalled lotus"—forms her mountainous breasts. In the tangle of mountains and jungles farther to the south lie her heart and womb, places said to be brimming with magical healing plants.[13]

To follow the course of the Tsangpo through its mist-filled gorges, the neyigs suggest, is to be absorbed into the anatomy of this "Mother of all Buddhas," and to be initiated into her mysteries.

When the pitch pine had burned low and stacks of barley bread for the morning meal had been piled high on the hearth, I retired to my tent, the light of the porters' fire flickering through the red nylon walls. As I was preparing for sleep, someone began pulling down the zipper of the tent door and I immediately imagined that either Ken or Sherab had come to announce another crisis such as we had had with the police officer. But instead it was a woman in a felt tunic whom I had seen earlier threshing grain by the river. She crawled in unbidden. "It's big in here," she said in a Kongpo dialect. "Are you going to sleep here alone?" Not sure if I had heard her correctly, I replied immediately that I was. Nonetheless, she stretched out on the floor and then reached through the shadows to run a hand along my arm.

Was this some kind of trial? The neyigs I had just been reading proclaim the women of Pemako to be emanations of Dorje Pagmo, initiatresses into hidden regions of the psyche. But like all dakinis, they are trickster figures that can lead the unwary dangerously off course. I reflected on the tertons who, to open the hidden-lands, had often availed themselves of local consorts; the alchemy of desire revealing hidden dimensions of mind and planet. The problem was I had no desire for my uninvited guest. Although wavering—I felt a bit like Galahad in the Castle of Temptations—I declined her advances. With a rough squeeze of my hand she crawled back out of the tent.

As I lay back in my down sleeping bag, I wondered whether I had passed a test or failed miserably by catering to my doubts and hesitations. My mind ran through a labyrinth of possibilities, not least of which was a concern that I was thinking too much. I recalled the words of a Scottish missionary who was active in Tibet in the late 1940s: "Tibetans were neither completely polygamous nor completely polyandrous. They were generally promiscuous."[14]

Descent into the Upper Gorge

WHEN I AWOKE THE NEXT MORNING, the skies were clear, and Gyala Pelri, the mountain invoked as Dorje Pagmo's head—"the crown center of infinite bliss"—gleamed above the northern walls of the gorge. The waterfall of Shinje Chogyal cascaded down the opposite bank, spilling into the Tsangpo which crested into small, shimmering waves. The neyigs described the section of the gorge we were about to enter as Dorje Pagmo's throat chakra,[15] the door into the hidden worlds farther downriver. For four or five days we would be on a track of some kind. After the ruins at Pemakochung we would be on unknown ground. As we headed out of the village, our gear loaded into freshly woven bamboo baskets, Olmula stood waving at us and muttering benedictions. Half jokingly, I told Sherab, walking beside me with his mala in hand, that Olmula might well be a manifestation of Dorje Pagmo. He nodded. "Dorje Pagmo's energies spread to all corners of Pemako," he said, "from the highest summits to the last blade of grass. To those of vision, whose channels are clear, all women are her emanations and these mountains are her palaces and charnel grounds."[16]

As we walked across sand dunes at the edge of the Tsangpo, I felt the sense of crossing an invisible threshold. We passed a rock outcrop associated with a local protector deity, a stone incense burner still smoldering with dawn offerings of juniper and fragrant herbs. The porters circled it before continuing, mantras flowing from their lips.

AN HOUR BEYOND GYALA we began to climb through a dense tangle of bamboo and rhododendrons with smooth bark that peeled off in our hands like red parchment. The ground was carpeted in a thick layer of damp leaves.

Rare sunlight drifted through the canopy, occasionally touching the green-tailed parakeets flitting through the delicate latticework. We contoured past a black cliff that Sherab referred to as an "iron gate" associated with a spirit entity who guards this entryway into the gorge.

We climbed over grassy ledges to a pine-covered spur high above the Tsangpo. Ken's altimeter showed us to be 11,200 feet above sea level. The porters called this pass Musi-La, in reference to cold sulfur springs that oozed over the rocks, leaving a thick, gummy deposit. In Kingdon Ward's day, the sulfur was collected and sent to Lhasa or paid as tax to the Powo rajahs. An eighteenth-century lama named Lelung Shepe Dorje had described the yellowish secretions as the secret water, or urine, of Dorje Pagmo, and he had rubbed it eagerly into his limbs.

WHEN KINGDON WARD entered the gorge in 1924 he was well aware of Tibetan myths of an earthly paradise. He wrote of Pemako as "the Promised Land of Tibetan prophecy," as "a land flowing with milk and honey . . . hidden behind misty barriers where ordinary men do not go." His own perspectives on the area, however, were hardly romanticized: "Not only is Pemako extraordinarily difficult to reach from any direction," he wrote, "it is still more difficult to penetrate and explore when reached. Surrounded on three sides by the gorges of the Tsangpo, the fourth is blocked by mighty ranges of snow mountains, whose passes are only open for a few months in the year. Beyond these immediate barriers to east and west and south, are dense trackless forests, inhabited by wild unfriendly tribes. . . . Add to this . . . a climate which varies from the sub-tropical to arctic, the only thing common to the whole region being perpetual rain, snakes and wild animals, giant stinging nettles and myriads of biting and blood-sucking ticks, hornets, flies and leeches, and you have some idea of what the traveler has to contend with."

Although Kingdon Ward's foremost ambition was to resolve the mystery of the fabled waterfall, his professional objective was "to collect seeds of beautiful hardy flowering plants for English gardens." Sponsored on his journey by government grants, seed companies, and wealthy patrons, including his companion, the twenty-four-year-old Thane of Cawdor, Kingdon Ward would discover at least ten new species of rhododendrons and numerous other plants including the blue poppy (*Meconopsis betonicifolia*), which ultimately thrived in Britain's wet and temperate climate.[17] The flora of the Tsangpo gorges, Kingdon Ward wrote, "covers the whole gamut from the tropics to the Arctic." Many species proved to be unique and have yet to be found anywhere else. Although some of the seeds that Kingdon Ward collected only blossomed twenty years later, flower species from the Tsangpo gorges continue to grace the world's gardens— from Kew in London to the Dalai Lama's Norbu Lingka palace in Lhasa.

Tibetan texts describe Pemako as a horticulturist's heaven, overflowing with life-sustaining and, at times, miraculous, plants. One of Padmasambhava's termas, *Wishfulfilling Light Rays,* makes bold claims for these uncatalogued species:

> This supreme plant . . . allows humans, wild animals, and even insects to attain Buddhahood. [Consuming] it will increase one's wisdom and lead to miracles such as leaving imprints of one's feet and hands on solid rock.
>
> In [Pemako's] secret chakra, a place blessed by the wisdom dakinis . . . bloom pink colored flowers. The sweet scent of these flowers can induce bliss. . . . Eating them one can survive for years.

Kingdon Ward took no particular interest in the ethnobotanical aspects of Pemako's plants, whether the plant poisons used by the Lopas on their hunting arrows or the healing herbs prized in the Tibetan medical tradition, but the flora intoxicated him just the same. When he first came upon the species of rhododendron named Scarlet Runner, he stood mesmerized: "For a moment we just stared at it," he wrote, "drunk with wonder." Lord Cawdor, however, became increasingly disenchanted by Kingdon Ward's obsessive plant hunting. On November 19, 1924, he wrote in his journal: "After eight months in this infernal country I shouldn't have imagined anyone would wish to see another rhododendron again—I'm damned certain I don't!"

ON THE FAR SIDE OF THE PASS, we descended into a grove of Himalayan fir, their massive trunks rising unbranched for nearly 100 feet. We made our first camp in the shadows of the trees. After dinner, the porters stood in a circle around an enormous fire piled high with fir boughs, chanting into the billowing flames the words of the *Barche Lamsel,* an ancient prayer attributed to Padmasambhava to remove obstacles on one's path. The brighter the blaze, the more intensely they chanted, until the radiating sparks threatened to ignite our tents.

I looked at the faces of our crew, illuminated in the light of the fire and unified in their common faith. Some were dressed in traditional Kongpo-style tunics fashioned from matted wool. Others wore Chinese military fatigues or Mao jackets. Amulets dangled around their necks. Machetelike swords were thrust through sashes and smaller knives hung in silver scabbards from their belts. Some carried pack baskets of split bamboo. Others tied their gear to aluminum frames that had been left behind by the expedition on Namcha Barwa. Several of the porters had been as far as Pemakochung—on pilgrimages or hunting trips—but each year the trail is reclaimed by jungle or altered by landslides and they proceed as much by intuition as by clear knowledge of the way.

Eric threw the packaging from a freeze-dried dinner into the fire and Dawa Tsering came up to tell us that such actions would offend the spirits of the land and could bring rain. Besides, there are *migyu,* large apelike proto-humanoids in the area, he insisted, and burning garbage irritates them. Normally they hide from human beings, Dawa said, but if angered they have been known to kill people. We promised to throw our refuse elsewhere. In the local worldview, every action establishes a relationship with the environment. Estrangement from nature is not an option. Even one's subtlest thoughts and intentions— whether positive or negative—are held to elicit a response from the animating forces within the landscape. Ill thoughts and selfish concerns can cause rock-falls and hail. Well-directed prayers, on the other hand, can literally stop the rain. A constant interchange occurs, giving rise to what Tibetans call *tukje*, great compassion for or empathy with all things.

THE NEXT MORNING, May 1, we awoke to birdsong filtering down from the trees overhead. Khamtrul Rinpoche and other lamas maintained that some of Pemako's avian species incant mantras. Some of the early tertons, Khamtrul Rinpoche said, had been guided deeper into the beyul by following their delicate songs.

We descended through strands of bamboo and rhododendron to the banks of the Tsangpo. Ken's altimeter gave a reading of 8,900 feet. The Tsangpo had transformed into seething rapids, an explosion of waves disappearing below us between steep cliffs. On the opposite bank, glaciers poured into a narrow valley, their meltwater merging into a gray torrent which disgorged into the Tsangpo. Earlier in the century, a small monastic complex called Vulture Hermitage had been built into the cliffs on the opposite bank, but no trace now remained. Sulfur springs oozed over the rocks at our feet while waves surging up from the Tsangpo drenched us in mist and spray. The porters had put down their loads and were staring raptly into the drifting mist in the valley on the opposite bank. Sherab told me it was a hidden né called Gyala Sengdum, where the faithful could receive visions. I looked up through the aqueous light, but all I could see was a wall of ice emerging momentarily from behind thick banks of cloud.

As we continued downriver through a forest of alder and willows Sherab pointed out an abandoned meditation hut built into a cliff on the other side of the river. Goltsang Tulku, the head lama of Vulture Hermitage, had once resided there, Sherab told me. He recounted a local legend that holds that a large fir tree downriver from Goltsang Tulku's retreat grew from the staff which he planted in the earth as he flew up into the sky. We had clearly entered the Tibetan dreamtime.

WE CONTINUED DOWNRIVER along the banks of the Tsangpo, forging our way among slick rocks soaked in spray. At a place the porters called De-nobanja we took out climbing ropes to ascend a short cliff. When sheer walls blocked further passage down the river, the porters paused to brew tea at a small side stream that wound through a ravine. Afterward we began to climb steeply through a dense forest of bamboo, birch, and rhododendron. The ground writhed with leeches. The lama Lelung Shepe Dorje had referred to them in a journal of his pilgrimage through Pemako in 1729: "Their bodies are round and thin like sticks of incence, but after sucking your blood, they become the size of a thumb. Unless they have their fill, they never loosen their bite. These leeches are everywhere."

A recent avalanche had cut a wide swath through the jungle and we climbed up through banks of snow and rubble toward the Tomtom-La, the second of the four major passes between Gyala and Pemakochung. In local belief, the 9,700-foot pass represents the route by which the Chinese bride of the Tibetan emperer Songtsengampo was carried in a palanquin on her way from Powo to Lhasa in the seventh century. On the far side of the pass the vegetation became more dense and layered. Pine, bamboo, maple, and birch covered the slopes, alternating as we moved between exposed faces and sheltered gullies. Omnipresent was the tangle of red branches and flowers that cloaked both sides of the gorge and which had led Kingdon Ward to refer to Pemako as a "rhododendron fairyland." Ken recognized several of the species that had delighted British horticulturists when Kingdon Ward first introduced them in 1925. Shrubs of *Rhododendron maddeni* sprouted from sheer rock walls. *Rhododendron thomsoni* was clearly distinguishable by its red dripping leaves while massive specimens of *Rhododendron grande* towered in places to more than forty feet.

Most of the rhododendrons' leaf buds were still closed to protect them from frost, but some were already flowering, their large bells opening into the light of spring. Green-backed tits and fire-tailed sunbirds, their tongues rolled into tiny tubes, pecked at the purple and red corollas, drawing up their hidden nectar. Looking at the fallen blossoms lying in glowing heaps beneath the gnarled trees, I recalled that the Pemako neyigs tell of raining flowers.

We descended through the trees in light drizzle and reached a glen called Tsongchenkega, where a series of notched logs brought us to the top of a cliff. We camped not long afterward among giant boulders near the banks of the Tsangpo.

I had brought Lelung Shepe Dorje's journal with me and I read more of it that night. For Shepe Dorje, the Laughing Vajra, the Tsangpo gorges spread out like a fabulous text that he interpreted with the signs, codes, and symbols at his disposal.[18] As he and his retinue entered deeper into the gorge in search of Dorje Pagmo's heart center, their world transformed along with their vision. During the day—"slipping down by holding on to dangling tree roots"— Shepe Dorje wrote of breaking into spontaneous song. At night dreams carried him farther into Pemako's hidden realms. But as he and his party ventured deeper, the hazards increased:

> The path now is very steep and difficult. My attendant Tsering Norbu was hit by a falling stone . . . but at last we reached our night's resting place. The others complained that the way is too dangerous and our destination too far away; that it would be better to return to Gyala. But due to the prophecies I received, the deities Oddan Karpo and Shingchongma promised to assist, and I resolved that if we are unable to reach our destination, it would be better not to return.

Eric sat by the fire silently making carvings on his walking stick. Ken was immersed in Wordsworth, sharing passages that resonated with what I had told him of the Pemako neyigs. Ken pointed out that Wordsworth's poetry had similarly transformed perceptions of landscape, his evocations of his native Lake District revealing "a new heaven and earth" in which "life's every-day appearances" could be redeemed in the act of creative perception.

As the porters chanted around a blazing fire, Ken and I sat in the rain and discussed how Tibetan literature concerning hidden-lands had promoted an indigenous, if unacknowledged, cult of the sublime. The poetry of the Romantics, like the neyigs, had pointed to the unity between mind and nature and helped transform the natural world from a resource to be exploited into an intimate expression of the Divine. Writing of the English Lake District, Words-worth described the valley of Grasmere as a "Paradise before him," echoing Milton's description of Eden in *Paradise Lost.*[19]

On his approach to the Tsangpo gorge, Lord Cawdor recorded in his jour-nal that he was reading a commentary on Milton's *Paradise Lost* that had been published in London's *Spectator* in March 1712. Despite such reading material, he was little affected by literary notions of an earthly paradise, nor by Kingdon Ward's ecstatic proclamations of the "paradise of primulas" and other plants which surrounded them. Along with extensive ethnographic notes that he con-tributed to Kingdon Ward's book, *Riddle of Tsangpo Gorges,* Lord Cawdor's journals illuminated their unrelenting hardships. On November 26, 1924, he wrote:

> Rain down here. Snow very low down—Jungle thoroughly sodden. This is without exception, the most depressing country I've ever been in. It may grow more weeds "per foot" than any other country, but what is that to me—Blast these showers! I'd sell my soul to see some honest weather again.

Tibetan pilgrimage guides liken Pemako's landscape to the unfolding petals of a mystic lotus emerging from the body of a Tantric goddess. Although the texts make reference to specific geographical features, their symbolic language re-orients pilgrims to their surroundings, transforming primeval wilderness into a realm of spiritual redemption. If for Wordsworth paradise could be recovered through the "internal brightness" of poetic imagination, for Tibetans like Shepe Dorje it demands a burning away of all false perceptions. In the Buddhist sense, imagination does not so much transform as reveal what is already present, the mind's inherent creativity realizing its essential unity with all situations. Paradise is thus not so much a place as liberation into the fullness and bounty of every-day experience—Eden in its etymological sense of a "garden of Delight."

For Kingdon Ward, the intrepid plant collector, the notion of paradise was in-timately linked to the luxuriant gardens that he supplied with exotic flowering plants. In the seventeenth and eighteenth centuries, English works on gardening bore titles such as *Paradise Retrieved* and *Paradise Regained;* botanical gardens were widely viewed as artificial paradises to compensate for the Eden that had disappeared. The earliest English gardens had been church sanctuaries that preserved memories of a lost Eden, walled gardens with a sense of order that reflected the Western myth of a realm impervious to suffering and death. As horticulture became inextricably associated with the expansion of the British Empire, cloistered gardens evolved into heated glass houses displaying exotic specimens appropriated from far corners of the globe. At the height of the British Empire gardeners often sought to create sublime landscapes where boundaries between the cultivated and the wild were purposefully blurred. The species of rhododendrons, magnolias, and other plants that Kingdon Ward introduced from Tibet enhanced the beauty of these woodland gardens with their meandering paths, ponds, and ravines. As new seeds flooded the market, wealthy landlords competed with each other for ribbons through foundations such as the Rhododendrons Society.

At his home at Cleeve Court in Berkshire, Kingdon Ward created a rock garden that simulated the great bend of the Tsangpo. He planted the steep banks of the stream with barberry, aza-lea, and rhododendron seedlings that he had brought back from Tibet. Although Lord Cawdor did not fully share Kingdon Ward's passion for collecting plants in the field, he was a zealous gardener, and rhododendrons, barberries, cotoneasters, and roses from the Tsangpo gorge still flourish in the gardens at Auchindoune, the Cawdor dower house a half hour's walk from Cawdor Castle along peat-black streams and through a forest of ancient oaks.[20] I went there one summer in search of the journals that the young thane had kept on his journey through the Tsangpo gorge.

The six clothbound diaries offered an intimate portrait of the conditions that the two explorers had faced in the gorge, but the most intriguing passages had been scratched out long ago by the thane's own hand. I'd learned far more from the countess herself.

Born into Bohemian aristocracy, Countess Angelika Illona Lazansky von Bukowa had married Jack Cawdor's son Hugh Cawdor, the sixth thane. She traveled to the Himalayas where she recognized many plant species that her father-in-law had brought back from Tibet. Using notes from the 1920s when the gardens at Auchindoune were first laid out, she restored them to their original glory. She had also created a "Paradise garden" near the entrance to the fourteenth-century castle that was immortalized in Shakespeare's *Macbeth*.

The countess guided me past a hedged labyrinth to a narrowing path that led beyond thorn bushes and towering thistles to a sanctuary where a fountain representing the waters of life spilled over into a wealth of flowers that she had planted according to the color symbolism of Goethe. "The Victorians and Edwardians were obsessed with exotic plants," the countess told me, "but for me, it is the sound and flow of water that is central to all existence."

Kingdon Ward's ambition of "enriching the beauty of his native land" with flowers from the farthest corners of the British Empire had been surpassed by the countess's grander vision. Lady Cawdor spoke of the peaceable kingdom, of communion between species. She told me of a local Benedictine saint who, rapt in prayer, would wade naked into the frigid waters of the North Sea and return to shore to be dried by sea otters.

When we parted on the castle drawbridge, she took nuts from the pocket of her tweed jacket as a flock of birds roosting in the castle walls swooped down to eat from her hands. For the countess, paradise was not something lost at the far edges of the earth, but a primal harmony to be realized on one's native soil.

In a like manner, the Tibetans had counteracted the corruption, worldliness, and war that had pervaded their centers of power by envisioning their borderlands as an immanent paradise. The thousand-petaled lotus held to bloom in Pemako's innermost center symbolized the blossoming of humanity's highest potential.[21] The flower is referred to in a poem by a fifteenth-century mystic named Kabir.

Don't go outside your house to seek flowers.
My friend, don't bother with that excursion.
Inside your body there are flowers.
One flower has a thousand petals
Centered there you will have a glimpse of Splendour
Inside the body and without;
Before and after gardens.

ON THE FOLLOWING DAY, May 2, we ascended steeply along precarious ledges covered in dwarf rhododendrons and wild roses to a pass called Nyuksang-La. On the far side, we cut our way through thick rhododendrons, their trunks and branches smooth like opaque red glass. Across the gorge, a glacier curled into the Tsangpo like a frozen tongue, the surging river carving away at its tip. Traversing on ledges along a mossy cliff we saw beneath us the carcass of a takin, a shaggy Himalayan ruminant related to the Arctic musk ox, which had fallen from a cliff. In a grim vision of the web of life, bushy-tailed martins pranced on top of it, devouring its flesh. Continuing on, we emerged into an open valley encircled by glacier-covered peaks.

The northern walls of Namcha Barwa glittered above us like an ice-encrusted palace. Ken and I lingered behind as the rest of the team made its way through bogs and open forest. When we tried to pick up the trail, there was no sign of their passage, nor any response to our calls. For more than an hour we bushwhacked amid flowering rhododendrons and crystalline streams. Finally we heard Sherab's calls and followed them up a stream which we crossed on fallen logs. The porters were brewing their midday tea under the arching roof of an overhanging cliff, huddled against the rock wall to escape a burst of rain. After eating we continued through dense forest and emerged at a sandy beach on the banks of the Tsangpo. A pair of leopards had left tracks in the wet sand.

We camped that night at an overhanging boulder. Hunters had etched inverted peace signs into the rock as a sign of the musk deer that they had killed nearby. A strange protuberance on the side of the rock was held by the porters to be a *rangjung*, or self-manifested, image of the *purba*, or magical dagger, wielded by Dorje Traktsen, the spirit guardian of this myth-drenched terrain. The porters invoked him again that night, seeking his protection by heaping fragrant branches of juniper and fir onto a blazing fire.

When they had finished their prayers, Sherab approached me on behalf of the other porters. They wanted to be paid now for taking us to Pemakochung even though we were still more than a day's journey away. They seemed to doubt that we would actually pay the double rates that we had agreed to. Gunn sat by the fire drying out his sneakers and studiously ignoring the proceedings. After much reassurance, the porters finally agreed to be paid the following day when, if all went according to plan, we would arrive at Pemakochung. We began to suspect that the porters had no real intention of going with us into the unknown tracts beyond the ruined monastery. That night it began to rain heavily and the Chinese tent supplied to me by Gunn's agency flooded with water.

THE FOLLOWING DAY we left the hunters' camp in thick mist and descended into a great cleft ravaged by landslides. The Tsangpo surged below us. As we reentered the forest, the tangle of rhododendrons grew ever denser. Kingdon Ward had noted that as the gorge narrows and the climate becomes wetter, the rhododendron species prevalent higher up in the gorge give way nearly entirely to Indo-Malayan varieties characteristic of temperate rain forests. The bulk of the forest was composed of *Rhododendron irroratrum* and a purple-flowering Aroreum. A less prevalent species, *R. maddeni*, had intrigued Kingdon Ward for its peculiar venation, the sunken channeled veins on the upper surface of the leaves leaving embossed images on the lower. To our porters the unusual patterns on the leaves suggested mantric syllables, more evidence, like the figures on the rocks, that we were on hallowed ground. Kingdon Ward wrote of the species that it "grows on the sheerest of cliffs and in addition to being uncommon, is often inaccessible." Ward had entered the Tsangpo gorge in autumn and saw only stray blooms of rhododendrons that had opened out of season. He speculated on how the gorge would appear in early spring: "The forest then, tier on tier from the dripping snow to the rocking river must be one incandescent lava stream of rhododendron blossom."

The rhododendrons were riveting. More than 154 species have been documented in the Namcha Barwa region along with 218 varieties of orchids and 20
different types of bamboo. This region of Pemako alone has been estimated to
contain more than 1,410 plant species, an unprecedented diversity. Still uncatalogued were the five psychotropic plants described in the Pemako neyigs.[22]

Bhakha Tulku had told me how two hunters who had run out of food had accidentally discovered one of these magical plants. Unable to secure game, the
hunters had survived by eating roots and flowers in the jungle. One of the hunters
ate an unknown plant and soon began to feel as if he was rising off the ground.
Startled and afraid, the other hunter told him to put the animal skin he had been
sitting on over the top of his head to dampen the effects. I asked Sherab and
Dawa whether they had ever come across such plants, but neither he nor any of
the other hunters had ever found them. "You have to be very lucky," Sherab said.

The hunters did rely on wild food, however, and they were particularly fond
of the large broom mushrooms that grew on cliffs and tree trunks. One porter
had eaten one of these fungi during our midday tea break and he was now lying on the trail in a fetal position, clutching his stomach. I sought remedies
from my meager first-aid kit and finally administered a dose of colocynthis, a
homeopathic medicine derived from bitter cucumber. Within ten minutes he
was on his feet again and shouldering his load.

IN STEADY RAIN, we proceeded down the right bank of the Tsangpo. Enormous boulders covered in slick moss made our passage progressively more difficult. The river was swollen, and splintered logs swept down in floods were
jammed into small bays. The rising water level soon forced us to leave the river
and to cut our way through dense jungle. Lord Cawdor had written unhappily
of his passage through this terrain in 1924:

> The going was very bad and steep, up ladders and slippery rocks for the most
> part. After that and naturally we came down the other side—The road through
> the jungle was of the usual order—Bogs, rocks, slippery tree trunks (some with
> notches cut), rocky ledges, landslides, etc. . . . quite enough to keep one busy

even if one hadn't a load to hump and we went very slowly for we had to keep hauling coolies over the worst places.

I thought back to David Breashears's description of this route into the gorge as more arduous than climbing Mount Everest. Although the route was often dangerous due to falling rocks and collapsing ledges, I couldn't help but suspect that his accounts had been meant to discourage us from attempting the journey that he and Wiltsie had been forced to abandon. We had seen curiously little evidence of their passage and when I inquired of Dawa he told me that two weeks ago the river level had been lower and that they had been able to follow the banks of the Tsangpo during the final push into Pemakochung. With the increasing rain Dawa feared that the route along the river would be submerged. The only way to reach Pemakochung now, Dawa claimed, would be by climbing over a pass to a swamp called Tsokalamembar—Lake of Burning Fire. The other hunters looked doubtful, but as Dawa was the only one who had been to Pemakochung in recent months, they agreed to go. Sherab talked of natural lights that appear in the marsh. If you follow them, he said, you're likely to drown in the mire. In the minds of our Tibetan guides the holy swamp was clearly a dangerous place.

One reason for their hesitation quickly became apparent when we reached the base of a rock wall that Dawa said we had no choice but to climb. The route, up eroding gullies and unstable ledges, was truly harrowing. Shepe Dorje had made the same ascent in 1729 and described rocks the size of sheep hurtling down the face of the cliff. Two thousand feet above the Tsangpo we finally topped out into a thick tangle of moss-covered rhododendrons with scattered birch and pine. We then followed an avalanche chute toward the great marsh of Tsokalamembar and the lake that lies cradled in its center.

It was raining, and banners of mist drifted through the trees. The swamp was infested with *Rhododendron irroratum*, bloodred flowers spilling into the bog. Beaded strands of Spanish moss hung like nets from the sodden branches. When the lama Shepe Dorje entered the bog in 1729 he described how his feet "sunk the length of a forearm" into the oozing mud. We crossed the marsh and entered a thick tangle of rhododendrons worthy of Tolkien's Middle Earth. We broke for tea under the dense canopy of leaves and smooth looping branches drenched with epiphytes. Afterward we forged our way through the forest and trudged through lingering banks of snow toward the 10,450-foot pass which would lead us into Pemakochung. As we crossed the saddle, Namcha Barwa appeared through a window in the dense tangle of branches. Glaciers poured down its northern slope and disappeared into jungle. Kingdon Ward had referred to this view as "coldly menacing": "The snow peaks enclosed us in a ring of ice. . . . Dense jungle surged over the cliffs . . . a maelstrom of river, forest, and ice fighting dumbly for dominion."

Hidden amid the swamps below us lay the ruins of Pemakochung's former monastery. We made the steep descent through rain and fog, clinging to branches and swinging our way down through a wet, bramble-filled forest. It was at this point that Lord Cawdor had written of porters falling through "a net work of roots, another time into a big hole. . . . The jungle was very thick— huge trees, masses of rhododendrons, with an undergrowth of tall ferns. Even at this time of year a great deal of verdure comes above one's head, and everything is crawling with ticks and leeches—What it can be like in the rains, I can't imagine—God! How I loathe all jungles."

As we descended toward the abandoned gompa a vast amphitheater opened around us. The pyramidal peaks of Namcha Barwa soared above us, and a granite wall—snow clinging to its upper slopes and red-flowered rhododendrons advancing up the slabs—framed the valley from the west. Great torrents poured off Namcha Barwa's glaciers into the marshes and forests. We proceeded through leech-infested swamps to a small hillock where the crumbled walls of the old monastery were slowly sinking into the earth. A pomegranate tree laden with overripe fruit spread above us while a headless statue of Tara, a female deity, sat perched on a moss-covered wall. Bronze butter lamps and a pair of broken cymbals lay amid the ruins. As the porters strung prayer flags between two fir trees, Ken, Eric, Jill, and I set up our tents, using cut bamboo to lift them off the sodden ground. When Lieutenant-Colonel Eric Bailey traveled into the gorge in 1913 he had referred to Pemakochung as an "abomination of desolation" and "one of the world's dead ends." Taking in the rain and mud and leeches, I reflected that little had changed.

Pemakochung

CAMPED AMID THE RUINS, I thought again of the first account of Pe-makochung that Kinthup had brought to the West, and of how in 1884, the Trigonometrical Survey Department had garbled his report and indicated that two miles below the monastery the Tsangpo pours over a 150-foot cliff. When Kingdon Ward and Lord Cawdor reached Pemakochung in 1924 the confusion concerning "Kinthup's Falls" had already been resolved. If there were a larger waterfall on the Tsangpo they would find it farther downriver. While Kingdon Ward scrambled up cliffs to collect seeds of new species of rhododendron, Cawdor descended to the Tsangpo to see the falls that Kinthup and Bailey had referred to in their reports. "I could see nothing in the way of a fall," Cawdor wrote in his cloth-bound journal. "There was rather a big rapids hereabouts, going down in steps but nothing more—I took a photograph of it—It was possible that I did not get to the right place for the falls, I had some difficulty in making them understand what I wanted." Either way, Lord Cawdor was not overly impressed by the prospects. "The Tsangpo is now merely a foaming tor-rent," he wrote, "a beastly greenish color."

I asked Sherab and the other porters about the falls below the monastery and Sherab told me that hunters and ambitious pilgrims still visited them to cleanse themselves of accumulated sins. All the porters were eager to go. So were Ken, Jill, and Eric. As we prepared for the descent to the Tsangpo a strange feeling came over me, and I remained behind. The lama Shepe Dorje had men-tioned in his account a nearby cliff with a golden waterfall representing the site of union of Dorje Pagmo with her consort. He described a red-colored image emerging from the rock and additional waterfalls like "silk threads" associated with Ekajati, the one-eyed protectress of Tibetan Buddhism's highest teachings.

Thermal springs were said to emerge from the snout of a nearby glacier with beds of crystals that Shepe Dorje and his retinue had shared as offerings.

Hoping to follow in Shepe Dorje's footsteps, I wandered alone into the gnat-filled swamps below the monastery and headed for a band of cliffs streaming with water that formed a wall at the southern end of the bog. Bloodred blossoms of *Rhododendron irroratum* blazed out from the mist. In this "sky-covered dense forest," Shepe Dorje wrote, "the tree leaves are marked with seven, eight, and sixteen spoked chakras and double-crossed vajras"—the strange venation of the *Rhododendron maddensi* that Kingdon Ward had mentioned in his notes.

This was no paradise, however. Leeches fell from the trees and climbed up from the swamp. Clouds of gnats flew into my eyes. Shepe Dorje had described this plague of insects in sobering detail: "This area is full of blood sucking leeches . . . and there are also swarms of poisonous insects. They make sounds like small bells. . . . When darkness falls, they sound like monks praying in a large hall."

I walked on through dense mist, inhaling gnats and surrendering my body to the leeches. I thought of the Mahasiddha Naropa, who had nearly been consumed by them during his initiation.[23] Even our porters viewed them with a certain respect: "They only suck out the bad blood," Sherab had insisted. The band of cliffs I was headed for seemed to recede farther into the distance as I often had to double back because of impenetrable thickets and knee-deep mud. The swamp began to seem more like hell than than any immanent paradise, and I finally gave up. With a torn poncho and blood-soaked legs, I headed back to camp and retreated into my tent. There I plucked off leeches and regretted that I had not gone with the others to the falls.

Soon, Ken and the others returned from the river. Due to high water they had been unable to get through the tunnel in the cliff. Apart from a distant view of Kinthup's Falls, which appeared, as it had to Cawdor in 1924, as merely a torturous rapids, they saw downriver to the massive spur of Namcha Barwa jutting into the Tsangpo which Breashears and Wiltsie had found no way around. The porters had completed their pilgrimage and were now standing restlessly around a feeble fire. They wanted to be paid. "We have only just begun," I told Sherab. "Our goal is to go through the gorge into Pemako."

Sherab was fidgity. "We don't have enough food," he said. "We can't make it." The porters had obviously determined that they would be better off returning to Gyala rather than facing the unknown dangers ahead. I reminded Sherab that our agreement of exorbitant wages only applied if we continued on around the headwall where Breashears and Wiltsie had turned back. Sherab countered that there was no way around the spur. He dismissed Olmula's account of the Khandro Sang-La, the Secret Pass of the Dakinis, as the ramblings of an old woman. The notes he had taken, it seemed, had been only to humor me. It now appeared that our porters had never had any intention of continuing on beyond Pemakochung, assuming that having reached this rain-drenched sanctuary we would be only too glad to return the way we had come. Gunn was hopeful. "We must think of safety first," he said. "Perhaps we should go back."

I proposed to Sherab that some of the porters go back to Gyala, leaving their surplus food with those who remained. Sherab immediately retorted that it was unsafe to travel in small numbers through such terrain and that no one would be willing to return alone. I held firm and told him that our deal was off unless we reached the headwall at least and attempted to find a way around or over it. I reassured him that we would be exceedingly generous if we managed to get to the other side and continue into Pemako. It began to rain and the porters retired to their makeshift shelter to discuss their options.

As I held an umbrella over the open fire, Ken stirred noodles into a stainless steel pot inherited from his father. Gunn ate one of his tins of black fish, casting the empty can into the forest. The porters were anxious. Eating fish brings bad luck in Tibetan belief and they blamed our Chinese liaison officer's eating habits for the worsening weather. Gunn, unfazed, retired to his tent to a blow-up air mattress more suitable for a holiday at the beach. Amazingly, he had also carried with him a small blue pillow that he propped above his haversack of tinned fish and our now largely useless permits. "I think we should go back tomorrow," he said halfheartedly, already resigned to our unfathomable resolve to make it through the gorge.

Mists descended from the cliffs and enveloped our camp. An owl hooted from a nearby tree. In Tibetan tradition owl-headed spirits are dispatched by Shinje Chogyal to herald misfortune. I drifted to sleep to the bird's eerie cries.

THE NEXT MORNING, negotiations continued with a new slant. The porters' main concern, Sherab told me, was not so much finding a route over the granite spur of Namcha Barwa into the inner gorge, but the much higher snow-covered pass—the Shechen-La—several days farther downriver. As no one had ever followed the Tsangpo into its innermost chasms, they rightly concluded that we would ultimately be compelled to return the way we had come or to cross the Shechen-La into Pemako. None of them had ever been there. No one knew the way. "There are snakes, cliffs, and glaciers," Sherab said, "and no path of any kind. We could easily die there."

Even though our own food reserves were minimal, it was unthinkable that we turn back and the uncertainties about the route ahead added significantly to its mystique. On the other side of the spur lay an area called Shekarlungpa—the Valley of the White Crystal. It was there that Bailey had been abandoned by his porters and where Kingdon Ward and Lord Cawdor had "lost" four days, as if having stumbled into another dimension. Shepe Dorje's party had searched there for the Hidden Forest of the Dakinis revealed to him in his dreams. Local spirits continually possessed the Kudanpas, or spirit mediums, who traveled with him. Khamtrul Rinpoche had spoken of a cave in Shekarlungpa said to conceal a key to Pemako's innermost heart and had dreamed of being transported there by ethereal muses. Farther downriver beyond where any explorers had reached was the area that Bailey had referred to as "one of the last remaining secret places of the earth, which might conceal a fall rivaling the Niagara or Victoria Falls in grandeur." Whether or not those innermost gorges would reveal such treasures, it would certainly offer a glimpse into what Kingdon Ward had written of as "the hidden heart of the Himalayas."

After much persuasion, Sherab agreed to send only two porters back to Gyala. The nine remaining men agreed to continue as far as the headwall and to search for the hidden path described by Olmula. If possible, we would then descend into the trackless jungles of Shekarlungpa. As they had no guns with which to hunt, Sherab asked for the climbing ropes so that they could set snares along the way to supplement their meager rations. It was raining heavily and we spent the day around the camp. Hordes of leeches converged on us from the saturated earth. We moved no farther than a shallow stream where we attempted to wash. At meal times we took turns holding the broken umbrella over a damp and struggling fire. The smoke offered partial relief from the clouds of gnats.

BEFORE LEAVING THE RUINED MONASTERY on May 5, the porters lit a pyre of fir boughs and prayed toward an ominous peak on the northern bank of the Tsangpo that they held to be a subsidiary abode of Dorje Traktsen. For the porters, negotiating the terrain ahead had less to do with strength and determination than with aligning oneself with this temperamental entity. We set out in rain through swamps and marshy undergrowth and descended 700 feet to the banks of the Tsangpo. Following faint trails left by migrating takin, we reached a deep, frigid torrent called the Talung Chu that streams down from the glaciers of Namcha Barwa. The porters sat down abjectedly on the rocks. Gunn was hopeful that we would now turn back. "There is no way across," he insisted. In a fit of exasperation I grabbed one of the porters' *apches,* their long machetelike knives, and began hacking at a large tree. An hour later we'd cut down two tall poplars and crossed to the other side.

We dried out on the far bank, where sulfur springs bubbled from rank pools along the shore of the Tsangpo. The river was wild and furious, with twenty-foot troughs and vast waves cresting into the sky. The whole area reeked of sulfur. As Shepe Dorje described it in his journal:

> The waves from the river resound with Ha Ha Hum Hum and Hang Uang, pounding against each other and crashing into rocks. This valley is called Talung, the upper and lower parts . . . smell of brimstone. We reached the bank of the river and crossed on a fallen tree trunk. A great rock rose at the water's edge like the skin of a tiger. On it were self-manifested images of a jewel, the syllable "AH," and golden fish. Other rocks were embossed with lattice grids and eyes of wrathful deities.

We soon reached a larger torrent, the Sanglung Chu. It emerged from a glacial moraine visible through the forest. Two trees that had been uprooted in a flood had fallen across the water and were lodged in place by boulders, and we crossed the river without incident. The forest on the eastern bank was dense and dripping, and we followed meandering takin trails to the edge of the Tsangpo where more sulfur springs oozed from the rocks. After some distance, the lead hunters spotted a herd of takin on the opposite bank. Lord Cawdor had seen these primordial-looking animals there on his journey with Kingdon Ward. "I had a look at one through the glass," he wrote in his journal. "It is a fabulous beast—about the size of a small cow with long shaggy hair; blackish on the back and reddish on the sides. It has horns that bend sharply and go straight back. Its head is much like a sheep."

There were signs of takin ahead of us as well. Excited at the prospect of fresh meat, three of the porters set down their loads and bounded ahead to set snares. Long before the advent of guns, Pemako's hunters snared their prey by rigging nooses made from woven bamboo along the takins' customary trails. In our case, the porters made do with our nylon climbing ropes. By the time we had caught up with them, they had herded a female takin and her two calves into the Tsangpo. One of the calves was swept into the rapids and lost down-

stream over a small falls, but they managed to lasso the two others with the climbing ropes and dragged them bellowing onto the rocks. The river was deafening, echoing off the cliffs above and swinging wildly to the north around the rock headwall which Breashears and Wiltsie had attempted to traverse. The bull takin—its snout bulging and short thick horns sweeping back over its head like those of an African gnu—appeared suddenly on the cliff face. With a final look over his shoulder at his doomed family, he ascended diagonally what seemed to be a smooth granite wall and disappeared into the jungle.

The porters skinned and gutted the two takin and began roasting their flesh on wooden racks which they built amid the boulders along the banks of the Tsangpo. We pitched our tents in a clearing above. Disturbed as I was by the killing, I knew that it was necessary. Without additional food, the porters would not have been able to continue. Sherab later climbed up from the river with his arms full of meat. Don't worry about the takin, he said. They are *ter* (dharma treasures) of Padmasambhava. When they are killed, Sherab insisted, their *lha*, or life-force, spontaneously reincarnates in Yangsang Né, Pemako's mystical sanctuary. He showed us a small perforation in the tip of one of the takin's horns. It was through this hole, he said, that the takin's soul was ejected. To eat the meat of takin here, Sherab said, is to receive the blessings of the hidden-land. "If we hunt elsewhere it's sinful," Sherab said, "but in Pemako it's different," the beyul's unique attributes freeing them of any adverse karmic repercussions.[24]

Hunters have always had an ambiguous role in the opening of hidden-lands. Despite their life-taking vocation, they have often discovered routes into beyuls' interior realms. In Pemako's oral tradition, hunters who have followed the tracks of takin and not returned are often said to have stumbled into Yangsang, although none come back to indicate the way.

Like Yangsang, the first "promised lands" were places with genial climates, fresh water, and, most important, abundant game. Etymologically, paradise stems from a Persian word for a walled park and originally designated a private hunting preserve. Only later did paradise come to be associated with a region or state of supreme happiness. Apart from its spiritual assets, Pemako retains the qualities of a privileged hunting ground where, despite the Buddhist injunction against taking life, hunters kill with supposed impunity.[25]

We boiled the takin meat in Ken's pot as rare sunlight faded from the northern walls of Namcha Barwa. The granite spur that we would have to cross remained hidden in shadow. The porters called the spur Gyama Taki and described it as the boundary between the Tibetan district of Kongpo and the regions of Pemako. The river exploded against the base of the great buttress before coiling northward and disappearing into a wilderness of rock and cloud. Gunn had been sitting at a distance, poring over a Chinese military map he refused to show us. When we called him over for food, he proclaimed almost hopefully that there was no way either around or over this granite barrier. He discoursed on its composition: white-and-black-banded gneiss, a coarse-grained metamorphic rock made up of feldspar, mica, and quartz.

If Olmula was right, hidden somewhere above us was the Secret Pass of the Dakinis. The future of our expedition depended on finding it. Sitting by the fire, Dawa Tsering revealed that Breashears had talked to the old woman through his Chinese guide, but their communication had faltered. After failing to round the buttress, they had tried to climb up to a notch between two pinnacles of rock but had been forced down by falling rocks and the steepening incline. Dawa wasn't optimistic about the route that Olmula had invoked. "There are only cliffs up there," he said. "Higher up there are treacherous glaciers." Nonetheless, despite Breashears and Wiltsie's failed attempt, Dawa retained some hope that we might still find a route across the cliff.

AT FIRST LIGHT on the morning of May 6 Dawa Tsering and three other porters made a final effort to find a route around the headwall, but returned dejected. Armed with freshly sharpened apches and a climbing rope, Sherab launched into the jungle with two other hunters to search for the Khandro Sang-La. The rest of the porters stayed in camp, drying takin meat over open fires or washing in the thermal springs. With a break in the rain and a supply of fresh meat, the porters' moods had visibly improved and the prospect of being paid double wages for the way ahead compensated for the uncertainty of the route. Even its etymology was obscure. Some called it Khandro Sang-Lam, the

Secret Path of the Dakinis. Others insisted it was Khandro Sang-La, the Daki-nis' Secret Pass. Either way, as the day progressed, we had doubts that Sherab would actually find a way through, or even tell us if he did.

Shortly before dark, we heard Sherab's calls echoing through the forest above us. Soon afterward, the three scouts stumbled into camp and sat down by the fire. They'd been out for eleven hours. They had found a route to the top of the jagged ridge and had looked down into the dense jungles of Shekarlungpa. It was late and they had not descended on the other side, but they were hope-ful that, with ropes, we would be able to enter into the hidden ravines below. In a last ditch effort to convince us to turn back, Gunn talked again about safety and suggested that it would be better to go back the way we had come.

ON MAY 7, WE ROSE EARLY and began climbing through rain-drenched jun-gle. Sherab had had inauspicious dreams and remained disturbingly quiet as he searched for the blazes that he had made the day before. The slope became progressively steeper, and we hauled ourselves up by tree branches and water-saturated shrubs. Leeches dropped down our necks and burrowed into our sod-den boots. Our hands bled from clinging to briars and serrated plants. Higher up, the eroding slopes were covered in delicate ferns, small purple orchids, and a variety of mushrooms. We ascended avalanche chutes and crossed into a zone of unstable rock outcrops. Rocks cascaded from above, engulfing us in the characteristic smell of pulverized stone.

WE HAD ALREADY CLIMBED more than 2,000 feet above the level of the Tsangpo. Sherab could no longer locate the blazes he had made the day before. We forged on through the green air, following the line of least resistance. The porters cut notches in a fallen log and raised it to ascend a short moss-covered cliff. Several of them removed their canvas shoes and climbed barefoot to gain better purchase on the slippery log. The pass which Sherab claimed to have found seemed as phantasmal as the lost Falls of the Tsangpo, "something ever more about to be," as Ken put it, quoting a line from Wordsworth's "Tintern Abbey."

After climbing for more than five hours we reached a narrow break in the ridge—the long-sought pass. Snow plumes streamed from the peaks above us like vaporous prayer flags, but our eyes were drawn downward into the abyss below where the Tsangpo surged through a torturous chasm. A snow-covered spur of Gyala Peiri—hidden now in clouds—formed the north side of the gorge. The spur terminated in a pyramidal peak which Olmula had simply called Dorje Pagmo. To the south, the gorge was framed by an eastern extension of Namcha Barwa that appears on Kingdon Ward's map as Sanglung but which the Tibetans called Kangla Karpo. A great spur curved down from the glacial heights, causing the Tsangpo to change its course and flow abruptly northward between the base of Dorje Pagmo and a similar peak called Dorje Traktsen on the spur descending from Kangla Karpo. Through binoculars, we could see waterfalls streaming down the granite slabs where the Tsangpo begins its great bend to the north between the two mythic sentinels. The cliffs marked the farthest point Kingdon Ward had been able to reach. Terrified of heights, he described his ascent up these dripping slabs as a nightmare.

Between us and the Great Bend lay a morass of cliffs and trackless jungle. The Tsangpo cut through this wilderness like a white, roiling serpent, the thunder of its rapids echoing up the sides of the gorge. Takin had traveled recently through the break in the mountain wall, and Sherab and others were convinced that game would be plentiful in the unfrequented ravines spreading out below us. Ken was elated at the prospect of moving through such untrammeled wilderness. Eric was more sober, pointing out that beneath the canopy of trees were deep ravines and cliffs that we couldn't even see. Although in the past there may have been some semblance of a trail, there were now only incipient animal tracks. Getting through would not be easy.

THE ABYSS THAT OPENED BEFORE US was referred to in the neyigs as Shekarlungpa, the Valley of the White Crystal. The eighteenth-century Terton

Rikdzin Dorje Thokme had referred to it as the right collarbone of Dorje Pagmo's throat chakra. "Secretly," he wrote, "it's the place where nectar flows from the dancing dakini of great bliss, Dechen Karmo. By tasting this nectar of her outflow, one experiences the coemergent wisdom of emptiness and great bliss."

On his journey in the 1950s Khamtrul Rinpoche had gazed into the valley and "beheld a floating goddess amid a vast expanse of sky and surrounded by . . . glorious rainbows. . . . To the east, a crystal reliquary mound (*chorten*) rose from the rocks and farther in the distance I beheld land rich in lush grasses, water, and amrita. Sublime Buddhas were subduing nagas, demons, and other beings of the six realms with their *vajras.*"

Although our vision of what lay ahead was far more modest, we had clearly begun to slip into mythic time ourselves. We descended into the trackless jungles of Shekarlungpa with both elation and dread, following the cloven hoof prints of migrating takin.

The Valley of the White Crystal

AS AGILE AS MOUNTAIN GOATS, takin can navigate rock faces that humans cannot, and we searched for alternative routes when their tracks descended over cliffs or dissipated into scree. At times, we lowered ourselves through the drizzling canopy by hanging on to boughs of trees. We reached a grottolike ravine where a waterfall cascaded into a dark pool, its waters swirling downward and over a cliff into the Tsangpo.

We climbed out using shafts of bamboo to ascend a plant-choked cliff, then dropped through mud to a sloping grove of bamboo. There the porters fashioned a crude shelter to escape the rain. The ground was steep and we leveled spaces for the tents by cutting rhododendron boughs and evening out the surface with bamboo and clumps of moss.

The porters made their customary offering of evergreen boughs in a sodden fire, but rather than excitement, there was now palpable anxiety, and their chants were more ardent. Parts of the gorge looked sheer, the rain was constant, and the jungle before us was a dense morass of interlacing limbs. From the top of the pass, we had seen to the beginning of the great bend but wraithlike clouds had now obscured all but the trees that surrounded our makeshift camp. The scat of the migrating takin indicated that they had passed through weeks before, and the hunters worried that there would be no fresh meat to supplement their dwindling supplies. As we shared a spartan meal of rice and lentils, Gunn informed us that unless we reached habitation within four days he would be out of food.

The next morning, May 8, we packed up our sodden tents and headed into the forest. Almost immediately we confronted a steep granite slab that we crossed on slippery holds. A narrow track used by takin appeared above us and we followed it through a tunnel of thick undergrowth and, afterward, down a series of

ledges. At the base, we entered a stand of alders, wading through a ground cover of waist-high ferns and stinging nettles. A maze of intractable cliffs soon blocked all progress. Gunn stared gloomily at his Chinese military map while the porters used their apches to scrape leeches from their legs, careful to avoid injuring either the blood-drunk creatures or their own limbs. The Tsangpo surged unseen beneath us between high cliffs, a constant thundering drone.

Sherab and I looked together at the zigzagging lines that he had made in my notebook during our interview with Olmula. It was our closest approximation to a viable map. Ken's aeronautical chart showed no contour lines and Kingdon Ward and Cawdor's map of 1924 gave only a rough estimation of the topography. Both maps were at a scale of 1:500,000 and, however expertly surveyed, were no real help to us. Gunn finally showed us the map that he claimed he had secretly photocopied from the Chinese Military Library in Chengdu. The cause of his glumness became immediately clear. He had photocopied the original map in two parts and glued them together, and the area we were now entering had fallen off the edges of the photocopy machine. Gunn stared at the map at regular intervals nonetheless, as if it were a kind of talisman that would eventually reveal our missing coordinates.

As best as Sherab could interpret the scrawls that he had made in my note-book, the rock buttress ahead of us was called Dotrakey. We cautiously tra-versed the slick rock face, grabbing at bunches of shallow-rooted grass that grew out of the cracks, until we reached a desolate cove where the Tsangpo surged up against massive boulders before cutting north and disappearing be-tween walls of schist and limestone. A conical peak, the Shekar Potrang, emerged from the mists above us.

Judging by their journals, Kingdon Ward and Cawdor had camped here, "hemmed in by river and cliffs." As we attempted to level out a space for our tents amid the stones and driftwood, a long yellowish snake slid out from be-tween the rocks. A porter lifted it up on a stick and, muttering prayers, cast it into the jungle. They referred to it as a *lu*, or naga, a serpent guardian of the hidden-lands. Dawa Tsering borrowed Ken's pot to collect water from the Tsangpo but the river ripped it from his hands. We now had no pot for cook-ing and had to use the porters' after they were through with brewing tea.

Khamtrul Rinpoche had described a cave on the slopes of the jungle-covered Shekar Potrang that rose above us out of the Tsangpo like a "nomad's tent." Ac-cording to Khamtrul Rinpoche's account, the three-pillared cave concealed scrolls that would ultimately help in locating Yangsang Né. Khamtrul had med-itated there and received "innumerable portentous omens and auspicious signs."

Olmula had not mentioned the cave in her account, Khamtrul Rinpoche had given no specific directions as to how to reach it, and the terrain was tan-gled and obscure, but I hoped that we would at least be able to look for it the following day. I drifted off to sleep to dreams of golden serpents.

The next morning, we climbed out of the small cave and directly up the ver-dant cliffs of the Shekar Potrang. I spoke to Sherab about the cave, but the ter-rain was intimidating even to him and, with little food left, he was clearly preoccupied by reaching the pass. We could search for days and never find it, he said. Despite his obvious interest in the gorge's spiritual assets, survival had be-come an overriding concern. I thought of Bailey, forced to retrace his steps out of the gorge when his porters had deserted him, his decimated boots strung to-gether with the strap from his hypsometer. Not for the first time, the image of Bailey's hauntingly incomplete map arose in my mind.

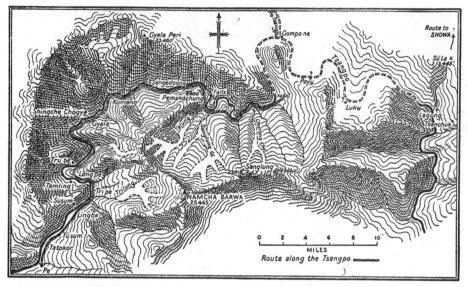

F. M. Bailey's map of the extent of his journey down the Tsangpo in 1913.
The dotted line represents the river's suspected onward course.

DESPITE THEIR NUMEROUS HOOFPRINTS leading into the jungle, we had
seen only one takin, which lumbered up a precipice before the porters could
pursue it. Sherab kept out the climbing rope in hopes of setting up a snare
should we come across a herd. We followed their tracks through a narrow saddle to a river which both Kingdon Ward's map and Olmula's account had indicated as the Churung Chu. It emerged from a wall of glacial ice that was visible
above through a canopy of gnarled, narrow-leaved rhododendrons. The river
was icy cold, gray, and foaming with glacial silt. Sherab brought out his string
of sandalwood prayer beads and performed a divinitory rite to determine
whether we should go up or down to find a way across. He blew on the polished beads and touched them to his forehead before counting off a set number. The beads indicated that we should go low. With no alternative theories of
our own, we picked our way down the bank of the river on spray-drenched
rocks. Before long, we dead-ended where the torrent poured off a cliff, spilling
vertically 200 feet down into the Tsangpo. We headed back upstream. Putting

down our loads, we felled two trees, lodged them precariously against boulders emerging midstream, and shimmied across over the surging waters.

On the far side of the Churung Chu the trees grew larger and wilder with flowering orchids spilling from moss-encrusted limbs. The leeches too became more voracious. They burrowed through our gaiters and the strips of green canvas that the porters had wrapped around their calves and ankles in an attempt to seal them out. It wasn't until the end of the day, when we took off our sodden and blood-filled boots, that we could see their handiwork. The saliva of the common leech harbors chemicals that anesthetize the area of the wound, while an anticoagulant called hirudin prevents the blood from clotting. The result is a painless incision that streams with blood. Only when the bleeding stops does the site of the leech bite begin to itch, often for weeks afterward.

Eager for some technological buffer against this primal terrain, Gunn fantasized that the Chinese government would construct a cable car through the Tsangpo gorge—from Gyala all the way to the confluence. "What good is it if so few can reach this area?" he asked. "And how can they enjoy it if they do?" The porters seemed to feel differently: they marked the trail only faintly, as if to keep it purposefully vague, a green veil that would close again behind us.

We were now in the heart of the gorge. The forest had become almost tropical. Magnolias with long pendulant leaves and vines and lianas formed a green lattice through which we forged a narrow passage. Weeping pines with long, slender blue-green needles shimmered in the rain. Peaks rose above us as waterfalls streamed through the ceiling of clouds and water poured down our collars and backs.

We followed a narrow rhododendron-covered ridge to a steep slope where the porters reached down sticks to haul each other up. We fanned out above in search of a viable route. Sherab and several of the other porters headed down with Eric, while Ken, Jill, and I climbed toward a narrow saddle visible through the trees. We soon heard shouts from Sherab, and we bushwhacked down to where they were pointing excitedly to a rhododendron trunk emblazoned with the deep slash of an apche. The blaze indicated that other human beings had traveled through here in the past. We continued through a tangle of magnolias, rhododendrons, and weeping pines, following other cuts which had been made in the trees until they petered out at the top of a 700-foot cliff dropping off into the Tsangpo.

Somewhat disoriented, we traced the edge of the cliff and before long stumbled into a small clearing with the remains of a primitive shelter and a wooden rack for drying meat. The porters were overjoyed, for along with the fire-blackened rocks it was a sign that either Monpas or Lopas from Pemako had come here to hunt. Amid the porters' excited talk of Pemakochung and the easy virtues of Lopa women, Gunn began to weep with relief, and went around shaking everyone's hands. Sherab maintained that we had found the trail due to our *Chod*, or Dharma practice. Ken held that it was due to our having followed the tracks of the takin—what Kingdon Ward had referred to as the "mystical bovine of the bamboo forests." Despite our dire circumstances in regard to food, Ken was vaguely disappointed. The forest and the surging river had entranced him, and the prospect of a route back to civilization was not altogether welcome.

KINGDON WARD WROTE EVOCATIVELY of this section of the gorge. As the gorge grew ever narrower and the gradient steeper, "the power behind the maddened river was terrific . . . Its blows fell on rock and cliff with frightful force; and at every turn a huge cavernous mouth seemed to open, and gulp it down faster and faster. . . . Already we seemed to be far below the level of the ground, going down, down, into the interior of the earth . . . nothing seemed more unlikely than that we should ever reach civilization again. Every day the scene grew more savage; the mountains higher and steeper; the river more fast and furious."

Lord Cawdor had described the enveloping jungle as "pestilential," and he and Kingdon Ward assigned names to their camps that accorded with their mood: The Heights of Abraham, Braefoot, Cold Comfort, Dismal Swamps. It was at a place they called the Banks of Rubicon, however, that Lord Cawdor reached a state of utter abjection. On November 29 he wrote in his journal: "Woken up by steady rain and large drips. My God! what a country. I only look forward to the day I shall see the last of it!"

AS WE CONTINUED THROUGH THE FOREST, the porters attempted to lasso mushrooms growing from the cliffs. One species—white on the bottom and reddish or honey-colored above—was said to be particularly nourishing, but all the attempts to secure them proved unsuccessful. As a consolation, I offered them one of my last remaining bags of Kashmiri almonds.

We descended through a narrow gap in the trees and dropped steeply toward a small stream at the bottom of a ravine. The creek led directly into the Tsangpo, and we followed it to where it was consumed in a sea of pounding rapids. I gazed out over the fury of white water. Less than a mile ahead, the Tsangpo surged against the enormous spur, laced with waterfalls, that we had seen days earlier from the top of the Khandro Sang-La. After crashing against the wall of rock the Tsangpo disappeared from view, surging northward into the narrowest and still unexplored section of the gorge, the legendary Five-Mile Gap—the last possible refuge of the fabled Falls of the Tsangpo and one of several routes which Tibetans hold to lead into Yangsang Né, the spiritual heart of the Tsangpo gorge.

The Great Bend

WE WERE NOW AT KINGDON WARD and Lord Cawdor's Banks of Rubicon, the site of their last camp along the Tsangpo on November 29, 1924. Kingdon Ward wrote of this critical impasse in his book, *Riddle of the Tsangpo Gorges:*

A quarter of a mile ahead a blank cliff, striped by two silver threads of water, towered a thousand feet into the air. The river came up against this cliff with terrific force, turned sharply to the left, and was lost to view. We scrambled over the boulders, crossed a belt of trees and a torrent, and made for the foot of the cliff in order to see what became of the river; but even before we got there our ears were filled with a loud roaring noise. As we turned the corner, and before we could see straight down the river again, we caught sight of a great cloud of spray which hung over the rocks within a half mile of where we stood. "The falls at last," I thought! But it wasn't—not *the* falls. A fall, certainly, perhaps 40 feet high, and a fine sight with rainbows coming and going in the spray cloud. But a 30 to 40 foot fall, even on the Tsangpo, cannot be called *the* falls, meaning the falls of romance, those "Falls of the Brahmaputra" which have been the goal of so many explorers.

Nevertheless, we stood spellbound, as well we might. The river here swung round to the west, boring its way between two mighty spurs which jutted out, one from Gyala Pelri, the other from Sanglung. Cliffs towered up on both sides, so close together that it seemed one could almost leap from crag to crag; and the cliffs were *smooth* as well as sheer. Only high up against the skyline did a few trees cling like fur to the worn rock surface. Obviously we could get no further down the gorge; to scale the cliff seemed equally impossible.

Kingdon Ward and Lord Cawdor did eventually scale the wall of rock that rose ahead of us now, streaming with delicate cascades. "Of that climb," Kingdon Ward later wrote, "I have only an indistinct recollection, beyond the memory that it was a nightmare." With their porters on the brink of mutiny, the two explorers forged on to the first village in Pemako, where they sheltered in a primitive temple. The abbot of the monastery at Pemakochung who had guided them through the gorge had told them of sacred texts that indicated that there were "no less than 75 waterfalls" in the section of the gorge below where they had been forced to exit and where the Tsangpo seemed to be "boring ever more deeply into the bowels of the earth." Kingdon Ward tried to urge his porters into this uncharted territory, but they insisted that there was no way through. He wrote that they were anxious "to divert our attention from this forbidden land!"

I SAT ON THE ROCKS at the edge of the Tsangpo, looking out over the cresting waves toward where the river began its great horseshoe bend to the north. Clouds sealed off the top of the gorge and silvery waterfalls streamed down the cliffs. Rainbow Falls, the farthest point on the Tsangpo that Kingdon Ward had been able to reach, was hidden behind the spur of Gyala Pelri that terminated in the pyramidal peak called Dorje Pagmo. The Tsangpo carved around this towering monolith and disappeared into unexplored territory, arching back on itself and flowing northwest into the part of the gorge that Morshead's map of 1913 showed only as a conjectural, dotted line.

Directly in front of me, a wave-polished cliff jutted into the Tsangpo, barring farther progress down the river. The earthquake that had obliterated the ledges around the headwall at Pemakochung had altered vast sections of the gorge. It was clear that we would have to climb high above the level of the Tsangpo before we would be able to descend again to river level. Some of the porters had gathered on the rocks and were staring across the maelstrom to where the Tsangpo, as in local folklore, seemed to disappear into the earth. I tried to convince them that after finding a way around the cliff we still had a chance of forging a route into this unknown territory. At the very least, I told

them, we could find a way up the stream-laced cliffs that Kingdon Ward and Cawdor had scaled in 1924.

The following morning we made an attempt to climb above the obtruding rock wall. The cliffs were sheer and dripping with moss, ferns, and runoff from the rains that were falling now in earnest. Every attempt to push farther down the river brought us higher up on the slopes of the gorge. We followed a narrow ridge through a tangle of wet rhododendrons, the cliffs below us dropping into mist and dense vegetation. Using our climbing ropes, we crossed a precarious avalanche chute but found no passage back down toward the Tsangpo. We followed the arete higher in hopes that the slope would eventually lessen and allow us to contour eastward toward the gap. But every effort led us upward toward the glaciated spurs of Sanglung or, as the Tibetans referred to it, Kangla Karpo—a white snowy peak representing the left breast of Dorje Pagmo. (Although other accounts locate her left breast to the east of the Tsangpo on a similarly named mountain, Kangrl Karpo.)

Olmula had described the Shekar-La, or White Crystal Pass, which leads over the spurs of Kangla Karpo into the valleys of Pemako, but had warned that at this time of year it was likely to be blocked by snow. Clouds hung against the mountains like a white veil, and we could see nothing above us. Still, we had no choice now but to climb higher toward the mist-shrouded pass.

In the afternoon, we stumbled into a small cave where hunters from Pemako had previously camped. Hair from a musk pod lay on the ground among the remnants of a fire. Sherab estimated from cut branches that the hunters had camped there less than a month earlier, so unless the rain that was falling in torrents here was falling above us as snow, there had to be a way over the pass. We sheltered under the overhanging rock to wait out a heavy shower and then continued through the tangle of roots, mud, and branches that had become our accustomed terrain. As we climbed higher, the rhododendrons grew lower and more densely, and we navigated through their interlacing limbs as if it were a forest of petrified snakes. When we rested, Gunn stared blankly at his map as if some clue would emerge from the empty spot caused by his inattentive photocopying. One of the porters, the only one who spoke Chinese, watched raptly over his shoulder.

High up a ravine, we came across a cave where half of the porters settled in for the night. The rest of us continued up the streambed in unrelenting rain. We found a larger rock shelter where the porters immediately began building a fire and drying out their wool tunics, which served as everything from blanket to sleeping pad to all-purpose outerwear. The matted felt shed rain at least as well as our own Gore-Tex jackets, which, though certainly lighter, had proved far less durable.

To escape the smoke, I set up my tent beneath a large boulder across the stream. The rain continued throughout the night and into the morning. When I wandered over to the cave, there was nearly zero visibility; a dense unmoving cloud had enveloped us. With no sense of the route ahead and the snowline only 100 meters above, we had no choice but to wait for a change in the weather. Jill lay curled up in her sleeping bag. Eric carved away at his walking stick with a Swiss Army knife. Ken was marking a passage in his copy of *The Prelude*.

"The Spirit of Nature was upon me
and the Place
Was throng'd with impregnations, . . .
And naked valleys, full of caverns, rocks,
And audible seclusions. . . .

DESPITE THE RAIN AND THICK CLOUDS, Sherab had left with two others at first light to scout the route ahead. I returned to my waterlogged tent and read through Kingdon Ward's account for possible clues as how to proceed. He had written in his journal that he had "only the dimmest recollection" of his passage through Shekarlungpa; the disorienting terrain having made it difficult to account for his movements. During our climb to the cave, we had seen through rents in the clouds the lower slopes of the spur that Kingdon Ward and Cawdor had crossed to reach the village of Bayu, but sheer cliffs had prevented us from getting there. The lama Shepe Dorje had also reached the Tsangpo's lower gorge by climbing over these spurs, but his account of his passage focused more on his visions than on the physical topography. Shepe Dorje ascended a "sky high track" where rocks fell continuously from ramparts above. One of his porters tumbled off the escarpment but was drawn back up unharmed. The Gyala headman who had accompanied him on his pilgrimage told him that "The Shekar-La is the most dangerous of all paths. When Lopas travel this route, almost every time someone dies, especially now in the spring." Shepe Dorje continued on undaunted:

> I have completely entrusted myself to the lamas, dakinis, and meditational deities; I recited mantras and asked for help from the dharma protectors. Blowing on our kanglings [thigh-bone trumpets], we climbed one by one up the near-vertical rock as if up a ladder. . . . Loose stones lay everywhere and the rock was very slippery. . . . Thick mist hung over the four directions and a rainstorm was imminent. I generated the vajra-pride of the deity Lokitri Pala and fiercely recited mantras to control the eight classes of spirits. . . . We moved forward very slowly as dense fog covered the mountains and sacred places. Although we could not see clearly the spectacle of our surroundings . . . they matched the descriptions in the *neyigs* and revealed that we were in the center of the throat chakra of enjoyment [*drimpa lungjod kyi korlo*], the palace of the lords of the hidden-land and a gathering place of dakinis and *mamos* [female spirits].

On the morning of May 12, the rain had intensified, and the roof of my Chinese tent collapsed under the weight of the water. I sought refuge in the cave where our porters were lying amid our gear, complaining that they had only a few days of rations left. Sherab's reconnaissance the day before had led them into vertical gullies and impenetrable mists where there was no sign of takin or edible plants. Some of the porters favored a dash back the way we had come. They sat amid pack baskets, coils of rope, and drying clothes, reciting mantras to appease local protectors whom—presumably along with us—they held responsible for the deluge of rain. Gunn sat by the fire, still staring at his map as if the crucial blank spot would miraculously fill in and reveal a way out.

Gunn had become more forthcoming with his map, and he pointed out places where it indicated forest resources for potential exploitation as well as strategic military positions near the border with India. Maps invariably reflect the interests of their makers; the early maps commissioned by the British Raj had similarly been created to lay claim to their frontiers. The Tibetans' textual maps—the neyigs—had a no less ambitious purpose: to convert wilderness into a sacred realm and to chart the interface between mind and landscape.

During a lull in the storm, I headed out with Sherab to look for a route to connect with the one Kingdon Ward had followed in 1924, or some clear line toward the snow-covered pass that Olmula had described. The snow above us was deep and unstable and boulders and small avalanches cascaded out of the mists. Sherab was eager to find a route below the snow line. We traversed through a labyrinth of cliffs and ravines, but after several hours the walls of rock became steeper and the visibility poorer. The porters sat down dejectedly on a ledge. "We're going to die here," said one, wrapping himself in his matted tunic.

It was becoming increasingly clear that we would have to climb into the snow and search for the Shekar-La as we had exhausted all our other possibilities. Olmula had given no specific directions, perhaps doubting that we would ever make it this far. The pass didn't appear on any of our maps, and none of the porters had ever traveled this way before. If we crossed the wrong col or gully we would end up trapped in the trackless glaciers, swamps, and jungles beneath the southern walls of Kangla Karpo.

As we walked back toward the cave, I lingered behind at a snow field on a moraine above our camp. Rocks tumbled down around me out of the mist. I walked into the whiteness, enveloped in rain and snow, imagining a route toward the pass. Snow gullies led off in various directions and it was impossible to guess which one would lead us to the Shekar-La. Perhaps Sherab would resort again to divinations. According to Tibetan accounts, we were near one of the doors into Yangsang Né, but the idea of a nearby Elysium seemed as improbable as that of a colossal waterfall. I returned to my tent, emptied my mind as best I could and, displacing thoughts with mantras, linked myself to the unseen presences of the gorge. One of the Tibetan texts that I had brought with me was entitled *Opening the Door to the Hidden Land: Relieving the Heart's Darkness*. One of its stanzas had left a deep impression on me: "Pemako's protector spirits will cause perilous circumstances to test the power of your realization.

They will assist those who abide by their spiritual commitments and will mislead those who do not."

We had only two days of food left, and in these higher altitudes there were no signs of takin. Several days earlier, at the stream by the Tsangpo, one of the hunters had walked up to a takin calf and killed it with a rock, but the meat had lasted them only a single meal. Since then the porters had subsisted on black tea thickened with spoonfuls of tsampa. Our own combined stores were minimal—three freeze-dried dinners, a box of pilot bread, a bag of almonds, and a few remaining energy bars. Gunn's supply of tinned fish had finally come to an end. It was still raining hard when Sherab came to my tent and said that whatever the weather, we would have to leave the next morning or stay where we were and starve.

The following morning, May 13, we climbed up the moraine above the cave and headed for a rock spur that led up into the snow. The crumbling conglomerate soon forced us into a snow-filled gully that steepened as we climbed. We had cut staves of bamboo in lieu of ice axes, while the porters used their apches to cut steps, burying their blades to the hilt in the softening snow. When the mists briefly parted, we saw a wall of snow cornices like milky waves far above us. The pass at last, we thought, only to have the vision recede into pale clouds. We climbed higher into the mists and rain, kicking steps into the snow. Enveloped in clouds, we finally reached a knife-edge arête that rose steeply on both sides, laced with cornices. It was cold, and our first instinct was to drop to lower elevations. A scree-filled gully dropped below us into mist. Sherab fashioned a small cairn to mark the way we had come. After each of us added a stone to the pile of rocks we let go and slid down into the clouds, snow, and broken rock, gliding with muttered or unvoiced prayers through a gray-white world between the breasts of Dorje Pagmo. Gunn's Chinese tennis shoes had delaminated in the snow and he looked to be on the verge of tears. I told him that according to Buddhist texts, we were on the brink of a paradise. He replied with a saying popular during China's Great Proletariat Revolution: "If this is heaven, where then is hell?"

Tselung

WHEN SHEPE DORJE CLIMBED toward the Skekar-La in 1729, the *kudanpa*, or spirit medium, who traveled with him began to sing, inciting local spirits to guide them through the perilous terrain. The lama wrote, "We entered a narrow passage through the snow, ascending one steep precipice after another. The rocks were wet and slippery. Nowhere could we step with a full foot, and there was nothing to hold on to. At every moment, we were likely to slip over the edge. One of the porters from Gyala fell down the height of five stories and injured his eye. . . . We passed through a mirrorlike rock where a special feeling came over my mind . . . [I later realized] that it was a palace of dakinis called Raga Ra Da Ling."

For Tibetans the key to pilgrimage is *danang*, the sacred vision that transfigures the environment into a pure realm of enlightened energies. Even the most miserable of circumstances invites this shift in perception.

In the Tantric tradition, the ideal of pilgrimage is not simply to visit sacred sites, but to facilitate an inner transformation at places that challenge conventional ways of seeing. In this sense, the more destabilizing the surroundings the better. As the fourteenth-century scholar and meditation master Longchenpa urged:

> *Go to mountain tops, charnel grounds, islets, and fairgrounds. . . .*
> *Places that make the mind waver,*
> *And let the body dance, the voice sing,*
> *And the mind project innumerable thoughts:*
> *Fuse them with the view and practice*
> *of spontaneous liberation*
> *Then all arises as the Path!*

The eleventh-century adept Padampa Sangey was even more emphatic in advocating this esoteric approach to pilgrimage, beyond divisions of sacred and profane:

> *Approach all that you find repulsive!*
> *Anything you are attracted to, Let go of it!*
> *Visit cemeteries and other frightening places!*
> *Find the Buddha within yourself!*

In the minds of Tibetans, Pemako had long been considered an ideal realm for undertaking this inner level of pilgrimage and transforming one's perceptions. Shepe Dorje had epitomized it: "Leaving our homes behind us we are self-abandoning yogis . . . As meditative experiences spontaneously arise, we travel joyously . . . without hope, doubt, or attachment as to whether or not we will succeed. We have no concern for our personal comforts . . . nor for the binding fetters of monasteries or the knots of worldly existence. Nor do we strive for nirvana. All places are joyous to us. We have no fear about dying on the way . . . nor will we have regrets when we have to return."

WE DESCENDED INTO THE MISTS below the pass, with little idea about where we would emerge. The clouds had enveloped us and we could only see a few feet ahead, yet I felt strangely surrendered to the unseen spaces around me. As we dropped lower, shafts of sunlight pierced through the veil of clouds, and we suddenly found ourselves in a glacial cirque. The mists slowly lifted, and we crossed the snow field to where it transformed into a half-frozen waterfall that poured down between black cliffs and disappeared into an abyss. We fashioned a platform from stones that had been pushed down by the glacier and erected our tents at the edge of the precipice. The waters of the melting snow coursed beneath us as we slept. Gunn had a rough night, as the sharp rocks punctured his air mattress.

The following morning we traversed to a line of trees and descended deeper into the ravines below. We had seen a valley far below us through breaks in the clouds, and we imagined that we could follow it to a village in the Tsangpo's lower gorge. We had seemingly missed the Shekar-La itself and had crossed the ridge too far to the west. Our only hope now was to find a way down to the

jungle-filled valley. Light strained through veils of mist and rain, revealing abstract patterns of mountains, clouds, and trees. I thought of something the critic William Hazlitt had written in the eighteenth century in praise of mist, of how humans could borrow "a more fine existence from objects that hover on the brink of nothing." As we descended, our world narrowed to a small circle in which orchids and wispy lichen floated from gray and ghostly trees.

We fanned out in search of a way down the ridge, our hands blistered and raw from cutting through the tangled forest. Ken fell down an eroding cliff, suspended by his armpits between boughs of rhododendrons. Lower down, I tried to climb down a short face only to have the holds crumble beneath my feet. I fell onto a narrow ledge, a vast gulf opening below me. Any serious injury here would have disastrous consequences, and we proceeded as cautiously as the circumstances would allow.

TOWARD NIGHTFALL WE FOUND OURSELVES on a steep slope covered with ancient, moss-laden rhododendrons. Rain dripped through the canopy of intertwining leaves and branches as the porters tried to start a fire in the hollow of a tree. The rest of us leveled a platform with cut boughs and clumps of moss. Nearly hypothermic, we set up a single tent, while the porters hunched like gnomes in notches in the moss-encrusted trees. "We will die here," one of them said. "You brought us here against our will. Now you must find a way out!"

After a nearly sleepless night, we left in rain, and with the aid of ropes descended lichen-covered slabs into an apocalyptic gorge, a place of mud slides, eroding cliffs, and vibrant orchids spilling from the trees. Raindrops beaded like pearls on the leaves of giant magnolias, while lianas and trailers of moss enveloped us in a net of vegetation. Mist swirled around us like ethereal veils.

In crossing the pass, we had entered Pemako, the Land of the Lotus and the body of Dorje Pagmo, and it seemed fitting that we had come in through a back door where there wasn't any path. We climbed down vines and rhododendrons, carpets of ephemeral moss dissipating beneath our feet. My watch had broken and time itself seemed to dissolve. We dropped through ravine after ravine. Leeches returned as we reached lower elevations, and we passed through swards of stinging nettles, oaks, tree ferns, and delicate orchids of a variety, Gunn claimed, once crushed in Chinese courts to make perfume.

THE ULTIMATE GOAL OF EVERY PILGRIM to Pemako is Yangsang Né, the paradise of Dorje Pagmo's innermost heart. According to Padmasambhava's prophecies, a future generation to inhabit the earth will emerge from this most sequestered of valleys—born again from the secret lotus of this "mother of all Buddhas." For some, Yangsang is an Elysian haven where fruits and self-sowing crops ensure freedom from toil, and life-giving waters confer longevity and everlasting health. For others, Yangsang refers to the innermost reaches of the human heart, a field of energy without boundary or end that certain environments can help reveal.[26]

We followed a narrow stream through tunnels of bamboo until we reached a wide and turbulent river that surged through the narrow gorge that we had seen from below the pass. A limestone cliff blocked passage along the riverbank. We tried to climb above it but soon recognized that it formed a continuous wall of rock rearing up through the canopy of trees. We turned back to the river and warily eyed the torturous silt gray waves, swollen in the recent rains. We fell to cutting down a large tree which hung over the bank, aiming our slashes so that it would lodge against a boulder in the center of the stream. But the span was too great and the tree was swept away in the flood. A second attempt led to the same result and the near loss of one of the porters when the log jammed against his leg, nearly sweeping him into the river. We also lost half of one of the climbing ropes that had been tied to the end of the fallen tree. Sherab cut it at the last moment when the log was lost to the surging waves. The porters had become slightly panicky. At nightfall we made a makeshift camp in the subtropical jungle, eating only the sauce to our last freeze-dried meal while the porters brewed tea and scouted the forests for mushrooms.

In the morning we began to construct a cantilever bridge, building a foundation of logs and boulders strung together with vines. As I pushed rocks into place, I could feel my arms trembling from lack of nourishment. Things would get very serious unless we got across the river, and there was no certainty about what we would find on the other side. The broad valley that we had imagined from above had been no more than a figment of hope, now dwindled into a dense and narrow gorge. From our current vantage point, we looked across at a wall of vegetated cliffs, although a small sandy beach farther downstream offered some promise of a way down the river. We could also see wild banana trees in the forest above.

Despite our precarious circumstances, my mind had been filled with lucid dreams, and I had awoken with a strange sense of exhilaration. I thought back to the waterfall at Gyala, and the image of Shinje Chogyal that appears to pilgrims through the veil of water. When meditated upon without preconceptions, Shinje's vast energies, the resources of the subconscious mind, offer a gateway to either heaven or hell. When we had crossed over the pass without coordinates, we'd stepped into a world that increasingly shaped itself to our projections and changed in character according to our shifting conceptions. The lama above Kyikar had asked us if we wanted to die here. Enveloped in this

green world teeming with life and death, the two states did not seem so opposed. "Without contraries is no progression," wrote Blake, and the surrounding jungle seemed to embody his vision of *The Marriage of Heaven and Hell.* (For Blake heaven represented reason while hell was a realm of uncensored and delightful energies.)

WE EVENTUALLY SUCCEEDED in bridging the river by pushing logs out on top of the shorter ones which we had anchored to the bank with boulders and vines. With three logs lodged against the rock in the center of the stream, we were able to cross to the other side, losing no more than a plastic water jug. We struggled up the jungled slope on the far bank, heading for the wild banana trees that we had seen the day before, only to find that they bore no fruit. But the porters discovered edible ferns which they harvested for a later meal. As we climbed back down toward the river, moss and earth matted over a network of roots and vines gave out beneath our weight. We used ropes to negotiate the final moss-covered cliff, first lowering our packs down to river level.

The prospect from this far bank was hardly reassuring. Where we had hoped to find clear passage beyond the sandy cove, cliffs rose directly out of the river. Lianas trailed from the trees and mists mingled with the spray of the waves, forming an ephemeral curtain.

Apart from their harvest of ferns and fragments of compressed tea leaves the porters were entirely out of food. They watched mournfully as we consumed the last crumbs of Ken's stale pilot bread. Who would eat who if things get worse? Eric wondered. They have the knives, Jill said.

I recalled again the consoling belief that those who die in Pemako will not pass through the bardo, a supposedly harrowing interim between one life and the next, but will be immediately transported to paradisiacal realms. Bolstered by these beliefs, pilgrims often take inordinate risks on their journeys. Despite their Buddhist faith, some of the porters were now visibly ill at ease. We had come to a moment of crisis and we all felt it.

Strangely, I found myself not wanting things to be other than they were. I was concerned for my companions, but my initial fears of becoming even more lost until we were living on roots and insects, had given over to some unfamiliar psychological state, a contentedness beyond anything I had ever known. Perhaps it was no more than the first stages of starvation.

Slightly disturbed by the selfishness of my thoughts, I shouldered my pack and we headed downstream in light rain, skirting the cliff at the end of the cove by wading up to our waists through churning water, our bodies insubstantial from lack of food. We reached a ravine, and as we contemplated whether to climb up it or to cut our way lower along the level of the river, we heard a sudden barking of dogs in the jungle above us. Two hunters appeared out of the trees, wearing animal-skin tunics and with primitive rifles slung across their shoulders. We told them where we had come from. No one goes over that pass, they said, but you are fortunate that you have, for it is called Tselung Pemadrak—Long Life Valley of the Wrathful Lotus—and the waters there confer longevity; you will live to be a hundred years.

The two Lopas were headed up the valley to hunt takin. One, who called himself Nima Dorje, Invincible Sun, had scars across his face and a gimp leg from a fall off a cliff. They wore amulets of musk to protect themselves against snakebite. Seeing our condition, they immediately gave us some of their cornmeal tsampa. As Gunn jumped up and down ecstatically at our good fortune, Ken and I looked at each other with the complicity of shared disappointment. "They've appeared two days too soon," Ken said. We were close to the edge, and salvation came before we had completely savored the experience.

One of the hunters agreed to lead us back to the village from which they had come. The other continued on alone up the valley. Only later did the hunter Nima Dorje reveal that at the head of this cloud-enveloped valley was a pass leading into Yangsang. They had never crossed it, Nima Dorje said. Without a qualified lama to perform the appropriate rites, the hidden way through the *dripyol*, or obscuring curtains, would never be found.

Following log bridges and treacherous catwalks of bamboo, Nima Dorje led us back toward his village. We crossed huge heights and dropped down again toward the river on trails that we would never have found on our own. Our hands pulsed with the toxins of thorns and stinging nettles. We passed steaming sulfur springs, moving quickly so as to reach the village before nightfall. Strengthened by Nima Dorje's chang and roasted corn flour, we made rapid progress. In the emerging twilight, I grasped tentatively at every vine. "The snakes come out after dark," Nima Dorje said, "we must hurry."

It grew darker and we pushed on, wary of vipers. There are black ones, Nima Dorje said, and if they bite you, you'll die within an hour. The first fields appeared. A primitive mill for grinding barley and a prayer wheel inscribed with mantras turned in a shallow stream. We crossed a plank bridge and passed the first of several rustic dwellings that were raised above the earth on wooden posts. Two bear cubs wrestled in a pile of firewood, the skin of the mother bear nailed beneath the eaves.

The Lower Gorge

THE VILLAGE WAS CALLED GOGDEM. Nima Dorje took us to his house, where we dried out by the fire. His wife brought us bowls of chang, refilling them three times per Tibetan custom. Having barely eaten for days, we were immediately intoxicated by the potent brew of fermented maize. Cornbread followed, and coarse local rice, yogurt from dzomo tethered beneath the house, and strips of dried bear meat. With food and alcohol streaming through the open door, takin skins for mattresses, and a roof over our heads protecting us from the ever-present rain, we were giddily content, although our shrunken stomachs soon rebelled at the immoderate feast.

The porters discovered relatives who had escaped from Kongpo after the Communist invasion, and they spread out among Gogdem's seventeen houses, built amid small plots of barley, corn, and vegetables and garlanded with vines of crimson chili peppers. Semidomesticated boars wallowed in the mud beneath the houses, and besides their stock of pigs and dzo, the villagers hunted in the jungle for takin, bear, muskdeer, and wild goats. Most of the residents were Lopas, descended from Pemako's original tribes, but they had intermarried with Monpas who migrated into Pemako from eastern Bhutan at the end of the eighteenth century, escaping feuds in their home valleys and following prophecies of the hidden-land. There was also a smaller number of Kongpopas and Khampas, refugees from their homelands after the Chinese invasion.

We stayed in Gogdem throughout the next day. The hunter with the bear cubs came in the morning and tried to sell us pods of musk and the dried gallbladder of the cubs' mother whose skin he had hung out to dry on the outer wall of his house. These glands are revered as potent medicine by both Chinese and Tibetans, but villagers came to us with ailments which no local plants or animal products had been able to cure. One had a necrotic leg from a viper bite. Others had septic infections caused by leeches. Although I asked them to describe their specific illnesses, they were more concerned that I read their pulses. Traditional Tibetan doctors examine eighteen different pulses to gain information about the health of specific organs and energy meridians. I had no idea how to read these pulses, but the villagers insisted on a hands-on approach. Besides an emergency reserve of antibiotics, I had only homeopathic and herbal remedies, and after disinfecting any wounds with iodine, I dispensed them as judiciously as I could. Most coveted were the *rinchen rilbu,* or Tibetan precious pills, that contain silver, gold, and semiprecious stones such as turquoise and coral. They are widely believed to cure a diverse range of ailments. Promised land or not, Pemako clearly offered no escape from old age, sickness, and death.

Gunn and the others stayed wrapped up in their sleeping bags by the fire. Ken had filled his journal and was scribbling notes in the margins of *The Prelude.* He looked up, firelight reflecting off his wire-rim glasses, and declaimed, ". . . the voice of mountain torrents; or the visible scene / Would enter unawares into his mind, / With all its solemn imagery, its rocks, / Its woods, and that uncertain heaven . . ."

Jill rolled over in her sleeping bag and, amused by these utterances, asked Ken whether he felt he had encountered the sublime. He replied that journeys take shape on reflection, but that yes, he had tasted what he had come for. Still, he said, he suspected that the ultimate journey, like the Tibetans' quest for Yangsang, could never be fulfilled. It would be, as Thoreau had said, "like chasing rabbits that you keep dragging out of your hat."

THE FOLLOWING MORNING Gogdem's headman handed us a cryptic note from Rick, who had apparently hobbled into the village ten days earlier. Rick's letter stated that the rest of the group had returned home, and that he was heading alone down the lower gorge, accompanied by two Monpa porters. The villagers had noted his injured leg and his trademark red bandana, and demonstrated how, in lieu of words, he had gesticulated with his hands in an effort to communicate to his porters.

The headman told me that a cable spans the Tsangpo several thousand feet below Gogdem and that Rick had crossed over to the village of Gande on the far side. News had already come back that local officials had not allowed him to continue south toward the border with India as he had planned, and that he had crossed over a pass called the Gawalung-La into the region of Powo. From Gogdem, we could see the Tsangpo far below us as it flowed southward into a maze of clouds and blue-gray peaks on its course towards the Indian frontier. There it would be referred to by its tribal name, the Dihang, and be joined by other Himalayan streams—the Lohit, Subansiri, Kameng, Bhareli, Dhansiri, Manas, Champamati, Saralbhanga, and Sankosh—to form the massive flow of the Brahmaputra before converging with the Ganges and Jamuna and emptying into the Bay of Bengal.

Nima Dorje described how the Tsangpo represents the life-force of Dorje Pagmo and interlinks the energies of her throat, heart, navel, and womb. As enticing as it was to be on the threshold of the sacred sites of the lower gorge, our permits had expired, and Gunn stressed that we must return to Lhasa as quickly as possible. Nima Dorje agreed to accompany us on the way out, telling us that it would be a five- or six-day journey up the gorge to its confluence with the Po Tsangpo and onward to the trailhead at the village of Trulung (Pelung).

WHEN SHEPE DORJE REACHED the lower Tsangpo gorge, he had planned to follow the river southward into the heart of Pemako, in accordance with the prophecies that he had received in his dreams and visions. But before he had even reached the Shekar-La, two Lopas had tried to make him turn back:

"Please Lama, don't go to Pemako. The Lopas there have no leader and the place has no laws. Even if you do reach there, there will be no benefit for you. We will help carry your belongings back the way you have come. . . . The Kanam Depa [the hereditary ruler of Powo] commanded that not even officials, lamas, or accomplished yogins should be allowed over the Shekar-La. If you let them pass, he told us, I will seize your property. You cannot succeed and

even if you try, we will lose everything." We argued extensively, but the Lopa
said that the pass and related areas along the Tsangpo were the domain [of the
King of Pwo] ... They held knives in their hands and insulted the Gyala
Depa ... saying, "Why do you and your son try to bring lamas to our village?"
They tried many way to stop us, but retreated when we persevered.

Once in the lower gorge, Shepe Dorje was better received:

The Lopa Pawo [shaman] sent Lopas named Tsesung and Kunga to invite us to
their village. They burned incense on a stone slab in greeting and, not far away,
Lopa Pawo himself brought tea and chang and greeted us with veneration. ...
That night we camped near the Lopa village. Apart from the Lopa Pawo, everyone is very poor. Some have injuries and swollen limbs. Some of our porters
had caught *sadug* [earth poison] which they healed with mantras and ointments.

The Lopa Pawo ... is different from the others. ... He has left foot and
hand prints in solid rock [as signs of spiritual accomplishment]. ... The
Lopas offered us tea, millet chang, millet thukpa, dzo yoghurt, honey, and
pork. ... The Pawo gave me deer musk, butter, millet, and rope and mats woven from bamboo ...

Despite his kind reception by the Lopa Pawo, Shepe Dorje's journey south was
blocked by a contingent of warriors sent by the ruler of Powo. The prophecies
that Shepe Dorje had received had indicated that "If you enter Pemako from
the western gate, you must have patience and perseverence. Then all wishes can
be fulfilled." Adamant that he should proceed, Shepe Dorje sent a letter to the
court in Powo stating his objectives and settled down to await the reply.

The thirty-one-year-old lama was not idle while he waited for the messenger to return. As he wrote in his account: "The Drejongpas (from Sikkim) were
practicing yogic exercises (*trulkor*). In the mornings and evenings, I perfomed
my own practices and gave the teachings of *Sangyig*, the profound generating
stage practices, and Guru Yoga to assembled dharma sisters and friends. I
passed the time with discussions of *Vajra Neluk* (the natural state of existence,
the changeless state of Dharmata). For the dakini, Pema Roltso and several

others, I gave the pointing out instructions on the Nature of Mind (*Rigpa Sel-
wang*)."

Shepe Dorje also spent time documenting numerous unfamiliar plants and
trees. He commented on the many varieties of fruits and also on the patterns of
vajras, lotuses, and wheels which he witnessed on leaves and exposed tree roots.
He also took note of banana trees which
are found nowhere else in Tibet. "The
leaves are two and a half paces long," he
wrote, "and shaped like swords. . . . They
offer a perfect place to avoid the rain."[27]

When the messenger returned with a
letter from the Powo court, he announced that if Shepe Dorje did not return
the way he had come, an army of Lopa warriors would come to stop them. The
letter stated: "Pemako belongs exclusively to the people of Kanam (Powo); it is
not a place that the inhabitants of U and Tsang (central Tibet) may enter."

Despite the protector deity Mentsun Chenmo's vow to assist Shepe Dorje
like "a shadow following his body" and the prophecies concerning the places
that he was to open in Pemako's heart and navel chakras, "the auspicious circumstances (*tendrel*) and conditions and opportunities did not allow us to reach
these [sacred] places." As Shepe Dorje wrote: "We tried every means possible,
but the Kanam Depa's representatives were too frightened to let us pass. All the
doors have now been closed and, in the end, we have decided to return the way
we have come." After final prayers "to increase the virtues and qualities of the
hidden-land as well as for the good fortune of all sentient beings," Shepe Dorje
began his journey back to central Tibet. "I journeyed here not for my own
sake," he wrote, "but in fulfillment of the dakinis' prophecies and to benefit all
sentient beings. Although it was prophecied that I was to open the chakras at
[Dorje Pagmo's] heart and navel, the auspicious circumstances failed to materialize . . ."

ON MAY 18 WE FELT SUFFICIENTLY RESTORED to begin our journey toward the confluence. We set out for Luku, the next village to the north. As we walked, Ken lamented the return to inhabited terrain and looked longingly up the valley that we had followed from the Shekar-La. Vast glaciers on the southern walls of Namcha Barwa appeared through the clouds. Although intrigued by the local culture, his heart was set on finding a way into the still unknown section of the Tsangpo gorge and laying to rest the mystery of the falls.

We reached Luku before midday. The village was slightly larger than Gogdem, with twenty-two houses spread out along the steep slopes of the lower gorge. Dorje Drolma, Olmula's older sister, had died years before, but our porters discovered other lost relatives who had come from Kongpo in the 1960s to escape the People's Liberation Army. We settled into a large wooden house where three local women—Tashi Tsomo, Sonam Wangpo, and Sonam Dekyi— plied us with chang, while their mother, dressed in a bloodred shirt woven from raw silk, stirred cornmeal and millet into an enormous pot simmering on the earthen hearth. Large bowls of the millet-based alcohol were passed around the room, which was painted with white *gakyils,* or coils of joy. Bearskins and antique weapons hung on the walls from iron nails. In Bayu, the next village to the north, Kingdon Ward had been similarly received. "Occasionally you taste a vintage which is just frolicking foam," he wrote, "One sip and the world is transformed . . . a fleeting glimpse of the golden age . . ."

Although the Monpas and Lopas spoke their own indecipherable language, they spoke enough Tibetan that I could communicate with them. Drinking games and dancing ensued, and even Gunn, well lubricated with the local spirits, was enticed into singing a Chinese love song. The chang continued to flow until we pleaded exhaustion and were shown to the family shrine room where we slept amid animal skins and a pedal-operated Chinese sewing machine. The revelry in the main part of the house continued throughout the night.

We tried to leave the next morning, but the porters were still drunk. When Chimé Gompo fell off the porch while shouldering his load, we realized that we would be marooned in Luku for another day. The chang again began to flow and the three sisters cooked up a delicious meal of wild mushrooms. On a trip out to relieve myself, I discovered opium poppies growing behind the house and was told they were used for medicine. Had they been brewed into the chang? Double rainbows arched across the Tsangpo amid spectacular cloud formations.

In Lopa folklore, a rainbow represents the movement across the sky of four lustrous, spring-dwelling *nagas*, or water spirits, in search of wives as radiant as themselves. The falling rain is held to be the ambrosial chang that they consume on their journey.

Back inside the house, the party continued. Eric, dressed in his newly washed Hells Angels sweatshirt, had passed out dreamily against a wooden pillar. Gunn was talking about his wife in Chengdu. Our porters sang and danced. The oldest of the three sisters, Tashi Tsomo, continued to ply me with chang and her beauty blossomed the more I drank.

A drunken Lopa with large ivory earrings came into the shrine room where we had sought refuge and, bowing his head to my knees, asked for *abhisekha*, initiation into the Tantric mysteries. Earlier I had given him a photograph of the Dalai Lama as well as Bhakha Tulku who is revered in Pemako and beyond as the reincarnation of Pema Lingpa, a fifteenth-century terton. Never having met any of the high lamas who had escaped to India after the Chinese invasion, the sinewy Lopa had convinced himself that the blessings and empowerments that I had received from them could be passed on. Amused, embarrassed, and nearly as drunk, I told him I could do nothing. But the Lopa was unrelenting and with his shaved head fixed to my knee, I brought out the sachet of mendrup that Chatral Rinpoche had given me the day before I left for Tibet. This consecrated elixir can only be prepared in elaborate Tantric rites and is highly esteemed in the Tibetan world. Suddenly the room was crowded with eager Lopas, Monpas, and Kongpopas, all insisting that I give them some of this coveted substance. Some ate it immediately. Others wrapped it carefully in bits of cloth and put it into their amulet boxes. During the proceedings, I learned that a forty-one-year-old incarnate lama from Kham named Wasadorje Tulku was staying in meditative retreat above the village. For three years he had not received visitors, and I began to understand why.

ON MAY 19 WE AWOKE to roosters crowing beneath the floorboards and soon began a grueling climb northward to a pass called the Gopu-La. A pilgrims' shelter had been built at a clearing at the top of the pass, and on the following morning, rather than beginning the steep descent to Bayu, Nima Dorje led us along the crest of the ridge to a rock monolith called Tsebum, the Vase of Life. It was a sacred site highly revered in the upper parts of Pemako, and we circumambulated it through tunnels in the rock and across notched logs spanning precipitous drops.

Following Nima Dorje's directives, we carried sticks with us, and near the top of the enormous outcrop we cut notches into them with our knives—one for every year of our lives. We then stacked them against the rock along with countless others that had been left there before, each one rising up like a ladder into the sky. Nima Dorje explained that by placing the stick there we were establishing a connection to the sacred energies of the place, and that powa, or transference of consciousness, would thus occur spontaneously at the time of our deaths.

Tsebum was a potent place. Nima Dorje showed me where a visiting terton named Tulku Dorje Tenzing had left imprints of his foot and hands in the rock after meditating there for a month, a physical testament that the world is more permeable than it appears. Three *koras,* or circumambulations, around the monolithic outcrop were said to confer the same spiritual blessings as a single circuit around Kundu Dorsempotrang, a sacred mountain deep in the wilderness east of the Tsangpo's lower gorge. The towering rock had been enveloped in mist and only as we were leaving did we see it arching into the sky. Beneath it was a cave with water dripping into a tranquil pool.

We continued back to the pass, but rather than begin the long descent to Bayu, a village still many hours away, Nima Dorje insisted that we now climb up the ridge to a sacred body of water called "the burning lake which removes all obstacles," where we should also perform ritual circumambulations. Snow lay in drifts in the forest, and Nima Dorje lost the way. It had begun to rain, but the porters were all eager to gain the blessings of this sacred site, a proxy to the remote mountain that local tradition claims to hold the key to Yangsang.

After thrashing through the forest, we eventually came upon the half-frozen lake. It was several hundred feet across and Nima Dorje said we would have to circle it thirteen times. As we began the first kora, the porters' prayer beads came out again from beneath their tunics, and their mantras reverberated through the still and silent air.

Long before Buddhism came to Tibet, the soul and vitality of Tibetan clans was connected to particular lakes, rocks, and mountains. Although the spirits of these places could be appeased with ancient shamanistic rites, Buddhism transformed an uneasy alliance with nature into one in which pilgrims could participate directly in the sacred presence, just as Tibet's primordial demoness, the Srinmo, had reformulated herself in Pemako as a bliss-bestowing goddess.

It was well past midday when we finished our thirteen rounds, and we were concerned about whether we would be able to make it to Bayu. We headed down through interminable ravines and gullies, following the faint semblance of a trail. Thousands of feet below the pass, we entered a forest of towering plantains, clusters of the green banana-like fruit dangling pendulently high above our heads. In twilight we climbed up a steep slope and emerged suddenly onto cultivated fields. Soon, we saw the first houses of Bayu. Takin skins and bearskins were nailed against the walls to cure. Firewood lay in huge stacks beneath the eaves. Villagers came out of their houses to greet us. In gathering darkness, they led us up a log ladder into a house raised above the earth where they handed us bowls of chang. As we sat ourselves around the fire, our raven-haired hostess served us bear meat and mustard greens. It had been a long day, and we spread out almost immediately around the fire on takin skins. I drifted off to sleep to the sound of boars grunting beneath the floorboards.

Gunn's senior colleague, Mr. Lo, had been waiting for us in Bayu for almost two weeks. Assuming that our route out of the upper gorge would take us directly into Bayu, he had stayed behind when Rick headed out on his own in an attempt to reach Medok, a remote outpost close to the border with India. Lo had been on the verge of sending out a rescue party when we stumbled into the village. He had been reasonably content in Bayu, he told us the next morning, as our pretty hostess, a Monpa woman named Nima Tso, Lake of Sunlight, spoke passable Chinese.

Over tea by the hearth, Lo told us that David Breashears had also come down the Po Tsangpo and had climbed up to the ridge above Bayu, scouting unsuccessfully for a route into the innermost gorge. Kingdon Ward and Lord Cawdor had crossed this same spur from the other direction, passing through a region of giant bamboo, palmlike Araliaceae, and unusual orchids. We were eager to make the 6,000-foot ascent up the ridge in order to look down into the area that no one had yet been able to reach, the forbidden land that Tibetan texts claimed concealed no less than seventy-five waterfalls. But the weather was still bad, and Lo, as our official liaison officer, would not allow it. Our permits had already expired, he said, and we would have to head straight back to Lhasa.

Over a morning meal of eggs and unleavened corn bread, Lo told us of a bizarre race that had occurred between Breashears and the twelve-year-old son of one of Rick's clients. Having been closed out of the inner gorge by the cliffs beyond Pemakochung, Breashears and Wiltsie had determined to reenter the gorge farther downriver. Like Rick and his clients, they planned to follow the river that drains the Powo and Yigrong valleys to its confluence with the Tsangpo at the apex of the Great Bend. From there they would try to enter the section of the gorge that had thwarted all previous explorers, and fulfill their mission for National Geographic.

The route down the Po Tsangpo to the confluence is well traveled. A village called Tsachu (Zhachu) lies thousands of feet above the river with spectacular views—when the mists lift—toward Gyala Pelri and Namcha Barwa. Kingdon Ward and Lord Cawdor had returned to central Tibet by this route in the last week of 1924. Despite the relative ease of the terrain and the fact that Westerners had been there before, the broad trail down the Po Tsangpo provided the context for a ludicrous parody of Scott and Amundson's tragic race for the South Pole. According to Lo, Rick was adamant that his team be the first to reach the area of the confluence. Unable to compete personally because of the torn ligament in his knee, Rick dispatched the two strongest hikers in his party—a forty-year-old secretary named Sharon Ludwig and Ry Larrandson, the twelve-year-old son of another of Rick's clients. The two snuck through Breashears and Wiltsie's camp before sunrise and began the seventeen-mile trek to Tsachu. Later that morning, Breashears spotted the tracks of their vibram boots and rose to the bait. Unloading his pack onto Wiltsie, he took off running in an attempt to beat Rick's clients to the village. Despite his efforts and the ensuing abuse he received from Wiltsie for being made to carry two packs, Ry and Sharon had reached the village hours before him. The confluence was still more than two hours farther down the ridge, but after reaching Tsachu—idyllically situated amid meandering streams and fields of barley and corn—the mission suddenly seemed absurd to all participants. "What a sad day for me, getting caught up in that silly game," Breashears later said.[28]

After Breashears's foray to the ridge above Bayu, he and Wiltsie returned up the Po Tsangpo and drove back to Lhasa. After several days based at the confluence, trying unsuccessfully to find a route upriver into the inner gorge, Rick's clients had also returned home. Rick stayed on and redirected his efforts toward the lower gorge. Unlike the wilderness upstream, the Tsangpo's lower reaches—from the confluence all the way to the border with India—are sparsely populated. Bailey and Morshead had seen parts of the lower gorge in 1913, but they were blocked from continuing north to the confluence by a Powo official who rerouted them over the Su-La pass. Rick was eager to document the sections of the gorge that they had missed. As we later learned, he had crossed the Tsangpo on the cable bridge below Gogdem and had ended up in the next village without any food or Chinese currency. Avoided at first by wary villagers, Rick had ultimately conviced some of them of the value of a $100 bill and secured porters to take him across a snowbound pass into Powo, where he arrived without a permit. He later claimed to have avoided frostbite by slipping Ziploc bags over his single pair of woolen socks.

WE LEFT BAYU ON MAY 21. A gnomish Monpa, sporting a red, three-pointed cap and twirling an oversized prayer wheel, came out of his house to see us off. Several other mantra-inscribed whirligigs gyrated along the ridgeline of his house, which was surrounded by banana trees and towering hemp plants that we were told were used for making rope. We walked past a wall of *mani* stones, carved with mantras, and along fields of ripening barley before plunging once again into jungle. Climbing through mist and rain, we began a long ascent through a forest of alders, oaks, and pines to a break in a ridge that runs out from a great cliff that looms over the Tsangpo–Po Tsangpo confluence. Through breaks in the trees, we could see snow ranges far to the north and the lower slopes of the eastern face of Gyala Pelri.

We descended toward the apex of the Great Bend, the Tsangpo surging beneath us with the additional waters it had amassed after merging with the Po Tsangpo, several miles upstream. When we reached the river, the altimeter registered only 5,247 feet above sea level—little more than the highest parts of Kathmandu. We found a 300-foot-long footbridge in place of the single cable that had previously connected these lower parts of Pemako with the regions to the north. In Kingdon Ward's day there had only been a rope of twisted bamboo. Lord Cawdor had written of the experience in his journal: "I was hauled across, thrashed like a fowl for the pot. Fortunately the distance was short, and the agony did not last long."

Once across the river, we climbed up through the steep jungle to the village of Tsachu, comprised largely of Lopas and settlers from Powo. We slept at the house of the village headman and could look out from the porch over pendulous banana trees toward the massive headwall called Shatidzong that blocks all views and passage into the Tsangpo's inner gorge. According to our host, the fluted cliffs conceal undiscovered terma, but villagers mostly visit them to collect honey.

Tsachu had been equally enchanting on December 17, 1924, when Lord Cawdor had written in his diary: "I shall ever remem-

ber this corner as the pleasantest spot we have struck—wonderful country, interesting vegetation, plenty of cultivation, and extraordinarily pleasant, friendly,
and cheerful barbarians."

We left our hosts at Tsachu early the next morning. After initial landslides,
the trail began to level into dense temperate rainforest and to wind back and
forth across the Po Tsangpo on primitive bridges. After fifteen days of rain, the
sun finally emerged from behind the clouds and a shower of butterflies hovered
over the path. Green and golden snakes stretched themselves across the trail
to soak up the rare sunlight. We walked through forests of towering bamboo,
cherry trees, and 200-foot cypresses, passing sulfur springs where vapors drifted
through the trees and warm velvet waters cut across a sandy beach to empty
into the Po Tsangpo. As we neared the road head, I lingered behind to walk
alone, crossing a catwalk of cables and wooden planks bolted into the cliffs. As
night approached, I emerged from the jungle and crossed a rickety bridge
strung with tattered prayer flags. Navigating the broken boards, I stepped onto
the road that connects Lhasa with western China. As I walked into the small
roadside hamlet of Trulung (Pelung), a Chinese Dong Feng cargo truck laden
with freshly cut logs rolled eastward along the narrow dirt road.

Lo had installed us in a makeshift room with cement floors and broken windows. The next day we drove to Powo and visited Bhakha Tulku's monastery,
situated on a small peninsula where the Po Tsangpo broadens into a tranquil
lake. Due to Chinese regulations forbidding foreigners to stay at Buddhist
monasteries, we drove to the district center of Pomi (Powo Dzong), where a local police official directed us to a designated hotel. The Chinese immigrants
who ran it were gruff and unfriendly. The official told us that Rick had already
been "caught" and had been sent back to Lhasa. We we were told to leave first
thing the next morning.

Lustrous, snow-covered peaks rose on both sides of the river that flowed
through Powo Dzong. Beyond the small outpost, the Po Tsangpo was lined
with peach trees and silver firs. As Lo negotiated on the black market to secure
enough gasoline to get us back to Lhasa, the police official told us we should
never have come and that we should go back to America.

Lamaling

ON THE THREE DAY DRIVE back to Lhasa, we made a detour to Lamaling, a Buddhist sanctuary built in a valley behind a seventh-century temple.[29] My first Buddhist teacher, Dudjom Rinpoche (1904–87), had been born in Pemako but had later moved to Lamaling, where he lived until the time of the Chinese invasion, when he fled Tibet and settled in Kalimpong in northeastern India. His daughter, Semo Dechen, and his chief attendant, Lama Chonyi Rinpoche, continued his work in Tibet when conditions for Buddhist practice improved after the Cultural Revolution. They had made Lamaling a flourishing retreat center where men and women from all parts of Tibet came to study and practice. Dudjom Rinpoche had built a three-tiered temple at Lamaling representing Sangdo Pelri, the celestial paradise of Padmasambhava, but the earthquake in 1950 had toppled it to the ground. In recent years the Chinese government had relaxed restrictions regarding the practice of religion, and Chonyi Rinpoche and Semo Dechen had begun rebuilding the historic temple. We could see its golden roofs glinting in the sun as we drove through open fields toward a small hamlet built on a ridge amid poplars, cypresses, and pines.

Red-clad nuns and yogis came out to receive us. Before we could account for ourselves, they led us through a wooden door into a hidden garden brimming with peonies and chrysanthemums, and pear and apple trees. Parakeets flew overhead and sat on branches above a small fountain. Chonyi Rinpoche, his long silvery hair tied into a yogic topknot, came out from a single story house and, after shaking our hands, led us into his shrine room.

Sitting on colorful Tibetan carpets, I told the lama that I had been a student of Dudjom Rinpoche after he had left Tibet, and that we had just come from Pemako after a month-long pilgrimage. Chonyi Rinpoche had lived in Pemako for many years. He held up one of his hands and with the other indicated the incessant ridges and ravines that we knew only too well. I described our route from Gyala to Pemakochung and over the pass to Gogdem and Luku. "Ah," he said, "you've been through the throat of Dorje Pagmo." He described it as the gateway into the heart of Pemako and the hidden-lands below. I asked him about Yangsang Né, Pemako's ever-elusive center, and whether it was located in the throat, the heart, or the vulva, as different accounts had suggested.

Chonyi Rinpoche's response helped clarify the conundrum. "Each chakra has outer, inner, secret, and ultimately secret [yangsang] dimensions," the lama said. There are thus doors at every focal point along Dorje Pagmo's body. "Each chakra, in turn, has four *lings*, or petals, each with their own outer, inner, secret, and ultimately secret levels. Each one, in turn, radiates outward. As Dorje Pagmo's throat center, the inner gorge must therefore conceal a door." But as far as he was concerned, to reach Yangsang one must journey first to a mountain called Kundu Dorsempotrang, the All Gathering Adamantine Palace, which rises at Dorje Pagmo's heart. According to Buddhist treasure-texts, the mountain holds the key to Pemako's innermost sanctuary.

I asked about the waterfall rumored to lie in the Tsangpo's innermost gorge, and he told me of the lama named Kanjur Rinpoche who had passed through such a falls in the 1950s while searching for Chimé Yangsang Né. In Buddhism, Chonyi Rinpoche explained, waterfalls symbolize the transitory nature of all phenomena. In Tantric yoga, they signify the descent of amrita, the glandu-

lar secretions that fall from the cranial vault and spread through the chakras, connecting what's above with what's below. Chonyi Rinpoche explained that to enter Yangsang, a place ultimately beyond geographical or anatomical co-ordinates, one would first have to open "secret gates" within the mind and body. One of the twelve yogis currently in retreat at Lamaling had been hav-ing dreams of Pemako, Chonyi Rinpoche said. His visions revolved around secret practices concerning the descent of nectar and the opening of the chakras. Perhaps that's the meaning of the waterfall, Chonyi Rinpoche suggested.

Semo Dechen served us a lunch of wild mushrooms, vegetables, and rice. Afterward, the lama led us through the garden to the temple of Sangdo Pelri, which was surrounded by fruit trees and banks of flowers. Inside, red and white blossoms overflowed from vases on an altar that was dominated by a gilded statue of Padmasambhava. A polished rock, embossed with what was said to be Padmasambhava's own footprint, lay at its base. Deities representing increasingly subtle states of awareness emerged from lotus plinths as we walked up through the stairs and galleries toward the roof. From the balcony beneath the gilded eaves, we could see the gardens laid out like a mandala around the temple. Far on the southeastern horizon, the summit of Namcha Barwa rose through clouds, while the Tsangpo flowed below like a distant, silver mirror. An old woman was piling juniper boughs into an incense burner at the base of the temple, and the smoke streamed into the sky like a fountain of fragrant vapors.

As Chonyi Rinpoche led us back from the temple, sun rays poured across a ridge of pines, illuminating gardens which would have sent Kingdon Ward into fits of rapture. Kingdon Ward had searched the gorge for exotic seeds to "beautify the gardens of England" and to placate his sponsors; Shepe Dorje had searched for a flower of another order, the thousand-petaled lotus said to bloom at its center. Pemako, a land arrayed like enfolded lotuses, guarded its innermost secrets from both of them, but the two explorers had been models for me, their opposing yet strangely complementary perspectives opening my mind to the depths and complexities of the Tsangpo gorge.

Lo had waited by the Land Cruiser during our visit to the temple. He urged us toward the open door, saying that we had many hours left to drive that day. As we drove off down the dirt road, Chonyi Rinpoche, Semo Dechen, and assorted nuns, yogis, and villagers all waved goodbye. I felt a strange lightness, as if the Land Cruiser was floating above the earth. I recalled the passage Ken had marked in Book Ten of *The Prelude:*

Not in Utopia, subterranean fields,
Or some secreted island, Heaven knows where!
But in the very world, which is the world
Of all of us, the place where, in the end,
We find our happiness, or not at all!

PART THREE

THE

MOUNTAIN

To reach this secret place, your meditation and insight should be confident; free of any fear or doubt. . . . In order to pass through the tunnel of obstacles, one's behavior and actions must be impeccable . . . otherwise [Pemako's] hidden places will never be revealed.

RINCHEN RIWOCHE JEDRUNG JHAMPA YUNGNEY
Clear Light: A Guide to the Hidden Land of Pemako

This enchantment of the human mind with archetypal landscape . . . is a phenomenon as old as myth and persistent as dream. . . . We seem to have an insatiable thirst for places that don't exist.

We must believe that the mountain exists; yet it must remain elusive, yielding to none of our usual means of entry. . . . One "gets there" only through extremity, by way of abandonment.

BELDEN C. LANE
The Solace of Fierce Landscapes

The sensible are never free.

NORMAN MAILER
An American Dream

July 1995
The Year of the Wood Boar

WHEN SKIES CLOUD OVER during the summer monsoon, Kathmandu's residents carry gilded deities from dark pagoda-roofed temples and parade them on covered palanquins through the rain-washed streets. The ancient rites are meant to protect the valley from landslides and floods, but nothing had prevented my old house from collapsing under relentless rains. I'd moved into a rambling flat with Hamid Sardar, who had taken a leave of absence from Harvard to study Sanskrit in Kathmandu. His tutor, a white-clad Brahmin pundit, would arrive early each morning, and the resonant sound of Sanskrit slokas would reverberate for the next two hours from the oval living room. As the monsoon rains intensified, mold grew on the plaster walls and spread across the surface of books and antique Tibetan furniture. Bamboo and banana trees in the garden reached unprecedented heights.

On my return from the Tsangpo gorge in 1993, I sought out Bhakha Tulku and told him how I'd been unable to reach the deepest section of the gorge. He told me that without the key I'd never find the passageway into Yangsang. Like Chonyi Rinpoche, he advised me to go first to the mountain Kundu Dorsempotrang.

The name Kundu Dorsempotrang translates as the All-Gathering Palace of Vajrasattva, a Tantric deity symbolizing pristine, unobstructed awareness. Tibetans often refer to the mountain as Kundu Potrang, the All-Gathering Fortress, or simply as Kundu. A neyig entitled *Guide to the Heart Center of the Great Sacred Land of Pemako* describes the mountain as the "indestructible, secret fortress of the dakinis . . . that liberates upon seeing." Echoing stories I had heard in Sikkim

and Tibet, Bhakha Tulku told me how the lama Longchen Yeshe Dorje, Adamantine Awareness of Vast Space, better known as Kanjur Rinpoche, had visited the mountain in the 1950s and been guided by visions to a tunnel behind a
waterfall that led him to a paradisiacal valley that he had identified as Chimé
Yangsang Né. When Kanjur Rinpoche tried to return there with his family, he
claimed to be unable to find the route.[1]

Bhakha Tulku had met Kanjur Rinpoche on his journey to Kundu Dorsempotrang in 1956. Although he was only twelve at the time, the mountain had left
a deep impression. He compared the peak to Mount Kailas, the world pillar in
the arid wastes of western Tibet that Buddhists and Hindus alike consider the
meeting place of heaven and earth. Unlike the snow-covered dome of Kailas,
which looms above vast, treeless plains, Bhakha Tulku described Kundu as being surrounded by swamps and rain forests. "The mountain is the heart of
Pemako," he said. "It's the key to its hidden realms."

In May 1994, I returned to Pemako with Hamid in an attempt to reach the
sacred mountain. Bhakha Tulku had returned to his ancestral seat and we visited him at his sixteenth-century monastery in the Powo valley north of Pemako. Together with Ken Storm, Laura Ide, a girlfriend I'd met during my
sojourn at Columbia, a climbing partner, Rob Parenteau, and his fiancée, Karen
Kung, we had followed the Tsangpo River south to Medok, the traditional
starting point for the pilgrimage to Kundu and, since the 1960s, a Chinese military base. Local authorities had forbidden us to proceed farther.

Claiming to be in need of a rest day, we headed into the jungle with minimal provisions on the pretext of bathing in a nearby waterfall. Avoiding detection, we climbed through dense forest and clouds of gnats until we reached a
remote golden-roofed temple that according to local tradition, lies in Dorje
Pagmo's navel chakra. Kundu lay several days' journey to the southeast, but
heavy snow on the passes and the Chinese military emissaries sent to reclaim us
thwarted our hopes of reaching the fabled mountain.

On our return, Bhakha Tulku told me about a more circuitous route to
Kundu that would take us deep into the wilderness, far from any Chinese military camps. We would have to travel during the summer rains, he said, the only
time when the passes that encircle the mountain would be free of snow.

As Bhakha Tulku's wife served tea with fermented honey, he described the stages of the journey to the peak from high snow-covered passes to dense jungles infested with snakes and tigers. "Unless pilgrims have traveled there recently," Bhakha Tulku said, "you will have to cut your own trail." He spoke of Kundu as the gateway to Chimé Yangsang Né. At the turn of the twentieth century, the lama Jedrung Thinley Jhampa Yungney Rinpoche, Precious Lord of Compassionate Enlightened Activity (Jedrung Rinpoche), had taken his bearings at the mountain and gone south with his followers

in search of the paradise. But Jedrung Rinpoche and his followers were repeatedly ambushed by Mishmi warriors and never reached the promised land. His next incarnation, Jedrung Trakpa Gyaltsen—Bhakha Tulku's father-in-law—returned to Pemako with no better fortune. "No one has yet been able to find the way," Bhakha Tulku said.[2]

Around this time, I had begun research for a book on Tibetan medicine, an amalgamation of Ayurvedic, Chinese, and Hellenic healing practices. Some of the more extraordinary additions to Tibet's *materia medica* appear in the Pemako neyigs that describe "five miraculous plants" capable of bestowing *siddhis,* the physiological and psychic powers arising on the Tantric path. According to Bhakha Tulku, these uncataloged species grow most plentifully in the area of Kundu and the valleys of Yangsang. One plant, called *tsakuntuzangpo,* the all-beneficent herb, is said to induce memories of past lives and bestow visions of other realms; others are said to "confer immortality . . . and the experience of emptiness and bliss." One lama I spoke with suggested that extracts from these psychoactive plants could be the mysterious key to Yangsang alluded to in Pad-masambhava's prophecies. According to Bhakha Tulku, animals that inadver-tently eat these rare herbs have left imprints of their hooves in solid rock.

Over the past year, my study of alchemical elixirs in the Tibetan Tantras had brought exotic substances into my kitchen larder. Concoctions of lotus seeds and wild honey, sautéed caterpillar fungus (*Cordyceps sinensis*), Indian snake-root (*Rauwolfia serpentina*), and preparations made from purified mercury, silver, and gold became a regular part of my and Hamid's diet. Some of the elixirs were only to be used in conjunction with specific Tantric practices. One, a formula from the Chandramaharoshana Tantra, caused eruptions of light in the frontal cortex when combined with certain yogas. A rarer recipe contained within the *Nyingtik Yabtsi,* a fourteenth-century compendium on Dzogchen meditation, pre-scribes a concoction made from the tropane-rich seeds of Himalayan datura (*Datura metel*) for opening the body's subtle energy channels and cultivating vi-sions, the final distillate to be dropped into the eyes through the hollow shaft of a vulture's quill. (European varieties of datura, or thorn apple, were princi-pal ingredients in the "flying ointments" and magical salves of medieval witches which promoted out-of-body experiences.) I asked Bhakha Tulku for more details, but he stayed silent, stroking his graying goatee and Salvador Dali–like moustache. He then uncorked a bottle of rice wine that had been steeping with various unidentifiable ingredients on his altar.

KUNDU DORSEMPOTRANG DOES NOT APPEAR on any map. My U.S. de-fense chart showed a large white section along the border between India and Ti-bet emblazoned with the word UNEXPLORED. Available satellite imagery was even less helpful, as the territory lay concealed beneath dense clouds. Con-cerned after our last experience, I contacted Mountains & Rivers Travel in Chengdu, the company that had arranged permission for our journey through the gorge in 1993, on the off chance that permits could be issued for the moun-tain itself. Gunn faxed back to tell me that he could not locate Kundu Dorsempotrang, even on the restricted Chinese military maps. He told me over the phone that permission could not be given for a place that from an official perspective does not even exist.

In the end, Kundu's obscurity assured our passage. I faxed Gunn a sketch map placing the mountain much farther to the north and away from the political line of control than it actually lay. Gunn wrote back telling me not to worry; he would arrange everything. With this vague assurance I began assembling a team.

I'D ADOPTED THE NAME Red Panda Expeditions, Ltd. to lend credence to my correspondence with the Chinese. When it came to communicating with prospective clients, Red Panda's policies were as elusive as the animal after which the company was named. Beginning in 1994, I offered trips to Pemako with only provisional itineraries and word of mouth as the sole means of promoting the once yearly expeditions.

I'd tried to convey the full spectrum of the upcoming journey in a letter to selected individuals who I thought might be interested.

In Tibetan tradition, the mountain Kundu Dorsempotrang—the "Palace of Adamantine Being"—lies at the heart of a Tantric goddess who guides initiates toward spiritual enlightenment. Tibetan prophecies refer to the mountain as a *Sachod Shingkam,* a terrestrial counterpart of the Buddhist Pure Lands, reachable only with great merit and faith. . . . Following rediscovered Tantric texts *(terma),* we will travel for more than a month through dense rainforests and over precipitous snow-covered passes to the luminous peak that rises at the heart of Dorje Pagmo, the dakini-goddess who presides over the Tsangpo gorges. . . . As we move farther and farther into the unknown, the journey will be both literally and figuratively a passage from one order of being to another. . . . The region is said to abound in an uncataloged wealth of medicinal and psychoactive plants as well as tigers, leopards, red pandas, and takin. Travelers should be prepared inwardly as well as outwardly for torrential rains, leeches, and venomous snakes. Most important, participants should have a deep and genuine commitment to the spirit of pilgrimage—recognizing that the destination is ultimately not so much a place as a new way of seeing.

In phone calls that followed, I actively discouraged several would-be participants who expressed doubts about their ability or sought assurances of any kind. I stressed the need for self-reliance, in no small part because of my and Hamid's plan to break off after reaching the mountain and continue on into the secret valleys of Yangsang.

Despite my admonitions and the uncertainty of the terrain, Pemako's allure was inescapable. Laura Ide declined a return trip, but she put me in touch with her brother-in-law, Christian Kuypers, a Dutch graphic designer living in New York who was eager to break out of his established routine. Ken Storm initially planned to join the expedition, but in the end decided to wait until the following year when we agreed we would make another attempt at the still unexplored section of the inner gorge and lay to rest the legend of the waterfall.

The first to commit to the expedition were two real estate developers from Phoenix, Arizona, whom I had met a year earlier in a hotel lobby in Lhasa—Gil and Troy Gillenwater. They had just returned with Rick Fisher from an ill-fated rafting trip on the Tsangpo 100 miles upriver from where we had scouted in 1993. Having rafted and kayaked extensively through the American Southwest—including a run through the turbulent Cataract Canyon on the Colorado—the two brothers were both seasoned adventurers, but the run they had just attempted with Fisher was more extreme than anything they had previously encountered. "The water was huge," Troy said, "beyond Class VI." They had roped through the worst rapids or portaged around them. When it became clear that it was too dangerous to continue, they stashed the raft under a rock and tried to climb out of the canyon. Rick had told them it would take only four hours, but in the end they walked for four days through the enchanting chasm often across narrow ledges in the cliff face. They subsisted on hard-boiled eggs that they bartered for with local villagers.

Gil, the elder of the two brothers, had studied Buddhism at Vajradhatu, the center founded in Boulder, Colorado, in the 1970s by the renowned Tibetan lama Chogyam Trungpa. He told me that he had been disappointed that apart from their limited contact with Tibetans, their trip did not touch on Tibet's culture or religion. Rick had been interested solely in the river and in gaining recognition for his achievements, Gil said. He and Troy were eager to return to Tibet and to learn more about its Buddhist traditions.

I told the two brothers about the legend of Yangsang and the mountain that Hamid and I would be attempting to reach again the following year, a mountain no Westerner had yet visited and one that wasn't on any map. They wanted in and eventually persuaded their younger brother, Todd, to go along as well.

A MONTH BEFORE OUR DEPARTURE, Hamid and I met a Thai naturalist of royal descent at a party in Kathmandu. Oy Kanjanavanit had received her doctorate from the University of London's School of Oriental and African Studies and had done pioneering work in Thailand in habitat preservation for the country's endangered tiger population. She later found her niche as a popularizer of natural sciences, focusing on the hidden life of plants.

Hamid led her outside to the veranda where jasmine flowers and night-blooming datura the color of moonlight spilled over a carved wooden trellis. He began telling her about the lush forests and goddess mythology of Pemako. She told him about a bestselling Thai novel called *Pet Pra Uma* (*Uma's Diamond*) that had captivated her as a child. The book describes a secret land that, like Pemako, lies on the border of India and Tibet and is presided over by a beneficent goddess. The book follows the adventures of a hunter who receives directions to the fabled land from a Tibetan lama wandering in Thailand's western jungles.

The site of Oy's research in the Huai Kha Khaeng Wildlife Sanctuary lies along the route to Tibet described in *Uma's Diamond*. One of the last remaining wilderness tracts in southeast Asia, the preserve lies within a range of mountains—the Tanasserim—that arcs northwestward through Burma and merges with the Himalayas. Oy had found inspiration in the novel's account of an enchanted land on the borders of Tibet but, she told Hamid, she never imagined that such a place might actually exist.

The next morning Hamid went to her hotel with translations of the

Pemako neyigs and showed her a photograph of the gilded temple at Rinchen-pung, set in subtropical jungle and arched over by a double rainbow. Two weeks later, Oy called from Bangkok. She'd determined that the Tsangpo gorges contain the northernmost extent of tropical and subtropical rain forest in Asia. The region was certain to harbor undiscovered species. But scientific interest aside, she couldn't pass up the opportunity to travel to the land of *Uma's Diamond*. "It seems like some kind of a dream jungle," she said on the phone.

One of Hamid's high-born girlfriends, a blond English aristocrat named Sophie, had been eager to join us and had offered to help sponsor the expedition through a British whiskey manufacturer. On principle, we'd avoided all forms of sponsorship, including the Explorers Club, of which I was a member, on the basis that it was a conflict of interest with our own idiosyncratic sense of pilgrimage. With Oy on board, Sophie would be a conflict of interest of another kind, and Hamid dwelled on the impending hardships until she decided to withdraw. He would meet her afterward, he promised, at her home in Notting Hill.

In the week before departure it rained continuously. My home, built on top of an abandoned rice paddy, had become so damp and flooded that Hamid and I had taken rooms in the dilapidated Shankar Hotel, a former Rana palace a few minutes away. Hamid entertained a lithe Korean dakini who had come back with him from an island in the Gulf of Thailand, and I made daily runs back to the house to check for faxes from Gunn.

Gunn finally faxed from Chengdu that the permits had come through, although closer inquiry revealed that permission had only been given for areas on either side of the great tract of wilderness where Kundu Dorsempotrang was actually located. Nonetheless, Gunn was optimistic. He assured me on the telephone that once we had entered the forests there would be no one to challenge our passage.

True to Red Panda tradition, whose motto was "confuse and elude," we would be journeying without real permission to a place that did not exist as far as governments and maps were concerned. What we would find there was even more uncertain.

ON JULY 25 OY ARRIVED on an afternoon flight from Bangkok. That evening, Christian and the Gillenwaters flew in on a Royal Nepal Airlines flight from Hong Kong. When I met them at Kathmandu's international airport, I reflected that perhaps my warnings regarding the expedition had been too extreme. The brothers emerged out of the customs area like a team of Navy Seals. All three of them had shaved their heads, and the tattooed dragons across Gil's biceps made him look like a cross between a World Wrestling Federation contestant and a Shaolin priest. Christian had spotted them on the plane, but he originally gave them a wide berth, even though he too had coincidentally shaved off his hair.

Once assembled at the Shankar Hotel, we spread out our gear for final packing. The food and heavier equipment would go overland with a crew of Sherpas and Tibetans. We would take the rest with us on the hour and a half flight to Lhasa. We packed everything into rubberized drybags. We would be entering one of the wettest places on the planet, a region that often receives more than thirty feet of rain each year, most of it during the summer.[3]

Having run out of food on their last trip in Tibet, the Gillenwaters had stocked up on energy bars and gourmet items such as oysters and assorted patés. Christian had brought jars of almond butter from New York. In Kathmandu, I'd bought brown rice from a local organic farm called Lotus Land, a twenty-kilo wheel of yak cheese, tins of tuna fish, walnuts, and freshly made black sesame paste. I'd stayed up late the night before mixing ground almonds and flax seed into bags of muesli. Hamid and I had also stocked up on *yogeshwar*, a Tantric formula made from purified gold that siddhas of ancient India had reputedly used in place of food.

Apart from standard items such as antibiotics, our medical kit included Tibetan *rinchen rilbu*, or precious pills, that contain sixteen metals and minerals including gold, silver, crushed pearls, and lapis lazuli, along with seventy other ingredients that have, in theory, been purified of their toxins so that only their therapeutic properties remain. The kit also included traditional Tibetan preparations made from musk to protect against venomous snakes. (The standard antivenom needed refrigeration.) I brought codeine phosphate and other drugs for emergencies and lots of aspirin for the inevitable requests for medical intervention.

Bhakha Tulku had asked me to deliver two large Buddha statues to his monastery in Powo. We slipped them in amid ropes and climbing gear. He also gave me wax-sealed letters for monks at his monastery. The letter to the acting abbot, Sangye Tenzing, requested that he help us by arranging porters for our pilgrimage to Kundu.

AFTER THE LOOTINGS and mutinies that had occurred on earlier trips, I had hired a Sherpa named Pemba to organize local porters in Tibet and to work as head cook. He arrived at the Shankar Hotel with a six-by-ten-foot dining tent that I had specially ordered for the journey. Lama, a monk from the monastery of Thubten Choling in Solu Khumbu who had given up his vows to marry Pemba's sister, showed up with him carrying bamboo pack baskets filled with pots, pans, spices, and a jerry can of cooking oil. Pasang, a half-deaf yogi from the Tibetan borderlands, trailed behind with coils of prayer flags and his eighteen-year-old son, who had been a novice monk in Chatral Rinpoche's retreat center in the mountains above Kathmandu. Other Sherpas would be arriving the following day.

I'd selected the crew carefully. Known for their reliability and innate skills in mountaineering, Sherpas have been recruited for Himalayan expeditions since the beginning of the twentieth century. Originally from Kham in eastern Tibet, Sherpas migrated to Nepal in the sixteenth century, settling in the high valleys near Mount Everest, which they revere as a sacred mountain called Chomolungma, Mother Goddess of the World. Although Sherpas' skills in climbing and camp etiquette have become legendary, it was equally important that they share our sense of Pemako as a sacred land. I thus bypassed the usual agencies and recruited friends from mountain villages and renegade Sherpa monks and yogis who would join us not simply as hired hands, but as fellow pilgrims. Pemba had recently returned from a Kalachakra initiation given by the Dalai

Lama. On his return from Pemako, Pasang planned to use the money he would earn to build a village stupa and undertake a prolonged meditation retreat.

THE EVENING BEFORE LEAVING KATHMANDU, Bhakha Tulku came to my house and performed a Tantric fire offering in the garden. Hamid dragged a tiger skin out of the living room for him to sit on, and blazing flames soon cut the dampness of the moss-covered stones and dripping bamboo. As Bhakha Tulku recited from the text of the *riwosangchod*, we each cast handfuls of juniper twigs and fragrant leaves of a dwarf species of rhododendron onto the smoldering fire. The pungent smoke curled through the damp air and misty rain, carrying prayers and aspirations for the success of the journey.

In Tibetan tradition, the rites of *riwosangchod* strengthen the life force and reveal a path where none is percievable. Dudjom Rinpoche, the lama from Pemako who had initiated me into Vajrayana Buddhism on my first visit to Nepal in 1977, had composed the text that we were now reciting, the same one the porters had repeated each night on our journey through the gorge, two years before. Outwardly the prayer seeks to remove obstacles in opening the way to hidden-lands, while inwardly it seeks to burn away all limiting perceptions.

The Sherpas also attended, uniting us on our common venture. As the fire subsided, Bhakha Tulku ladled out amrita from a human skull bowl lined with silver. Christian, the three brothers, and Oy, her black hair flowing around her face like a Khmer apsara, drank deeply from the blood-colored elixir that Bhakha Tulku gently poured into our open palms.

Afterward, Bhakha Tulku spoke about pilgrimage; how the journey to sacred places opens a path of heart and mind and removes the veils of ordinary vision. He talked about pilgrims who had died while journeying to Kundu Dorsempotrang, content in their knowledge that they would be reborn in the realm of the Buddhas. When I asked whether this was really true he just laughed, as if to say that doubt itself was the surest barrier.

Into Tibet

OUR EIGHT SHERPAS were originally to travel overland with the bulk of our gear and meet us in Tibet. In the heavy monsoon, rocks and mudslides had blocked the road between Kathmandu and Lhasa, and at the last minute I had to arrange seats for them on the twice-weekly China Southwest Airlines flight to Tibet. The Sherpas arrived at my house at 6 A.M. to load the duffel bags and other gear into a van and take it to the airport. They had already picked up Christian, Oy, and the Gillenwaters from the Shankar Hotel.

Traveling light on journeys to Pemako was never easy. In addition to tents, sleeping bags, and other personal gear, we had food supplies for six weeks; plastic tarpaulins for local porters; climbing gear for ascending cliffs and crossing rivers; and ritual thigh-bone trumpets, cats' eyes, and other semiprecious stones to give away to Pemako's villagers. Hamid had been out late, escorting an ex-girlfriend from Nepal's former ruling family to the Kathmandu Valley Heritage Ball. He was still madly packing in the black caftan he'd worn to the party. As the van waited outside, he stuffed Gore-Tex pants and capilene shirts, gaiters for mud, snow, and rain, a machete and an umbrella into a Patagonia Black Hole bag. At the last minute he rolled up a leopard skin to sleep on in place of his punctured Therm-a-Rest.

In the chaos of departure, the Brahmin pundit who tutored Hamid in Sanskrit arrived in the rain and stood outside the house under his umbrella as we loaded the last of the gear into the van. Hamid paid him for the last week of classes, and the Brahmin held up his hand in benediction as we drove off over rutted roads toward the airport.

We flew over the Himalayas through thick clouds and descended onto a rain-swept runway. Gunn, once again our guide and liaison officer, met us at

the Lhasa airport with two Land Cruisers and a flatbed truck for the Sherpas and our gear. Since I'd last seen him, he'd grown a sketchy moustache and sported brand-new tennis shoes that he had bought for the expedition. His freshly cut hair looked blow-dried from the back forward. We piled into the Land Cruisers for the two-hour drive to Tibet's capital city.

After checking into the Snow Lion Hotel, we dispersed into the Barkhor, the pilgrims' circuit and ancient market surrounding Tibet's most revered temple. We joined the throngs of Tibetans that were pressing through the Jokhang's dark corridors toward the jewel-encrusted image of Sakyamuni Buddha that lies at its center. According to the Pemako prophecies, a single circuit around Kundu Dorsempotrang is equal to thirty-nine visits to this seventh-century temple, the Lourdes of Tibet. Outside, we changed money with swaggering Khampas and bought final provisions—apricot kernels, tsampa, and dried yak cheese. Christian bought a green Hapsburg-style felt hat from one of the stalls to shield him from rain. The next morning we began the long drive eastward, crossing high passes, washouts, and landslides to Kongpo Gyamda, our first stop on the road to the Tsangpo gorges.

The following day we continued east along a tributary of the Tsangpo until we reached Bayi, the administrative center for the Kongpo and Powo districts of Tibet. Its cement buildings rose like mistakes against a stunning backdrop of mountains and forests. Built by the Chinese military on a strip of land along the Nyang Chu river, Bayi means August First in Mandarin, named in honor of the foundation day of the People's Liberation Army. By coincidence, we'd arrived on July 31, the eve of their annual celebration. We needed road permits to continue, and the chief officer was out of town preparing for the festivities. He would be back, Gunn reported, some time the following evening.

Bayi had anything but pleasant associations. Apart from its garish architecture and the oppressive military presence, Hamid and I had been robbed there on our previous trip. Khampa thieves had climbed into our supply truck during the night and made off with our sleeping bags, mattresses, and large portions of our food. We'd replaced the down bags and Therm-a-Rests with Chinese army blankets and sheep skins that we found in the Bayi market, but after weeks of Pemako's constant rain, they doubled in weight and slowly began to rot. On our return through Bayi, we had found that the thieves had been caught and some of our gear recovered. The Tibetan police detective who had handled our case, dressed in a trench coat and fedora hat, had insisted that when we next returned to Bayi we bring him a "prize." We were very much hoping to avoid him.

We negotiated with our drivers to take us on to Lamaling, an hour to the south. Chonyi Rinpoche was sitting in his walled garden among cages of parrots and parakeets. He would feed them mendrup for a week or two, he said, and then return them to the skies, carrying the blessings of the Buddhist Dharma. He remembered our conversation two years earlier and was pleased that we were headed to Kundu Dorsempotrang. "Although outwardly we might see only a mountain," he said, "inwardly Kundu is a mandala of Dorje Sempa [Vajrasattava in Sanskrit], a supreme expression of enlightenment." Circling the peak would open doors to new awareness and, by extension, the hidden realms beyond. When the others had gone to visit the temple, Chonyi Rinpoche told me of a cliff on Kundu's eastern wall where the key to Yangsang is said to be located. "What is the key?" I asked. Somehow my question seemed to miss the point, and he smiled back as if to suggest that if I had to ask I would never find it. Although I'd become accustomed to such Buddhist paradoxes, another part of me still sought literal explanations. Does the key refer to a particular terma, a ritual text, a map, an inner revelation? Touching his forehead to ours, he sent us off with his blessings but without answering.

Back in Bayi, Gunn informed us that the local Public Security Bureau (PSB) had insisted that we take a police escort with us for "protection." Gunn introduced a small unsmiling man dressed in camouflage fatigues and a Mao cap who, as Gunn translated, said that he would be our "friend" on the journey. Hardly convinced of that, we retired for dinner to a vinyl-seated restaurant attached to the single hotel designated for foreign visitors. We'd seen longhaired rats being sold for food in Bayi's central square, and no one had much of an appetite. Music pulsed from the floor above, and we went upstairs to a surrealistic dance hall. The room was empty except for two Chinese men, dancing arm in arm to wailing disco music.

The next morning we crossed a 15,440-foot pass and descended steeply on the other side to a logging camp where Chinese army personnel and Tibetan prisoners were reportedly engaged in cutting down old-growth forests of cedar, spruce, and fir. We ate in a wooden shack where immigrants from China's Szechuan province had set up a makeshift roadside restaurant. One of the ingredients in our midday meal made us all very drowsy, and we nodded off as we descended lower into the gorges leading toward Powo. Through heavy lids, our driver looked up continuously to avoid falling rocks, at one point swerving in the mud tracks and nearly driving off a precipice.

Soon after, the road ended at a great landslide several hundred meters across. Many roads built by the Chinese to harvest Tibet's vast timber reserves have been abandoned as too difficult and expensive to maintain. But this was the southern highway between China and central Tibet, and road crews had shored up part of the track with interlaced logs and were cutting through the steep waste of mud, boulders, and uprooted trees. The PSB officials in Bayi had told us about the slide and said that we would most likely have to cross on foot and hire new vehicles on the other side. Dodging falling rocks, we ferried loads across the eroding mountainside and negotiated with truck drivers marooned on the other side to take us on to Powo. But in the meantime, our drivers determined to get across the landslide and, free of passengers and excess weight, careened across the precipitous slope.

The road continued as a tilting, muddy track through streambeds and dense forests until it emerged at the village of Trulung where a footbridge connects to a trail leading down into Pemako. This was the same route by which I had emerged from the Tsangpo gorges in 1993, but our journey to Kundu now meant continuing east on the road toward Powo.

We drove along the northern edge of the Po Tsangpo, crossing the Yigrong River at 7,680 feet and continuing on through washouts and waterfalls that plunged into the river below us. Despite the hazards of the road, Oy was in near ecstasy, stopping the car frequently to examine plants or point out a band of macaques crossing a sandy beach on the opposite bank. When she discovered six species of lichen on a single tree, she declared the area a botanical paradise.

The valley gradually widened into lush fields of ripening barley and peach and apple trees. We came upon the first timber-framed habitations in Powo, until 1931 a semi-independent feudal kingdom whose hereditary rulers claimed dominion over the tribes of Pemako.[4] Powo is connected to Pemako by a range of high snow-covered passes. In the vision of Pemako as the body of Dorje Pagmo, Tamer of Serpents, the valley of Powo is the snake that she wields in her left hand.

The Valley of Powo

BHAKHA TULKU'S ANCESTRAL SEAT, Bhakha Gompa, is one of Powo's principal monasteries. It sits on a promontory on the southern bank of the Po Tsangpo river, surrounded by glittering snow peaks and lush forests of hemlock and fir. To the east, sandbars reach out into a wide and placid section of the Po Tsangpo. Where the river narrows again into fierce rapids, a wooden suspension bridge strung with colorful prayer flags connects the monastery to the northern bank and the road from Szechuan to Lhasa.

We carried the Buddha statues, still hidden in duffel bags, across the bridge and climbed the hill to the courtyard in front of the main temple, where monks and carpenters were reconstructing the sixteenth-century temple. (It had been destroyed in the great earthquake in 1950 and again by the Chinese during the Cultural Revolution.) As workmen shaped trees into timber planks, monks painted images of Buddhist deities on either side of the wooden entrance doors.[5]

Sangye Tenzing, the acting abbot, received us in Bhakha Tulku's absence. In a private room away from the watchful eyes of our "friend" from the PSB, I gave him Bhakha Tulku's letters. He eagerly opened the one addressed to him, the first news in many months from the departed Rinpoche. Outside, other monks had lined up porcelain cups on wooden boards to serve us tea. Rain showers skudded across the river below.

WHEN WE HAD LAST VISITED in May of 1994, Bhakha Tulku had been overseeing the monastery's reconstruction from a family home in the upper Powo valley where glaciers descend toward the edges of ripening fields of barley. The same idyllic valley also contains a Chinese high-security prison. A Tibetan student from Middlebury College in Vermont who had received a Watson fellowship to record traditional Tibetan dances and music had been accused by the Chinese of espionage and was confined there for several years. The valley was restricted and we left hurriedly, concerned that our presence might put Bhakha Tulku in danger.

Later that year, Chinese authorities accused Bhakha Tulku of being a spy for the U.S. government and forced him to leave Tibet. He had traveled back to Nepal by truck and public bus, laden down with whatever possessions he and his wife, Sonam, could carry. Immediately afterward, the local administration began cutting down old growth forests in the vicinity of the Bhakha monastery, turning what had been a protected forest into lumber for export. The Chinese call Tibet Xizang, the Western Treasure House, and since their "liberation" of Tibet in 1950 they have systematically plundered its vast forest reserves and ravaged its earth for uranium, gold, and other precious metals. In Tibetan culture, mining was largely forbidden. Instead, the earth was regularly empowered and enriched by filling *sechu*, or earth treasures vases, with jewels and other precious substances and burying them underground—a covenant with the landscape in radical contrast to Chinese policies of extraction.

Sangye Tenzing folded up the letter from Bhakha Tulku and concealed it in his robes. Most of the resident monks, those who weren't needed for overseeing the construction of the monastery, were up in the mountains on meditation retreat, he told me. Nonetheless, he would spare whomever he could from the construction site to come with us as porters. Sensing a rare opportunity, he said he would personally come with us to perform the religious rites to open the way (*go-che*) to Kundu and beyond.

We'd intended to spend the night at the monastery and leave the following morning, but our new "friend" from the Public Security Bureau, Mr. Zang, would not allow it. It wasn't specified on our itinerary, he said. We would have to drive another hour to Pomi, the local administrative center. We left after arranging to send the truck back the following afternoon to collect Sangye Tenzing and whatever porters he could recruit.

As we crossed the rickety bridge leading back to the road, I shared with Gunn my concern that, even with the abbot's best efforts, we would not have sufficient porters for the journey. A crew of ragged Monpa coolies who had been repairing a washed-out section of the road were resting under towering fir trees. After a short negotiation, Gunn hired them, and they squeezed into the back of the truck with the few meager possessions that they carried in their bamboo baskets.

AFTER PILING INTO THE LAND CRUISERS, we drove to Powo Dzong, known as Pomi to the Chinese, and settled into the soulless designated hotel— as Christian noted, "a euphemistic way of saying you can't stay anywhere else." As we divided food supplies and other gear into manageable loads, police officials came into the room and told us not to leave the hotel. The streets in Pomi are dangerous, they insisted. We thanked them for their concern and soon went out to explore.

Cradled beneath soaring moonlit peaks, with the Po Tsangpo River meandering through its center, Pomi seemed like a Klondike boomtown. Dingy restaurants littered with empty Chinese beer bottles lined the mud-filled streets. The restaurants' proprietors hailed from China's Szechuan province. They'd been lured into the Tibetan outback by Chinese government incentives that left many Tibetans unemployed. We rounded a corner and came upon a makeshift disco with revolving strobe lights. Behind the curtained doorway, Szechuan nymphs cupped their hands around glasses of hot jasmine tea. As Gunn explained, it was so the "cats" hands would be warm when they touched you. We passed on in search of other locales.

The restaurants all looked questionable. Scandal had erupted in Pomi earlier in the summer when a dog unearthed a human head from a rubbish heap behind one of the more popular restaurants, reinforcing widespread rumors that Tibetan children were being served as food in Chinese eateries. In Lhasa, there had been demonstrations in the Barkhor against what we were told was an increasing incidence of street children, itinerant nuns, and other untraceable persons ending up as mincemeat in Chinese Muslim restaurants. Bhakha Tulku had been the first one to tell us about this, relating how a fat nun in Nakchuka, a region north of Lhasa, had entered a Muslim restaurant and not come out.

The previous night, when the chief of police in Bayi had turned up to issue our road permit, we had questioned him about a foreigner that we had heard had been arrested for traveling without a permit in the lower Tsangpo gorge. He was from Austria, the police officer told us, and he had been collecting medicinal plants. But exactly where he was arrested and what the penalty had been for his illicit journey was all "secret." When the official remained silent on the subject of his punishment, Hamid offered that we'd heard he'd been eaten. The chief officer got up abruptly and left the room, not sure, if seemed, it we were joking. Life in Tibet held uncertain perils. As we plied the streets of Pomi in defiance of the local police, Oy reflected on our apparent danger of ending up as an ingredient in some cadre's noodle soup.

Nonetheless, we were eager for a solid meal as we had carried little more than rice, lentils, noodles, and dehydrated vegetables for the journey to Kundu. The Gillenwaters wanted meat. We ordered chicken stew and several other dishes at a roadside restaurant. Perhaps to reassure us of what we would be eating, the Chinese cook appeared from the kitchen with two squawking hens. A few seconds later they uttered their last sounds. When the pot of chicken soup finally arrived at the table, it was decidedly disappointing; an assortment of claws, necks, and heads, and very little meat. The Gillenwaters looked dismayed. Christian picked at it with his chopsticks.

Apparently, the cook was preoccupied by a more lucrative enterprise. A large stack of white and gold mushrooms was pickling in brine in the corner of the restaurant, to be sold to traders who would export them to Japan. In July and August, Pomi's entrepreneurs engage in a brisk trade in what we took to be maitake mushrooms. The cook had fresh ones too, but he wouldn't let them go for less than $100 a kilo. Communicating through a Tibetan who had wandered into the restaurant to inspect our little group, the Chinese man claimed that the mushrooms, which he had harvested from the surrounding forests, were "like gold beneath his feet." "The mushrooms grow from a fungus underground, and if you don't damage the earth more come up each year," he said. An expert in fungi, Oy clarified that maitake can't be grown commercially, as the mushrooms sprout from a network of threadlike fungal cells that feed only on the living roots of pine trees. Foregoing the house specialty, we started back for the hotel along a pitch black street, stopping in briefly at a surrealistic wood-floored roller skating rink erected beneath a vast tent, which was being patronized by teenage girls and three underage monks.

BY THE NEXT DAY, August 2, several of the Monpa porters we'd hired from Bhakha had already disappeared. Some of them, it seemed, had just wanted a ride into town. Others now asked for an advance so they could shop for food for the journey. Although Gunn wrote down their names in his yellow note-book, we had no way of knowing whether they would actually show up later that afternoon when we would drive to the road head.

After setting aside as much gear as we could to send back to Lhasa, we drove to Dungchu Lhakhang, a seventh-century border-taming temple that had served as a staging ground for the earliest journeys into Pemako and where several of the Pemako neyigs had been discovered.

THE SOUTHERN REGIONS OF PEMAKO into which we were now headed were not opened until the late 1700s. A lama named Dorje Thokme, Limitless Vajra (1746–97), discovered a yellow scroll in a pillar of the Dungchu Lhakhang entitled *The Luminous Web: The Seven Profound Teachings that Open the Gate of the Hidden-land.* He transmitted his teachings to two other renowned lamas— Orgyen Dudrul Lingpa (b. 1757), the abbot of a monastery called Daglo Gampo, and Kunzang Garwang Chimey Dorje, the reincarnation of Choeje Lingpa who, after dying in the jungles of Pemako, had been reborn in 1763 to a local Monpa family. Collectively, the three lamas became known as the *Beyul Rigdzin Nam Sum,* the Three Knowledge-Holders of the Hidden-Land, and their teach-ings spread among the Monpa clans that were migrating into Pemako from eastern Bhutan at the end of the eighteenth century.

With the patronage of Powo's king, Nyima Gyalpo, the three lamas jour-neyed into Pemako, converting hostile Lopas and opening the pilgrimage route to Kundu Dorsempotrang, the mountain described in the neyigs as "the heart center of the great sacred land of Pemako." Through their efforts, the mountain became renowned as the ultimate Tantric pilgrimage site. A sixteenth-century meditation master had defined the benefits of pilgrimage through such perilous terrain: "Progress can be achieved more rapidly during a single month amid terrifying conditions in rough terrain and in the proximity of harmful forces" than by meditating for three years in towns and monasteries.[6] As we left the temple, a rainbow arched over the valley to the east in the direction we were headed.

When we arrived back at the hotel, Gunn looked nervous and distressed. The Monpa porters were demanding higher wages than they had agreed to the day before. The abbot had arrived from Bhakha monastery along with another senior monk, but the local powers had intervened. The monastery was being rebuilt, and Sangye Tenzing was responsible for overseeing it, the police officials said. The other monk could go with us, they said, but not the abbot.

We were already sitting in the Land Cruisers, and we made room in the front seat for the maroon-robed monk. At this point, Zang interjected, saying that it was illegal in China for Westerners to travel with monks or lamas. The monk offered to dress in lay clothes, but Zang was unmoved. He flatly forbade us to take him. Gunn sat glumly in the front seat.

We were disappointed that none of the monks from Bhakha Gompa would be coming with us and concerned that no one in our entourage knew the way to Kundu Dorsempotrang. Still, we were happy to be leaving this remote outpost, one of the most fertile and beautiful parts of Tibet, but as unaccommodating under Chinese rule as it was when Bailey and Morshead had visited here in 1912 during the reign of the Kanam Depas. One of our Monpa porters had been over the first pass to a valley called Chimdro. We would find people there, he said, who would know the way to the sacred mountain. There was an uncertainty now to every step, but the unknowing contained a strange joy, a trust in the unfolding of the journey.

The Dashing-La

SOON AFTER LEAVING POMI the road opened into a spectacular valley overhung by glaciers and granite spires too steep for snow to cling to. The Po Tsangpo, swollen by the summer rains, flowed beneath them. As we turned south and drove across the river on a cantilevered wooden bridge, the eastern extension of the Himalayas that seals Pemako from the north rose in front of us like a burnished wall of rock and ice.

Only a few passes lead through the mountains into the hidden-lands beyond. The year before, we had come in May, and all routes into Pemako were blocked by snow. No one had crossed over the passes since the previous autumn. When we left Bhakha Tulku at his residence above his monastery, he had held a silver amulet box containing sacred relics on the top of our heads and said prayers for the success of our journey. We had continued on to Pomi to try our luck. Wandering through the markets, we met a Lopa hunter who had crossed over the snow-covered ranges from Pemako to sell a leopard pelt. Some of the proceeds of the sale had visibly gone to Chinese alcohol, but he agreed, somewhat reluctantly, to guide us into Pemako over a high pass called the Gawalung-La[7] that he claimed to have crossed several days earlier. We enlisted a crew of road coolies to carry our provisions. They were Chinese and had little idea where the Lopa hunter was leading them. They carried our gear on bamboo poles that they slung across their shoulders. Near the top of the pass, an avalanche of collapsing cornices had forced them to bivouac, and they caught up with us the next day, partially snowblind.

We were now headed for a pass farther east on the Kangri Karpo range—the left breast of Dorje Pagmo—that would connect us with the route to Kundu that Bhakha Tulku had followed in 1956. It was getting dark, and we'd driven past a small village called Dashing, the "field of arrows," looking for flat ground on which to camp. Although jeep tracks clearly continued deeper into the forest, the drivers suddenly refused to proceed any farther, insisting that we had come as far as vehicles would allow. The one Monpa who claimed to know the route over the Dashing-La pass insisted that the road continued for another day's march. A raging feud ensued between our drivers and the elderly Monpa, who eventually fled into the bushes. One of the drivers had threatened to kill him for imparting such inconvenient facts.

Using the Land Cruisers' headlights for illumination, we set up our tents in the middle of the jeep track, while Gunn, Zang, and Cookie, Gunn's personal cook, went back to Dashing village to arrange for additional porters. They returned the next morning, ravaged by bedbugs after sleeping on old Tibetan carpets. Surly and demanding additional pay, the drivers proceeded another ten miles on the rough logging road, struggling through a deep forest of towering spruce and tsuga hemlocks until the track petered out into yet denser forest.

After unloading duffel bags, bamboo pack baskets, and sacks of provisions from the Land Cruisers and truck, the Sherpas sorted out the loads. Beyond the eight Sherpas and Tibetans who had come with us from Kathmandu, we had hired twelve additional porters, seven from the crew of Monpa road workers and five from the villages around Bhakha. Gunn's porters from Dashing had brought horses and mules. They would go only as far as the Chimdro valley on the far side of the Dashing-La pass, they said. They would return with dried chili peppers to sell in the market in Pomi.

As we were weighing loads, a small green jeep appeared, lurching up the final stages of the logging road. We feared it was the police from Pomi telling us we would have to return. Instead, a portly lama wearing a sun hat with a red rose ribbon emerged from inside the car. He was accompanied by two attendants, the elder one twirling an enormous prayer wheel. They installed themselves in a clearing in the forest and brought out wooden bowls, tsampa, and a thermos of tea. After eating, the lama approached us and introduced himself in Tibetan as Kawa Tulku, Reincarnation from the Snows. He was the abbot of Neydo Gompa, a Nyingma monastery in Riwoche, several days' drive to the north. His whole life he had heard about Pemako and the sacred mountain Kundu Dorsempotrang, he said. It was now the Tibetan Year of the Wood Boar, and he had decided to undertake the pilgrimage to the lands of the pig-headed goddess, Dorje Pagmo. Neither of his attendants knew the route, and as the trail to Kundu is notoriously rugged and ill defined, we agreed to travel together. The senior monk from Bhakha monastery had not been allowed to come with us, but we now had a reincarnate lama along in his place. This time there was no illegality; we would simply be following the same itinerary.

The porters told us that it would take us four or five days to reach Chimdro, and from there another seven days to Kundu Dorsempotrang, figures that roughly agreed with Bhakha Tulku's account. All additional efforts to establish distances and time had been in vain. Popular Tibetan wisdom maintains that Monpas cannot count, and it's true that their estimates had varied so greatly as to be virtually useless.

WE WALKED LESS THAN AN HOUR to a campsite in a large meadow at 11,000 feet. The seven Monpa porters laid claim to a dilapidated wooden shelter and burned several of its floorboards to brew their tea. Kawa Tulku ensconced himself in a blue and yellow Chinese dome tent. When we went to greet him, he was sitting in the tent door, slicing chunks of meat from a shank of dried mutton and drinking chang. He smiled broadly, and the Gillenwaters referred to him ever after as the Jolly Lama.

Hamid and I asked him about Pemako's nés, or sacred places. There are many nés in Pemako, he said, and he planned to take his time visiting as many as he could. After Kundu, he would continue on to the monastery of Rinchen-pung and stay some weeks there in retreat. Afterward, he would cross the Tsangpo and leave Pemako over the Doshung-La, the Pass of Sharp Stones.

I asked him about the location of Chimé Yangsang Né, Pemako's "innermost secret place." He looked up with an air of surprise. Yangsang is in disputed territory between India and China, he said protectively. No one can get permission to go there. He returned to his shank of wind-dried meat. I pointed out that permission can hardly be given for a place that no one has yet located. He changed the subject to the weather. One of the Monpas who had been loitering nearby announced confidently that it wouldn't rain for fourteen days. As Pemako is notorious for its incessant rainfall, the proclamation was extreme enough to be taken seriously. Kawa Tulku laughed and returned to his leg of mutton.

Hamid and I took our leave at nightfall and joined the others in the dining tent. The horses that would carry our gear over the pass had been put out to pasture. The tinkling of the bells strung around their necks merged with the roar of waterfalls that poured from glaciers, lost now in darkness above the Dashing-La pass.

Despite the Monpa's proclamation, we awoke on August 4 to rain drumming on the roofs of our tents. After loading the horses, we headed into a deep, mossy forest of hemlocks and firs, framed above by high, glacier-covered peaks. Kawa Tulku walked slowly through the rain with unrufflable composure. The green dye in Christian's Hapsburg hat poured down his head in thin rivulets. The weather slowly cleared, but we knew that the rains would be heavier on the other side of the pass. Monsoon clouds race unobstructed up the Tsangpo valley from the Bay of Bengal, drenching the mountains and swamps of Pemako and turning it into a place that Kingdon Ward described as having only two seasons: "wet and more wet."

We stopped at midday by a foaming river where the Monpas brewed their salted tea, and we ate our packed lunches of yak cheese and unleavened bread. Afterward, we climbed steeply for 1,000 feet to a crude wooden shelter used by pilgrims and traders before they cross the Dashing-La into Pemako. The altimeter showed 12,850 feet. A great wall of rock rose behind us to the north. Black clouds streamed over a barrier of mottled glaciers to the south and east. We set up our tents in a boggy meadow as the porters spread plastic sheets on the floorboards of the rough lodge.

The Sherpas had built a smoldering fire, and we came in from the rain to dry our clothes. Large bags of tsampa were tied to the rafters; food caches of local traders in a place where community loyalties discourage theft. Kawa Tulku had set up his tent on wide planks beneath the dripping roof. Oy had collected orchids along the trail and set them out to dry. "They're very advanced plants," she claimed, and went on to describe the various chemicals that they exude to attract insects and birds. The whole flower, as Oy described it, was an elaborate snare of sex and death.

Kawa Tulku had watched Oy inspecting primroses and other flowers along the side of the trail. With her wire-rimmed glasses perched on her nose, she had pressed samples between the pages of her journal or placed them carefully in Ziploc bags. And now she'd laid out others to dry by the fire. Kawa Tulku asked what qualities the flowers had and whether they were medicinal. It turned out he too had come to look for plants, albeit of another order.

Like an Eastern incarnation of the intrepid plant collector Frank Kingdon Ward, Kawa Tulku intended to scour the forests of Pemako for rare flowers; not blue poppies for beautifying distant gardens but plants described in the Pemako neyigs that could heal the body of disease and catalyze physiological, psychological, and even spiritual transformation. Kawa Tulku had brought a copy of the treasure-text that the Terton Dorje Thokme had discovered in the temple in Powo. The terma offered descriptions of five "nectar-bestowing" plants that the lama hoped to identify on his journey.[8]

AS WE CARRIED ON with our heady talk of plants, Christian returned from the glacier. He'd crossed a stream of melted ice to check out a furry mass he'd seen on the opposite bank, spurred on, he said, by thoughts of newspaper headlines such as NEW YORKER DISCOVERS YETI. What he found was a five-foot carcass of a female *Ursus thibetana*—an Asiatic black bear—curled on her side and rotting on the ice.

Immediately, a large party of Monpas set out for the glacier with the lama and his young monk attendant trailing behind. Oy, Hamid, and I followed afterward along a river that issued from beneath a vast snow field, the remnants of a large avalanche earlier in the year. The snow seemed firm, and we crossed the submerged river to where the bear lay curled up on its side, presumably having been swept away in the avalanche and only now emerging with the summer thaw. As the Monpas dragged the frost-stiffened bear into an upright position, the lama performed a rudimentary powa ceremony to ensure the safe transit of its soul. Then the Monpas set upon it with knives, cutting a long gash down its chest and reaching in with their hands to extract the gallbladder, a prized organ in traditional Chinese and Tibetan medicine. They then cut off the paws. In a few weeks they would be able to sell them in one of the small Chinese garrison towns. By the time it reached the market in Hong Kong or Guangzhou, a dried gallbladder would fetch as much as $500.

The bear was rotting, yet the porters began dividing it limb from limb. They extracted the heart and liver and set them aside on the ice. Thinking that they were nearly done, we headed back to camp for dinner. An hour or so later, the Monpas filed by the dining tent with huge chunks of bear meat slung across their shoulders. A great feast ensued inside the shelter, although the Sherpas would have no part of it, speculating that the bear might have been poisoned, in which case its flesh would be toxic. We were more concerned that the meat was rancid, although Hamid pointed out that hunters often hang game up for weeks to give it "noble rot." The Monpas had no worries; the meat was *tsok sha*, manna from heaven. While the lama sat by the fire reciting mantras, they smoked the meat on racks of branches that they built over the flames. They placed the bear's head in the rafters like an eerie totem.

We retired for the night under a half moon. Dark clouds billowed over the ridges from Pemako as smoke streamed through the walls of the shelter and rose into the sky. If our porters survived the bear feast, we would be in Pemako by the following afternoon. The pass ahead of us seemed increasingly like a portal. Moonlight bathed the lower slopes, and from its upper levels, concealed in mist, came the rumbling sound of avalanches.

WHEN WE AWOKE ON THE MORNING of August 5, the porters were still roasting the last of the bear. Some of them had stayed up the entire night. With 100 pounds or more of dubious meat added to their loads, they climbed slowly toward the pass. One of them had tied the bear's head to the top of his bamboo basket.

We ascended steep snowfields, the remains of the avalanche that had swept

away the bear. We then began a steep climb toward the pass itself, switchback-
ing across small streams, gullies, and bands of rock.

While the Monpas carried the bulk of our supplies, the Sherpas carried our
personal gear. A sixty-two-year-old Sherpa named Ongel shouldered the dry-
bag containing my sleeping bag, pad, spare clothing, and film. He had been on
six Everest expeditions and innumerable climbs throughout the Himalayas.
Small, with a leathery face and piercing black eyes, his mountaineering skills
would be crucial in avoiding circumstances such as those we experienced the
year before on the Gawalung-La when, without Sherpa support, we had nearly
lost our entire regiment of porters. Ongel's most distinguishing feature was a
cigarette-sized hole through the middle of his two front teeth, the more
poignant since even at these altitudes he smoked like a chimney.

When the Sherpa clans originally migrated from eastern Tibet, they followed prophecies of a hidden-land in the vicinity of Mount Everest, or as they
know it, Chomolungma. The heart of the beyul has yet to be found, Ongel
said, but all of Solu-Khumbu, the region they settled in, is thought to be part
of it. They found fortune there. Although Sherpas number only a few thousand
in the Nepalese population of twenty-two million, their standard of living is

one of the highest among the kingdom's many ethnic groups, due largely to their hazardous work on mountaineering expeditions.

AT THE TOP OF THE 15,000-FOOT PASS, dark rain clouds obscured the view into Pemako. A horse caravan emerged from the mists carrying tsampa and chiles from the Chimdro valley. Along with them came a Chinese man dressed in a khaki field suit. We learned that he was a zoologist named Qui Minjiang, and he had spent the last month studying Chimdro's growing tiger problem. Pemako is the last place in Tibet that has tigers, Qui said. He claimed that elsewhere in China they are on the verge of extinction, with no more than twenty to thirty scattered over a large area. The Khampas of Chimdro hunt them illegally, he claimed, not for their skins or bones, which are considered medicinal, but because they are the major threat to their livestock.

Until the Khampas settled in Chimdro in the early twentieth century, Qui explained, the valley was a prime habitat for tigers. They preyed on takin, red goral, and other wild species that inhabited the valley. With their natural habitat usurped by humans, they now preyed on the Khampas's horses and cattle. The previous year, marauding cats had killed 15 percent of Chimdro's 947 head of cattle. Qui feared that with human retribution, the tigers' numbers would dwindle. His stated mission was to ensure that they did not, even if it meant darting them and relocating them by helicopter into the wilderness to the south—the area of Kundu Dorsempotrang.

It was raining heavily now and the porters had all gone ahead. We parted company with Qui at the top of the pass and descended into the clouds. After an hour, a lone herder's hut appeared in the valley below. Approaching it through deep mud and the barking of a fearsome one-eyed Tibetan mastiff, we heard the sound of a drum and bell. Inside the stone dwelling, Kawa Tulku was performing a ritual ceremony to strengthen the life force of the the small family of herders. He sprinkled them with water from a consecrated urn, and afterward they served him yogurt made from the milk of their cattle.

It was still pouring when Kawa Tulku and his attendants readied themselves to leave. "Come with us," the older man said, "the trail is uncertain." We were still soaked from the descent from the pass and we told him we wanted to dry out first by the herders' yak-dung fire. "It only started raining when Rinpoche came inside," the attendant said. "Now that he's leaving, the rain will stop." We shouldered our packs and headed out into the rain. In less than five minutes, the rain had stopped completely.

An opening in the clouds revealed a lush valley far below us, a wide stream flowing through its center like a silver ribbon. We descended through thickening fir forests; to the west waterfalls streamed down the faces of moss-covered cliffs. A lone man emerged from below, carrying nothing but a string of wooden prayer beads and a plastic jug filled with chang. When we told him we were headed for Kundu Dorsempotrang, he told us he was returning from there himself. He had cut a trail through the jungle and felled trees to cross the swollen streams, he said. "The way is clear. You will find the mountain." He offered us swigs of his elixir and continued upward toward the pass.

We camped at 12,000 feet at the edge of the stream that we had seen from far above. The ground was wet and spongy, but the weather was clearing. Towering rock walls rose above us into a world of ice and snow. A circle of blue sky hovered above the valley as streamers of diaphanous mist drifted through the trees. The lama, it seemed, was at work. Even Gunn conceded that he seemed to have some uncanny power over the weather. "Every time I've been in Pemako," Gunn said, "it's been like hell. Now it's like paradise. We must stay with this lama." Gunn's conversion had begun.

The Valley of Chimdro

WE STARTED OUT THE NEXT MORNING on a track of rough-hewn planks that led through a thick swamp. The Sherpas had bought rubber Wellington-style boots in the market in Pomi, as had Kawa Tulku, who now set the pace, ambling ahead with an enigmatic smile, mantras spilling from his lips, while above us hung the improbable circle of blue sky.

The valley of Chimdro lay 4,000 feet below. The mule trail wound through bogs and swamps and crisscrossed a glacier-fed stream overhung with hemlocks and birch. Gunn's Chinese tennis shoes had begun to decompose in the mud, but he followed the lama closely, convinced that he had some kind of influence over the environment. When he found him resting on a log beside the trail, Gunn asked him to bless a small jade Buddha that he wore around his neck. "I believe in science," Gunn told me, "but this lama is special. I want to gain something of his power." Oy marveled that Kawa Tulku's boots had remained relatively dry, while her own feet were soaked through despite neoprene dry socks and Gore-Tex gaiters.

For their midday meal, the porters stopped by a stream cascading down from the glaciers above the Dashing-La. They started a steaming fire with damp branches and placed a blackened kettle on the flames to brew their tea. With their long knives they carved chunks from the dismembered bear, but it was becoming clear already that some of the meat was rancid; a nun from Bhakha who had attached herself to our column was retching in the bushes.

As we sat amid the thick horsetail grass that lined the river and feasted on our more prosaic fare of yak cheese, bread, and dried apples, the Monpas boasted that the bear's gallbladder would fetch them as much as 3,000 yuan (nearly $380). They disclosed that after hunting trips, they had sometimes mixed the gallbladder of a bear with that of a pig. If it's done well, they claimed, no one can tell the difference.

The trail continued along islands in the braided stream, switching back and forth between the banks on fallen logs. We entered a dense forest of firs, sycamore, and maple. At 10,000 feet above sea level it transformed into an almost impenetrable thicket of towering bamboo. It challenged the imagination to think of the intrepid Khampas who first entered this jungle in search of a promised land, yet shortly before dark and 2,000 feet lower, the forest opened into a vast field of artemesia framed by magnolia trees, tall cliffs, and tiered waterfalls. A reddish glow infused the sky as a rainbow arched across the valley to the south.

We approached a small village with sloping wooden roofs and stopped to make camp. A woman appeared carrying a bamboo basket filled with fodder. Last night a tiger had killed one of her dzos on the same spot, she told us. The villagers had carted away the carcass.

SETTLERS IN CHIMDRO had cleared and partly cultivated the once densely forested valley floor and driven local wildlife onto the steep mountainsides where tigers could no longer prey on them. The tigers preyed instead on the Khampa settlers' horses, pigs, and cattle. The Tibetans were hesitant to kill the tigers, not only because they were protected under Chinese law, but because they considered them to be manifestations of Pemako's protector deity, Dorje Traktsen. According to the Khampa woman who had wandered into our camp, Chimdro's tigers have never killed a human being and few of the villagers had even seen one. They come like ghosts, she said.

At these lower altitudes, Pemako's notorious leeches and clouds of flying insects posed a more immediate threat. When the woman returned to the village, we retreated into our tents as a thunderstorm illuminated the green walls of forest that sealed the valley on all sides.

In the morning we headed into the village to look for Kawa Tulku. Half a dozen wooden houses, each encircled by white prayer flags and raised above ground level on posts, sat among small plots of barley and corn. Hedges made from stacked thorns had been built to ward off monkeys. Dzos and mithun cattle roamed the surrounding fields. Enormous spiderwebs stretched across the paths and from the houses' wide, overhanging eaves.

We found the lama in the home of the village headman, eating tsampa and drinking whey. The headman, Orgyen, had been telling him about a dzo that he had lost to a tiger two nights earlier. "Each year, every household in Chimdro loses at least one horse or head of cattle to a tiger," Orgyen said, but in the last three years he alone had lost forty of his livestock to predatory cats. The previous year—1994—Chimdro's tigers had killed 113 cattle and 29 horses, and this year the rate had been even higher.[9]

In response to our prodding, Orgyen told us that he had been born in Pemako to Khampa parents who had arrived there in the first years of the twentieth century as followers of the lama Jedrung Jhampa Yungney, who had unearthed a guidebook to Pemako called *Clear Light* from a cave in eastern Tibet. The lama had led them on a search for Chimé Yangsang Né that came to naught. In a lengthy story with familiar echoes, Orgyen told us of the peregrinations of this group of devout Tibetans buffeted about by outside forces, from hostile tribes to border disputes between India and China.[10]

From oral history, the conversation turned suddenly to the weather. Strange atmospheric phenomena had occurred in the three days prior to our arrival, Orgyen said. The only time that rainbows appear in the sky while the sun is shining and while, at the same time, it is raining is when someone dies or when a great lama is coming, he maintained. And now also when Americans first come to Chimdro, he added jokingly. Kawa Tulku, perpetually amused, said nothing and continued to eat his tsampa and whey.[11]

However welcome we might have felt, we were eager to continue on toward Kundu Dorsempotrang. Gunn arrived at Orgyen's house and expressed concerns about our permits. He was clearly nervous about the small Chinese military garrison in Gutang, where a bridge crossed to the other side of the Chimdro Chu River. Orgyen told us of a cable that stretched across the Chimdro Chu several hours' walk upriver from Gutang. If we crossed there, he said, we could avoid the Chinese altogether. On the other side, a gorge leads up through dense forests to the Pungpung-La, the pass leading toward Kundu. I asked Orgyen about finding someone who knew the way to the mountain. "The young people from Shingke have all left," Orgyen said, "and we're too old now to go. You might find someone in Samdrup, the village above the cable."

As we prepared to leave, Kawa Tulku announced that he would be staying in Shingke for several more days, waiting for some monks from Kham. I couldn't blame him. If his idea of pilgrimage involved any modicum of solitude, it would definitely have been compromised by our presence. When I told Gunn, he was clearly disappointed. Zang refrained from comment.

WE FOLLOWED THE VALLEY WESTWARD through dense broad-leafed forests and open grazing land where dzo and dzomos foraged warily, perhaps aware of the perpetual threat of tigers. After several hours we reached the village of Samdrup. We set up our tents on a shelf of ferns below the site of a ruined temple dedicated to the lineage of Taksham Nuden Dorje, the "tiger-skirted" treasure-revealer who had opened routes into Pemako in the latter part of the seventeenth century. The altimeter showed 7,500 feet. Below us a cable stretched across the seething river that we would have to cross the next day to begin the ascent toward Kundu Dorsempotrang.

Gunn confessed that our permits did not technically cover the way ahead. No one in our entourage knew the way to the sacred mountain, and our attempts to find a guide in Samdrup had been unsuccessful. As in Shingke, the villagers claimed to be too old for such a pilgrimage. You'll have to find someone in Gutang, they said.

Gunn had hoped to avoid the authorities in Gutang but, apart from our pressing need for a guide, the porters he'd hired in Dashing-La had refused to go any farther, and he'd been unable to recruit others in either Shingke or Samdrup. He would find someone in Gutang who knew the way to Dorsempotrang, he promised, cross the bridge, and meet us on the other side of the river the following day. It seemed a reasonable plan.

Another problem remained. Before leaving Shingke, Kawa Tulku had warned us that as an outsider, meaning one unsympathetic to Buddhism, Zang would cause obstacles on the pilgrimage to Kundu. He urged us to find some

way of divesting ourselves of him. We had already decided to send three
porters down the Chimdro Chu with food supplies that we would need when
we reached Medok in the lower Tsangpo valley. I proposed to Gunn that Zang
accompany them to guard the loads. Unfortunately, he failed to take the bait.
"We must take Mr. Zang," Gunn said anxiously.

After Gunn and Zang left for Gutang, we sat outside our tents as a rainbow
appeared over the gorge leading toward Kundu Dorsempotrang. Not only were
we inspired, but it gave the people of Samdrup—who were encountering Westerners for the first time—confidence that we were not unwelcome weather patterns often being viewed as a direct expression of the mood of local protector
spirits.

Equally auspicious was the arrival of three Tibetans who had gone with us
the year before on our journey to Medok. They had heard news about us in
Pomi and, traveling without loads, had taken only three days to catch up.
Puntsok, a Khampa, wore a black woolen chuba, a threadbare straw hat, and a
boar's tusk and amulets around his neck. The two others were from Powo. One,
Chimé Gompo, had a distinctive scar across his face. His friend wore his green
cap at a jaunty angle. With a cigarette dangling from his mouth, he bore a faint
resemblance to Humphrey Bogart. Given our difficulties finding porters in
Chimdro, their arrival was as welcome as it was unexpected. But they had no
more idea than we did about the route to the mountain.

Crossing the River

WE AWOKE ON AUGUST 8 to clouds and drizzle. By 8 A.M. it had turned into a steady rain. A group of villagers appeared at my tent door and told me that Chinese soldiers were on their way from Gutang to prevent us from continuing to Kundu Dorsempotrang. "Go across the river quickly," an old man said. "Once you're across the river, they won't follow."

The cable stretching across the Chimdro Chu was intimidating; it sagged across several hundred feet of deafening white water, all headed for the Tsangpo and afterward into the Brahmaputra and the Bay of Bengal. Last year the cable had broken, the villagers informed us, and a Chinese soldier had fallen into the river and drowned.

Despite the ominous tidings, we were eager to cross as quickly as possible. We decided to send the Sherpas first and ourselves last in case we had to negotiate with local officials. A one-eyed Khampa led us to a precarious staging platform of rotting wood built between two trees. He placed a notched section of rhododendron wood over the top of the steel cable and tied leather straps around Pemba's torso and neck. We attached a 180-foot climbing rope to the dubious apparatus so that it could be hauled back across for the next person.

The climbing rope was too short, and we had to add three lengths of local hemp and a long strip of leather in order to stretch it across the river. As the rope would otherwise dangle in the water and be pulled downstream by the force of the rapids, the Monpas made a loop of woven saplings that held the rope above the full force of the white water. With all in place, Pemba slid out over the void, waves leaping around his ankles as he hauled himself and the first load across the river.

It took the better part of the day to relocate our entire crew and all of our

supplies. The Chinese soldiers had failed to materialize, although we could see figures on the other side of the river and worried that they had instead gone with Gunn to accost us on the opposite bank. There was no way of knowing, as there was only one-way communication across the rope bridge. We waited out of sight on the banks of the Chimdro Chu, where one of the Monpa porters busied himself plucking fish from the eddies with his bare hands.

When our turn came to cross the cable, we backed up the notched piece of rhododendron with carabiners and nylon webbing, despite the one-eyed Khampa's protestations that it would create too much friction. He had stood for hours on the rotten staging platform like an executioner at a gallows. He placed the leather straps and ropes over my head with a lavish grin, and I slid out over the waves and hauled myself up to the opposite bank.

Gunn was waiting on the other side. With Zang's assistance, he had pacified the authorities in Gutang, found several porters, and recruited a slightly manic Khampa named Yonten who claimed to know the way to Kundu Dorsempo-trang.

We set up camp above the river amid towering ferns and sorted through piles of what seemed increasingly like extraneous gear. The Sherpas, dressed in expedition hand-me-downs, played cards in the green nylon cook tent. Gunn,

Cookie, and Zang formed a separate camp with meager Chinese pup tents and a stove that had lost its base on the way across the river. Gunn's large inflatable air mattress—the kind one might use for lounging around on a lake—was perhaps their most impressive piece of equipment.

The porters from Bhakha, with amulet boxes around their chests and swathes of green canvas wrapped around their legs to ward off leeches, had encamped under one of our surplus tarpaulins. The Monpas camped deeper in the ferns, where they feasted on the now definitively rotting carcass of the bear and made beds of matted foliage. The slightly demented nun hunched over her prayer book while sitting on a throne of deep green ferns. In terms of technological development, our extended camp was a study in evolution. But any thought of romanticizing the Monpas' ease with their environment was undercut by the sight of two of them retching up the putrifying bear meat.

Over dinner Hamid regaled Oy and the Gillenwaters with tales of his Caspian homeland. "The cloud forests of the Caspian are very much like Pemako," he told them, "they're full of snakes, leopards, and wild boar." He elaborated on the region's charms: "The mountains there are so remote that during Persia's medieval period, they served as a base for the renegade Assassin sect. The Assassins' teachings were a blend of Neoplatonism and Sufi mysticism, and were much maligned by Islamic historians, who claimed that the sect's leader fed hashish to his disciples as a foretaste of paradise to come, and then sent them out to terrorize and kill his enemies much in the manner of Japanese ninjas. But the Persian historian Juvaini reported that his forest fortress had contained a great library with unique manuscripts in various languages including the works of many Greek philosophers, until they were put to the torch by Mongol invaders in the thirteenth century."

SITTING BY THE SHERPAS' FIRE, the guide that Gunn had enlisted to lead us to Kundu, Yonten, described the route ahead of us, pointing up the gorge and naming the various passes, swollen rivers, and swamps that we would have to cross en route to the mountain. He spoke of the tigers that we would likely hear but never see and the poisonous snakes that we would be lucky to avoid—

Russell's vipers and king cobras. But he evaded all our attempts to determine how many days it would take us to actually reach there. "The trail grows over every year," Yonten said. "No one from Chimdro has gone this year. We will have to cut our way through dense jungle."

Further complicating matters, Yonten explained that Kundu could not be approached directly. Before climbing to the mountain's inner circuit, tradition dictates that pilgrims complete a multiday circumambulation of eight lakes that surround its base. This *Chi-kor*, or outer circuit, extends into disputed territory between India and China, Yonten claimed—the legendary region of the *Lo-nag*, or Black Savages.

The rumours of the trials ahead circulated throughout the camps. The porters from Gutang had demanded 100 yuan a day, and the ones from Bhakha now demanded the same. It may have been a pilgrimage, but along with religious merit the Tibetans wanted to accumulate as much cold, hard cash as possible.

Other than the dubious claims of the drunken "pilgrim" whom we had met on his way toward the Dashing-La, we had no sense about whether the trail to Kundu would be passable. We had no accurate maps, and our guide, Yonten, was unproven. Christian suspected that he had never actually been there. We were poised at the threshold of the inner beyul. The trees beyond our sea of ferns were silhouetted like brush strokes against descending mist. The forest above was shadowy and silent, uninhabited for hundreds of miles. I divested myself of leeches and crawled into my sleeping bag; the dark sinuous forms inched across the nylon netting of the tent door. Before falling asleep I thought of the Buddha's words in the *Dhammapada* regarding crossing the river of Samsara for the boundlessness of Nirvana: "Leave the past behind; abandon all thoughts of the future, and let go of the present. You are ready then to cross to the other shore."

The Gates of the Beyul

ON AUGUST 9 WE LEFT THE REFUGE of the fern garden in heavy drizzle. Within minutes of setting out several of us had taken different paths on what turned out to be no more than animal tracks through the dense undergrowth. We called and whistled to each other and wandered in circles trying to find the actual trail. Yonten, the guide, was nowhere in sight.

Not only was the way blocked by almost impenetrable foliage, but the ground—when we could see it—was crawling with leeches. Blind but heat-seeking, the blood-sucking worms extended themselves from wet leaves and dropped down on us from the tree limbs, tunneling through layers of clothing until they found bare skin. It was impossible even to count how many we might find on our bodies at any one time.

Several varieties appeared, from ones so small they could hardly be seen to four-inch-long tiger leeches. We stopped every few minutes to divest ourselves of as many of them as we could—dozens at a time—but, as Christian exclaimed, they seemed to be raining from the trees. Even the most hardened of the porters raced through the ferns as if speed alone would keep the leeches from adhering. "They're like wrathful guardians testing our resolve," Christian shouted. I told him the stories of Dulshuk Lingpa, Chatral Rinpoche's father-in-law, who, in similar circumstances, had urged his fellow pilgrims to let the leeches have their fill of blood until they fell off of their own accord, swollen to several times their original size.

Ever the naturalist, Oy spoke about the anesthetic that the leeches inject before engorging themselves on mammalian blood. "That's why you don't even feel them at first," she said. "But it wears off and that's why they itch terribly once they've fallen off." They also inject an anticoagulent, causing the wounds to bleed profusely for several hours after they've been removed. Oy referred to them as marvels of specialized evolution and commented that Thai villagers sometimes use them to purify their blood.

YONTEN HAD STUMBLED UPON some semblance of a trail and called out from up above. There was no sign of any recent human passage, and the porters in front had to hack through tangled undergrowth and overgrown ferns with their long machetelike knives. We followed as best we could through the jungle, parting the wet, leech-filled foliage with bamboo staves. It was a purgatory worthy of Dante. We followed a ridge through serpentine moss-covered rhododendrons and entered a realm of dense bamboo that in places, we had to crawl through on all fours. The Monpas pointed out several spots where bears had feasted on the stalks.

We then entered a narrow ravine gouged by landslides and climbed steeply into mist-filled forests. Yonten referred to the narrowing gorge as the *ne-go*, or gateway, to the inner beyul. The neyigs compare the surrounding mountains to "a fence of swords, rice stalks, crystal stupas, the manes of demonesses, breasts of dakinis, kings on thrones, and swords piercing into space." But the mist and tall bamboo prevented us from seeing all but a narrow circumference. For hours, we hauled ourselves up along the streambed of the narrow gorge, rocks tumbling down from the slopes above.

The porters stopped to build a fire and eat tsampa beneath an overhanging rock that Yonten called Drakartrodzong. Yonten had said it would be a long day and we continued on ahead in mist and rain. The gorge steepened and landslides had cut large swathes through the forest, whole sections of which had slid into the mud-filled river. The deadfall and unstable gray rubble that had been left behind was saturated with water. Sheered, splintered bamboo stuck up out of the mud like spears. We moved across the eroding slopes as quickly as possible in the pouring rain.

I passed four Sherpas who had been walking in front of me and continued on to a recent mudslide that looked like gray, molten lava. I climbed to the top of the slide and descended on the other side to the original trail, where I caught sight of several porters in the mists ahead of me. Suddenly—at a point where the trail disappeared into yet another landslide chute—I lost sight of them, as well as where the trail continued. I finally found it lower down where it disappeared into jungle, but there were no footprints or broken branches indicating that the porters, or anyone else, had come this way. I was disturbed that the Sherpas were so far ahead when it was 4:30 P.M. with no sign of Yonten or the other porters behind us. To my relief, Hamid, the Gillenwaters, Oy, and Christian appeared behind me, together with Pemba. Nobody seemed to know who was in front and who was behind. Confusion and disagreement reigned as to whether to go on or to wait for the porters who were still behind. But we believed that the porters with our tents and sleeping bags were the ones still ahead of us, and we were eager to catch up.

I followed Pemba up the trail until we found footprints and then proceeded across treacherous landslides until we regained the original trail by ascending a short, vegetated cliff. Christian and the others were behind, traversing a steep eroding mass of unstable rocks and tree roots protruding from gray mud.

I turned around when I heard Gil yell, "Man down! We've got a man down!"

The ground beneath Christian's feet had given way and he'd somersaulted toward the river, pitching headfirst into a rock. Gil rushed down to where he was lying in the mud, dazed but lucid. In addition to the injury to his skull, his hand was bleeding and badly bruised. He'd broken his watch and the small compass fixed to its band. Troy checked his pupils for signs of a possible concussion. Unable to resist a joke, Christian terrified Troy by calling out wildly, "Who am I? What's my name?" A moment later Hamid yelled, "Rocks! Look out, rocks!" and Christian and the Gillenwaters darted out of the way of a cascade of falling boulders. They slowly climbed back up to the trail in the rain. Christian may not have had a concussion, but he was soaked to the bone and caked with mud, and he looked like an initiate in a New Guinea mud dance.

We continued on up the ravine. Gunn and the Chinese police officer caught up with us in the gathering dusk and reported that some of the porters were following behind them, but that others had stopped to carve out sleeping platforms from the side of the gorge.

As we climbed higher, the terrain became progressively wilder and steeper.

Our steps loosened the mud conglomerate and sent it hurtling down into the stream below. Hauling ourselves up on thin bamboo saplings, we eventually caught up with two of the Sherpas. Apparently they had thought that we were ahead of them and were trying to keep up. Two more were farther ahead, they said, also trying to catch up. Clearly the protector spirits were at work to disorient us.

AS IT TURNED OUT, the four Sherpas were carrying neither tents nor sleeping bags. They had traded their loads for food supplies that they feared the local porters might otherwise pilfer. It was too late to return the way we had come, and we had no choice but to stay where we were and hope that some of the porters would soon appear. It had been raining off and on all day and the ground was saturated with leeches.

Pemba set about chopping down glassy-stemmed rhododendrons to rig a makeshift shelter with the plastic sheets that had been covering the Sherpas' bamboo pack baskets. One of the other Sherpas began making a fire, initially with little success. At 8 P.M., Lhakpa, one of the younger Sherpas, appeared out of the mist with news that the porters who had been behind us had turned back at the landslide where Christian had fallen. Lhakpa claimed to have made it in less than an hour from where Yonten and the rest of our party had set up camp. But no one wanted to make that descent in the dark.

The fire hadn't taken, and suddenly I began to shiver. The clothes I had with me were soaked through, and I decided to descend with Lhakpa to the lower camp. The fewer of us there were at our makeshift bivouac, the more chance that the night would be bearable for those who did stay. I relinquished my poncho as a ground sheet and left with Lhakpa at 8:20 P.M.

In the gathering darkness we made fast progress through the tangled ravines, landslides, and uprooted trees. Lhakpa was sure-footed, but I slid and tumbled frequently, nearly impaling myself on the rhododendron and bamboo stalks that had been sheared off by the mudslides. One to two feet in height and an inch or less in diameter, they stuck up out of the ground like small spears.

We reached camp after 9 P.M. The porters had rigged simple shelters from tarpaulins and the plastic sheets that covered their loads. The Sherpas had used the dining tent as a fly and suspended it between moss-encrusted rhododendrons. In heavy rain, I pitched my tent on a rough framework of tree limbs that one of the Sherpas had suspended over the mountainside. I emptied the water from my boots, deleeched, and spent the night in fitful sleep, unable to banish the thought that my precarious shelter might wash into the stream below.

A Treatise on Paradise

AS EARLY AS 50 C.E., the theologian Philo cautioned against a literal interpretation of the Garden of Eden, writing, "To think that it here meant that God planted vines, or olive trees, or apple trees, or pomegranates, and any trees of such kinds, is mere incurable folly."[12] The fourth-century Christian thinker St. Ephraem, in his *Hymns on Paradise*, similarly cautioned that, "It is with the eye of the mind that I saw paradise . . ."

But theologians who argued for a symbolic reading of "the divine garden" remained a distinct minority. St. Augustine registered the conflicting points of view. "Some interpret [Paradise] in an exclusively corporeal sense," he wrote. Others give it "an exclusively spiritual meaning," and still others take it in both senses, "sometimes corporeally and at other times spiritually . . ."[13] St. Augustine personally favored the literal reading, and shaped the convictions of later generations of Christian theologians who maintained that the earthly paradise had not disappeared, but had only become inaccessible as a result of mankind's fall from grace.

Centuries later, in 1617, John Salkeld synthesized prevailing views on the reality of the Garden of Eden in his work *A Treatise on Paradise and the Principle Contents Thereof.* Relying on theological authorities such as St. Augustine, Salkeld set out to prove that the earthly paradise was "a real and corporeal place" and not merely metaphysical. Catholic dogma at the time supported the same literalist point of view, insisting that descriptions of Paradise were "not allegory but history." John Calvin, the sixteenth-century Protestant reformer, similarly declared that the Garden of Eden was "situated on the Earth, not as some dream in the air."

In the fifth century St. Augustine admitted that, "It is probable that man has no idea where Paradise was." Medieval geographers located the lost garden everywhere from the North Pole to the middle of the Atlantic Ocean, although the prevailing Church view held that the earthly paradise lay "in the east," in the regions of the Tigris and Euphrates rivers or in the farthest reaches of Asia, at a great height so as to have been unaffected by the waters of the flood. Like Yangsang, the terrestrial paradise was described as a place of eternal spring, neither hot nor cold and filled with fruit-bearing trees and healing waters. Early in the eighth century, St. John Damascene wrote that Eden "was temperate in climate and bright with the softest and purest of air. It was luxurient with ever-blooming plants, filled with fragrances, flooded with light, and surpassing all conception of sensible fairness and beauty."[14]

Throughout the Middle Ages and into the Reformation, the Vatican dispatched friars into the depths of Asia in pursuit of Eden, hoping to discover vestiges of the vanished Paradise. After all efforts had proved futile, St. Thomas Aquinas maintained that:

> *The situation of Paradise is shut off*
> *from the habitable world by mountains, or seas,*
> *or some torrid region, which cannot be crossed;*
> *and so people who have written about*
> *topography make no mention of it.*[15]

In the fourteenth century, Sir John Mandeville made an even stronger case for Eden's inaccessibility. He wrote that "wastes and wilderness and great crags and mountains" surround the earthly paradise. Of those who had tried to follow the raging rivers leading into Eden, "some had died through exhaustion . . . some went blind and deaf through the noise of the waters, and some were drowned through the violence of the waves."[16] Even with advances in cartography in the fifteenth century, beliefs regarding the story of Genesis remained tenacious. The Garden of Eden appeared consistently on maps at the eastern edge of India, where it was shown as being separated from the rest of the earth by an impenetrable wall, not unlike that of the Himalayas.

Pemako enjoys many of the attributes of the lost Eden—a promised land

east of India sealed in by towering mountains and hazardous terrain, duplici-
tous serpents and magical flora somewhere at its heart.[17]

John Salkeld's early-seventeenth-century *Treatise on Paradise* explained why
such promised lands can rarely be reached:

> What may be the reason why Paradise was never found? Why, it was the huge-
> ness and insuperable height of the mountains, which are betwixt us and Par-
> adise, secondly, for that there be mightie wilderness full of all kind of most
> venomous sepents and wild beasts. Thirdly, because there is no way but through
> large regions of most pestiferous aire in which no man can live.[18]

The belief in a geographical paradise persisted widely until the end of the seventeenth century when the Church conveniently declared that the Garden had
been erased from the surface of the planet by the Great Flood. The question
then remained not where Paradise lay, but what it meant. Although the expul-
sion from Paradise is the core western myth, the notion of the fall was a later
accretion. At the end of the second century, Christian writings by St. Theophi-
las of Antioch and St. Irenaeus reveal an understanding of the story of Genesis prior to the invention of original sin. According to these erudite bishops,
Eden was "a means of advancement" for "maturing and becoming perfect."
The eating of the fruit of knowledge did not condemn humankind to suffering, but the act of disobedience ultimately furthered its maturity and capacity
to perfect itself. Eden was thus not so much a perfect place, but a place where
being could be perfected. Mankind's departure from the enclosing walls of Paradise and its bucolic luxuries led the first couple to become all that they could
be. As the philosopher Immanuel Kant wrote in 1785, it was a necessary transi-
tion from an unreflective, animal state to one of full humanity. Freedom, he
suggested, begins when the nostalgia for a perfect place ends and one embraces
the present moment.

Nonetheless, Paradise persisted as a perennial dream and an incentive to geographical discovery. The religious dissidents who abandoned a repressive Europe for North America discovered what seemed a blessed land, where history
could begin anew. They described New England as being "like the Garden of

Eden, a new Eden." In a more literal sense, when Columbus sailed close to the isthmus of the Orinoco in South America, he believed he had discovered one of the four rivers that issue from Eden. As he wrote to Queen Isabella of Spain during his third expedition, "I believe that the earthly paradise lies here . . . which no man can enter except by God's leave."

The belief in Eden, the widespread conviction of an impending apocalypse, and the desire for gold and fortune led to voyages of discovery in which explorers saw in the lands that opened before them the shape of a lost paradise. Following Columbus, Amerigo Vespucci (1499–1502) surveyed the coast of Surinam and Brazil and wrote that: "If the earthy paradise exists anywhere on earth, I think it must not be very far from this area."[19] Yet as D. H. Lawrence recognized, to believe in Paradise was to consign oneself to Purgatory, to be forever seeking something beyond the horizon, beyond life itself. "Why pin ourselves down on a paradisal ideal?" he wrote in 1953. "It is only ourselves we torture. . . . Love is never a fulfillment. Life is never a thing of continuous bliss. There is no paradise. Fight and laugh and feel bitter and feel bliss."[20]

Hell Night

THE NEXT MORNING, after climbing an hour and a half above our precarious camp, I caught up with Hamid, Oy, Christian, and the Gillenwaters. They had rigged up a perfunctory fly to shield them from the rain, but the night had been hell. Hamid had screamed out in the middle of the night when he discovered that a bloated tiger leech had fixed itself to the inside of his mouth. Rallying to the crisis, Gil had produced a lighter and as Hamid—wild-eyed—held down his lower lip, Gil carefully scorched the leech, bursting its contents of human blood. No one quite managed to sleep after this nightmare.

As we stomped around the fire trying to warm our feet and stay out of the rain, Christian said that the time since we had left the river had probably been the most confounding twenty-four hours in his entire life. "Maybe we aren't wanted here," he mused. "Perhaps some 'wrathful force' is trying to tell us something."

Hamid told Christian about the year before when we had crossed the Gawalung-La and our Chinese porters had been caught beneath collapsing snow cornices. "The guardian spirits are compassionate," he tried to convince him. "They only keep out those they feel are harmful to the land. If they don't want you here, they'll first try to manipulate your thoughts and dreams. Only if that fails," Hamid insisted, "will they resort to unleashing avalanches and rock falls to keep you out."

"Or molest you with leeches," Christian countered. "It's hard to accept that we're on the edge of some paradise. This seems more like hell."

"In Tantra, hell *is* paradise," Hamid said, thinking perhaps of Padmasambhava's words that "adverse conditions are a practitioner's true wealth."

THE FIRE WAS STILL SMOLDERING, and the Monpa porters took the opportunity to cook their midmorning rice. "These Monpas stop five times a day to eat," Pemba reflected. "Tea, tsampa, chiles, bear meat in the morning; then rice or corn gruel in the middle of the day; more tsampa or bread in the afternoon; tea, and bear meat in the evening; and before sleeping, another big bowl of tsampa. They'll run out of food at this rate."

We left ahead of the Monpas and proceeded up the gorge, eventually crossing over on a fallen log to the left bank of the river. The trail began to contour westward, and we crossed two smaller streams on moss-slick trees. Bhakha Tulku had told me stories of the many pilgrims who had lost their lives while crossing Pemako's notorious tree bridges. They're serviceable so long as they're covered in bark. When it wears off, the logs become perilously smooth. It is safest to cross them barefoot, he had advised.

Deep sphagnum mosses carpeted the forest floor. "It's like an elfin realm," Oy exclaimed. We walked through stands of moss-clad fir trees and evergreen oaks and drank from crystalline rivulets, as the Monpas gathered a variety of mushrooms that they insisted were edible. The increasingly strangely behaved nun, Ani-la, pulled leaves from plants along the trail and stuffed them in her mouth. Yonten warned of the bears that frequent these forests. "The tigers won't bother us," Yonten said, "but the bears may come after our food."

Troy told of how he'd once woken up in the Arizona desert with a mountain lion gazing down at him from a nearby rock. "I don't know why he didn't kill me."

"He probably saw you were peaceful," Oy said. "In Thailand many monks befriend tigers during their forest walkabouts." She herself had had several close encounters, one while napping beneath a tree. When she awoke there were three tigers playing a short distance in front of her. "It was one of the most magical moments of my life," she said.

All day we had been enveloped in mist and an endless expanse of pine trees, but at last we emerged out of the forest into an open valley. Suddenly, as the mists parted, we could see huge, granite ramparts rising above us. For a moment there was even a patch of blue sky, but it vanished again as quickly as it had come. The trail was equally ephemeral and it often disappeared entirely. Happily we had climbed higher than the range of leeches.

The Pungpung-La

AT DUSK, WE REACHED A LARGE overhanging boulder surrounded by weathered prayer flags. Mantras had been carved into the rocks. An eerie light filtered through a stand of silver fir and a shallow cave offered partial shelter from the rain. Yonten called the place Gyayul, Realm of Victory, and said it was the door to Kundu Dorsempotrang. It was the first sign of any religious conception of the environment since we had left Samdrup. The trail for the past two days had been so faint that at times we had doubted whether it was more than an animal track. But now at our first né, or portal to inner Pemako, the preceeding two days seemed a passage through the outer rim of a mandala—a disorienting trial to test our resolve. The altimeter showed 11,760 feet.

During breakfast the following morning, August 11, Kawa Tulku suddenly appeared out of the forest. The monks from Kham who were originally to join him on his pilgrimage had sent word that they couldn't come for another month, and he had made the decision to catch up with us. "The journey to Dorsempotrang is arduous," Kawa Tulku said, "and you already took the only willing guide." He joked that he had no choice but to team up with us. The one-eyed Khampa who manned the cable across the river had agreed to guide him as far as Gyayul but said that he was too old to go any farther. Everyone from the porters to Gunn was in high spirits. We had come to associate the lama with good weather and favorable conditions, and after two days of perpetual rain and drizzle while climbing through the leech-infested gorge we were ripe for a change in circumstances.

Until Kawa Tulku's sudden appearance, we had decided to stay another night at the door. It was raining hard, and almost nothing we owned was dry. Mists clung to the surrounding cliffs and the pass we now had to climb—the

Pungpung-La—was hidden in clouds. Kawa Tulku, however, was resolved to continue, and so we rolled up our sodden tents and began climbing up a talus-filled ravine toward the cliffs below the pass. Waterfalls fell through rents in the clouds, the largest cascading in 200-foot tiers from the cliffs to the south. At 13,500 feet, we reached a glacier-carved valley filled by a mile-long lake dotted with small islands that rose like reefs from the clear, black waters. We followed Yonten up rock slabs to the south of the lake as several smaller bodies of water appeared out of the mists, interconnected by streams and waterfalls with the larger lake below.

Possessed of new vigor, Kawa Tulku walked ahead, mantras and incantations issuing silently from his lips. As we neared the pass, a flock of ten or twelve bright blue birds flew in formation directly toward him, circled once around him, and disappeared as quickly as they had come.

AT 15,100 FEET (Bailey had put it at 14,395), the Pungpung-La was a treeless, rain-swept divide demarcating, in Yonten's words, outer Pemako from inner Pemako. Four-foot high cabbagelike plants (*Rheum nobile*) rose out of the otherwise shrubless terrain. The Monpas claimed that their presence indicated the proximity of Pemako's more arcane healing plants. The plant's stem, they said, reduces swelling and fever, but if you tear off one of the leaves, torrential rain will immediately fall. No one wanted to perform the experiment. The porters also claimed that eating some of the root would protect us on the way ahead, and I joined them for the rite. One porter said, "The plants of Pemako can heal you, kill you, or make you crazy." I worried that the slightly demented nun, Ani-la, had eaten one that caused the latter.

We descended from the pass into what was now inner Pemako and entered a valley carpeted in alpine flowers of every describable scent and color. We walked along the edge of a lake where primroses and white, pink, and purple asters cascaded from the tall grass along its banks. According to the neyigs, Kawa Tulku said, this area below the pass is called Sangye Menla and is filled with healing plants. He began inspecting the flowers closely—yellow ones, pur-

ple ones, white ones—and then began eating what looked like small, blue hare-
bells. He urged me to join him. They tasted of pepper and spice.

As we walked, Kawa Tulku spoke of *tsaludadorje,* the indestructible naga demon grass, one of the miraculous plants described in the Pemako neyigs. A single blade of this grass can cure innumerable diseases, he said, and open one's
eyes to other realms. As stated in Padmasambhava's terma, *Clear Mirror for Identifying the Five Miraculous Plants:*

> Any deficiency of the five sense organs will be healed and one will attain mirac-
> ulous powers. One's body will transform like a snake shedding its skin.

By this time we had lost sight of our Monpa porters who, though unbear-
ably slow while ascending the pass, had forged ahead in the rain to look for
some place to camp. We followed their footprints and cut branches through
bogs and streams and emerged at a meadow where the Sherpas were stringing
up the cook tent between two towering firs. The lama's two attendants—the
young monk who was carrying his supplies and the old man with the prayer
wheel—erected the lama's tent under the protective boughs of another large fir.
Gunn pointed out that a small patch of blue sky had mysteriously opened
overhead. We dined that night in high spirits.

The Wrath of the Nagas

ON AUGUST 12, after three days of nearly incessant rain, the sun rose from behind the mountain wall and flooded our camp with light and warmth. After the relentless, mist-wreathed jungles and ravines leading up to the Pungpung-La, we found ourselves in a broad, grassy valley with a stream as clear as crystal meandering through its center. A place worthy of the prophecies, Hamid remarked.

Trees, grass, and clothing steamed with evaporating moisture, and we strung climbing ropes between the firs to dry out belongings that otherwise might have decayed before we reached Kundu. The Tibetans hung their sheepskins and tunics of matted felt next to our high-tech Gore-Tex jackets and the lama's heavy woolen chuba. As the nun waited for her robes to dry, she walked out into the meadow in her undergarments to pick small flowers and toss them as offerings into the sun-drenched sky. At least she had abandoned her habit of wandering around with her mouth full of leaves, Christian commented.

A short distance beyond the camp, the Monpas stopped by the stream to make a fire and brew tea for their midmorning meal. Kawa Tulku stopped to bathe. The lama's body was covered from head to toe in tiny red insect bites, but he smiled radiantly as he basked in the sun while his attendants applied a mysterious salve to his back and arms.

We continued on. Gradually the meadow transformed into an unnavigable swamp, and the trail entered a dense, sunless forest where we saw footprints of bear and takin. At intermittent sedge-filled bogs we often sank up to our knees in mud. Kawa Tulku plugged along in his customarily jovial mood. As conditions worsened, Gil expressed wonder at Kawa Tulku's unshakable composure. Several days before, Gil had written in his journal:

Today was particularly bad for me as the rain would not let up and the leeches were relentless. At one point I counted twenty-two of them sucking on me at the same time. . . . Sloshing along the muddy trail in the pounding rain I came upon a large, slimy log that had fallen chest high across our brush-choked path. In my agitated state I viewed the log as a menacing obstacle that was clearly separate, in my way and against me. With no way under or around I jumped, stomach first, and slid over the top. Regaining my balance on the other side, I was infuriated at the mud and decaying mush that seemed to have covered the entire front of my body. Rubbing off the crud I cursed the log and the goddamned rain. It was my brother Todd who suggested that we wait and see how the Lama would handle this formidable impediment. Surely this test would break him.

Hiding off the trail we peeked through the underbrush just in time to see him trudge up to the log. Ever smiling he took a couple of steps back and tried his jump with a running start. With not enough momentum—coupled with a portly belly—he slid back down on the same side of the log and landed on his back in a large puddle. Shaking his rain-drenched head he burst into spasms of uproarious laughter. Staggering to his feet he repeated the same maneuver—with the same results—no less than three times. With each collapse back into the puddle his laugher grew stronger and louder. On his fourth attempt he made it over the top and slid headlong into the muddy puddle on the other side. Again, the laugher was knee-slapping. Continuing to chuckle, he wiped himself off as best he could—lovingly patted the log as though it were a dear friend—and proceeded up the trail—*smiling*. Todd and I just stared at each other.

Deeper into the valley, we crossed to the left bank of the stream descending from the Pungpung-La and soon emerged at a slender shallow lake that was more than a mile long and blocked at its southern terminus by an enormous logjam. Bailey had seen the lake in 1913 and attributed it to the breaking of a glacial tarn in the valley that opened above us in a spectacular display of cliffs and glaciers reminiscent of the Canadian Rockies. One of the Sherpas spotted a bear on the opposite bank, our first such sighting. Another Sherpa drew giant

Om Mani Padme Hums in the sand at the edge of the water. Hamid staged crazy photo-ops with a bewildered Ani-la, as Kawa Tulku sat on a rotting log and watched in amusement. The sun continued to shine despite a brief rain shower and deep thundering over the cliffs above. Gunn was by now thoroughly convinced of Kawa Tulku's powers as a weatherman par excellence, and he stayed near him whenever possible. Zang said the atmospheric effects were only coincidence, he believed only in science. Putting away his cameras, Hamid retorted that there are many levels of science: the science of observing natural phenomena and the science of controlling phenomena. Gunn translated Hamid's comments to Zang, but our friend from the PSB remained resolutely silent.

Oy was sitting on the sand on a small Therm-a-Rest and overheard Hamid's comments. "Science tries to define what life really is," she said, "but it changes decade to decade; it's only a working hypothesis."

Gunn was not interested in perpetuating the dialogue. "We must get going," he said. "Yonten has already gone ahead."

WE FOLLOWED THE SOUTHERN EDGE of a narrow lake, Rirung Tso, through a thick tangle of bamboo and descended along the stream that disgorged from its southern end. In less than a mile, a second river flowing from a valley to the southeast merged with the one we had been following. Their confluence was marked by torn and faded prayer flags that hung from bamboo poles. This was a holy place called Yanggyap Né, Yonten said. As the river curled around a mound of lichen-covered rocks, it turned into gentle rapids and at one point formed a pool of deep green water bordered by a sandy beach. Thick grass covered the banks, along with wild irises and delicate bamboo. Small spruce trees sprouted from the rocks like sculpted bonsai. While we pitched our tents, the porters busied themselves weaving new pack baskets from the pliant bamboo. The altimeter showed 11,380 feet.

According to my U.S. Defense Service Map, we were camped at the border of India and China, but with the closest habitation to the south more than a week away, issues of national boundaries seemed mildly ludicrous. Until Ti-

betans entered this region in search of Yangsang, it had been a wilderness frequented only by Mishmi and Abor hunters. During the period of the British
Raj, the Bengal Eastern Frontier Regulation Act of 1873 cordoned off India's
relatively uncharted northeastern frontier—from the basin of the Brahmaputra
to the crest of the Himalayas. Forty years later, in 1913, Captains F. M. Bailey
and H. T. Morshead pushed into unexplored territory in the watershed of the
upper Dibang (a tributary of the Brahmaputra) and, when they returned from
the Tsangpo gorges, crossed back into Indian-held territory along a route that
became known later as the Bailey Trail. Their surveys led to the establishing of
the MacMahon Line, drawn along the crest of the Himalayas by Sir Henry
MacMahon and based on a supposedly tripartite convention between British-
Indian, Tibetan, and Chinese representatives in Simla in 1914.

China never ratified the outcome, creating an amorphous autonomous status for Tibet while laying down its border with India on the basis of British
"ridge and river" surveys. The tribal territory between the MacMahon Line and
the northern banks of the Brahmaputra was only loosely administered. Once a
year, expeditionary trips went up the Brahmaputra from Dibrughar to wave the
British flag and meet with Tibetan officials.

With India's independence in 1947, the need for effective governance led to
the creation of the Indian Frontier Administration Service. The job of polic-
ing what became known as the North East Frontier Agency (NEFA) was assigned to the Assam Rifles. Since their war over the contested region in 1962,
India and China had yet to establish an actual border, relying on the post-
conflict Line of Control to demarcate their respective territories. NEFA metamorphosed into Arunachal Pradesh, becoming a Union Territory in 1972 and a
state of India in 1987. Beijing lays claim to the entirety of its 90,000 square
kilometers (34,750 square miles).

A rainbow arched across the valley to the southeast. As I read Bailey's diary,
this seemed to be the same valley that he and Morshead had followed on their
route from Mipi, and where they had came across the remains of pilgrims returning to Tibet after their failed attempt to reach Yangsang. Yonten disagreed.
He maintained that we would not reach the valley leading to Mipi until we had
crossed Adrathang, a notorious bog still several days away. Yonten claimed that

the fir-filled valley that sloped above us led into the territory of the Tranak, fierce Lopa tribes that, a British colonial officer had written in 1899, "kill Tibetans on principle." Yonten spoke about a mountain in the land of the Tranak called Shelkichorten, the Crystal Stupa, that Jedrung Rinpoche had tried to reach in the first years of the twentieth century. According to Yonten, the Tranak Lopas make pilgrimages to the mountain and have successfully kept outsiders from coming near. After circumambulating the mountain, Yonten claimed, they press their palms into the sand in the shape of the hand, hoof, or paw of any creature they want to become, then bodily transform into that being.

It sounded like a dark vision of Yangsang, and I asked Yonten why no one since Jedrung Rinpoche had tried to go there. Yonten's answer seemed to sum up our mission: "If you have the key," he said "Yangsang can be like paradise, if not you'll be lucky to come out alive."

Hamid threatened Gunn with another expedition in search of the fabled crystal mountain. "If we were able to reach this mountain," Hamid prodded,

"what would you like to become?" Gunn said he would like to transform into "a rich man, a holy man."

Throughout these proceedings, Kawa Tulku, the Jolly Lama, laughed quietly. Our quest for Yangsang Né obviously amused him, even though it was something he himself was actively seeking. Was it our approach that he found so humorous? According to tradition, the key to Yangsang can be found on the circumambulation route around Kundu Dorsempotrang, but what the key was could only be guessed at.

"What is this Yangsang?" Christian finally asked as we sat along the grassy banks above the river. "Is it a real place or was it just a fantasy to inspire Tibetans to travel to these wild lands?'

Hamid attempted an explanation: "It seems more like a hypothesis, a vision of what lies in potential. Although no one has found Yangsang yet, it doesn't mean it doesn't exist. It may simply mean that no one has looked for it in the right way." In tribute to Oy's earlier comments by the lake, he added, "It's simply not perceivable to science as we currently know it."

"Maybe that's what the key is all about," Oy said, joining the conversation, "a new way of investigating nature. Maybe Yangsang actually is some unknown dimension of time and space. If we limit ourselves only to what we can perceive, or prove, we rob reality of all its magic. Science is sometimes like a blind person claiming there's nothing there, or like someone who is deaf claiming that music does not exist. Just because something can't be proved scientifically doesn't mean it doesn't exist."

"It may be linked to the plants that Kawa Tulku is looking for," Hamid suggested. "Like the vision plants used by shamans in the Amazon, the plants described in the neyigs may offer a missing ingredient in how we percieve reality; something that bridges the gap between what we imagine to be real and what actually is real."

Oy interjected, "You mean between what we know to be true intuitively and what can be empirically measured. Empirical knowledge is only one kind of knowledge. It's not truth. Even with microscopes, what we see with our eyes is only a narrow spectrum of light between red and violet. We see only five percent of the 'real' world. Most of what's out there remains hidden."

"Maybe Yangsang's like particle physics," Christian offered, "in that it conforms to one's method of observation, and that one only sees what one expects to see."

"Whatever Yangsang is," I added, "we certainly wouldn't find it using compasses and maps."

GIL WAS USUALLY THE FIRST to initiate such discussions, but he had gone to the river with his brothers to perform their daily washing ritual, a holdover,

I suspected, from their Mormon ancestry. The trio emerged from the shady pool beneath the rocks and, with towels draped over their shoulders, squished by in shorts and Teva sandals. Kawa Tulku looked up anxiously. "Did they bathe in that pool below the prayer flags?" he asked. The lama was clearly disturbed, and I asked him what was wrong. "That's the place of a powerful Naga spirit," he said. "They should not have bathed there." He went back to fingering the beads of his mala.

Pemba had climbed up some nearby trees and harvested a load of bright orange *ashamu*, or chicken mushrooms, and transformed our noodle dinner into a delicious feast. We took off our boots and sat in a circle on the floor of the dining tent. Gil was wearing a fresh T-shirt of a yowling skeleton riding on a dead horse. Tipping his cowboy hat, the specter shouts, "Have fun. I'll see you in five minutes." I kept what Kawa Tulku had told me about the water spirit to myself.

GUNN APPEARED IN THE MIDST of our banquet and confessed his anxiety about the route ahead. Yonten had told him that in the following days we would be passing through vast swamps with mud up to our thighs. Gunn's porters had also insisted on making the *kora*, or ritual circuit, around the mountain with Kawa Tulku, adding three days to the itinerary. "Those days are not scheduled," Gunn lamented. "If we go around the mountain, we won't reach Medok on time."

Adding to Gunn's frustration was the palpable languor that had come over the rest of us. Like Odysseus's crew in the Land of the Lotus Eaters, we were in no hurry at all to leave: we had discovered troves of edible mushrooms, the weather was clear, and we were camped in one of the most beautiful spots imaginable. As much as Gunn seemed bound to a tight time frame, we had a growing sense that as long as the weather held and we had food we could stay here happily indefinitely.

The weather didn't hold. The following morning, August 13, the skies turned ominous again, and soon after we had crossed the river on a series of roughly hewn cantilever bridges, it began to rain. On the opposite bank we entered a moss-encrusted forest and followed a route along the trunks of ancient, fallen trees. Mushrooms grew in profusion on the rotting logs and in the leaf litter of the forest floor.

Some of the mushrooms bursting from the ground looked clearly like psilocybin, a consciousness-altering fungus used by Mazatec shamans in the mountains of Oaxaca, Mexico, to communicate with the spirit realm. When I'd first visited Nepal in 1977, the same psychotropic life forms sprouted from cow patties on the grass runway at the airport in Pokhara. Enterprising Nepali children collected them after the rains and sold them to unwary travelers. I put some into my pack for later evaluation.[21]

The porters had pressed on ahead through the dense undergrowth, the faint tracks of their often laceless canvas shoes overlapping at times with the paw prints of bears. Yonten, as usual, had disappeared somewhere far ahead. "We must slow this man down," Gunn said. "It is not safe. We could get lost here."

Five hours later, we came to a clearing in the forest where the Monpas were stringing up the plastic tarpaulins that we had given them as protection against the rain. Kawa Tulku settled into a primitive shelter with a roof of rough-cut boards. Yonten called the place Adralatsa—the base camp for crossing the bog. The altimeter showed 10,900 feet. Hooves and tufts of skin of a musk deer lay outside the wooden shelter. The Tibetans from Chimdro were concerned. This is a sacred area, they said. Only Lopas coming up from India would dare to hunt here. If they've killed a tiger, Yonten muttered, it will rain for days.

The porters had nearly depleted their stock of bear meat and had been supplementing their tsampa and chiles with berries, nettles, and a large leafy plant favored equally by bears. They borrowed our climbing rope from the Sherpas and went off into the forest to lasso blood mushrooms from where they grew, high on dead trees.

As the other porters busied themselves making a fire, Gunn hounded Yonten for a clear assessment of the route ahead. Standing by the fire, Yonten described the next day's journey through the infamous Adrathang, a vast swamp that we would apparently reach after crossing a forested pass several hours climb above our camp. "The mud is deep and there's no way around it," he told Gunn. "Don't walk alone; there are tigers there." At the end of the day, Yonten said, we would cross another pass called the Kangkang Sam-La. From there, if the weather was good, we would be able to see Kundu Dorsempotrang. The kora, Yonten explained, would begin there.

When Gunn came up to me afterward, he looked thoroughly dejected. "Why do we have to go around this mountain?" he asked, his lip curling upward under his wispy moustache. "After seeing it, why can't we just go directly to Medok?"

Hamid tried to think of something that Gunn could relate to. "If we don't, Mr. Gunn, it would be like ordering a great feast of your favorite dishes and and never even getting to taste them."

Whichever way it went, Gunn was emphatic that this would be his last trip to the Tsangpo gorges. Cookie too, who had come on the trip to qualify himself as a guide, had no intention of coming back. "It's too difficult," he said, "and the weather is always bad."

IT BEGAN TO RAIN AGAIN, and we retreated to our respective tents. I was sharing mine with Hamid, and as the rain pounded on the sagging nylon, we began to reconsider our long-held plan of breaking away from the group. After circling Kundu Dorsempotrang, we had hoped to cross the border to the remote valley in Arunachal Pradesh where Jedrung Jhampa Yungney had staged his journeys in search of Yangsang, and where, decades later, Kanjur Rinpoche had entered through a waterfall into the mystic sanctuary. We had told a contact in the Indian government to expect us to emerge from the headwaters of the Dibang, even though no permits are ever given for the region. "The Indian government will be happy to have information about this area," our contact assured us. "I'll make sure you don't have any trouble." We had no illusions of what we would discover, but just because Yangsang might not exist in strict geographical terms seemed no reason not to explore the region that had inspired the myth.

At this stage, however, the weather and dwindling food supplies were threatening our resolve. Furthermore, our maps had proved to be thoroughly useless, and no porters would be likely to go with us. We would have to carry our own

gear on a kind of commando operation, such as when we had crossed surrup-
titiously into Tibet in 1989. There would be repercussions for Gunn if he had
to account for us at the end of the journey, and it could jeopardize our chances
of returning to Tibet in the future.

There was also the question of how we would be received by the Lopas. Tibetans have always held a dark view of the Chulikata Mishmis who guard the
portals into Yangsang. They accuse them of being cannibals who, in the absence
of ready victims during their marriage ceremonies, kill and eat the mothers of
the brides.[22] When Jedrung and his followers attempted to reach Yangsang at
the turn of the century, hostile Lopas had ambushed them with pitfalls and
poisoned arrows. We reached no conclusion except to wait until after the kora,
to see what would be revealed on the cliff where the key to Yangsang was said
to be located.

We went to visit Kawa Tulku. He was reclining on a sack of clothing and
had stretched his tent across the roof of the shelter to keep out the rain. He
had spread his texts out on a plank and was asking Yonten about the five mystic plants described in the neyigs. The descriptions were suitably vague. I wondered if they could be the psilocybin mushrooms that I had found along the
trail. I showed them to Yonten and to Puntsok—the Khampa with the boar's
tooth—but neither of them knew what they were. Only the Lopas know about
these plants, Yonten said.

Yonten claimed that the Lopas had plants that allowed them to live to extraordinary ages—by his reckoning, as long as the third growth cycle of bamboo. Puntsok was skeptical and pointed out that bamboo takes up to one
hundred years to mature and that the third cycle would mean that they could
live to be more than two hundred years old. Hamid asked Yonten if he had ever
gone south into Lopa territory to find these special plants. "You'd make a good
profit," Hamid assured him.

"No one can go into that area," Yonten said. "The Lopas would kill you."

Yonten said that he had met Lopas when they had come north toward
Kundu on hunting trips. Although Tibetans hold the area to be sacred and re-
frain from killing even the smallest insects there, Abors and Mishmis from
across the Indian border hunt for tiger, takin, and musk deer in the surround-

ing valleys. To Yonten's way of thinking, the killing of animals around the sacred mountain had caused the mystical plants to go into recession and become harder to find.

THE ANCIENT LIFE FORMS that Kawa Tulku was seeking recalled the Tree of Knowledge described in Genesis. The Bible is not specific about the nature of the tree, nor its fruit that "made [Adam and Eve] as gods, knowing good and evil." (Genesis 3:4) Long before apples were shown hanging from the mythic tree, the forbidden fruit was depicted as *Amanita muscaria,* as revealed in a thirteenth-century fresco on the wall of a ruined chapel in Plaincouralt, France, where the red-and-white flecked mushroom "is gloriously portrayed, entwined with a serpent, whilst Eve stands by holding her belly." The noted Bible scholar from Cambridge University who first published material on the subject claimed that: "The whole Eden story is mushroom-based mythology, not least in the identity of the 'tree' as the sacred fungus."[23]

Had the identity of Pemako's mystic plants been similarly lost? Were they possibly the small tryptamine-rich fungus that I had unearthed the previous day?[24] A traditional Tibetan doctor in Kathmandu had told me that there are particular mushrooms in Tibet that "bring bliss to the body and realization to the mind," but he had not specified their appearance. A section of Dorje Thokme's *Luminous Web* misleadingly titled *Clear Mirror for Identifying the Five Miraculous Plants* simply states that: "[These plants] cannot be found by ordinary people, but only by great, highly-realized Bodhisattvas." In Yangsang, thirteen "nectar-bearing trees" are said to grow. "Due to the interconnected power of these trees," the terma states, "one can obtain the *siddhis* [Tantric powers] of heaven and earth."

The search for consciousness-expanding and rejuvenative elixirs has long been linked with Taoism and Tantric Buddhism. Alchemical preparations made from cinnabar, or mercuric sulfide, are common to both traditions, as is the use of specific fungi. Early Tantric siddhas are thought to have used *Amanita* (which contains the tropane alkaloids mascarine and muscimal) in their elixirs of immortality, and the eighth-century *Vima Nyingtik*—The Secret Heart Essence of Vimalamitra—describes various concoctions of mind-altering substances, including datura and oleander, which can be formed into pills or placed directly in the eyes to induce visions and illuminate hidden contents of the psyche.[25] Yet the plant and mineral preparations only reveal their true potential in combination with yogic practices that harness the flow of subtle energy within the body's neural pathways and activate the true *elixir vitae*—the mysterious secretions of the pineal gland called *amrita*, or nectar, which often manifest internally as luminous spheres.

The blissful, visionary states resulting, in part, from the integrated flow of betacarbolines and other neural chemicals take symbolic form in Buddhist paradises such as those of Padmasambhava and the wisdom deity Dorje Pagmo. Dorje Pagmo's limbs and chakras form Pemako's esoteric geography as well as a map of the Tantric adept's subtle nervous system. The Tsangpo represents the central meridian called the *uma*, while lateral streams form the solar and lunar channels, the *roma* and *kyangma*. Through control of the breath and subtle physical energies called *tigle*, the Tantric practitioner activates the chakras, or neural energy centers that lie at major nerve plexuses along the body's central meridian, from the sacrum to the crown—a process uniting him or her with the realization of ultimate reality, personified in Tantra as the great goddess.[26]

YOGA COMES FROM THE ROOT *YUJ*, to yoke, or join together, and its practices unite individual consciousness with the source of consciousness beyond all concepts of "I" or "mine." The joyful awareness arising from the practice of Tantric yogas is never an end in itself, but a means for expanding deeper into the vast, open, nondual nature of *anatta*, or egolessness.

Before leaving Kathmandu, Hamid and I had gone to see Chatral Rinpoche in Pharping, at the cave where Padmasambhava had attained liberation together with his consort Sakyadevi. The daughter of a Nepalese queen who died in childbirth, Sakyadevi was reputedly raised from infanthood by monkeys in the forests surrounding an ancient temple dedicated to the great goddess Vajrayogini. Padmasambhava first saw her perched on the branch of a tree and dressed in nothing more than leaves; he immediately recognized her as an ideal spiritual companion.

The narratives of Padmasambhava describe his numerous liaisons as parables of the Tantric path, in which desire is transmuted into radiant compassion and expanding levels of spiritual awareness. In Tibet, when ministers threatened to cast Padmasambhava into the Tsangpo for his disregard for conventional morality, he retreated to an ice-bound cave with Yeshe Tsogyal, the Tibetan emperor's youngest queen. Practicing under his guidance, she attained enlightenment through *tummo*, the yoga of mystic heat.

According to Tantric precepts, practices such as tummo dissolve the illusion of an isolated, independent self. When practiced in union or through visualization, desire itself transforms into luminous rapture, and becomes an offering of joy, beyond conceptions of self and other. Tertons, the male and female treasure revealers, often developed their intuitive powers to their highest capacity through consorts who served as channels or intermediaries between the adept and the full expanse of reality. In accord with Tantric vows, they almost invariably kept their consorts' identities secret or referred to them only obliquely. Yet as Padmasambhava declared in one of the neyigs, no one follow-

ing the code of a monk would ever be able to open the doors to Pemako's innermost realms: they remained the province of the noncelibate yogi-terton. As his consort, Yeshe Tsogyal declared "Let male aid female, female aid male; let each penetrate the other as in weaving . . . merge emptiness with bliss . . . and allow the vital essences to pervade your being . . . Realize the fruit of passion, the Great Bliss (*Mahasukha*) . . . and let doubts and confusion disappear!"[27]

When I had first approached lamas for instruction in these secret yogas, they told me they could be dangerous. They're similiar to a snake in a hollow piece of bamboo,

I was told: one can fall to the lowest hells or travel upward to the highest Buddha Realms. In other words, the bliss may either inflate the ego and result in spiritual complacency or dissolve all sense of separation and lead deeper into the mystery of *sunyata*, or emptiness. ("Translating sunyata as Emptiness," wrote Octavio Paz, "is something worse than a misuse of language; it is a spiritual infidelity.") As desire without compassion can sabotage the subtle unfolding of higher states of awareness, the yogas of union are often regarded as the most deceptive of all Tantric practices. If practiced correctly, however, and the woman's energies penetrate the male's, neural energies flow through a fractal network of synaptic pathways called *tsa* (nadis), dissolving subtle physiological, psychological, and energetic impediments and uniting at the heart center, the nexus of the body's estimated seventy-five trillion cells. In the illuminated heart, illusions of separateness vanish and, what Buddha called *avidya*, or not really seeing, transforms into a radiant realization of the dynamic interconnectedness that unifies all life.

With or without a consort, practitioners of the inner Tantric yogas arouse the dormant energy in the lower chakras and cause it to rise like a flame through the body's central meridian, "melting" the luminous secretions (*tigle*) in the brain which, in turn, stream down like nectar (*dudtsi*) and give rise to increasingly subtle states of consciousness and, ultimately, to the realization of the nondual expanse of emptiness and luminosity, the Clear Light, held to be the mind's innermost essence.

In the 1980s, in order to delve more deeply into these arcane practices, I studied in South India with a Tantric master who placed me on a diet of cinnabar and gold dust. My assigned consort, Uma Devi, had been raised in a temple since the age of six. In the weeks before initiation, she lived on crushed rose petals and powdered pearls that had been dried under the rays of the moon. In later retreats, I used preparations from the Chandramaharoshana Tantra that transform seminal essences into a bioluminescence that lifts the mind from habitual perceptions of time and space.

Hamid had eaten the same alchemical preparations of purified mercury and gold with a girl of exceptional beauty from India's northeastern frontier named Minring. Minring had come to Nepal to work as a pilot for one of the kingdom's airline companies. Despite her training at a Texas school of aviation, Minring was deeply connected to her tribal roots in Nagaland. Soon after she'd returned from America, fellow villagers had killed her uncle as he devoured a goat on a night when he had allegedly transformed into a tiger. It's still commonly held in India's northeast frontier that certain human beings have a propensity for turning—literally—into wild animals. According to Minring, her aunt and nephews had locked her uncle in his room at night on full moons, but in the mornings the inside of his bedroom door would be gouged with claw marks.

Minring's remarkable stories—along with the fact that her maternal grandfather had the largest collection of human heads in their ancestral village—had impressed Hamid sufficiently that he relented to her requests for a formal consecretion of their union. Bhakha Tulku performed the rite, giving them five-feathered arrows of long life to hold in their hands and seating them on the moulting skin of a Himalayan brown bear that he had brought back to Kathmandu from Powo. After performing the ritual, Bhakha Tulku had his doubts. "Lopa girls are too wild," he told me after the ceremony, "they rarely stay with one man."

HAMID AND I RETURNED TO CAMP, where the others had gathered in the dining tent. Despite the weather, there was enthusiasm for the way ahead. By Yonten's estimates the mountain was only two days away, and even the infamous bog that we would have to cross to get there had captured everyone's imagination. Only the Gillenwaters remained quiet, despairing over another meal of lentils and brown rice. They had resorted to a secret stash of Gummi Bears. After dinner we retired to our tents, rain pooling on the sagging nylon walls.

ALTHOUGH EVERYONE HAD FELT WELL the preceding evening, Kawa Tulku's prediction concerning the disgruntled naga seemed to be coming true. On the morning of August 14, Gil appeared at my tent door to tell me that Todd had become violently ill. He had severe stomach cramps and had been vomiting throughout the night. I informed Pemba that Todd was too sick to move and that we would have to spend another night at Adralatsa. Pemba was nervous about our dwindling food supplies. Unlike Yanggyap, there were few wild mushrooms here, he said. I proposed that we try to move in the afternoon, but Yonten claimed that there would be nowhere else to camp until we were through the bogs.

Even as we spoke, Pemako's notorious weather descended upon us: mists and pouring rain sent us scurrying back to our tents. We resigned ourselves to spending another day and night in the mist-laced forest, catching up on our journals, meditating, sleeping, and hoping that Todd would quickly recover.

Gunn became very agitated. "If we lose another day you will never make your flight back to Nepal on August 26," he said. "I will have no way of contacting Lhasa to change your reservations. You might lose your tickets." The fact that none of us seemed particularly disturbed by the delay seemed to agitate him all the more.

Once the announcement was made throughout the scattered encampment, Kawa Tulku's attendant appeared at our dining tent where we were finishing breakfast. He put down his oversized prayer wheel and silently began to unwrap his feet, which he had encased in plastic bags and strips of green canvas. Eventually, he revealed a staggering display of swollen, infected blisters in place of toes. We sent him to the stream to wash his feet with soap and doused them afterward with liberal quantities of iodine. He remained completely composed, despite the inevitable pain. "He must have picked up his equanimity from Kawa Tulku," Oy mused.

All our tents were leaking badly, and in the afternoon Hamid and I ventured down the rain-soaked trail to visit Kawa Tulku again in his wooden hovel. The Monpa porters had strung up their tarpaulin from the roof and were huddled around a damp fire, not entirely pleased with the prospect of another day and night in their sodden confines. Kawa Tulku was quietly biding his time reciting mantras and poring over his collection of neyigs. His countenance never lost its quality of joyful repose.

"If from the point of view of ultimate truth, all is empty without any nature of its own, how can Yangsang exist?," I asked him, following up on our discussion of the previous evening.

Kawa Tulku responded in typical Buddhist paradox: "Sunyata, great emptiness, is inconceivable. It neither exists nor does it not exist. It transcends both being and nonbeing."

The doctrine of universal emptiness, or *Sunyata-vada,* that Kawa Tulku was invoking is less a philosophy than a dialectical practice that strips the world and self of every theoretical construction. Just as one cannot say of sunyata that it exists or that it does not exist, Yangsang is neither real nor unreal, but is closer to being a quantum truth that does not itself exist and that simultaneously does not not exist.

Hamid tried a slightly different approach: "Just as bodhisattvas vow to liberate beings that don't in truth exist, the adept searches for a place that he already knows is neither real nor unreal. Is that how it is?"

"Yes," Kawa Tulku said. "That's exactly how it is." He smiled and went back to cutting strips of meat from the dried haunch of mutton that he carried in his bag.

"To doubt Yangsang's existence," he then said, "would be the same as doubting its reality within ourselves," to fall from Vajrayana's sacred outlook.

It seemed to come down to a great leap of faith.

"Is finding the key to Yangsang ultimately just a matter of overcoming all doubts?" I asked Kawa Tulku, hoping for some definitive answer.

Several Tibetans who were sitting nearby were hanging on the lama's every word but attention was suddenly diverted when Christian appeared out of the rain like a wandering friar, the hood of his rain jacket pulled down in front of his bearded face. He sat down on a broken plank next to me and Hamid. "Ever since the porters cut up the bear, I've been eyeing their knives," he announced.

"Not the machetelike knives," he clarified, "but their daggers with the silver scabbards."

At Christian's request, Hamid asked the bedraggled throng of porters if any of them would be willing to sell their knives. The porters' knives were among their most cherished possessions, and they used them for everything from dissecting bears to constructing pack baskets.

Yonten, our phantom guide, slowly took his knife from his leather belt and let Christian inspect it. Like all their knives, its silver alloy sheath was engraved with stylized representations of a tiger and a dragon.

Christian offered Yonten 200 yuan, or roughly $25, for the ten-inch dagger. The other porters talked hushedly among themselves. Yonten looked a bit confused and made a counteroffer: "One hundred yuan!"

Hamid burst out laughing before he had a chance to translate, and Christian looked bewildered. Some of the other porters started slapping Yonten around, but he remained totally perplexed. He turned to Kawa Tulku for arbitration, and the price was finally set at 200 yuan.

Christian pulled out a wad of yuan and, as Yonten carefully counted and re-counted it, the others porters suddenly smelled a good deal. Puntsok, the Khampa with the boar tusk hanging from his neck, pulled out his dagger from beneath the folds of his chuba and handed it to Christian. "Damn!" Christian said "this is nicer than the one I just bought. The silver work is more intricate. The proportions are better. And it doesn't have a rough bolt on the head."

Through Hamid, he asked Puntsok how much he would sell it for. Puntsok looked hesitant, most likely because his knife was an essential tool along the trail. Christian was adamant. "I'll give you four hundred yuan," he said.

Yonten looked worried, thinking perhaps that Christian would ask for his money back. Christian had another idea, however, and proposed it to Puntsok: "I'll pay you two hundred yuan and give you Yonten's knife in place of yours."

Puntsok appeared amenable to the idea, but Yonten sensed he was losing out. He yanked the knife from Christian's hands and extolled its virtues. "The bolt makes it stronger," he said. "The leather strap is better . . ." To the amusement of the entire group, he began to perform various tests to demonstrate the superiority of his knife over Puntsok's, cutting one blade with the other to show which metal was stronger.

Christian tried helplessly to indicate that it was not an issue of the knife's function, but a matter of aesthetics. "They're the same!" Yonten retorted, pointing out the tiger and the dragon. In the end, the other porters were making too much fun of him, and Yonten gave up. Christian handed Yonten's knife to Puntsok and paid him 200 yuan. Yonten retreated under the tarpaulin, thoroughly perplexed.

The Bogs of Paradise

THE FOLLOWING DAY, August 15, Todd was still weak, feverish, and retching from the door of the tent that he shared with his two brothers. The rain hadn't stopped, but as we were short on food, we had to move on. During a brief break in the rain, we put on our neoprene oversocks and nylon gaiters and packed up our tents. The porters shouldered their loads, and we started out across a precarious tree bridge. Afterward we climbed steeply through the tangled roots and branches of enormous rhododendrons with nine-inch leaves. The backs of the leaves were veined in delicate patterns that Yonten claimed were auspicious mantric syllables. Kawa Tulku looked unconvinced.

I dropped behind and let the stillness and silence of the forest envelop me. My breath misted in the saturated air, and I paced myself so that it flowed evenly through my nostrils as my eyes drifted over the spaces between the leaves. Whatever the outcome of the journey across the bogs, we were finally converging on a mountain that I had dreamed about for years—the heart of the goddess.

After two and a half hours, I emerged from the rhododendron forest into the much anticipated Adrathang, literally the flat place shaped like an AH. Indeed, as I walked out into the vast, primeval swamp, the white chalky banks of a river that wound through its center approximated the shape of this most primal of Tibetan syllables. My immediate concerns, however, were to avoid sinking up to my knees in mud and not to lose my way across the bogs which seemed to stretch endlessly into the distance. Fog drifted over the open, marshy expanse, and small streams meandered through the low swamp growth. There was no trail, and the bog seemed to have swallowed the footprints of all who had gone ahead.

The neyigs compare the sedge-filled swamp to Sitavana, or Cool Grove, an ancient charnel ground in India where many Tantric adepts deepened their realization. When I caught up with Christian and Oy, Oy compared it to the Urschleim, the primordial ooze posited by late-nineteenth-century scientists. "Urschleim was the protoplasmic half-living matter from which one-celled organisms first emerged," Oy said, in her Thai-British accent with its the distinctive rolling r's. "It happened more than three thousand million years ago."

Christian suggested that she was thinking about her favorite childhood book, *Uma's Diamond*. He pulled the brim of his hat down over his dye-streaked forehead and plunged forward through the muck, eager to reach the campsite that Yonten said we would find at the far end of the marsh.

THREE HOURS INTO ADRATHANG, the porters stopped at the edge of the swamp to brew tea and to warm themselves by a smoky fire. They pressed ahead in the mist and rain while Hamid, Christian, Oy, and I waited for the three brothers to catch up. The band of siblings looked pale and drawn when they came in off the swamp. Gil and Troy had come down with the same mysterious illness, giving credence to the Kawa Tulku's fears that they would become ill after bathing in the naga pool at Yanggyap Né. They had been vomiting and wanted to rest by the fire. We had to press on, however. Yonten was the single person who knew where we were going and, as usual, he was somewhere far ahead, as he refused to carry a load.

At 3 P.M., we reentered the bog, thinking we would easily locate our campsite at the far end. Very soon, however, we lost the track and became entangled in dense underbrush that seemed to be floating on a layer of brackish water. Even more disturbingly, the marsh appeared to branch out in different directions. The seven of us fanned out to look for signs of the porters, plunging through mud and thigh-high streams. Cold fog and rain lashed across the pale reeds and saturated grass.

By the time we discovered the porters' tracks on the north side of the main river, we were completely soaked. At the crest of a grassy plateau far ahead of us, we saw a line of prayer flags. We assumed that it was the Kangkang Sam-La that Yonten had spoken of and that we would find our camp on the other side of the ridge.

When we arrived at the line of prayer flags, it was raining hard, and there was no sign of our porters or camp. We had no idea which way Yonten and the porters had gone, as footprints and other signs of passage had dissolved in the swamp grass. Had we missed a turnoff? Bhakha Tulku had told me in Kathmandu that the route to the mountain branches off near this pass, and it appeared that a track headed west from the crest of the ridge. But after following it some distance it petered out, and it seemed impossible that our entire regiment of more than thirty pilgrims and porters could have gone that way. Hamid and Oy continued to head south and shouted through the rain that at least some of the porters seemed to have gone that way.

According to my notes from Bhakha Tulku, the route we were now following would lead us not to Kundu, but into Arunachal Pradesh and the territory of the Chulikata Mishmis. Did Yonten know where he was going? Had the Sherpas gone this way?

Todd, Gil, and Troy were lagging far behind, but when we were sure that they had seen the direction we had gone, Hamid, Oy, Christian, and I followed the faint track through the reeds until the swamp suddenly ended and transformed into a narrow rocky chute dropping steeply into a slope of enormous talus. A vast valley of seemingly endless jungle opened below to the south.

"I can't believe the porters have gone on ahead like this," Christian said with a hint of panic. "It's probably Yonten trying to get revenge for the escapade with the knife!"

IT WAS FROM HERE that Hamid and I had planned to break away from the group on our secret mission into the valleys leading toward Yangsang. Alternating currents of dread and exhilaration filled us as we gazed below into the abyss. The mountain was washing away behind us in a veritable deluge, and we slid down slabs with no sense of whether or not we were on the right trail, or even on a trail at all. Our surroundings felt like Pangaea, the primeval supercontinent that incorporated all the earth's major landmasses before they began drifting into their current locations more than two hundred million years ago. After clambering down rocks and sliding down waterways, guided by occasional footprints, we entered a dense tangle of rhododendrons and followed more tracks into the forest.

We doubted strongly that all of the porters, let alone Gunn or Kawa Tulku, had come this way. We began to suspect that we were following only the three Sherpas who had left after the others from our fire at the edge of the swamp. We also suspected that the others had followed a path that we had somehow missed. At this point, however, it was too late to turn back. Our only hope of avoiding hypothermia and a night out in the forest with neither fire nor shelter was to keep going and hope that we could catch up with whoever was in front of us.

We were now in a dense bamboo forest and Oy pointed out clearly demarcated tracks of a Bengal tiger. "This is just the kind of environment they love," she said.

Hamid and I ventured ahead in hopes of catching up with the porters. An hour or more later, Christian came up from behind. With green dye from his hat streaming down his cheeks and forehead, he breathlessly announced that Oy had fallen headfirst off a log while crossing a large stream. The straps on her backpack had caught on a rock and prevented her from being swept down the river, but she was nearly hypothermic. Christian was having flashbacks to the day after crossing the Chimdro Chu. "I can't believe this is happening all over again. I'm drenched. It's getting dark. I'm on a muddy forest trail with no end in sight. We don't know who is ahead of us, or even if we're on a trail at all."

What's more, Christian had seen no sign of the Gillenwaters. "The last time I saw them, they were huddled in the mud and bamboo. They seemed unable to move."

As we debated whether to continue on or go back for the three brothers, Oy appeared out of the bamboo. Her lips were blue and her body was steaming. "I can't believe this! Where's the damn camp!" she yelled in her lilting accent.

We had no food, no shelter, no dry clothes, and no way to make a fire. Our only compass had broken when Christian fell from the trail, landing on his head and wrist. We were not even sure that we were on the right trail. By this time, we were all shivering; a night out without fire or warm clothing would have meant certain hypothermia. We had no choice but to continue on as fast as possible and to overtake whoever was in front of us. Words came to mind from Padmasambhava: "The time has come to recognize that negative circumstances can be transformed into spiritual power and attainment. . . . Utilize adversities and obstacles as the path!"[28]

OUR CIRCUMSTANCES WERE DIRE, yet I felt as oddly peaceful as I had on the journey two years earlier when Ken Storm and I had run out of food and lost all signs of a trail. At a high spot, Hamid yelled ahead into the forest, but the trees immediately muffled his voice. We continued to climb steeply through the forest, our senses alert. As we climbed higher, the trees began thinning and gave some promise of open ground where we might get some sense of our surroundings.

Suddenly, there was a faint smell of smoke. Was it our camp? Christian still doubted that our whole troop could possibly have come along this track, and he imagined that we were about to descend, unannounced, on a Mishmi hunting party. We continued on, and before long we arrived at a primitive wooden shelter. Kawa Tulku and the Monpa porters were there, huddled around a fire. The Sherpas had set up tents just beyond, commandeering the sleeping place of a bear at the base of a gnarled oak tree. Yonten called the place Pongkhang Sapa. The altimeter showed 12,500 feet.

We told Pemba that the Gillenwaters were still somewhere behind, and he immediately arranged for two of the younger Sherpas, Tika and Lhakpa, to search for them. While we huddled around the fire and poured water from our boots, Tika and Lhakpa loaded a tent, sleeping bags, food, and thermoses of hot water into a bamboo pack basket in case they found the brothers but were unable to return.

Just after the two Sherpas headed off into the twilight, Todd miraculously walked into camp. He had recovered from his illness, he said, but Troy and Gil had fallen into a stream and were severely hypothermic.

At 10 P.M., after walking for fourteen hours, Gil and Troy finally trudged into camp with Tika and Lhakpa. Without a word, without eating anything, shivering uncontrollably, they immediately crawled into their sleeping bags. As they walked by, gaunt and exhausted, Kawa Tulku looked up as if in surprise and said, "Oh, they didn't die."

The Outer Kora

DAWN BROUGHT THE PROMISE of lifting clouds. Yonten, our phantom guide, also had welcome news.

"It's not far now to the base of Kundu," he promised, "only four or five hours." I asked him to pace himself with the slowest in the group, but before we had finished breakfast he had already disappeared ahead.

All three of the Gillenwater brothers had vomitted intermittently throughout the night. It wasn't clear whether their symptoms were only those of hypothermia or, as the Tibetans maintained, an illness caused by bathing in the naga pool at Yanggyap. As the rest of us were completely healthy, it seemed unlikely that it was caused by anything that they had eaten, unless it was something from their own private stock.

Gil, Troy, and Todd started out early, knowing that they would be slow, but hoping to keep up with the first wave of porters. Not long afterward, the rest of us began climbing up the trail, following the left bank of a roaring cataract. As we entered a zone of scrub rhododendrons, I turned a corner and found the Gillenwaters sitting on a rock and looking pale and exhausted. They asked me to send back a Sherpa with their tent and sleeping bags in case they weren't able to make it all the way to camp.

Yonten had disappeared after making his pronouncement that we would camp that night at a lake beneath Kundu Dorsempotrang and begin the kora the following day. Yonten's estimates of time and distance had been sketchy throughout the trip, and none of us had any real sense of how long the day would be or where we would actually camp. Christian was convinced he was winging it. "How can we put faith in time estimates from a man who has never in his life owned a watch, or even thought in terms of hours and minutes?" Christian asked.

As we climbed higher through the scrub to catch up with the Sherpas, we passed several small lakes and eventually crossed a grassy ridge at 14,000 feet. The clouds had lifted and from the top of the pass we could look northward toward an extraordinary mountain with a summit like a black anvil with two lakes wrapped around its lower slopes. Bailey had referred to Kundu Dorsempotrang as "a slender snow peak rising into the clouds," but the mountain I was looking at was solid rock. Was this the mountain that we had come so far to see, the jewel in the heart of Dorje Pagmo? We had pursued it like a femme fatale into the depths of the Tibetan wilderness, only to be struck with uncertainty when we finally saw it.

Clouds had formed, and the peak disappeared and reappeared as if in a dream, each time looking slightly different. "It looks like a black castle," Oy declared. Hamid thought it looked more like a Buddhist reliquary box. Soon it disappeared altogether in the swirling clouds. If it was Kundu Dorsempotrang we had circled far to the south of it. And the lake where Yonten had said we would camp looked very far away.

We crossed the ridge and followed a worn track leading away from the mountain that we had seen through the clouds. Perhaps it wasn't Kundu after all. We had still not caught up with the Sherpas and although we were above treeline on a definable path I was worried about the Gillenwaters. As I dropped down a steep slope beneath overhanging rocks, I came around a corner and saw in the distance that the Sherpas had set up our tents at the edge of a small pond beneath overhanging cliffs. I also saw a line of porters climbing up the ridge beyond.

When I reached the tents, I asked Pemba what was happening. The Sherpas had reached the small body of water and, in consideration of the Gillenwaters, had tried to convince Yonten to camp there, but he had refused. Unless we reached a shelter several hours farther on, he told Pemba, we wouldn't reach the mountain the following day. Concerned at his own dwindling food supplies, Kawa Tulku had gone with him. Gunn became anxious that we would lose the only ones who knew the way and possibly be further delayed. He had gone racing after them.

Our party was unraveling along the trail. The trying circumstances and lack of clear communication from Yonten were pushing everyone's limits. None of the porters at the Sherpas' camp had any idea where the mountain lay. As concerned as I was about the Gillenwaters, I knew that if we lost Yonten we might well founder in the wilderness.

Christian and Oy stayed back to wait for Gil, Troy, and Todd. Although it was already pushing 5 P.M., Hamid and I started out with the two Monpas who were carrying our gear and climbed up beneath the cliffs to another 14,000-foot ridge. When we reached the top we were puzzled to find that the trail swung away even farther to the west—away from the mountain that we had thought might be Kundu Dorsempotrang. If it was the holy mountain, we were clearly circling it on an extensive outer kora.

The Tibetan word for pilgrimage, né-kor, means to circle around a sacred site and, throughout the Buddhist world—from the Jokhang in Lhasa to revered features of the landscape—pilgrims seek religious merit by performing koras around places or objects that they consider holy. Guided by an intuition that the sacred cannot be approached in a straight line, still less by linear thought, pilgrims emulate the path of the sun and circumambulate in a clockwise direction, beginning as we had from the east.

Yonten had mentioned that the outer kora around Kundu takes several days to complete. The inner kora, he said, takes only one day. According to the Kundu neyig, a single circuit of the mountain yields the same merit as thirteen koras of Pemako as a whole. Thirteen circuits around the mountain are held to establish one at the thirteenth bhumi, the level of a realized bodhisattva—perhaps something akin to the lines of poetry by Wallace Stevens in which he writes: "and round and round, the merely going round / Until merely going round is a final good . . ."

Because of time, we had stressed to Yonten the importance of heading to the mountain directly and foregoing the lengthy outer kora, but Yonten clearly had no intention of breaking the protocol. By tradition, a pilgrim must first successfully complete the outer kora before attempting an inner one. I now better understood why Yonten had been so vague when it came to estimating distances and why we had headed south at the end of the Adrathang marshes rather than directly west. I also understood why we hadn't yet reached the mountain.

There was no sign of those who had gone ahead of us. As we were unsure of the route, we followed the natural contours of the landscape and followed the high ridges that seemed to inscribe the mountain that we were now quite sure must be Kundu. It stood far off to the northeast like a dark sentinel, its summit a perfect horizontal block.

The skies had cleared, revealing lush ravines and slopes of silver-green grass that were drenched with pink, yellow, and blue flowers. High snow peaks rose in the distance into the evening sky. As we turned northward, the glacial massif of Namcha Barwa seemed to fill the horizon, its 25,436-foot summit turning purple and gold as the sun set over the horizon.

We had walked quickly, but despite our efforts we had seen nothing of Yonten, Gunn, or the lama except for occasional footprints. And now, as night fell, it became harder to follow their trail. Six hours after we had left the Sherpas, we began to descend toward a lake at the bottom of a deep valley in the hope that we would find the advance party camped along its shore.

When we reached the lake, we called out into the darkness, but there was no sign of Yonten or the others. We continued by flashlight along the water's edge and saw footprints that entered a bog as dismal as Adrathang. With wavering batteries, we trudged on through what all of Pemako had begun to seem—a vast, primeval swamp. If the ultimate purpose of pilgrimage was, as Bhakha Tulku had said before our departure, to move deeper into the equanimity of the heart, we still had a long way to go.

Hamid's flashlight batteries had given out and mine were about to, and we hastened our steps through the marsh. After some time we saw a brief flash of light far ahead of us that disappeared again as quickly as it had come. Gradually the light appeared like a distant campfire. But as we stumbled forward, multiple fires suddenly flared across the horizon as if the entire mountainside had been set on fire. The fires vanished again just as quickly. The two porters from Chimdro stopped short, staring into the blackness. Suddenly they began reciting prayers.

As the fires across our field of vision continued to appear and disappear, we had no idea what we were up against. In Tibetan tradition, such seemingly magical occurences attend the *ganachakra*, or Tantric feasts presided over by dakinis. In our exhaustion no more plausible explanation for the strange lights came to mind. All four of us began reciting protective mantras until, deeper into the marsh, we suddenly realized that we were approaching one of the primitive pilgrims' shelters whose locations had defined the length of our days. The light from the central fire had filtered through the wooden slats and created an optical illusion. We felt somewhat foolish for succumbing to the mirage. Kawa Tulku, sitting by the fire, gave us a knowing smile. Yonten called the place Shula Pongkhang. The altitude was just over 13,000 feet.

As we settled by the fire to dry our boots, Gunn announced that he had decided to bypass the mountain and travel directly toward Medok, the Chinese administrative center and army post in the lower Tsangpo gorge. He could contact his head office from there, Gunn announced. He would leave early the following morning with Zang and one of Yonten's men. "We are very late," Gunn said. "I will have problems when I reach there." Before we left Chimdro, Kawa Tulku had expressed concern about Chinese visiting the sacred mountain, and he now sat contentedly by the hearth, silently reciting mantras.

ON THE MORNING OF AUGUST 17, I left a note by the fire pit, informing those trailing behind us of Gunn's decision to go directly to Medok and of ours to continue on to Kundu Dorsempotrang with Yonten and Kawa Tulku. Yonten assured us that we would reach the base of the mountain that day, but as he'd given the same estimate for three straight days, no one got overly excited.

With Gunn's departure, our expedition had separated into three independent groups. The fate of those behind us was uncertain, but our own core group had been distilled to me, Hamid, and the lama. Along with Hamid's and my two porters, Yonten, and Kawa Tulku's attendants, we started out through high-altitude marshes that were punctuated frequently by large, unusual shaped rocks that had been marked with prayer flags. Following Kawa Tulku's lead, we circumambulated each of them three times to ensure a favorable reception by Kundu's guardian spirits.

We soon had our first clear vision of the mountain that we had been circling for days. Far from the tall slender snow peak that we had initially expected, Kundu rose in front of us like a black, tectonic obelisk of ophiolite rock, thrust up from ancient sediments of the seabed from which Tibet had formed.

Kundu reminded me of the mountain in Norway where, at the age of fourteen, I had first learned to climb, a cylindrical tower of dark, lichen-covered granite with a waterfall flowing from its slopes into a lake dotted with mossy, birch-covered islands. Eight years later, on a return visit, I'd fallen from its heights.

Days after being released from the hospital, a red pulsating lotus appeared on the ceiling above my bed and I felt that I was being pulled through a door into another reality. I was rushed back to the hospital with a blood clot in my heart. I had been ambivalent about the return to life. The fall had left me shattered, and death held a strong attraction. Ultimately, though, my wounds initiated a journey into a richer life and unsought visions in which boundaries between worlds seemed only habits of thought. As much as I resisted these eruptions from my subconscious, I began to think of mountains, rivers, and finally myself, in different terms, so that when I went to Sikkim, the stories of the beyul had resonated deeply.

WE DESCENDED THROUGH a rhododendron forest where a few trees were still in bloom and entered a meadow teeming with lilies, begonias, lavender, and wild ginger. Yonten found some wild rhubarb and soon we were all sucking on the stalks. After crossing through more marshland, we reached the edge of the lake that we had seen from a distance the day before. Kundu rose directly above us, its summit hidden by cliffs and forest. Yonten told us of a shelter higher up the mountain and, after staking a note to a tree for those who were behind us, we began the climb toward the inner kora.

We climbed steeply through a forest of rhododendrons. Leopard prints abounded in the soft earth. As we rose higher, the forest abruptly ended and we found ourselves above the tree line looking at a row of ghostly prayer flags waving in the misty wind. A simple, unwalled shelter sat on a tiny plateau jutting out from the steep slope. Yonten called it Osel Pongkhang, the Shelter of Clear Light. Perched at nearly 13,000 feet, it would be our base camp for the circuit around Kundu.

Beneath the roof of the shelter, a lone Monpa yogi sat by a small fire, turning a prayer wheel in one hand and counting mantras on a string of beads on the other. A row of butter lamps burned on a simple altar. Small prayer flags hung down from the beams. A blackened tea kettle sat on a rock beside him. With his thick woollen chuba and penetrating eyes he looked like an emanation of Kinthup, the legendary surveyor spy that the British government had dispatched to the Tsangpo gorge in 1881.

The yogi indicated with hand gestures that he had undertaken a vow of silence. Kawa Tulku set up his tent beneath the prayer flags. Hamid and I rolled out our sleeping bags on the earthen floor of the shelter and after a quick bowl of tsampa retired early in anticipation of the inner kora that we would begin the following day.

The Heart of the Goddess

WHEN WE WOKE AT FIRST LIGHT, Kawa Tulku had already departed. To maximize the merit, he'd resolved to circle the peak three times and needed to make an early start. Hamid's and my zeal for merit was countered by our desire to experience the mountain at a slower pace. We had decided to go on our own. Before heading out, we asked the yogi-in-residence for hot water from his kettle.

The mute hermit had not accompanied the lama because of an injured foot. With the hilt of his prayer wheel imbedded in the ground, he watched intently as Hamid took out some small, bluish bits of organic matter from a plastic bag. It was the psilocybin that we had harvested several days earlier from its mycilium bed. Although neither of us had consumed anything similar since college (my roommate and I had tried unsuccessfully to grow them in canning jars in our dorm room closet), we had decided to eat a small amount before beginning the kora.

As we washed down the decomposing mushrooms with the hermit's tea, he put out his hand, indicating that he would like to share whatever it was we had so carefully ingested. Hamid explained that the small mushrooms are akin to the revered but ever-elusive plant *tsakuntuzangpo*. They can induce visions, but not necessarily pleasant ones, Hamid told him. The yogi became even more eager. You might see demons, Hamid warned him. Or get sick. The yogi stretched out both of his hands insistently. Hamid and I looked at each other and realized that we had no choice but to allow him to share in our experiment. Hamid measured out a small portion onto the yogi's blackened palm. He washed them down with tea and, with a big grin on his face, went back to spinning his prayer wheel.

THE KUNDU NEYIG DESCRIBES six distinct regions, or *lings*, encircling the mountain like petals of a lotus and demarcated by lakes and intervening rock ridges. In Tibetan sacred geography, mountains and rocks represent the structural, or masculine component of a landscape. Streams and bodies of water express the feminine element. Kundu's six lings unite form and essence and enfolded within lie six additional "secret regions," perceivable only to illuminated adepts. Each of the lings, the neyig claims, contains undiscovered termas. One of them contains the key to Yangsang. The mountain as a whole represents the heart essence of Dorje Pagmo, the great goddess of Pemako.

Hamid and I left the shelter and followed a trail up a series of crude log ladders through a landscape of mist, rocks, and tumbling streams. After an hour, we reached the edge of a placid, cloud-enveloped lake. This was the Kundu Lhatso, the All-Gathering Essence Lake, and the first of the six lings. "Whoever washes and drinks from this lake," the neyig informed us, "can purify lifetimes of karmic defilements and pacify the obstacles and disturbances of this life."

Where the water flowed from the lake into a series of small waterfalls, we drank deeply and splashed ourselves in the clear, transparent water. Our ablutions over, we began contouring around the Lhatso on a faint track at the water's edge, passing between a tiger and a peacock-shaped rock held to be the doorkeepers of the first ling. Suddenly, a tunnel opened in the mists and—like a door opening into Avalon—revealed a snowfield clinging to black cliffs on the far side of the lake. A moment later, Kundu's square summit block appeared out of the swirling clouds. The entire mountain towered out of the tranquil lake like a majestic altar.

A cluster of prayer flags hung from bamboo poles at the top of a rise, and we meditated there, gazing into the mists. The mountain came in and out of view, its polyhedral summit swallowed by clouds only to appear again in its reflection in the black waters of the lake. It seemed like the long-sought *lapis philosophorum* of medieval alchemists, the jewel that would allow them to see into other dimensions of time and space.

According to the *Guide to the Heart Center: The All-Gathering Palace of Vajrasattva that Liberates upon Seeing*, a secret, black-bodied form of the wisdom goddess emanates from the center of the Kundu Lhatso with a retinue of dakinis while surrounding rock formations represent Padmasambhava in eight varying manifestations. Unlike most neyigs, the *Guide to the Heart Center* is not a terma, but was authored by a shaman-yogi from Powo named Pawo Orgyen Chongon. After Dudrul Dorje and the three knowledge holders (*vidyadharas*) of the hidden-land—Rigdzin Dorje Thokme, Orgyen Dudrul Lingpa, and Kunsang Ozer Chimey Dorje—first opened Kundu as a pilgrimage site in the eighteenth century, the way had been lost. In popular accounts Pawo Orgyen rediscovered it by following a takin that led him along the kora path. Possessed of supernatural powers, Pawo Orgyen communicated directly with Kundu's protector spirits and—in departure from customary Buddhist practice—had climbed to the summit to place a banner of victory.

In *Guide to the Heart Center*, Pawo Orgyen Chongon writes how each of the three knowledge holders of the hidden-land had perceived the mountain as Tantric deities in ecstatic embrace with their consorts. Representing the dynamic synergy of form and essence their alchemical passion gives rise to forty-two peaceful and fifty-eight wrathful deities (*shidro*), freeing those who can perceive them from the blinders of conventional vision. "The most fortunate beings will see Padmasambhava and the deities directly," Pawo Orgyen writes. "Others will hear their voices. Ordinary beings will see only earth and rock."

Modern science's mechanistic conception of nature has generally been taken for granted as the basis for any realistic experience of the world. Contemporary physics and depth psychology both reveal, however, that this assumption, and the dualistic worldview it supports, is ultimately a selective construct of the human mind, conditioned by its own unconscious processes. In its passage through a landscape lush with symbols, the inner kora represents a movement inward toward a more participatory and empathic consciousness in which imagination reveals forms of awareness and layers of reality hidden to the objectifying mind. The Tantric pilgrim familiar with the meditative rite of *Tromo Nagmo* (in Sanskrit, *Krohakali*)—the three-eyed goddess issuing from Kundu's essence-lake—invites her to sever his or her head and transform it into a skull bowl in which she distills his or her dismembered body into enlightening nectar which she bestows to spirits of earth, air, fire, and water. Freed of an egoistic reference point, and radiant with fearless compassion, the pilgrim recognizes his or her essential being as no different from that of the goddess. Adorned with anklets of snakes, flaming hair, and a skull garland of outmoded thought forms, the pilgrim continues the journey through the black rocks and waters of the sacred mountain, converging on the pristine, unobstructed consciousness of the heart.

On a fundamental level, the world conforms to our inner vision, just as chemicals that bind with certain receptors in the brain alter how we see. Pilgrimage, in this sense, becomes a journey from ordinary perception into full consciousness of our interpretive role in determining reality, to recognize, as Padmasambhava states, that "all phenomenon are, in essence, the magical display of mind." As we contoured through the green-black metamorphic rocks, we witnessed suggestive shapes of sinuous goddesses and sign letters in the secret language of dakinis. In distinction from the prosaic descriptions of science, in which words are confined to a single, precisely rendered meaning—the hermeneutic descriptions of the neyigs invite simultaneous levels of perception. Through a poetic mode of thought and communication that Thomas Mann referred to as moon grammar, they urge the pilgrim to see beneath the surface manifestations of the landscape into an open dimension, not unlike the implicate order of quantum physics, in which all is interconnected, luminous, and unbound—a primal matrix beyond the grasp of objectifying consciousness.

The tryptamine alkaloids of the mushrooms had seeped into our cells but revealed no more than what was already present, dissolving what Aldous Huxley had called the "cerebral reducing valve" that shuts out perceptions not required for biological survival. As we skirted Kundu's western wall, the path swelled and opened beneath our feet and a lush radiance emanated from the boulders that lined the trail. Sections of the rock had been worn smooth by the hands and foreheads of passing pilgrims. Other depressions represented the body prints of early tertons.

The neyigs, it could be argued, fictionalize the landscape as much as they reveal it, but we were willing sojourners through the mytho-poetic terrain. The neyigs were keys to a topography that in turn required further keys—a landscape of the heart beyond divisions of perceiver and perceived where pilgrims imagine themselves into a larger existence.

We entered a cave that sloped upward into a narrowing fissure. Faded prayer flags hung from bits of string. Offerings of rice and copper coins lay on tiny ledges on the rock wall. Was this a portal into the heart? The texts mentioned two tunnels: a Bardo Path representing a symbolic journey from one life to the next and a Liberation Path signifying spiritual rebirth. Eager pilgrims had worn the rock smooth, but we could find no way through. Not knowing the ritual protocol, I made a small offering and placed my head into the dark crack to receive whatever the mountain would offer in return. Like all Tibetan pilgrimage circuits, Kundu's inner kora offered numerous opportunities for dissolving the *sgrib*, or obscuring, psycho-physical shadows that veil the full expanse of earth and psyche, and for experiencing the *chinlap*, or flood of power, that issues from sacred sites.

The *Guide to the Heart Center* stipulates that in order not to disturb Kundu's energies, one cannot urinate or even spit except at two designated spots on the kora, marked by cairns. We hadn't yet located one, and to avoid any potential calamity Hamid had peed into a spare water bottle. Accounts of offended guardian spirits proliferate in Pemako. Bhakha Tulku had told us a story about a prince in Powo who, due to his position, had thought himself exempt from the usual protocol. He had urinated where he wasn't supposed to and was immediately crushed by a boulder. "The hardships you've endured coming to this place should not be wasted by incautious behavior," the neyig adds. "What should be a cause of virtue and happiness should not turn into a cause of suffering."

AS WE MADE OUR WAY around the mountain we climbed toward the rim of what seemed like a crater; mist billowed up from the third ling, the Valley of the Dakinis. Before entering Khandro Ling, we stopped to eat on the rocky precipice, where I took out my one gourmet delicacy: a tin of alligator meat that my sister had given to me the previous Christmas. We consumed it along with *chyawanaprash*, an Ayurvedic concoction made from more than forty different herbs.

After finishing our meal, we descended over the ridge into the Valley of the Dakinis. As we threaded our way through fields of boulders, the landscape opened into an abyss of swamps and vast gulfs. Spring water bubbled up from the sloping ground and drifted in small streams amid towering rocks. There was no clear trail, and Hamid and I wandered along separate routes, heading for a pass that would lead us to the next ling.

As I wove through the undulating landscape, mists curled through the rocks and gave shape to the saturated air. Birds with glossy blue-black wings danced on slabs of rock, veering around me in close circles. The mist condensed into a shimmering drizzle. I followed intermittent piles of rocks that indicated what I hoped was a trail.

Hamid had contoured lower down on the mountain, and I hadn't seen him for the last hour. When I called out there was no response, only muffled echoes off the walls of mist. I climbed higher to the top of a large boulder and called again. Like elsewhere in Pemako, the slightest deviation from the marginal paths—even here where there were no trees—could mean disappearing altogether. Had the siren calls of dakinis led him to other realms?

I was fairly certain that I was now on a route of sorts and that I was headed toward the pass leading to the fourth ling. Perhaps the route that Hamid was following would converge there from the marshes below. When I reached the rock cairn that marked the pass, I called out in the mist and heard a faint voice far below me. We continued a dialogue of calls, but Hamid's grew ever fainter. Perhaps he was convinced that he was on the right track and that I would descend.

As rain poured down ever harder, I waited by the cairn where a near-vertical spur curved upward into the clouds. I wondered whether this was the ridge that the shaman from Powo, Pawo Orgyen Chongon, had reputedly followed to the summit to place his banner of victory. The rock looked thoroughly unclimbable.

As I waited at the pass, Kawa Tulku appeared out of the mists along with Yonten and his attendants. They were midway on their second circuit around the mountain. Not long after, Hamid emerged from his adventures in the Valley of the Dakinis, his eyes wide and blazing. A few minutes later, Christian also appeared out of the fog banks with a retinue of porters-turned-pilgrims. The self-effacing nun trailed behind them, quietly mumbling to herself and carrying a glass jar filled with water and herbs that she had collected along the trail.

CHRISTIAN GAVE A QUICK REPORT of what had happened over the last several days. Todd had largely recovered from his illness, but Gil and Troy had not been able to hold down food or water for the past forty-eight hours. They'd resorted to an exclusive diet of Gummi Bears, Christian told us, and had camped by the lake beneath the mountain to recover their strength.

Christian was determined to do the inner kora, he said, and had set a fast pace from Shula Pongkhang, the shelter in the marshes. He'd lit out ahead of the others and found the note that we had staked to the tree by the lake. I had written that Hamid and I had gone ahead with Kawa Tulku to complete the kora, and that if they could not make it up the mountain, we would meet them at the campsite by the lake on our way back down. For a moment Christian had been dismayed. "Not to reach the object of one's journey would be exasperating under any circumstance," Christian wrote in his journal, "but [the kora around Kundu] means far more to me now than . . . an abstract notion in a foreign mythology. If pilgrimage for Tibetans is a spiraling path drawing you ever nearer to a place of great significance, both physical and of the mind, then for me it has become something similar; if I came on this trip mostly out of a desire for adventure, something else is facing me here . . . I came to escape the comfort and routine of an urban, working life; [and] through the challenging conditions I've come to . . . understand very well the true meaning of those wrathful forces said to roam these hidden lands. If you are not 'pure' of mind, if your intentions are petty and selfish, the perilous circumstances will get the better of you. I was drawn here by the lure of the unknown, but it is revealing the unknown within me, and I've become a true pilgrim too."

OY HAD CAUGHT UP WITH CHRISTIAN at the lake and, although they both felt badly about leaving the Gillenwaters behind, they decided to continue on up the mountain. They left another note for the three brothers and began the ascent to the House of Clear Light with two of the Sherpas.

Christian raced ahead. When he reached the shelter, he was surprised to find a total stranger sitting by the fire in meditation posture. "From the looks of him he's a monk, and he's either in deep meditation or he is fast asleep," Christian wrote in his journal. "I'm kind of shocked by his presence; he is the first person we've encountered in all this time on the trail. He sits by the smoky fire in lotus postion, holding his prayer bead necklace. . . . The monk stirs as I put down my pack. . . . He doesn't seem at all surprised though by my presence, and he continues rocking back and forth, counting his beads and reciting mantras. He greets me with a slow, wide grin. I try in vain to ask him what time the others left, a difficult concept to explain when using only hands and feet. In reply he just nods gently and smiles even more broadly."

Despite the clouds that had engulfed the peak, Christian headed off with six of the Tibetans—including the one he called Humphrey Bogart—who had followed him up the trail and were as determined as he was to make the circuit. Freed of their loads, the Tibetans leaped from boulder to rocky ledge as Christian struggled to keep pace. The porters stripped to their waists at the first stream and cleansed themselves of accumulated grime. At the cluster of prayer flags by the lake, they had prostrated themselves before the holy peak and prayed and meditated. Some had written on small scraps of paper which they left under rocks at the edge of the water. One made an offering of a cob of corn that Christian confessed to coveting. It was the first nondehydrated vegetable he had seen in weeks.

At the back of the wedge-shaped cave where I'd stuck my head, they'd reached into the narrow opening and came back with their fingers covered in a gold-colored dirt that they examined for signs. They had collected water from every stream—the heart nectar of Dorje Pagmo—scooping it into glass bottles with small green leaves of a particular plant that they added to the mingled waters. They had hurried on until they saw Kawa Tulku ahead of them through a break in the clouds.

The Key in the Wall

KAWA TULKU SAT ON A ROCK in the rain, smiling his characteristic smile, his bamboo walking stick resting against his thigh and his umbrella perched over his shoulder. The porters who had arrived with Christian filed by to receive his blessing—a perfunctory tap on their heads.

Kawa Tulku had already completed one kora around the mountain. The cairn where we sat marked the border between the third ling, the Valley of the Dakinis, and the fourth ling, the Valley of the Prophecy, *Lungten Ling*. Kawa Tulku said that we would soon be reaching the site said to conceal the *dimi*, or key, to Yangsang.

Long before the trip began, the enigma of the key had worked in my mind like a Zen koan. What is it that unlocks the innermost secret? Why had Chonyi Rinpoche, Bhakha Tulku, and other lamas insisted that I journey to Kundu before descending deeper into the gorge and the region of the suspected waterfall?

During a solitary meditation retreat at Taktsang, the Tiger's Nest sanctuary in Bhutan, my first Tibetan teacher, Dudjom Rinpoche, had visions of the innermost secret heart of Pemako. A rectangular rock had appeared containing the mystic key to Yangsang, but due to lack of *tendrel*, or auspicious circumstances, he was not able to open it. Was it this summit block of Kundu Dorsempotrang that he had seen in his mind's eye?

Chatral Rinpoche and Bhakha Tulku had both told me that the key refers to a concealed terma—a ritual object, text, or teaching, whether in the mind or hidden in rock, that would open a path to the heart of the beyul. But the door would only open, they had assured me, to one whose awareness had fully ripened through meditation and the practices of the inner yogas.

On our journey toward the mountain, Kawa Tulku had spoken of Yangsang as a mysterious interworld between the mind and physical reality. To reach it, he implied, is not simply a matter of decoding the neyigs; it involves a transformation of vision, recognizing external appearances as mutable apparitions of consciousness. Circling the mountain was clearly a process of entering this new awareness. The essence lake, the cave, the marshes, the cliffs all offered fulcrums where perception could turn to revelation and open the gates to some previously inaccessible space, whether within the outer landscape or the mind.

IT POURED RAIN AS WE SAT amid the rocks waiting for everyone to assemble, mist curling around our limbs. We started out from the pass across narrow ledges at the base of Kundu's western face and entered the fourth ling. Rocks plunging into the depths below punctuated the deep silence. Far beneath us, the pale outline of a lake emerged fleetingly through the mist. This is the lake of Dorje Pagmo, Kawa Tulku said, before the mists reclaimed it from our sight. The clouds condensed until we could see no more than thirty feet in front of us. I followed the lama through a world narrowed to shifting mists and the dark, basaltic walls of rock that loomed above us.

Kundu's western wall gradually formed into a steep slab laced with rain water. Kawa Tulku suddenly began climbing directly toward its base. He was breathing heavily, and his mantras seemed to take shape in the mist in front of him. The slab rose through the watery air and diffused into bright clouds several hundred feet above. With the water streaming across its surface, the rock seemed more acqueous than solid. Green, red, and yellow trails of lichen formed patterns like an unknown script. "This is the place," Kawa Tulku said.

I looked up through the mists at the glistening slabs; waters coursed down the rock and rose again as vapors. "Where?" I asked.

He pointed 100 feet up to where the lichen had etched scriptlike patterns across the wall. "There," he said, "the place of the key."

BHAKHA TULKU HAD DESCRIBED THE KEY to Yangsang as some kind of crucial dream, vision, or meditative experience that would arise symbiotically

with the landscape and open the door to more subtle dimensions. "The door to these other realms opens rarely," Bhakha Tulku had said. "When it does you must be ready." Was there a terma, or some key experience, hidden on the wall of rock above that could unlock the secrets the beyul?

The Tibetans had already begun to ascend a series of small ledges leading across the yellowish, lichen-covered slab. When they reached a point where the holds seemed to dissolve into a blank wall, they stood still and faced the rock. I watched through the mists as they slowly descended again the way they had come. Chimey Gompo, the scar-faced Tibetan from Powo, stayed the longest on the tiny ledge. Others returned impassive. Had they got it, I wondered? This elusive key or subtle instruction without which one can proceed no farther?

Kawa Tulku headed up toward the cliff in his rain-drenched woolen chuba. A large stone lay at the base of the wall and, like the others before him, he lifted it three times and placed it back on the earth. Leaving his bamboo staff against the side of the cliff, he started up the thin ledges in his rubber boots. Despite his girth, he ascended the diagonal line with the ease of a takin until he reached the point where the slab rose upward like a smooth granite wave. I watched through the veils of mist as he stood facing the rock and imagined the mantras that he was reciting; I half expected that the rock would open and that he would descend with some golden key. But after only a few minutes he began his descent along the moss-covered fissures. I had reached the base of the rock myself, and as he made the last steps down to the saturated ground I asked whether he had found the key. He smiled enigmatically, as if to ask: Do you really think there is something material there to be found?

I began climbing up the slab. I was surprised that, though streaming with water, it offered good friction. Two Khampas had stayed above at a critical point to help the lama over a tricky section, and they stood there now to help others. I moved up through the thinning ledges until I came to the lichen patterns on the rock wall. I let my eyes drift over the tiny crystalline protrusions that composed the rock. From below it had seemed as smooth as a mirror, but closer inspection revealed a microscopic landscape of valleys and ridges, a conglomerate of the upthrust of millions of years of subterranean forces. Lichen, a primeval organism formed from the union of algae and fungi, had taken root on the rock, nurtured by mist and light.

Instinctively, I sought out small protrusions by which to ascend farther into the brightening mists. Perhaps if I could reach a point above the others, I thought, something hidden would be revealed. I stood higher on small holds until they ended in a blank wall stretching ever upward.

I watched the mental graspings that cause us to miss what is right before us by seeking what is always just out of reach. In my climbing days, I had meditated on ledges halfway up cliffs, emptying my mind of thoughts and conceptions before embarking on the next pitch. And I stilled my mind now. Whatever was to be revealed on the cliff would not come by exceeding my reach or through the peregrinations of my mind, but by remaining receptive.

The rock felt thin and insubstantial, as if the mind's habits of perception were all that obscured its deeper strata. Soon there was only breath and mist. My eyes opened to the growth of fungi and algae that flowed across the crystal extrusions and beneath the water streaming down the slab. The suggestive scriptlike shapes of lichen that weave across the surface of leaves and rocks and reflect the unique energies of particular places are often said to reveal the location of termas. I held my hands open against the rock.

The mist, the rain, the rock wall, the vegetal growth, the microorganisms veiled from sight, all entered through the pulsations and cuts in my scratched and torn hands, and where I could not go I could only yield and be entered. The rain poured down my sleeves and neck and along my spine. The elements saturated me. All Pemako seemed to coalesce into the square foot of rock directly before me, and all its hidden depths were concealed only by my limited awareness and the mechanisms of mind itself.

The surface of the rock seemed to be turning to water beneath my touch and my vision began to waver and become porous, like a veil lifting. I felt at the edge of something just out of reach, but even as this thought intruded the feeling passed, and I was again standing against the rock, now aware that a small misstep would send me plummeting into empty space.

IN THE TERMA TRADITION, spiritual treasures often remain hidden until the terton unites with a consort who serves to open the subtle channels through which ordinary perception transforms into revelation, receiving through surrender what the mind can never grasp. Visualizing his paramour as a land of infinite promise and experiencing her eyes like the sun and moon and her limbs like celestial continents, the terton embraces the entire universe. In an unimpeded flow of energies larger than self or other, doors open into the hiddenlands of the heart that, like Yangsang, exist only in potential until realized in the fullest, fearless, unbounded expanse of one's innermost being, beyond the productions of intellect or faith or divisions between what's external and what's internal. In the full openness of the unknown there are neither curtains nor doors, still less a need for any key. For the key is the surrender itself, and yearning for it elsewhere only seals the doors. As T. S. Eliot wrote in *The Waste Land:* "Thinking of the key, each confirms a prison."

WE WALKED ON THROUGH the enveloping mist, as thunder rumbled over the peak above. Having passed the climax of the pilgrimage, we came to a sanctioned urinal, marked by a pile of stones. Lifting up the multiple layers of his robes, Kawa Tulku relieved himself into the great beyond. Hamid emptied out the water bottle that he had filled earlier when he couldn't hold it in any longer.

Christian considered this a theological dilemma. "Strictly speaking, isn't that cheating, Hamid? Maybe you've been causing this bad weather."

We ascended a fifty-foot cliff, which tradition dictates that one climb without using one's hands. When my balance faltered I leaned against the cliff, grinning at the absurdity of the mission. Christian scrambled up using all four limbs, having decided that it was better to invoke the ire of the goddess than to fall to his death.

At the top of the cliff we came to a small grassy platform at 14,500 feet that marked the border between the Valley of the Prophecy and Trakpo Kagye Ling, a region associated with eight wrathful Tantric deities. A lone prayer flag hung languidly beside a giant cube-shaped boulder. The very moment the last of the porters pulled themselves up onto the platform, bolt of lightning seared through the clouds. The sky behind the boulder lit up brilliantly, illuminating us like a scene from some Wagnerian opera.

Kawa Tulku was clearly unsettled by the synchrony. Christian worried out loud that his disregard for local protocol in ascending the short cliff had angered Kundu's protector spirits. Hurriedly—we had become human lightning rods now—we descended from the electricity-saturated ledge into the fifth ling.

In less than half an hour the trail opened into a grassy meadow encompassing a house-sized boulder draped with faded prayer flags. A worn track circled around the giant rock, which widened sharply from its base to create a natural overhang that proved welcome when the rain turned into a violent hailstorm and we gathered under its shelter.

After the volley of hail had passed, Christian continued on with the porters and Hamid and I stayed back with Kawa Tulku. Circling the rock thirteen times is held to equal one kora around the entire mountain, Kawa Tulku told us. In accord with the arcane mathmatics of Tibetan pilgrimage, Kawa Tulku was eager to make up for the third kora that, due to the lateness in the day, he would not be able to complete. Hamid and I resolved to do the equivalent of two full koras around the mountain, twenty-six circuits around the monolithic rock.

As we circled the boulder, the sky opened and shafts of sunlight perforated the clouds. A luminous thunderhead took shape over the lake at the base of the ling. Like a sculpture emerging from a block of marble, the full shape of Kundu, including the boxlike summit block, appeared as a reflection in the clouds of vapor rising from the lake. Kawa Tulku stood entranced.

AT 7 P.M., WE STARTED DOWN through the sixth and final section of the kora—Pagmo Drodrul Ling. As we wound through a passage between the rocks, Oy appeared in front of us in her green Gore-Tex jacket. Undeterred by rain, hail, or thunder, and in her usual good spirits, she had chosen not to attempt the kora but to explore the mountain in her own way. She had wandered about not really knowing where she was or where she was headed. "I slipped through a kind of keyhole," she said from beneath the hood of her parka.

When she reached the lake beneath Kundu's northern wall, a huge raptor had circled above her and, when it disappeared, she found an eagle's feather lying at her feet. "I didn't see any trail going to the left," Oy said, "so I just followed the edge of the lake going to the right—the direction the bird had come from. I hadn't gone far at all—just some sixty feet—when the sky began to cloud over. I kept moving and it began to rain and thunder and then turned into a hailstorm. The more the storm built up, the more energized I felt. But then I ran into the crazy nun coming from the other direction. She looked very concerned, and then I realized that I had been going around the mountain counterclockwise. As soon as I turned around and started going the other direction, the storm cleared up immediately. Within five minutes the sun was shining and a brilliant rainbow appeared right in front of me. What's going on here?"

As we descended through the slanting light toward the small shelter where we had left the silent yogi to his fate, banks of mist hovering over the lake in the valley far below slowly began to dissolve. Distant peaks appeared within an orange-and black-streaked sky as the sun lowered toward the distant ridges that we had descended on our approach to the mountain. As we gazed out over the vista of lakes and mountains, Kawa Tulku came from behind, beaming.

As we approached the House of Clear Light, I reflected on the whole crazy journey that was both necessary and absolutely unnecessary at the same time. We'd traveled to the far ends of the earth in search of a key that—in truth— could be found anywhere. I recalled something Franz Kafka had written: "Remain sitting at your table and listen. Do not even listen; simply wait. Do not even wait; be quite still and solitary. The world will freely offer itself to you to be unmasked; it has no choice; it will roll in ecstasy at your feet."

WHEN WE REACHED THE SHELTER, we found the bearded yogi sitting crosslegged in the same position we had left him. His eyes sparkled in the firelight. He gave Hamid and me a thumbs-up sign with his right hand while his other four fingers streamed over polished prayer beads. In his left hand he spun his prayer wheel.

As the fire burned down to coals, I lay down in my sleeping bag. The sky had remained clear, and rare moonlight spilled down through the loosened roof boards. Oy's voice rose out of the silver shadows: "In the novel *Uma's Diamond*, the entry point to the lost valley appears when the cresent moon touches the tip of a mountain shaped like Uma's breasts." The glow of the embers mixed with moonlight as we drifted into dreamless sleep.

Rinchenpung

AT FIRST LIGHT ON AUGUST 19, we left the House of Clear Light and descended to the lake where we found the Gillenwaters hovering around their campfire while two of the Sherpas were rolling up their tent. Gil's Hulk Hogan frame had withered under his Gore-Tex parka. "I know that pilgrimage is about accepting whatever comes," Gil said pensively, "but I'm still disappointed that we didn't reach the mountain."

Hamid attempted some esoteric consolation.

"Gil, to know Dorje Pagmo you have to surrender to her completely. If you try to conquer or possess her, she will always elude you. Pemako isn't a place you can seduce. The place seduces you."

"Thanks Hamid," Gil said. He didn't sound convinced.

OUR NEXT DESTINATION WAS RINCHENPUNG, a temple perched above the lower Tsangpo valley in Dorje Pagmo's topographical navel. To reach it, we had to cross the Zigchen-La, the Great Leopard Pass. With Yonten leading the way, we entered a morass of swamps and began climbing up a rocky defile.

Gil had recovered sufficiently from his illness to question Hamid on nuances of Buddhist doctrine and the nature of pilgrimage. "All the Buddhist texts talk about duality," Gil said. "Can you explain this to me?"

Hamid had become more preoccupied by Oy, who had stopped to photograph the paw prints of a large tiger that had preceeded us toward the pass. "They're very fresh," Oy said, "but the prints are probably all we will see."

Gil persisted. "Does it mean that whatever we see is actually taking place inside our heads and therefore does not really exist?"

"Something like that," Hamid responded, watching Oy as she sauntered up the trail. "Buddhist philosophy reveals that what appears as external and self-existing is ultimately a function of consciousness; it has no inherent existence. To say that reality is nondual doesn't mean that all is illusion, but that appearances arise in conjunction with our perception. When we recognize that perception dictates our reality, the forces of greed, anger, and delusion lessen and we attain a freer responsiveness to the events around us."

"You mean we don't get attached?"

"Right, we just recognize them as the play of consciousness, a kind of virtual reality. This isn't just artful fantasy," Hamid continued. "Science recognizes the same thing; that reality does not exist separately from our perception."

"So what's real then?" Gil asked. "Just this collective and intersecting delusion?"

"No," Hamid answered. "That's the whole point of Buddhism—to wake up from this collective dream and to recognize that there are no inherent boundaries between external reality and the circuitry of consciousness. If we could live in full awareness of this nondual reality, there would no longer be any basis for alienation, greed, anger, fear, and all the other mental poisons that Buddhism speaks about. We would take responsibility for our own perceptions and begin to work with them, in full consciousness of our interconnectedness with other beings."

Gil remained pensive, digesting this bit of Buddhist wisdom.

"I really wanted to reach that mountain, Hamid. But I can see that ultimately, it doesn't really matter."

"That's right, Gil, it's actually just a mountain."

I HAD WALKED BEHIND, amused by the philosophical bent of their conversation. Christian had stopped beside the path to jot down insights in his journal. Oy walked ahead, scouting the ground for more signs of large cats, the raptor's feather she'd found on Kundu dangling from her daypack.

AT THE CREST OF THE ZIGCHEN-LA, the trail dropped precipitously into a morass of mist, mud, and stunted trees. Sinking halfway up to our knees, we descended on a path through towering bamboo plants, their joints ringed in half inch spikes. I cut one down to use as a staff and another one to bring back to Bhakha Tulku, who would fashion it into a *shakuhachi*-like flute.

At dusk we came upon a crude shelter where Kawa Tulku and the advance porters had taken refuge. A small spring bubbled up from the earth. In the absence of any level earth, we formed precarious tent platforms from bent bamboo and slept suspended several feet above the ground. Gil's voice boomed out from the yellow North Face dome tent he shared with his brothers: "You mean to tell me that all this is my head, Hamid?"

The following morning we continued the steep descent toward Rinchenpung. The forest became ever denser and higher, full of ficus trees, colossal rhododendrons, and blossoming magnolias garlanded with moss. Oy found delicate orchids growing on dark tree limbs. "There are more than 36,000 types of orchids in the world," she announced with authority. "They are epiphytes. They grow on trees, but they get all their nourishment from air and rain." Like lichen, however, orchids cannot exist without their fungal partners, she said. In order for orchid seedlings to mature, the vegetative portion of a fungus—the hypha—penetrates in between the orchid's root cells or into the cells themselves. "Certain types of orchids rely on their fungal partners for chlorophyll and would perish without them. Exactly what the fungus receives in exchange is a bit of a mystery."

"It sounds like the Tibetan Yab Yum images," Christian said, referring to the statues and thangka paintings of Tantric deities in sexual union.

Soon afterward, we reached a line of cliffs that we could only cross by holding onto large vines that had grown across the rock. We had reached a sacred site called Tapak Né, where an image of Dorje Pagmo in union with her Tantric counterpart, Tamding (in Sanskrit, *Hayagriva*) was said to have manifested spontaneously on the colossal boulder.

In the Tantric view of life, the world is charged with the union of male and female energies, and the entwined form of Tamding and Dorje Pagmo (*Ta-Pak*) symbolizes the dynamics of the fully integrated psyche. Kawa Tulku stopped to perform a short ceremony, seating himself on the water-saturated ground.

Graphic icons of nonduality, Tantric images inspire practitioners to transcend habitual divisions between subject and object. As Jesus repeatedly instructed his disciples: "When you make the two one, and when you make the inside like the outside and the outside like the inside, and the above like the below, and when you make the male and the female one and the same . . . then you will enter [the Kingdom]." As I tramped around the rock through oozing mud, I overheard Hamid explaining to Oy the explicit, if universal, symbolism. "Sexual passion masks a spiritual longing for an end to duality and a return to wholeness," Hamid told her. "But unless there is intense presence the synergy can easily turn into compulsive grasping and the underlying sense of incompleteness remains. For true realization to arise in the heart and mind, these volatile energies must be fully encountered; only then does the illusion of separation disappear and transform into openness and radiant compassion. That's why in Tantra, the chakras connected with these largely unconscious energies must be opened first; just as we have to journey into these nether regions of Pemako before we can enter the innermost gorge."

AS I WADED AROUND THE ROCK, I recalled a story that Bhakha Tulku had told me about a Tibetan nun whom he had met during his stay at Rinchenpung in 1956. The nun would disappear into the forests around Tapak Né for several days at a time, Bhakha Tulku related, and return as if intoxicated, bearing fruits and flowers that no one had ever seen before. No one had followed her on her journeys, but all assumed that she was attending Tantric *tsok* feasts in the halcyon realms of the dakinis—beyond the conventional limits of time and space. Later, as I walked through billowing vapors rising up from the valleys below us, I realized that I had not seen our own flower-bestowing Ani-la for the entire day.

The Gillenwaters, eager to reach the imagined comforts of the monastery, had walked ahead with Kawa Tulku and the Monpa porters. When I reached a stream less than half an hour from Rinchenpung, I stopped to wash off the layers of mud that had encased my boots and gaiters. As I soaked in the birch-fringed waters, the blast of a distant conch shell roused me from my reverie. Kawa Tulku must have arrived at Rinchenpung, I thought. I set off to join the others.

The gilt-roofed temple sits on the crest of a grassy spur in the center of a bowl-shaped hollow filled with marsh reeds and small plots of ripening barley. In the sacred geography of Pemako, we were now in the navel of the goddess.[29]

AT DAWN ON THE NINTH DAY of the fifth month of the Wood Tiger Year (1794), the treasure-revealer Orgyen Dudrul Lingpa—better known as the Fifth Gampopa—who had journeyed down the Tsangpo to open Pemako's sacred sites, dreamed of a woman dressed in rags. The dakini instructed him to build a temple on a nearby hill "shaped like a heap of rice." The spear-wielding tribes that hunted in the region of Rinchenpung resisted Gampopa's plans, claiming that the sounds of the lamas' drums and conch-shell trumpets would scare away the game. But with backing from the king of Powo, the Tibetans finally secured rights to the land through gifts of animals, woolen cloth, swords, knives, axes, and copper cooking utensils. Surrounded by valleys that fanned out like petals of a lotus, Rinchenpung gradually became the center of religious life in Pemako, propogating the spiritual lineages of the Fifth Gampopa and Jatsun Nyingpo.

Hamid and I had visited Rinchenpung a year earlier after climbing up from Medok, the Chinese-occupied village perched on a plateau above the Tsangpo as it flows toward the Indian border only a short way downstream. Our requests to visit the temple had been refused and we had been forced to break away from our Chinese liaison officer, the beloved Gunn, and head into the jungle. To reach Rinchenpung, we climbed more than 3,000 feet above Medok, assaulted by leeches, stinging flies, and swarms of gnats. When we reached the top of the ridge, we entered a forest of flowering rhodedendrons, but no trail indicated the way toward the temple. At that moment, a hawk swept above us with a snake clutched in its talons. Lacking any better guide, we headed north in the direction from which the hawk had appeared.

When we finally emerged from the forest, we saw a double rainbow leading directly to the gilt-roofed temple. Uncannily, a maroon-robed yogi had already climbed halfway up the hill to greet us with a copper bowl overflowing with fermented chang. Rainbows like that only appear when someone is coming, he said. We drank deeply, as much to stave off the uncanny events as to refresh ourselves. The yogi led us to the temple where a monumental image of Padmasambhava in the wrathful form that he assumed in Pemako dominated the assembly hall. Above the head of the golden, four-armed statue was a repoussé image of a celestial hawk with a snake clutched in its beak and talons.

ONE OF PADMASAMBHAVA'S TERMAS describes Rinchenpung as the "gathering place of dakas and dakinis . . . the preeminent Tantric pilgrimage site. . . .

Whoever practices meditation here can accomplish in one night what in other places can be attained only after a year. Here, you will easily attain siddhis." As we sat on the porch of a primitive shelter behind the temple, Kawa Tulku told us that he planned to remain at Rinchenpung for several weeks to practice *metok chu-len,* an alchemical yoga in which he would subsist on the essences of wildflowers and various herbs. The plants and flowers that grow around Rinchenpung are considered especially efficacious for this practice. The *Luminous Web* revealed by Dorje Thokme describes one flowering plant called "severing the five poisons (of desire, anger, delusion, pride, and envy)." By eating this plant, the text claims, adepts can release the psychophysical *mdud*, or knots of the subtle channels that obscure perception of the myriad Buddha fields.

Apparently, the Monpa yogi at Kundu had given Kawa Tulku a favorable report about his experience with the psilocybin. Kawa Tulku asked Hamid and me whether we had more, and we gave him the remaining ones that we had collected. I explained that Lopas in our own country have used similar mushrooms to communicate with the spirits of their land and to open channels of perception. Kawa Tulku mused that perhaps these mushrooms would help him to find the other miraculous plants described in the Pemako neyigs.

In the practice of chu-len, consecrated substances such as the white-petaled *takmu* flower are consumed with hot water from a skull bowl and their effect further enhanced by meditating on the five elements and the flow of amrita throughout one's body. As a Tibetan healer had told me in Kathmandu, mushrooms described in their own pharmacopoeia can support certain kinds of meditation. But as I knew from my own experience, they can also be profoundly disorienting.

That night it rained torrentially. The Gillenwaters broke out the last of their gourmet cuisine (smoked oysters), Christian wrote feverishly in his journal, and Oy and Hamid disappeared into a neighboring storage shed. The following morning, August 21, as we left Rinchenpung, I mused that the fall from the Garden of Eden—the state of humanity in its infancy—had begun with the ingestion of the fruit of the tree of knowledge. But as as Milton suggested in *Paradise Lost*, the last chapter in the history of the world will be when we eat of it again, in what the poet Rimbaud might have meant by a "calculated disordering of the senses."

The Fortress of Flowers

WHEN WE HAD SET OUT FROM RINCHENPUNG the year before, the presiding lama had warned Hamid and me of the leeches in the jungles above Medok. When they infest your legs and hair, he counseled, imagine that they are drawing out your karmic impurities. If we could maintain this attitude of intrinsic beneficence, he implied, our journey through the hidden-land would bring great merit. Otherwise, we would simply suffer.

As we descended abruptly into the moisture-laden valley of the lower Tsangpo, bamboo and rhododendron forests yielded to a subtropical environment of tree ferns, wild plantains, and ubiquitous leeches. At times the leeches seemed to be raining from the sky, and we walked quickly to escape their predations.

In 1994, I had arrived in Medok at dusk, and my first encounter amid the bamboo-thatched houses was with a Monpa with a monkey on his shoulder and a sinuous green snake in a bamboo tube—one of the archetypal similies of the Tantric path, symbolizing the mind's potential, when freed of conventional boundaries, either to rise to celestial heights or fall to the lowest of the Tantric hells. Hamid had disappeared before we reached the village, and as night fell Ken Storm and Gunn mounted a search party to look for him, concerned that he might have been bitten by a venemous snake. Before Ken and Gunn returned, Hamid showed up inebriated and announced that he may or may not have just been wedded to an elf. He had followed the sound of drums and soon found himself in a thatch-roofed house, in which a chang-fueled religious rite transformed with his presence into an apparent nuptial ceremony with a Monpa sprite. Bhakha Tulku had alerted us to Pemako's easy blendings of the sacred and the sybaritic. His previous incarnation—the 9th Bhakha Tulku—had lived near Medok for several years and had many local liaisons. When Bhakha Tulku traveled through Pemako at the age of twelve, one of his predecessor's consorts had come to meet him near Medok singing, dancing, and bearing gifts. She had introduced him to her son, Bhakha Tulku's child from his previous incarnation.

MEDOK DZONG LIES ABOVE THE TSANGPO on a broad plateau studded with rice paddies and stands of bananas and bamboo.[30] Now we made our way through the village to a line of derelict wooden buildings raised ten feet above the ground and reachable by decaying sets of steps. Gunn and Cookie had taken up residence in one of the rooms to await our arrival. The Sherpas set up a makeshift kitchen in the one adjacent, while Hamid, Oy, Christian, the Gillenwaters, and I occupied two others. After hanging our wet clothing out to dry, we went out to explore our surroundings. Hamid tried unsuccessfully to locate the house of his alleged marriage the previous year.

After we had all fallen asleep, a drunken, overweight Chinese official accompanied by two police officers, all brandishing guns, broke into the Gillenwaters' room and demanded their exposed film. The trio gave them a few rolls of unexposed film, which seemed to placate the official's need to express his authority. He stumbled back out and nearly careened down the steps when a rotten board collapsed beneath him.

Medok would be a frustrating posting for any petty official. Many villagers still carried guns in the town despite a 1989 directive ordering that firearms be turned in to local authorities in an effort to control illegal hunting. The region was only sparsely settled until two hundred years ago, when Monpas from eastern Bhutan moved into the area, following Padmasambhava's prophecies. At that time the Monpa settlers had sought isolation, but they now wanted a road connecting them with the outside world so they could market their rice, plantains, and chilies. In the late 1980s and early 1990s, the Chinese had constructed a road between Powo Dzong and Medok, where they hoped to establish a banana plantation, but continual landslides, tree falls, and year-round snow on the Gawalung pass soon made it impassable, and the road reverted to a jungle track. A more logical route to the outside world would be south to India, but even if this were politically feasible, a road would put great pressure on Medok's timber resources and create easier access for poachers. It would also deprive many families of the income they receive from transporting goods with pack animals or as porters.

On the morning of August 22, the Chinese official who had relieved the Gillenwaters of their film came early and conversed with a nervous Gunn. Gunn urged us to pack quickly, offering as explanation only "He is not a good man."

We needed little persuasion to leave this border town and its frustrated officials. We headed out through the rice paddies and descended toward the Tsangpo. We intended to cross the river where we had the year before—on a hanging bridge made of woven bamboo.

When we reached the Tsangpo, we found that the bridge had collapsed several months earlier, killing several Monpas. The local villagers had not rebuilt it, and they directed us to another bridge a day's journey downriver. As we headed south along the Tsangpo, Yonten mentioned that we were headed into the heart of the poisoning district. In the settled areas of Pemako, villagers offer bowls of fermented chang to travelers and pilgrims. Members of the secret poisoning cult—usually women—conceal under their thumbnails a deadly toxin made from aconite, snake venom, and poisonous mushrooms, which they slip into the chang after sipping it themselves to show that it isn't contaminated.

Before my first trip to Pemako I had learned that the wife of Tenzing Norgay, who, along with Sir Edmund Hillary, completed the first ascent of Mount Everest in 1953, had met her end after allegedly being poisoned by a Pemako witch. Adherents of this ancient cult believe that they inherit the good fortune of those they poison. The higher their victims' status, the more luck accrues. Lamas and prosperous traders top the list of desirable victims, and foreign pilgrims are by no means exempt. If no suitable recipient appears, the *dugma*, as she is called in Tibetan, is compelled through a vow taken at the time of preparing the poison to use it either on one of her family members or on herself.

The previous year, we had entered the Medok region over the Gawalung pass and traveled down the Tsangpo through scattered Monpa villages. In nearly every settlement, villagers had greeted us with hollow gourds or large brass bowls filled with fermented chang and urged us to drink, with the recurring claim that they hadn't poisoned it. We mostly avoided the Monpas' potentially deadly hospitality, but sampled the potent brew in households known to our Monpa guide. We watched carefully for any sleight of hand. In a land known for its miraculous healing plants, the female practitioners of this pre-Buddhist cult tempt travelers not with the forbidden fruit that can make humankind as gods, but with the proverbial poisoned apple.

THE MONPA HUNTER WE HAD RECRUITED in Powo Dzong enlightened us to the particulars of the cult: like an inverse image from the Garden of Eden, the dugma hangs a snake from a tree and over a course of days allows its venom to drain into a bowl. She then mashes in a rotten egg, poisonous roots, and frogs and buries the concoction underground. She digs it up again under a full moon. With half of her face painted black and the hair on one side of her head braided and the other half left wild, she vows to use the poison within a fortnight— before the moon turns dark—on someone of the highest possible standing. The poison acts slowly, the Monpa hunter told us, and it's difficult to determine when and where it might have been administered. Depending on the proportion of ingredients, the victim dies within a period of anywhere from three days to three months.

The hunter further claimed that if the dugma isn't able to slip the powdered toxin into a traveler's chang, she often resorts to putting it under a fingernail and scratching her victims while they sleep. For this reason, our porters refused to sleep on the floors of Monpa houses and posted sentries at night to avert any potential sharp-nailed assailants.

In one infamous village, our porters insisted that we camp a safe distance away. That evening the most notorious of Pemako's dugmas—a woman ominously named Sonam Deki, Meritorous Joy, appeared at our tents to ask for medicine. Our guide whispered to me that she had reputedly poisoned fifteen people, among them several husbands and her own daughters. A short woman in her late fifties with long gray pigtails and dressed in a sleeveless chuba of black felt, the alleged witch seemed disarmingly docile. We gave her the medicine she had requested but turned down her invitation to come to her house for tea.

AS WE DESCENDED TOWARD THE BRIDGE that would lead us to the west bank of the Tsangpo and onward over the Doshung-La, tree ferns, magnolias, and dense vine-choked jungle tumbled down toward the Tsangpo, which meandered below us through veils of mist. An old Monpa with a single tooth claimed that large reptiles lived in a lake an hour above the trail. From his account, they sounded like crocodiles. Gunn was skeptical. "We haven't seen any crocodiles up till now. I don't believe there can be crocodiles here," he said. Snakes abounded, though—green and black serpents more than six feet long that stretched across the trail to absorb the feeble sunlight that penetrated the canopy overhead.

Gunn had waited for us on the outskirts of Bepung, the village above the bridge. A Chinese military cantonment lay amid rice fields and banana trees below the village, and Gunn had brought out his sheaf of permits to account for our presence. "We aren't supposed to be here," Gunn lamented, "This bridge is too close to the border."

We walked along the perimeter of the army camp but encountered neither soldier nor villager. Only at the site of an old bunker directly above the suspension bridge did we finally run into four young soldiers who examined Gunn's papers and sullenly let us pass. The liberation bridge had been constructed after border skirmishes with India in 1962 which established the current LOC, or Line of Control, a day's walk farther south at the village of Geling.

MY FIRST TIBETAN TEACHER, Dudjom Rinpoche, had been born just out-side of Geling in a village called Tirkung in the Year of the Water Dragon (1904), in accordance with the prophecy left by his previous incarnation, Dudjom Lingpa (1835–1904). Dudjom Lingpa had died on the verge of journeying into Pemako, but had urged his followers to continue without him, vowing that in his next incarnation he would be reborn there to lead them into the heart of the hidden-land.

The young Dudjom Rinpoche received Tantric empowerments from Jedrung Jhampa Yungney after his return from Mipi and established a training center for

ngakpas, or Tantric practition-ers, at his seat in Tirkung. He also established a college for ordained monks—the first of its kind in Pemako. But whereas the ngakpas thrived, the ordained monks soon lost their vows due to the ubiquity and great popularity of Pe-mako's justly famous chang.[31]

In the 1930s, the govern-ment of central Tibet sent representatives to Tirkung and forced Dudjom Rinpoche to leave the hidden-land. Only the state-sponsored Gelugpa order can found monasteries in Tibet, the monk official told him. After a period in Lhasa, Dudjom Rinpoche established his seat at Lomaling in Kongpo, where he built a replica of Pad-masambhava's paradise, Sangdopelri. It was destroyed in the great earthquake of 1950, and nine years later Dudjom Rinpoche fled Tibet in the wake of the failed uprising against a decade of Chinese occupation. He first settled in the Indian hill station of Kalimpong and later in southern France. The tower representing Padmasambhava's paradise that had collapsed during the earthquake lay in ruins until the 1990s, when Dudjom Rinpoche's chief attendant, Chonyi Rinpoche—whom I had met after my first journey into Pemako in 1993—began its reconstruction.

The Pass of Sharp Stones

TO LEAVE PEMAKO we had to cross back over the Himalayan barrier, this time over the Doshung-La, or Pass of Sharp Stones, on the western flank of Namcha Barwa. We began the ascent from the liberation bridge and climbed along the right bank of a river that cascaded through dense tropical foliage droning with cicadas. After climbing 2,000 feet above the Tsangpo, we reached a small plateau at 4,150 feet and camped in fallow rice fields swarming with moths and gnats. Oy had picked banana flowers and wild lemons along the trail, and her cooking added new dimensions to the evening meal. We retired close to midnight under heavy clouds. The temperature remained oppressive throughout the night, as did the plague of tiny gnats that penetrated the netting of our tents. Christian complained bitterly from within the dome tent he shared with Oy. "The world does not favor mammals," I overheard her say, "It favors insects; they proliferate while warm-blooded species face gradual extinction." Christian hardly seemed mollified.

In the morning we set out again, climbing through dense forests of bamboo. High on the ridge above lay the village of Marpung, where Kinthup had worked as an indentured servant to the local lama. In 1994, we had crossed the Tsangpo on the hanging bamboo bridge below Medok, and our route had led us through this village. On our arrival Marpung's presiding abbot had emerged from the monastery's dark interiors, flanked by village lamas dressed in brocade robes and bird-headed masks.

I had asked him about Yangsang Né. He told me that some neyigs indicate that Pema Shelri—the Lotus Crystal Mountain at the heart of Yangsang—lies

to south of Kundu Dorsempotrang, while others say it lies to the north beneath the walls of Namcha Barwa. He told me that during the 1960s many Tibetans had searched for Yangsang amid Namcha Barwa's cliffs and glaciers. Some had heard the jangling amulets of dakinis dancing invisibly in the air around them and took it as a sign that they were approaching the fabled portal. The lama himself had been part of a group that had journeyed up a narrow gorge to a white cliff that many believed to conceal the door to the hidden paradise. They performed elaborate rites for weeks at the base of the mountain, but the door never opened, the lama said; the time had not yet come. Some of the Tibetan seekers had died of starvation; others survived by eating the leather of their shoes.

When we arrived at a bridge leading across the Doshung Chu, villagers from Marpung recognized Hamid and me from the preceeding year. They pointed up a gorge with steep ridges receding into the distance and asked if we were headed toward Pema Shelri. The route was overgrown by jungle and no one had gone up the gorge in years, they told us. Unless the right lama went with you, there was no point, they said. You will see only rock and ice.

We told them that we had been to Kundu Dorsempotrang and were now headed back to Lhasa. The realm to the north would have to await a future visit. The temptation to venture into the unknown, inhospitable terrain was strong, and Hamid and I almost lamented the pull that Yangsang continued to exert on us. On one level we knew it was an unattainable realm, as fanciful as Shangri-La, but its obscure promise was impossible to deny. We knew that we would soon return.

We had journeyed to Kundu Dorsempotrang to find a key to penetrate deeper into the mysteries of the beyul, and as we climbed through the forest we asked ourselves what we had found. Beyond the ostensible merit of having circumambulated the sacred mountain, the journey had conferred a sense of wonder and magic that more than compensated for any hardship we might have endured. Although we were fatigued and ravaged by insects and stinging plants, the endless days of trudging through leech-infested swamps and along treacherous cliffs had granted us an uncommon peace, a sense of having been to the heart of things. We could now approach the Tsangpo's innermost gorge, the last secret place, with a new attitude. The gnostic Gospel of Thomas sums it up as well—and as cryptically—as any neyig: "The Kingdom is inside of you, and outside of you. When you have come to know yourselves, then you will be known . . . Recognize what is before your eyes, and what is hidden will be revealed to you."

Four hours from our campsite, the trail began to climb steeply along the side of a narrow canyon. Horse caravans passed us along the dizzying track, some carrying supplies for the Chinese army but most transporting cigarettes, liquor, and instant noodles for consumption in the Medok region. The Monpa horsemen had forsaken traditional clothing for Chinese military fatigues. Many carried guns.

At 7 P.M., we arrived at Hami, a small military post 7,800 feet above sea level. Monpa traders spilled from surrounding shelters strung with blue and white striped plastic sheeting. Chinese soldiers appeared and insisted that we stay in a derelict building that they tried to pass off as a guesthouse. Damp, motheaten mattresses lay on top of rotting floorboards. Claiming allergies to mold (a bold if somewhat exaggerated performance by Oy), we convinced them to let us pitch our tents in a nearby field. Last year we had eaten a snake here, a black viper killed by the Chinese cook dispatched by Gunn's Chengdu-based tour company. Tomorrow would be our last night on the trail, and we were as ambivalent as ever about the prospect of returning to civilization.

Oy cataloged her orchids—the word derives from the latin *orchus*, which means testicle, she announced—while Gil informed us that he'd calculated that we had already climbed more than 75,000 feet over the course of our journey, two and a half times the height of Everest from sea level.

The following morning, August 25, we headed out from Hami in heavy mists that soon dispersed into feeble sunshine and intermittent rain. The trail wound through a Tolkienesque forest of moss-covered rhododendrons. After eight hours of steady walking, we emerged into open marshland that snow and avalanche debris had covered the year before. Avoiding a cement shelter overflowing with crushed tin cans, we set up our tents on beds of flowering weeds at the base of a large boulder. The route over the Doshung-La wove up through a circle of snow peaks that rose behind us. It turned cold, the sky grew overcast, and it began to drizzle. As we ate our last supper in the hidden-lands, our thoughts turned inward as we, each in our own way, tried to fathom the significance of the journey, its hardships as well as its joys, from Gunn's incomprehension as to why Americans would spend so much money to suffer so inordinately in so remote a place to Hamid's and my own speculations as to how the journey would help us secure passage into the innermost depths of the gorge. Throughout our journey, inner and outer experience had merged into a kind of dreamtime continuum in which familiar appositions no longer pertained and anything seemed possible. Tibetans call it *rochik*, or one taste, and we suspected that it was the key to the deeper reaches, and meanings, of the beyul.

BEFORE DAWN ON THE MORNING of August 26, the porters cut boughs of juniper and heaved them onto a smoldering fire, sending columns of fragrant smoke into the shrouded sky. The year before we had crossed the Doshung-La on Sagadawa, the full moon in May commemorating the Buddha's birth, death, and enlightenment. We'd come across a corpse frozen in the snow as well as a dead horse and the wreckage of a downed military helicopter. This year we began the ascent back out of Pemako in mist and rain. Avalanches echoed from surrounding slopes as we wound our way through dwarf rhododendrons, ghostly rocks, and windswept snowfields. At the top of the pass, we followed Tibetan custom and left bits of our clothing or obsolete possessions on a cairn of stones marking the gateway out of Pemako.

As we descended from the pass, we looked back toward the fluted snow peaks that guard this hidden-land, a place of infinite promise for both pilgrims and explorers. Already, the ridge we had just crossed, the snowy flanks of the goddess, was veiled in impenetrable mist.

We followed switchbacks through a dense forest until late in the day, when we emerged from the trees and saw the Tsangpo flowing placidly in the distance at the base of bare, rocky hills. We climbed down through the pines to Pe-Doshung, a Tibetan village near the banks of the Tsangpo and the site of a small police station where our drivers had been waiting for us for days.

Gunn was excited that we had spanned the Great Bend, rising in altitude from a little more than 2,000 feet where the Tsangpo flows beneath the liberation bridge to more than 10,000 feet at Pe-Doshung. "The Chinese can build a great hydroelectric station here," Gunn announced enthusiastically. "It would be much greater that Three Gorges project on the Yangtse."

The local police displayed little interest when Gunn showed them our permits. They were overseeing a local funeral rite. Two friends or brothers—it wasn't clear—had killed each other in a knife fight the night before we arrived. In observance of local custom, villagers were cutting up their bodies and throwing them into the Tsangpo, where they flowed downriver into the throat of Dorje Pagmo and the unknown parts of the gorge. Was this the only way to penetrate those uncharted depths?

As we climbed into the jeeps, engines revving in the thin air and diesel fumes flooding through the cabin, Christian brooded on the image of bodies disappearing into the currents of the great river. "I guess the pilgrimage is over," he said. But equally, it was beginning anew. I'd arrived where I had started from in 1993, and though we were now driving back toward Lhasa, the current of my life still pulled me downstream, to where I had watched the bodies flowing toward the undiscovered depths of the gorge, and the dream of a waterfall uniting earth and heaven.

As we drove along the banks of the Tsangpo into the setting sun, I thought of a poem by the tenth-century Mahasiddha Naropa:

> *The way of the Buddhas manifests as a great river.*
> *The dazzling display of unfulfilled desire,*
> *Samsara's wave, of its own has passed away.*

PART FOUR

THE
WATERFALL

When truly sought even the seeker cannot be found. Thereupon the goal of the seeking is attained, and the end of the search. At this point there is nothing more to be sought, and no need to seek anything.

PADMASAMBHAVA
The Book of the Great Liberation

I reckon it is about 500 to 1 against falls, and I would lay it in guineas. . . . How the old chap who invented these infernal falls must chuckle in his grave when mugs like us go looking for them! And what a number of people have had a miserable time looking for this mythical marvel!

THE EARL OF CAWDOR
Journal entry for December 13, 1924

The waters symbolize the universal sum of virtualities; they are *fons et origo,* "spring and origin," the reservoir of all the possibilities of existence.

MIRCEA ELIADE
The Sacred and the Profane

If you do not expect it, you will not find the unexpected.

HERACLITUS

October 1998
The Year of the Earth Tiger

IN 1924, THE YEAR THAT KINGDON WARD journeyed into the Tsangpo gorges and declared the Falls of the Tsangpo a "religious myth," a novelist and ex-ivory poacher named Talbot Mundy immortalized the waterfall in a work of fiction. *Om: The Secret of Ahbor Valley* chronicles a disenchanted British civil servant's journey to a hidden monastery overlooking "the tremendous Tsangpo Falls." Emerging from a limestone tunnel beneath "a sheer wall of crags, whose edges pierced the sky," the protagonist, Cottswold Ommony, confronts the legendary waterfall:

> ... like a roaring curtain, emerald green and diamond white, blown in the wind, the Tsangpo River, half a mile wide, tumbled down a precipice between two outflung spurs that looked like the legs of a seated giant ... their roar came down-wind like the thunder of creation. Below them, incalculably far below the summit, the rising spray formed a dazzling rainbow; and where, below the falls, the Tsangpo became the Brahmaputra, there were rock-staked rapids more than two miles wide that threw columns of white water fifty feet in air, so that the rocks looked like leviathans at war.

At once an adventure story, a critique of British imperialism, and a treatise on Buddhist philosophy, Talbot Mundy's novel centers on a sequestered monastery where treasures of East and West have been preserved for posterity. Perched against cliffs at a height so high it "made the senses reel," the monastery is filled with Chinese carpets, Ming vases, paintings, and silk curtains "as perfect in material as craftsmanship could contrive." Infused with theosophical musings drawn from the teachings of the Russian clairvoyant Madame Blavatsky, *Om: The Secret of Ahbor Valley* focuses on the quest for the Jade of the Ahbor, a supernatural stone whose radiance reveals the highest as well as the basest qualities of all who gaze upon it. The "jewel of pure perception," the monolithic stone lies concealed in a hidden grotto behind the fabled Falls of the Tsangpo.

Mundy's descriptions of the topography of the Tsangpo gorge and the savage tribesmen who guard the valley "as cobras guard ancient ruins" drew on Bailey and Morshead's well-publicized accounts. Reinvoking in art what explorers had ultimately dismissed as a romance of geography, Mundy's novel envisions the lost waterfall "where rainbows dance" as the gateway to a paradisiacal sanctuary offering refuge from avarice and war. At the novel's end, the high lama, Tsiang Samdup, leads Ommony down a rock-hewn staircase amid "the rush and roar of water pouring into hollow caverns." They pass through an interminable tunnel that leads to the mystic stone in which one sees one's "higher nature shining through the lower." After parting prophecies concerning the fate of the world, the aged lama—a model for Father Perrault in Hilton's *Lost Horizon*—vanishes into a limestone passageway behind the fabled waterfall while Ommony, his spiritual heir, stands before the stone with the "sensation of waiting on a threshold of a new world—waiting to be born."

Om: The Secret of Ahbor Valley was a primary source for James Hilton's "wild dream" of Shangri-La in the novel *Lost Horizon*, published less than a decade later, in 1933. Borrowing from another little-known work, a play called *The Green Goddess* written by William Archer in 1920,[1] Hilton transposed the utopian realm from the Tsangpo gorge to northwestern Tibet where a hijacked government plane crashes with jaded British diplomat and ex-Oxford don Hugh Conway—and three mismatched companions. A Tibetan rescue party leads them over a high mountain pass to a monastery built against cliffs overlooking an idyllic valley. Shangri-La's library and salons overflow with great works of art, literature, and music, preserved, says the 250-year-old Capuchin who founded the monastery, for a time when "men, exultant in the technique of homicide, would rage so hotly over the world that every precious thing will be in danger."

Father Perrault espouses a doctrine of moderation based on Christian and Buddhist values and foresees a time when there "will be no safety in arms, no help from authority, no answer in science." At that time, the "lost and legendary treasures" preserved in Shangri-La will fuel "a new Renaissance." Father Perrault bequeaths his legacy to Conway, who conceives of Shangri-La as "a living essence, distilled from the magic of the ages and miraculously preserved against time and death."

The mystical romanticism embodied in *Om: The Secret of Ahbor Valley* and *Lost Horizon* originated with eighteenth-century reports by Tibet's first Jesuit missionaries—the inspiration for Shangri-La's and the Ahbor Valley's presiding abbots. Physical inaccessibility, diplomatic isolation, and fantastic legends of levitating monks and precious jewels transformed Tibet in popular imagination to a land of compelling mystery. Figures such as Francis Younghusband, one of the last great imperial adventurers, returned from Tibet in the early years of the twentieth century to promote interfaith dialogue, envisioning, decades before Hilton, a realm where Eastern mysticism and Western pragmatism could merge into a new paradigm. The legacy of these hopes lives on in Western imagination, as strongly as Tibetan belief in a Buddhist Pure Land in the heart of the

Tsangpo gorges—a place that Kingdon Ward, the last explorer to look for the falls, described as "hidden behind misty barriers where ordinary men do not go."

THE WESTERN SEARCH for the Falls of the Tsangpo in the first decades of the twentieth century paralleled a growing disillusionment with imperialism and an increasing interest in Eastern thought. During the period between the First and Second World Wars, books such as *The Tibetan Book of the Dead*, published in 1927, and Alexandra David Neal's *Magic and Mystery in Tibet* were great successes, and Tibet transformed in the popular imagination into a realm of timeless wisdom. *Om: The Secret of Ahbor Valley* and *Lost Horizon* (the first book ever printed in paperback) placed these transcendental ideals in the context of a utopian geography and gave birth to the modern notion of a paradisiacal Himalayan realm conforming less to the actuality of Tibet's landscape or culture than to the reality of Western fantasies.

Hilton described Shangri-La as a place "strange and half incredible," a place "touched with mystery . . . the whole atmosphere more of wisdom than

philosophy," where a monastic elite had discovered the key to longevity through esoteric breathing regimens and purple berries with mild narcotic properties. A storehouse of sacred wisdom and the greatest achievements of both Eastern and Western civilization, the sequestered valley was presented as a source of light and illumination in an age of impending darkness. Even the president of the United States, Franklin D. Roosevelt, was seduced, naming his Maryland hideaway (what is now Camp David) Shangri-La. Shangri-La had its Hollywood apotheosis in Frank Capra's 1937 film version of *Lost Horizon* starring Ronald Colman and Jane Wyatt. In one scene, the two lead actors swim in an Edenic lake fed by a sixty-foot sinuous waterfall—actually located in Tahquitz Canyon in Palm Springs, California.

Closing the Gap

IN 1993, KEN STORM AND I had penetrated no deeper into the Tsangpo's innermost gorge than Kingdon Ward had in 1924.

Lured by the prospect of the seventy-five waterfalls described in the Buddhist texts at the monastery at Pemakochung, Kingdon Ward and Cawdor had climbed out of the upper gorge at the Banks of Rubicon and, two weeks later, entered it again below the impenetrable chasm. "We had only one object in coming here," Kingdon Ward wrote, "to explore that part of the gorge which had been hidden from us. . . . Here if anywhere were the 'Falls of the Brahmaputra' which had been a geographical mystery for half a century; and the final solution—falls? or no falls?—was now within our grasp."

They descended to river level at a point where the Tsangpo "after hurling itself through the gap, rushes headlong into a gorge so deep and narrow that one could hardly see any sky overhead." The Tsangpo narrowed there to less than thirty yards across and poured over a ledge approximately forty feet high. Kingdon Ward measured the altitude by boiling point and found it to be 5,751 feet: 1,347 feet lower than their camp above Rainbow Falls. Unable to proceed farther upriver, Kingdon Ward determined that the forty-foot pour over was the highest falls that would ever be found on the Tsangpo. He and Cawdor returned to London and reported to the Royal Geographical Society that: "We are . . . unable to believe that there is any likelihood of a greater fall in the remaining 5 miles which we did not see." For his efforts Kingdon Ward was awarded the Society's Gold Medal of Exploration and effectively ended the search for "a falls of 100 feet or more" in the still unknown depths of the Tsangpo gorge. Lord Cawdor had written in his journal on December 13, 1924, of the futility of their quest:

How the old chap who invented these infernal falls must chuckle in his grave
when mugs like us go looking for them! And what a number of people have had
a miserable time looking for this mythical marvel!

Since Kingdon Ward's expedition, the Falls of the Tsangpo had shifted, by
general consensus, from the realm of fact to that of fiction, but the Five-Mile
Gap that Kingdon Ward and Cawdor had left unexplored still remained "one
of the last remaining secret places of the earth," as Bailey described it in 1913.
After our journey in 1993, Ken and I had resolved to return and definitively explore the unknown tract. The possibility of a waterfall on the Tsangpo of "a
hundred feet or more" still did not seem altogether impossible.

IN AUGUST 1993, three months after my first journey into the gorge, I met
with David Breashears at Lily's Restaurant in the Roger Smith Hotel on Lexington Avenue in New York City. In the mural-filled interior, he showed me
slides he had taken with a telephoto lens of a section of the Tsangpo below
Rainbow Falls. Shot from a vantage point thousands of feet above the river,
Breashears's photographs revealed a wildly turbulent river flowing through a
narrow canyon hemmed in by towering walls of rock. In the depths of the abyss
was what had looked to him like the crest of a surging waterfall, but intervening cliffs had prevented him from descending lower and he had not considered
it significant enough to report to National Geographic. Although his IMAX
work on Everest would mean putting it off for at least two years, Breashears
proposed a full-scale climbing expedition to reach the hydrolic event that he
had viewed through his binoculars and telephoto lens. Afterward, he wanted to
push through the Five-Mile Gap. I was equally set on exploring this unknown
region, but I wanted to experience it on different terms. In accordance with
Chonyi Rinpoche's counsel that ascending the heights of Kundu Dorsempotrang would reveal the key to Pemako's innermost depths, I put off the search
for the waterfall until after I had traveled to the sacred mountain.

I returned to the Tsangpo gorges in May of 1996, eight months after the journey to Kundu. To ward off competition, Ken Storm had told an interviewer from *Outside* magazine that a full traverse of the Tsangpo's innermost gorge "would require an army of explorers with big-wall climbing experience and massive river support," but simultaneously we were planning a far simpler expedition. I enlisted the support of my brother Ralph Rynning, who was born in Norway and whose zeal for mountaineering led to a forty-two-day crossing of the Patagonian icecap in the footsteps of the legendary explorer Eric Shipton. Enterprising in other ways too, he arranged to finance his trip by excavating a rock from the bottom of the gorge and selling it to a Swiss geologist at the Zurich Institute of Geology.

Ralph, Ken, Hamid, and I planned to follow the route that Kingdon Ward and Lord Cawdor had pioneered in 1925 when they reentered the gorge from the north. From the forty-foot falls that Kingdon Ward had determined to be the highest on the Tsangpo, we intended to continue upriver with climbing gear into the section of the gorge that Kingdon Ward and Cawdor had not seen. Hamid and I trained on limestone cliffs at the edge of the Kathmandu valley. Ken reacquainted himself with rappelling and jumar work at his island retreat in northern Ontario. Hearing of our intentions, Gunn deputed a Chinese colleague in his stead. "I have had enough of Pemako," he told me over a crackly phone line from Chengdu.

On the drive in from Lhasa, we ran into a band of British plant collectors who had extended Kingdon Ward's work into the Powo region and several passes leading toward Pemako. The team's leader, Kenneth Cox, came from a family of Scottish plant collectors and had distinguished himself as perhaps the world's foremost authority on rhododendrons. He aspired to introduce plants to the British Isles that Kingdon Ward had discovered but whose seeds had not survived, as well as rhododendron species that Kingdon Ward had overlooked. He rattled off names like *Rhododendron laudandum, Rhododendron bulu, Rhododendron cephalanthum, Rhododendron dignabile,* and *Podophyllum aurantiocaule.* He hoped to draw attention to the botanical diversity of the Tsangpo gorges and to encourage its conservation. While sharing a meal in the town of Nyingtri, Kenneth revealed that the local police had placed them there under house arrest

pending the arrival of their Chinese guide and travel permit. The roadside restaurant was as far as they were allowed to go.

From the road head at Pelung, we crossed the footbridge and followed the Po Tsangpo River to its confluence with the Tsangpo. At Mondrong, a small village emerging out of fields of millet, we recruited Monpa hunters to lead us into the region of the gap. A village lama told us of caves that we would pass where yogins had meditated beneath the walls of Gyala Pelri. From Neythang, as he called it, a perilous descent would lead us to the cove that Kingdon Ward had reached in 1925. Sheer cliffs line the gorge, the lama told us, and no one had ever penetrated farther upriver. When we asked the lama about the texts from Pemakochung describing the seventy-five waterfalls reputed to cascade through the innermost gorge, he told us that thirty-five years before, the Chinese had forced him at gunpoint to throw all his scriptures into the Tsangpo. He had no recollection of that particular text and disclaimed any knowledge of the seventy-five waterfalls.

Discouraged by the lama's account, Hamid resolved to travel deeper into Pemako on his own and search for Buddhist texts that might have survived the Chinese predations. Following the Red Panda motto "confuse and elude," we convinced Gunn's replacement that he would be of the most service to us if he remained in Mondrong as we divided into two groups. Hamid enlisted a Lopa and his daughter to guide him downriver and carry his sleeping bag and a tarp. They crossed the Tsangpo on the bridge below Tsachu and, battling gnats and the occasional viper, headed south toward Luku, the village that Ken and I had visited after our passage through the gorge in 1993. Impressed by Hamid's knowledge of Tibetan, a local lama urged him to cross the Tsangpo on a dizzying cable and to consult a colleague, a reincarnate lama in the village of Gande. In the archives of the small temple, Hamid discovered a text that described Pemako in terms of the five chakras of Dorje Pagmo. But apart from referring to the innermost gorge as the goddess's throat, the manuscript offered no account of any waterfalls.

Meanwhile Ken, Ralph, and I headed upriver from the confluence into the innermost gorge. Rather than descending to the Tsangpo where Kingdon Ward had, we continued on to Neythang, where the hunters led us to the meditation caves on the walls below Gyala Pelri. Herds of takin roamed the grassy plains below the caves, and the hunters killed three of them for food and stretched their hides on racks of bamboo. The area was also full of birds, many of which

migrate up the gorge from India. Ralph had received partial funding from Cornell University's Department of Ornithology to record the fire-tailed sunbirds, pygmy blue flycatchers, giant laughing thrushes, and other species that inhabit the area. Chinese sources had listed 232 species in Pemako and acknowledged that there were probably many more. According to our hunter guides, some of the birds sing mantras that can lead the attuned to Pemako's secret realms.

We continued over another pass, hoping to descend into the gap at a point higher upriver. But after a precipitous traverse across landslides and ice-choked gullies, we could find no way to reach the Tsangpo, let alone see down to its hidden depths. We retraced our steps and descended along the edge of a waterfall toward the small bay in the Tsangpo that Kingdon Ward had visited in 1925. On the climb down we nearly lost one of our porters as he tumbled thirty feet down a fern-drenched cliff. Lower still we reached a sheer 300-foot drop in the forest. We lowered ourselves inch by inch, hanging on to tree branches.

As we approached Neygyap—the bay in the Tsangpo—the oldest of the hunters, Dungley Phuntsok, revealed that his grandfather had led two Britishers to the same spot more than seventy years ago. In an astounding display of oral history, he pointed with his bamboo stick to a shallow cave high above the Tsangpo where they had slept as they descended toward the river. He described their terrier and the small pistol that one of them had used to shoot two pheasants for their evening meal. He also pointed out accurately that one of them (Cawdor) had not made the final descent, but had waited behind on the narrow shelf of rock. (Kingdon Ward and Cawdor had named the precarious campsite Birdcage Walk.)

Great plumes of spray arched above us as we reached the river. We traversed out on a spit of granite and gazed down at the thirty- to forty-foot cascade that Kingdon Ward had thought to be the highest waterfall that would ever be found on the length of the Tsangpo. Kingdon Ward had calculated that the river falls 1,700 feet in the eight miles from Rainbow Falls to Neygyap—a drop of more than 212 feet per mile. We pushed upstream, but as waves surged against the steep vegetated walls, it was clear that there was no way to cover the missing section on the Tsangpo's left bank. The cliffs across the river looked equally sheer.

As Kingdon Ward had noted in 1925, the only access to the area, if there was one at all, seemed to be from higher up on the right bank of the Tsangpo, and we would have to leave that for a future journey. The Five-Mile Gap remained, as it had for centuries, a place of inaccessible mystery.

I RETURNED TO TIBET TWO MONTHS LATER and visited a mountain sanctuary north of Lhasa. As I sat on a limestone outcrop above a bubbling hot spring flowing with slender green snakes, a Tibetan woman with long dreadlocks and a thick woolen robe came down to the pool to bathe. Her name was Ani Rigsang, and she had lived for years in meditative retreat in a cave above the springs.[2]

Toward the end of my stay at Terdrom, I invited Ani Rigsang to come with me to Gompo Né, a pilgrimage site marking the northern door into Pemako. Gompo Né lies near the confluence of the Po Tsangpo and Tsangpo rivers, a two-hour journey from the village of Mondrong. The texts describing the Tsangpo's inner gorge may have vanished, the lama in Mondrong had told me, but he had suggested that clues to the area could be found by meditating at

Gompo Né. If I had learned anything in Pemako, it was the limits of linear thought, and I had taken the lama's advice to heart.

The Po Tsangpo had swollen in the summer rains, and vines and foliage grew lavishly along its banks. Faced with unrelenting leeches, two fellow pilgrims turned back at the outset and two more a day later as we approached the confluence. At Gompo Né, rock pinnacles worn smooth by floods rose from a small sandy plain. A circuitous pilgrims' path led through tunnels and passed by dark springs. Adepts had left handprints in solid rock as signs of their passage; mantras and images of snakes had been carved into the granite walls. Flood waters of the Tsangpo had swept away a small temple that once sat amid the towering rocks.

Ani Rigsang followed the lineage of Jatsun Nyingpo, the treasure-revealer who had uncovered the first Pemako neyig in the early seventeenth century. The revealed scroll had presented an exalted view of pilgrimage and Buddhist practice: "In any circumstances good or bad abandon all hope from Buddhas and give up all fears of suffering in Samsara. Recognize that hope and fear are the magical display of your own mind of Primordial Purity [kadak] . . . . Remain in the state where there is neither perceiver nor object of perception. Let go into the immaculate space of Great Perfection . . . beyond meditation or distractive disturbance."

I later asked the dreadlocked nun to come with me the following summer, when, along with Hamid, I hoped to enter the gap from the ravines south of Namcha Barwa. We had learned of a bamboo rope bridge that spanned the Tsangpo several days' walk below Luku, where Ken and I had emerged from the gorge in 1993. A remote hermitage called Mandeldem once lay on the other side, Bhakha Tulku told me. The eighteenth-century treasure-revealer Choeje Lingpa had reputedly set out from there on his search for Yangsang, crossing a pass into the unknown section of the Tsangpo gorge before passing away in the sunless jungles.

Since returning from Kundu Dorsempotrang, I'd asked several lamas for their theories about Yangsang's coordinates, and no two had the same perspective, though all insisted that, like the Tantric power places (pitha) of ancient India, Yangsang was no mere metaphor, but an actual place, albeit not strictly geographical. Some maintained that only the specific incarnations stipulated in

Padmasambhava's termas would be able to reveal it, but others claimed that was only another veil to protect Yangsang from outsiders.

IN AUGUST 1997, Ani Rigsang came to the Yak Hotel in Lhasa where I had arrived with Hamid, Ken Storm, Gil and Troy Gillenwater, and two additional recruits who would help defray the cost of the expedition. Claire Scobie, an English journalist, had traveled the year before with the British plant collecters we had met in Nyingtri. Waltraut Ott, a German Buddhist, claimed to be seeing visions of Dorje Pagmo after a yearlong meditation retreat near Kathmandu. We drove to Bhakha monastery in Powo and set out the next day for the Su-La pass that leads into Pemako. I'd begun working with a new company in Lhasa, and our Tibetan guide, Nima, proved a loyal and dedicated ally, despite the fact that we had to carry him down the Su-La due to crippling knee pains. On the far side of the pass we entered the now-familiar dense, leech-filled jungles. It rained unrelentingly. "I can't believe we're doing this all over again," Gil said.

After a night at what they dubbed insect camp (more than 2,300 species of insects have been found in Pemako and a vast number of them had infested our tents), Gil and Troy had had enough; they were going to return to higher ground. We split our rations, and with two Sherpas to assist them they started up the Tsangpo to where they could cross by cable to the right bank. From there, they would trek upriver to the confluence that they had visited with Rick Fisher in 1994. Ken, Hamid, and I continued with Claire, Waltraut, and Ani Rigsang to a Lopa village called Chutanka from where we hoped to cross the Tsangpo and enter the valleys to the south of Namcha Barwa.

Chutanka lies on a shelf of land thousands of feet above the Tsangpo River. The conical moss-clad peak that rises above the village makes it look from afar like the ancient Incan capital of Machu Picchu. Foregoing tents, we settled into a house and dried our clothes around a smoky fire. Sitting on skins of large white monkeys, Nima, Hamid, and I spoke with the Lopa headman about the route across the river. "No one has crossed the cable in years," the headman said, sitting naked from the waist up; "the anchors are loose and rusty now." In

the past, people from his village had made pilgrimages to Choeje Lingpa's hermitage at Mandeldem, but it had long since fallen into ruin. The valley was now the haunt of monkeys and lumbering takin that descend from the slopes of Namcha Barwa to drink from thermal springs at the base of the glaciers. "Even if the cable could be crossed," the headman added, "the ravines beyond are impassible in summer; they're infested with venomous snakes and trees that cause unbearable blisters if one brushes against them or rain drips on you from their leaves. No matter how much you paid us," he said, "what good would it do if we died?" He told us of another cable several days downriver. "Maybe you can cross there," he said.

Ken was discouraged and decided to catch up with the Gillenwaters. He hoped to convince them to take a detour to the Shechen ridge, where they could look down into the Five-Mile Gap. Hamid and I held out, determined to try our luck at the next cable crossing.

As we left Chutanka, we passed a circle of sharpened, head-high stakes that had been painted the color of blood and thrust into the earth above the village to harness the energies of local spirits. For two days we contoured along high paths above the Tsangpo, passing through scattered villages. At Druk, villagers told us

that the cable there had also rusted and
no one had crossed the Tsangpo in years.
Even if the cable doesn't break, the headman told us, no trails lead through the
mountains on the far side of the river.
Waltraut speculated that the villagers
did know of a secret path leading to
Mandeldem and to Yangsang, but would
not tell us about it. Claire, a pragmatic
journalist, said that Yangsang existed
only in the mind, a will-o'-the-wisp, like
the Tsangpo Falls, that receded as you
approach it. I translated their comments
to Ani Rigsang, who laughed and continued eating the wild grapes that grew
along the trail.

We'd reached an impasse. It was too
late to retrace our steps and follow the route north toward the confluence and
the ridge above the Five-Mile Gap. We resigned ourselves to trekking down the
lower Tsangpo gorge, retracing the route that Kinthup had followed in 1882
during his clandestine attempt to follow the river into India.

As we continued down the slopes of the gorge, side streams spilled from
dense jungle and transformed into waterfalls that plunged into the Tsangpo. At
one silvery cascade overhung with subtropical foliage, naked children bathed in
the spray amid peals of laughter. As we approached, they scampered through the
rocks and water and disappeared like sprites. The sun tilted through the vine-
strung trees at the top of the falls and formed halos in the cascading water.

IN 1982, AS I PREPARED FOR MY STUDY of sacred landscapes in Sikkim,
the anthropologist Dr. Michael Harner told me of his experiences among the
Jívaro Indians in the Amazonian rain forests of eastern Ecuador. The Jívaros'

principal initiation rites occur in the spaces behind waterfalls, Dr. Harner told me. Holding a balsa wood staff, the shaman crosses back and forth between the translucent curtain of water flowing on one side and the solid rock wall on the other, the cacophonous roar of the cascading water (and often the combined use of decoctions of the hallucinogenic vine *Banisteriopsis caapi*) leading him into an altered state of consciousness.[3] I learned of similar initiatory rites that take place in Haiti, where white-robed Vodoun initiates descend a limestone escarpment and enter the waterfall of Saut d'Eau where a serpent deity held to be the repository of wisdom offers renewal and transformation amid the thundering waters.[4] In Japan, adherents of the Shugendo sect stand under icy waterfalls to assimilate the energies they believe to pervade the entire universe, while African chieftains placated their gods by throwing offerings over the brink of the 355-foot high Mosi-oa-Tunya, the Smoke That Thunders, that David Livingstone renamed Victoria Falls when he "discovered" it in 1855.

Even animals experience the awe of waterfalls: a noted animal behaviorist described the journey of a solitary chimpanzee to a waterfall in East Africa, "evidently for the sheer pleasure of communing with it."[5]

WE CONTINUED DOWN THE TSANGPO and crossed again over the Doshung-La pass. Chinese police officers met us on the other side and escorted us to the Public Security Bureau in Bayi, where we discovered that Ken Storm and the Gillenwaters had been arrested for deviating from the stated itinerary.

Bayi's head detective, Tashi, who had recovered some of our stolen belongings in 1994 and had requested a "prize," was still there. The gaudy plaque that Hamid and I had brought him in 1996 still hung from the office wall. Tashi was dressed, as usual, in a trenchcoat and a fedora. In our past dealings with him he had been friendly, if odd, but on this occasion his Chinese superiors were present, and he acted accordingly. Translating their demands, he asked that we hand over all our film and he forced Hamid to read aloud from Claire's journal. Gil's Tibet guidebook contained a foreword by the Dalai Lama, and the police confiscated it as a subversive document. They examined Ken's video footage at length and expressed disappointment when it revealed no more than images of mountains and rivers. Through sleight of hand, we managed to conceal most of our film. I pushed in the tails of several unexposed slide rolls and passed it off as film that I had shot on the trail. I could not resist asking what the chief detective thought I could possibly have taken pictures of that would be strategically sensitive; U.S. satellites can secure much better images of bridges than I can with my camera, I assured him.

"Yes," he said triumphantly, "but not the underside of bridges."

After writing obligatory "self-criticism" letters for having broken the laws of China and promising to honor Tashi's request to bring him a video of *The Godfather* when we next returned, we piled into the jeeps and headed for Lhasa. That night at a roadside restaurant Ken, Gil, and Troy related their experience. After crossing to the west bank of the Tsangpo, they'd learned of a hunters' trail that winds along a knife-edge ridge to Shechen-La. They'd followed it until the weather opened and they gazed out over the glacier-covered peaks of Namcha Barwa and Gyala Pelri and down into the dizzying depths of the Five-Mile Gap. With the aid of a local hunter whom they had met in the mists, they descended lower and reached a point high above the Tsangpo where they could look downriver toward the crest of the hydrolic feature that David Breashears had photographed from a similar vantage point in 1993. Beyond that point the Tsangpo disappeared from view, but the plumes of spray suggested the presence of a large waterfall. Intervening cliffs prevented them from descending closer.

Gil and Troy had tried to see into the gap from the north on their expedition with Rick Fisher in May 1994. After their aborted raft trip farther up the Tsangpo, they had trekked down to the confluence. Rick had read about the seventy-five waterfalls described in Kingdon Ward's book, Gil said. They'd followed a trail above the village of Mondrong, and in an article in *Men's Journal* in September 1994, Rick claimed to have seen into the innermost sections of the gorge. "There were no waterfalls!" he had declared. Gil clarified that they had followed the trail for no more than a few hours and hadn't even gone far enough to see the river, let alone its hidden depths. On this occasion they'd seen only a small portion of the Tsangpo from the Shechen-La, but had been tantalized by the sight of the foaming cataract where it disappeared around a headwall and entered the Five-Mile Gap. We looked repeatedly at the video footage that Ken had shot and, over dinner in Tsedang, agreed to go back together to the gorge in October 1998 to investigate more closely.

On the Trail of the Takin

IN THE WINTER OF 1998, in the first days of the Tibetan Year of the Earth Tiger, I traveled to Cambridge, Massachusetts, to meet with Hamid and Robert Gardner, the founder and director of the Film Study Center at Harvard University. In 1990, a year before beginning his doctoral program at Harvard, Hamid completed a yearlong course at the Anthropology Film Center in Santa Fe, New Mexico. Robert Gardner's lyrical film on ritual warfare among the Dugum Dani tribe in New Guinea (*Dead Birds*, 1964) and his cinematic essay on the cremation ghats in Benaras, India (*Forest of Bliss*, 1984) had left lasting impressions, and Gardner, in his turn, had been intrigued by Hamid's accounts of the Buddhist hunters of the Tsangpo gorge. Gardner had agreed to partly finance a film that Hamid and I would help direct. Gardner had recruited an award-winning cinematographer named Ned Johnston who joined us in Cambridge.

Hamid and I told the seasoned filmmakers what we knew about the Pemako hunters' quest for takin, the horned blue-eyed ruminants they believe Padmasambhava placed in the gorges for their benefit. According to the hunters' stories, the takins' life force travels at death through an aperature in one of their horns to Chimé Yangsang Né, Pemako's Secret Place of Immortality. Legends abound in Pemako of hunters who have followed their tracks into the mystic sanctuary. As they never return, the way is lost to all who would follow.

Hamid spoke eloquently of the importance of documenting the Tsangpo hunters' vanishing way of life and exploring their beliefs that link the quest for game with a spiritual search. The film should invoke the hunters' sense of living at the threshold of another world, Hamid argued.

Gardner's groundbreaking films had been made with minimal or no narration. *Forest of Bliss* unfolds without commentary, subtitles, or dialogue and of-

fers a magnified sense of participation in ceremonies, rituals, and vocations associated with death and regeneration. *Dead Birds* focuses on a Stone Age society
in the highlands of West Irian living an isolated existence based on intertribal
warfare between neighboring clans. As Gardner described the making of the
film, "Certain kinds of behavior were followed, never directed. . . . It was an attempt to see people from within and to wonder, when the selected fragments
of that life were assembled, if they might speak not only of the Dani but also
of ourselves."

We hoped that the film on the hunters of the Tsangpo gorge would have a
similar allegorical dimension. When Frank Capra induced Columbia Pictures
to buy the film rights to *Lost Horizon,* he allegedly claimed that the story "held
a mirror up to the thoughts of every human being on earth." We felt that the
hunters' quest for an idealized realm ever beyond the horizon spoke of the
same universal longings.

During the two years that Hamid lived in Kathmandu, he created a powerful film about the masked dances of Harisiddhi, a temple on the edges of the
Kathmandu valley that's still rumored to practice human sacrifice. Gardner
urged that Hamid take charge of sound for the film on the Tsangpo gorge and
that we both assist Ned in shaping its themes—from the preparation for the
hunt to the quest for Yangsang. If Yangsang could not be found literally, we
would try to evoke it through art.

WHEN WE LEFT FOR TIBET in May of 1998, we planned to film the takin
hunt in the area of Neythang which Ken Storm, Ralph Rynning, and I had visited in 1996. Hamid had traveled alone that year to Bayu, where he spent the
night in the home of a Khampa hunter named Tsering Dondrup whose
brother, the local lama, had directed him across the Tsangpo to the texts expli-
cating Dorje Pagmo's five chakras. By chance, we ran into Tsering at the trailhead in Pelung, where he was attending a local festival and drinking large
quantities of chang. Hamid told him of our intention to film takin in
Neythang.

"Don't go to Neythang!" Tsering said in drunken enthusiasm, "I'll show you where there are more takin in the valleys above Bayu."

In Tibetan deeply inflected by the local dialect, Tsering claimed that as the snow begins to melt on the high passes, the takin migrate out of the deepest section of the gorge where they shelter in caves during the winter. When Hamid and I pressed him, Tsering told us of a network of takin trails through the area that Kingdon Ward had referred to as a "forbidden land." This was a revelation to us: it shattered the long-standing myth of the inaccessibility of the Tsangpo's innermost gorge. Since the middle of the nineteenth century, Tibetans had categorically denied any knowledge of the legendary gap, but now Tsering, lucid with chang, began to name the caves and rock shelters where he and other hunters slept on their hunting expeditions into the world's deepest gorge. As he described an improbable route through precipitous jungles and across towering, moss-covered cliffs, our excitement mounted. If he was to be believed, the Himalayas' ultimate terra incognita was in fact its best-kept secret.

We hired Tsering on the spot and began the trek down toward the confluence. As we followed the gallery of bridges down the Po Tsangpo River, Tsering described the game trails into the depths of the gorge that the takin forge during their spring migrations. I scribbled the names of the various sites in my notebook: Benchi Pagmo, Zadem, Hugudurung—remote outposts reclaimed by jungle in the months when the stinging nettles, bamboo, and underbrush grow too densely to allow passage.

In the course of his descriptions, Tsering mentioned three waterfalls on the Tsangpo that he and other hunters had only seen from ledges high above. One of the waterfalls fit Kingdon Ward's description of Rainbow Falls; another seemed to lie at the point where Ken and the Gillenwaters had lost sight of the Tsangpo the previous summer. Using his arm to indicate its shape, Tsering described the third waterfall as a plume of water farther down the gap. Could one of these three waterfalls be the fabled Falls of the Tsangpo?

Tsering measured on his fingers the respective heights of the mysterious cascades. "The middle one is the highest," he said. "It's twice as high as the first, and the third one is smaller than the other two." He admitted, though, that neither he nor anyone else had ever gone all the way down to the falls. They'd only looked down on them from the cliffs above. "Powerful guardian spirits (*suma*) reside there," Tsering said. "It's not a place to go without a lama."

Tsering said that until now they'd never told any outsiders, Chinese or otherwise, that there was a way down into the innermost gorge. Hamid and I had returned year after year, he said, we spoke their language, knew their ritual practices and, most of all, we had undertaken the *né-kor*, or pilgrimage to Kundu Dorsempotrang. He said that the people of Pemako had accepted us now as *nangpa*, or Buddhist insiders.

WHEN WE REACHED TSACHU, the village perched above the northernmost arc of the Great Bend of the Tsangpo, we climbed through sloping fields of buckwheat to the house of Lama Topgye, one of Pemako's oldest and most respected lamas. I produced from my pack a letter from Bhakha Tulku that he had sealed with wax and wrapped in a silk khata. Lama Topgye read the letter carefully several times. It was the first news that he had had in years from a compatriot who had been forced to leave Tibet. As he read, Lama Topgye's wife, an imposing woman garlanded in cats' eyes and gzi stones, produced the requisite bowls of a particularly intoxicating variety of chang, brewed from local millet.

Lama Topgye sat cross-legged on a worn Tibetan carpet in front of an open window. The ponderous leaves of a banana tree rustled against the sill. Across the subtropical valley, the ice-fluted walls of Gyala Pelri rose to nearly 24,000 feet above sea level. Encouraged by Bhakha Tulku's letter explaining that Hamid and I had come as Buddhist pilgrims, Lama Topgye pointed to a gilded statue on an altar at the opposite end of the room. "Many centuries ago," he said, "the Tantric master Padmasambhava composed texts that foretold the way to a paradisiacal sanctuary that will only open when the right circumstances all converge. When the Chinese first came to Tibet, many people tried to find the innermost secret heart of Pemako. Some came back disappointed. Others disappeared into the jungles and never returned. The Chinese told us it was all superstition. They forced us to throw all our books into the Tsangpo."

I asked Lama Topgye if he remembered a text describing seventy-five water-falls in the Tsangpo's innermost gorge, and he lamented that it had in all likeli-hood been consigned to the waves or destroyed in the earthquake in 1950 that toppled the monastery at Pemakochung. I mentioned the three waterfalls that Tsering had told us about, and Lama Topgye suddenly became pensive. Look-ing out across the deeply forested valley toward the wall of snow mountains that seal Pemako from the rest of Tibet, he said, "According to Padmasam-bhava's prophecies, there are several né-go, or doors, that lead to Pemako's in-nermost center. One of them is said to be the largest of three waterfalls in the Tsangpo gorge. But just reaching there doesn't mean the way will open. The lost termas described specific rituals to open the door. If the right rituals are not performed or one's motivations are not pure, things could go wrong and the way into Chimé Yangsang Né might close forever."

Lama Topgye opened a leather box and took out thin red cords called songdu, the talismanic strings that, when tied around the neck, help protect the pilgrim from adversities. "This whole realm," he said, "belongs to the goddess Dorje Pagmo. She will protect you, but you should go carefully, the way is dan-gerous." A false step, he suggested, could lead to one's plummeting into the Tsangpo as it roars between vertical walls of rock.

As we climbed down the ladder from Lama Topgye's hut, his sonorous chanting filled our ears. Beating on a double-headed drum suspended from the rafters, he had begun the invocations of local protector spirits that we had asked him to supplicate on our behalf.

WE CROSSED THE TSANGPO on a bridge below the confluence and trekked south along the forested slope of a spur descending from Namcha Barwa. Shortly before nightfall, we arrived in Bayu, where we settled into Tsering's rough-hewn home and began recruiting hunters for the journey into the gap. Ned filmed them as they packed their meager supplies into bamboo pack bas-kets, cleaned their primitive Chinese rifles, and offered wild roses at the altar of the local temple. Tsering spread ink on a carved wooden block and printed

miniature prayer flags on squares of cotton. He would place them along the path of the takin as offerings to the spirits of the land.

Before beginning the climb to the Shechen-La, we visited Tsering Dondrup's brother, a lama named Kongchok Wangpo. Dressed in blood-colored robes, he told us that hunters bring the takins' heads to him after they're killed to consecrate the meat and ensure the safe passage of the takins' souls on a crystal pathway to the heart of Yangsang.

ON THE MORNING of our departure, the lama performed a fire ceremony in front of the village temple. As great clouds of fragrant smoke rose and merged with the mists, the hunters prayed for the success of our journey. As we climbed through dense forests toward the Shechen-La, Ned's filming focused on the hunters' deep intimacy with the landscape through which they moved. They recited mantras at welling springs where we filled our water bottles and Tsering fixed prayer flags to the overarching trees. Our second day out they showed us the remnants of snares where takin strangled themselves to death in their efforts to break free. They spoke of Yangsang Né as a realm beyond the dichotomies of life and death, a place where takin and those who hunt them are mysteriously united, where fruit falls from the trees of its own accord, and a primal harmony exists between man and beasts—the fulfillment of Thoreau's advice to "hunt until you can do better."

As we descended off the snow-covered ridge into the region of the gap, Tsering and the other hunters looked for signs of the takins' passage. Less than an hour below, with the distant roar of the Tsangpo filtering through thickening mists, they came across tracks that led south, contouring along the slopes of the gorge. Tsering expressed surprise. "They are moving early this year," he said.

After picking our way across landslides and snow-choked gullies, we reached a narrow shelf where Tsering determined we should camp. We spent hours carving a ledge large enough for a single two-man tent that Hamid, Ned, and I were compelled to share. The hunters sheltered under tarpaulins stretched between trees. It began to rain during the night, and by morning we were caught in a deluge. In a region where metereological events are held to signify guardian deities' response to human intercessors, the weather was definitely not in our favor.

For the next three days, we holed up in the single tent in weather that seemed like the end of the world. A torrent of rocks and boulders tumbled down on either side of the camp and knocked out the supports of the plastic tarpaulins that the hunters and the Sherpas used for shelter. When we ventured out from the tent, clouds of gnats descended upon us, inflaming any bit of exposed skin. The hunters huddled by the smoky fire, which offered partial relief. Lama, the former monk who had come with us on the pilgrimage to Kundu, performed endless fire offerings, as much to keep the gnats at bay as to appease the local spirits.

Across the gorge, flitting in and out of the swirling gray mists, was the triangular-shaped peak that Tsering called Dorje Pagmo Dzong. Its jagged ridges and crowning pyramid of slate-black rock formed a citadel of the great goddess of the Tsangpo gorges. "Beneath that peak lies the largest of the three waterfalls," Tsering said. From where we were camped, at the edge of an abyss, the falls seemed as inaccessible as the peak itself.

I'd waited out storms in ice caves near the tops of mountains in Norway and the Alps, but this collapsing, gnat-plagued ledge was beyond anything I had encountered. Claustrophobia drove Ned from the tent, and now he sat under the tarpaulins on pine boughs amid clouds of smoke, immersing himself in Salman Rushdie's *The Satanic Verses*. By wearing gloves and exposing little more than his eyes, he evaded all but the most persistent gnats. Whenever Hamid and I joined him, he discoursed passionately on favorite films such as *The Passenger*, whose themes of cultural and personal displacement seemed increasingly relevant to our current circumstances. As we waited out the storm, Ned invoked Werner Herzog's *Aguirre: The Wrath of God*, a film about the search for El Dorado in the jungles of Peru by a party of conquistadors. As civilization vanishes in their wake, restraints dissolve and the men—led by their greed and a demoniacal Klaus Kinski—descend into the vortex of their darkest beings.

Looking down into the cloud-wrapped depths of the gorge reminded me of another film called *The Valley (Obscured by Clouds)* that had even odder parallels with our journey. Produced and directed in 1972 by the iconoclastic French filmmaker Barbet Schroeder, the film opens with a tantalizing overhead pan of the New Guinea highlands, shot through banks of mist and accompanied by an ethereal soundtrack by the rock band Pink Floyd. An unseen narrator describes a lost valley from which previous explorers have never returned, a blank spot on the map perpetually covered by clouds that legend says may be paradise on earth. But even the primitive tribes who live closest to it dare not venture there, as it is the dwelling place of their gods.

The film chronicles the Dionysian odyssey of a small band of French and European dreamers who venture into the primeval mountains in search of the legendary valley. Joined by a French consul officer's bourgeois wife who is searching for plumage of the endangered bird of paradise, the adventurers encounter Stone Age tribes and imbibe hallucinogenic tree sap as they journey ever deeper into morally and geographically ambiguous terrain. The film ends as they reach the rim of the long-sought valley, abandoned by their guides and divested of food and bearings.

Like a cross between *Lost Horizon* and *Acopolypse Now*, *The Valley (Obscured by*

Clouds) has all the trappings of fantasy, but much of it was unvarnished reality, shot on location and spontaneously scripted. Our vision for the *Buddhist Hunters of the Tsangpo Gorges* was strictly documentary, but like *The Valley*, we hoped to use it to explore modern society's yearning for a primitive golden age. By sharing the traditions of the Pemako gorges with those who would never come here, we hoped to introduce a wholly different worldview, in which the possibility of Yangsang is an ever-present reality.

AFTER THREE DAYS, the storm abated and we set out across the fresh landslides that had formed around our bivouac site. Buluk, one of the hunters, drove the end of his matchlock into the mountainside, balancing himself under a swaying basket of blackened pots, ropes, and climbing gear supported only by a fraying tumpline of woven bamboo. Behind me, another hunter, less stable on his feet, chanted mantras as he crouched down with his hands against the steep, eroding slope. As we moved across the landslide, scree slid out from beneath our feet—a continuous cascade of rocks, crystals, and frozen snow tumbling downward into the depths of the Tsangpo gorge, hidden below us under veils of mist.

The hunters searched for the hoofprints of the takin, but the torrential rain had washed most of them away. By following the line of least resistance, we picked up the trail again and followed it across a series of ridges and ravines. At one point, Tsering pointed down into the mists and said that from a ledge below one could see two of the waterfalls that he had told us about.

Ned adamantly wanted to continue on ahead to catch up with the phantom herd of takin. Hamid and I couldn't resist the opportunity to scout the route that had eluded Ken and the Gillenwaters the year before. We convinced Ned that the thundering waters would provide a compelling background for the film, even if he could only shoot them from high above. Begrudgingly, he agreed to make the side trip.

We wove our way down through a tangle of twisted growth along a spur that dropped precipitously toward the yet unseen river. Steep cliffs flanked the sides. As the drop steepened we lowered ourselves from moss-covered branches and after more than an hour we reached a sloping ledge perched approximately 2,000 feet above the Tsangpo River. Holding on to thick rhododendrons, we peered out over the edge and looked a quarter mile upriver to the first of the waterfalls that Tsering had described. A wide curtain of green-gray water poured over a ledge that was bisected in the middle by a protruding granite block. Judging by the spur descending from Gyala Pelri and the photograph taken by Kingdon Ward in 1924, we determined that it was the waterfall that he and Cawdor had seen only from upstream, known ever since as Rainbow Falls.

Directly below us, and hidden from Kingdon Ward's vantage point on the wall above Rainbow Falls, was a larger cataract that surged through a narrow breach between opposing spurs of the gorge. Doubling back on itself, the Tsangpo plummeted down into a grottolike alcove, but our view was fore-shortened by being perched directly over the drop and it made it impossible even to guess at the waterfall's height. Despite its magnificent setting, we were fairly sure that the falls below us were well under 100 feet high, which meant, sadly, that it was not the long-sought Falls of the Tsangpo. If it *was* more than 100 feet high, then Kingdon Ward's conclusions had been premature. We were resolved to find out either way.

The hunters had never descended lower than the ledge to which we now clung like the narrator in Poe's short story "The Maelstrom." The falls were still thousands of feet below, but the surging waters resounded off the over-hanging walls on the opposite side of the gorge. Even had we been able to dis-cover a route to river level at this time, we had no equipment for measuring the waterfall's height. And we had made a commitment to journey there only in October with Ken and the Gillenwaters. Ned shot footage of the two waterfalls but was eager to climb back up to where we had left our packs and to resume our quest for the takin. "Unless we catch up with this herd," he said, "we won't have a film."

Tsering too wanted to leave the ledge as soon as possible. "Takin don't go there," he said. "And humans going there could anger the protector spirits." He looked up at the towering cliffs of Dorje Pagmo's citadel.

I asked about the door into Yangsang Né. "It's no use," he said, "unless a qualified lama performs the appropriate rites; it would just be an impenetrable veil of rock and water."

We began the long climb back up to where we had branched off from the tracks of the takin. I looked back: the plume of mist that rose from the base of the falls made it look more like a fountain. Whatever the waterfall's actual height, there was an air of mystery about the place, and I looked forward to returning in the autumn when we would try to find a route down to its base and continue afterward through the gap.

As we made our way back through the gnarled jungle and hung from vegetated cliffs, Buluk offered to carry Ned's movie camera, which he'd bumped against innumerable rocks. Ned wouldn't relinquish it, and it became increasingly battered, to the point where he wondered whether its focusing mechanism was still intact. Further darkening Ned's mood, he had scratched an expensive Baume & Mercier watch that he had bought shortly before the expedition. Hamid had commented at the outset that the watch seemed more suitable for a black tie dinner than the inner depths of the Tsangpo gorge, but Ned had insisted on wearing it.

Close to dark we reached a small waterfall pouring down through cliffs to a level spot where Tsering had told the others to set up camp. No one was there. We found fresh footprints leading up a steep embankment, following takin tracks into the jungle. Night was upon us, but we had no choice but to follow the footprints up the narrow ravine. We called out into the darkness but heard no reply. In pitch darkness, we began to fashion a makeshift bivouac for ourselves beneath rocky, moss-covered boulders, but as we did we heard distant voices and, eventually, with only a single, fading flashlight, we made a hazardous descent to a snowfield where the Sherpas had set up a precarious camp. We crawled into our tents and disappeared until the morning.

THE NEXT DAY we followed the takin tracks farther upriver and away from the gap. They seemed to be headed toward a high pass on the eastern flanks of Namcha Barwa.

"Where are these animals!" Ned shouted, irritated that we could not keep pace with the elusive beasts. Although takin most closely resemble the African gnu, they are distant relatives of the Arctic musk ox. Shaggy and powerfully built, they climb cliffs as sure-footedly as mountain goats. A Tibetan folktale accounts for the takin's odd appearance. A saint named Drukpa Kunleg entered a remote Himalayan village and demanded a goat, which he ate in one sitting. Still hungry, he demanded a cow, and just as quickly finished it off. He then took the head of the goat, placed it on the carcass of the cow, and slapped it on its rear end to send it off to graze, thus accounting for the takin's goatlike head and bovine body.

We emerged out of the tangled undergrowth and crossed snowfields until we reached a series of ledges where the hunters traced the takins' tracks to the bottom of a near-vertical eroding cliff. The takin had disappeared over its crest.

The unscalable band of cliffs continued above us as far as we could see. Below, the slope plunged vertically into the depths of the gorge. It was already late afternoon, and the hunters, who seldom balked at the extreme terrain, said that the takin had gone too far and that we couldn't follow them over the cliffs. Ned was in near despair. "We've come all this way for nothing," he said. "That damned waterfall. If we hadn't lost all those hours, we might have reached here before the takin disappeared over that cliff!"

The loss of the takin disappointed us all. But it was the days that we had spent pinned to the side of the gorge in a raging storm and not our side excursion that had led to the takin's outdistancing us. Tsering now had more immediate concerns. He said that by following the takin's hoofprints we had descended far from where he had instructed the porters to set up camp and that we would have a difficult time making our way up through the ravines and watercourses. We looked up and saw cliffs, landslides, and steep unstable slopes. With no more chance of stumbling into the herd of takin, Ned packed away his camera.

The climb up the side of the gorge was treacherous. In near darkness we crossed an enormous landslide with nowhere to anchor our ropes. At one point Ned lost his footing and began to slide toward the cliff below us, rocks plummeting beneath him into an incredible void. Had he not grabbed on to the small tufts of vegetation that grew up through the mud, snow, and scree, he would have catapulted down to his death.

Ned cursed continuously as he picked his way across the collapsing mountainside. As his knees shot up and down like a sewing machine, Tsering and Buluk climbed below him in their thin-soled Chinese sneakers and placed his feet on small protrusions of rock and earth that held for only a few seconds, forcing him to move rapidly across the shifting surface of the slide.

We eventually reached the far side of the landslide. From the ridge beyond, we could see in the distance the small fires where the Sherpas had set up camp. We made our way through the darkness to shallow caves recessed beneath looming boulders.

That night around the fire, Tsering lamented that we had not been able to catch up with the migrating takin. In the warming weather, they had crossed early over high passes into the regions south of Namcha Barwa. The jungle there is so dense that we could never follow, Tsering said. Even if we found them, we would never be able to carry the meat back out. Perhaps on another trip, Tsering continued, we could travel that direction. The weather had improved and, in their perception that Pemako's guardian deities are arbiters of meteorological events, the clearing weather indicated that if we were not fa-vored, we were at least tolerated by the local spirits.

Ned filmed Tsering as he sat by the sparkling fire and recounted how in their own local mythology, the takin will eventually lead them into Yangsang Né. Following their footprints in the snow, they will find a still-hidden pass and cross it into the promised land.

Without footage of the takin, the film was incomplete. But Hamid already had in mind how he would supply the missing shots with his own Bolex cam-era. In October, he would go off alone with one or two of the hunters, he said, when the takin return to the Five-Mile Gap. My own reveries turned more toward the hidden waterfall. Although I doubted that it would turn out to be more than 100 feet high, and I had no clue as to how the mythical door might actually open, I had faith that if we could reach it something momentous would be revealed.

The Exploration Council

DURING THE TREK DOWN THE PO TSANGPO with Ned Johnston and Hamid Sardar, I had met Steve Currey, the owner of a wilderness rafting company who was scouting for a major descent on the lower Tsangpo River. After Rick's failed rafting venture in 1993, *Outside* magazine had determined that "The Tsangpo Gorge . . . given its abundance of Class VI rapids, will likely never be run. . . ." But Steve Currey was set on running the section of the river below its confluence with the Po Tsangpo. He had enlisted two top kayakers—Scott Lindgren and Charlie Munsey—who launched their boats near the bridge in Pelung and ran several miles of the Po Tsangpo before the raw power of the waters drove them back to shore.

As we watched them from a decrepit footbridge spanning the river, Tsering Dondrup commented on the boats' usefulness. "If I had one of those, I would use it to cross the Tsangpo at Hugudurung," he said, referring to a river-level cave in the depths of the Five-Mile Gap. Herds of takin cover the slopes on the opposite bank, he said, but neither he nor any of the hunters had any way of reaching there. He claimed to be the last in his village to know how to make a boat by burning the centers of fir trees and lashing them together with bamboo cords.

After the kayakers pulled out of the thrashing waves, they continued on foot toward the confluence to scout the area where a Japanese kayaker, Yoshitaka Takei, had perished on the Tsangpo in November 1993. If feasible, they would put in at the junction of the two rivers and make a run for the Indian border.

We did not tell them our own plans of making a film, or of the rumored waterfall in the heart of the gap. We told them that we had come to continue our research into the cultural history of what, for Tibetans, is a promised land.

Oddly, Currey's Chinese liaison officer had remained at the road head in Pelung, and Hamid and I translated for them as they negotiated rates with their porters and told them where they wanted to go. We left them when they crossed a bridge leading west to Mondrong, exchanging addresses before parting.

Two months later—in July 1998—Currey called me in Kathmandu. He told me he would be making a presentation at the National Geographic Society, seeking sponsorship for an expedition on the lower Tsangpo River. Knowing that I had traveled through the villages of the lower gorge, he asked if I would show slides and talk about the indigenous peoples living "in the deepest and most remote valleys on Earth," in the hope that this would help persuade National Geographic to sponsor his expedition. He also asked if I would organize the land portion of the expedition if the grant went through. I had already planned to come to the United States the following month, and I agreed to meet him in Washington, D.C., on August 10.

I took the Metroliner from New York City and, late at night, checked into a hotel a few blocks from the National Geographic Society. In the morning, a few hours before our scheduled presentation, I reviewed Currey's prospectus: a $577,863 bid for full funding of an ambitious, multipronged expedition that would "make history by rafting/kayaking the Lower Yarlung Tsangpo gorge (which includes the first-ever descent from China to India)." I was ambivalent about involving myself in such an expedition. Whereas Currey was primarily interested in the area below the confluence, I was focused on what lay above. But I was curious as to how National Geographic would receive our presentation and grateful that he had asked me to participate.

Assembled in a small auditorium with a panel of senior National Geographic personnel, Currey began the presentation with video footage of Scott Lindgren maneuvering his kayak through the seething froth of the Po Tsangpo. I followed with slides and spoke of the region's cultural and religious history—the legacy of the beyul.

It felt odd speaking of these matters in National Geographic's hallowed halls, but my audience was attentive. Somewhat embarrassingly, it quickly became evident that the society had no interest in sponsoring The Currey Expedition, because they were already sponsoring a kayaking expedition on the Tsangpo that coming fall. But several on the review board had taken a great interest in my slides that revealed a cultural dimension to the Tsangpo gorge that they had not been previously considered. "Why haven't you contacted us before?" asked Rebecca Martin, director of National Geographic's Exploration Council (now known as the Expeditions Council). "When are you planning to go back?"

I told her that I hadn't been interested in publicizing the area before making a thorough survey and that only recently had I learned of a route into the legendary gap. I said I would be returning to Pemako in October to attempt to make my way through this unexplored section of the gorge. Purposefully, I mentioned nothing about the waterfall that we had seen the previous May.

"That's exactly the kind of trip the Exploration Council sponsors," she told me, and encouraged me to submit an application. She would call a special meeting, she told me, and the council would decide quickly.

I had always been wary of obligating myself to a third party and in the past had rejected sponsors who desired something from me in return. The Exploration Council struck me as different and seemed genuinely committed to promoting worthy journeys that would lead to National Geographic's stated mission—dating back to 1888—to increase and disseminate geographical knowledge of the planet. I would be returning to Nepal in early September to lead a Himalayan Kingdoms tour for the Smithsonian Institution, and I agreed to complete the application before I left the States.

As I would not be returning to Washington, Rebecca Martin urged me to meet with members of the kayaking expedition that National Geographic had already agreed to sponsor. The team proposed to make the first attempt to kayak through the chasms of "Tibet's forbidden river." The expedition leader, Lieutenant Colonel Wickliffe W. Walker, an ex-Special Forces officer, had previously applied to another institution, the Henry Foundation for Botanical Research. By coincidence, I had met Susan Treadway, the foundation's director, a year earlier when she was staying at my parents' home in Bedford, New York. She had told me then about Walker's plan to kayak through "the Earth's deepest canyon" and asked me whether I thought it would be feasible. Sections of the gorges are definitely runnable, I told her, but to attempt its innermost chasms would be suicidal. My words haunted me as I drove to the home of Harry Wetherbee, Walker's partner in organizing the expedition.

A former state department employee, Harry Wetherbee had privileged access to restricted maps and high-resolution satellite photography. A StairMaster stood prominently on the living room floor in front of the fireplace. Wick Walker was out of town, but Harry's wife, Doris, and Tom McEwan, one of the expedition's four world-class kayakers, were present as we pored over their state-of-the-art imagery. When they reached the area of Rainbow Falls, they planned to portage along the Tsangpo's left bank, Harry told me.

I found it curious that the satellite imagery gave little indication of the actual terrain: even Kingdon Ward's photographs from 1924 show sheer cliffs rising from the left bank of the river and I knew from our foray earlier that year that what Harry proposed would be impossible.[6] Without revealing what Tsering had told us of hunters' trails through the region of the gap, I told of them of a crucial escape route should they need to exit the gorge farther upstream: the pass across from Pemakochung that Ken, Ralph, and I had gazed down from in 1996.

I submitted my grant application to the Exploration Council on September 4. I titled it "Secrets of the Tsangpo" and revealed for the first time what Hamid and I had learned on our previous expedition:

> The culmination of seven previous trips to the Pemako/Tsangpo gorge region in southern Tibet, this expedition will document what has been referred to as "the missing link": the last unexplored section of the world's deepest gorge and a blank spot on the map of world exploration. . . . Traveling with Tibetan hunters who, until now, have guarded this region from inquisitive outsiders, the expedition will document for the first time the topography of the Tsangpo gorge between Rainbow Falls and the confluence with the Po Tsangpo. . . . The expedition will take accurate measurements of all waterfalls . . . and shed light on a region that has confounded geographers and fueled the Western imagination for more than a century.

I included résumés of my fellow teammates Hamid Sardar and Ken Storm. The Gillenwaters had opted out. They were on the cusp of a major real estate transaction. If it went through, Gil said, they might never have to work again. They were also concerned that the waterfall would turn out to be a red herring and did not want to backtrack on terrain they had already covered. "We're Pemakoed out," Gil told me over the phone.

The per-person cost of our Pemako expedition decreased with the number of participants and, with the Gillenwaters' withdrawal, the possibility of funding from National Geographic took on renewed importance. I had budgeted liberally in the application, requesting funds for camera equipment, high-tech measuring devices, and hundreds of feet of climbing rope. Some of it would go to film so that Hamid could complete the footage for the work we had begun through the Film Study Center at Harvard University.

Several weeks later, I was in Tibet lecturing to a group of thirty people in the Smithsonian program when a fax arrived for me at the Lhasa Hotel from Rebecca Martin. She wrote that the Exploration Council had agreed to finance our entire expedition. She also informed me that National Geographic Television would be sending a cameraman to document our journey. Attached to the letter was an eight-page contract.

As pleased as I was, I also felt a vague foreboding. The only sponsorship that I had accepted in the past was from a Colorado-based manufacturer of climbing equipment. In 1996, Black Diamond had supplied us with ropes, carabiners, and other climbing gear when we imagined that the only way into the depths of the gap would be to rappel down thousands of feet of vertical rock. They had asked for nothing in return. The multipage contract sent by the Exploration Council, on the other hand, bordered on the draconian, and National Geographic assumed all rights to our experience. When I called Ken to tell him the news, he was particularly concerned about the agenda of National Geographic Television.

"This is our experience," Ken said from his desk at Alladin Distributors in Minnesota. "How are we going to be able to control what they do? They may be a nonprofit institution," he said, "but their focus is totally commercial. All the nuance will be lost." In the end, Ken never signed the agreement, adamant about preserving his own right over his slides, images, and experience.

Hamid was far off in northern Central Asia and unavailable for comment.

AFTER RETURNING TO KATHMANDU, I began making preparations for the trip, putting together a team of Sherpas, organizing a supply truck, and laying in food. Due to work obligations, Ken would arrive in Nepal only two days before our intended departure date, with barely enough time to secure his visa from the Chinese embassy in Kathmandu. I had still heard nothing from Hamid. A month earlier, he had called me from Mongolia to say that he would be heading into remote parts of Tuva, a Central Asian state in the Siberian steppes, to investigate an isolated tribe of reindeer herders.

Less than a week before our departure date, David Breashears called me from his home in Boston. He told me that this year had seen devastating floods on rivers throughout China and Tibet. Destabilized topsoil from torrential rains and excessive logging had washed into the rivers, raising their levels and diminishing their ability to absorb the monsoon rains. The Tsangpo had risen to unprecedented heights but, eager to stake their claim on this "Mount Everest of rivers" and with obligations to their sponsors, Wick Walker's team had forged ahead. Within the first days of the expedition, one of the lead kayakers, Doug Gordon, a brilliant research chemist, had drowned in the turbulent waters. The rest of the party was pulling out, and we were asked to look for the body on our journey through the gap. I thought back to my grim prophecy to the chairman of the grant committee to which they had first applied.

Other ominous signs proliferated in the days before departure. The Chinese embassy in Kathmandu, under new directives from Beijing, refused to issue visas to our key Sherpas because the surnames given on their passports was Lama, a common caste name in Nepal indicating no more than Tibeto-Burmese ethnicity. This meant finding replacements for Pemba, our invaluable cook, and several other loyal allies. Furthermore, a young and deferential

Sherpa named Dawa, whom I had enlisted as an assistant to the National Geographic cameraman, had been jailed after a knife fight with a billigerent rick-
shaw driver. All attempts to spring him failed, and Bhakha Tulku offered to
send a relative of his, Lekshey, in his stead.

Oblivious to these proceedings, Hamid called me from a crackling phone at
an airstrip in Tuva. He had traveled by boat up the Shishget Khem River with
a local guide, a carton of ammunition, and a case of vodka, the only valid currency in the areas into which he was traveling. Due to contaminated fuel, the
boat engine had died. The Russian boatman left Hamid and his Tuvan guide on
the riverbank with a rusty fishhook and a shotgun and ten shells as he floated
back downstream to make repairs. His last words, Hamid reported, were, "Be
careful, the pine nut harvest has been bad this year; the bears are aggressive."

As they waited for the boatman to return, it began to snow. They kept a fire
going to ward off the cold and predatory wildlife and shot grouse until they
ran out of ammunition. (They kept two shells in reserve in the event of a bear

attack.) Five days later, the boatman
still had not returned, and they survived on an ancient species of trout
called leenok that they ate raw with
vodka, salt, and onions. Valodya, the
boatman, never materialized, and a Tuvan shaman called Ak Boghadan, the
White Old Man, eventually discovered
them while tracking a wild boar that he
and his two sons had wounded with a
primitive Russian rifle. They led them
back to civilization on the backs of
reindeer.

Hamid appeared in Kathmandu
only a few days before our scheduled
flight to Lhasa. It was mid-October
and the height of Kathmandu's festival

season. Nepalis feasted and, to ensure prosperity after the harvests, made blood sacrifices to ancient Mother goddesses—Durga, Bhagwati, Mahakali—at street-side shrines. Even the wheels of Royal Nepal Airlines' fleet of Boeing 707s had been splattered with goat's blood. A month earlier the living goddess Kumari—an incarnation of Taleju—had anointed the king, investing him with divine power to rule. The weather was also at its height; the Himalayas glittered on the horizon above emerald fields of rice.

In early June, I'd returned from our previous trip to the Tsangpo gorges and found that my house, built atop what had once been a rice paddy, had been flooded by monsoon rains. My cook and housekeeper, knee-deep in water, were bailing out the front hall when we returned. Before my trip to Washington I had moved into a new house.

My landlord, a Tibetan who had settled in Nepal after the Chinese invasion, had transformed a turn-of-the-century cottage into a fantastical multistoried structure of stained-glass windows, elaborately carved rosewood panels, and Victorian era mantelpieces salvaged from collapsed Rana palaces. A water buffalo head hung above the back stairs; an art nouveau lamppost held up the living room ceiling. A spiraling wrought-iron staircase ascended into an upper salon—curtained with heavy velvet drapes—that felt like a cross between a monastery and a maharaja's palace. Hamid kept the original apartment downstairs; outfitted with an elaborately carved fireplace, six-foot-high Belgian mirrors, and broken chandeliers, it had once served as a playhouse for dissipated Rana princes. Rental costs in Kathmandu are cheap, and we paid less than $500 a month for the entire house.

WHEN BRYAN HARVEY, the thirty-one-year-old National Geographic Television cameraman, arrived in Kathmandu, he wanted to start filming immediately. He shadowed me through the streets as I bought additional gear in trekking shops in Thamel and sat me in front of a tree in a hotel garden to ask me to describe on film the purpose of the expedition. What could I say? Over the past fifty years, Everest and K-2 and most of the world's highest mountains had all been climbed, men had walked on the moon and explored the ocean's trenches, but the final five miles of the Tsangpo gorge remained a complete mystery. Ostensibly, we intended to close the gap and resolve the enduring issue of a phantom waterfall in the world's deepest gorge. Inwardly I was in search of something beyond the parameters of geography, but I could only frame it in terms of the Tibetan myths of Yangsang.

Departure for the Gorge

ON OCTOBER 26, 1998, the night before our flight to Lhasa from Kathmandu, Hamid and I were invited to a black tie soirée at a certain Princess Malla's, where a Hollywood action hero turned incarnate lama would be present in his Tibetan silk brocade robes. I declined the invitation and stayed home to mix tsampa with ground almonds, concentrated goat whey, and assorted Himalayan herbs.

Frustrated by the pretensions of the evening's gathering, Hamid had left early for Dutch Bob's, the infamous watering hole and home of one of Kathmandu's most-storied old-time expatriates, a dealer in antique Tibetan carpets, furniture, and silver artifacts. Bob's house sat in view of the towering Boudhanath stupa and felt like a cross between a museum and a lavish if somewhat dissolute temple. Visitors congregated around a low eight-foot-long central table that presented a shifting still life of antique skull cups, exquisite burl wood bowls, and bottles of Famous Old Grouse and Old Smuggler whiskey that Bob poured for his guests into silver and ivory drinking cups. Often, a bevy of attractive young Nepali women would be sitting around the table on colorful Tibetan carpets.

Toward midnight, Hamid returned to the house with a winsome new acquaintance named Monsoon, whom he had ostensibly recruited to help him pack. He retired to his quarters as I measured out my fortified tsampa into gallon-size Ziploc bags, and stashed it along with other food into locking waterproof duffel bags. When the van arrived at 5 A.M. to take us to the airport, we were still in disarray, but the disorientation seemed strangely correct. And when Monsoon rushed off to attend a Pentacostal church service, it felt like a scene from *The Canterbury Tales*.

AFTER CLEARING CUSTOMS at the Tribhuvan International Airport, we soared high over the Himalayas in a Chinese Southwest Airlines airbus, the luminous walls of Everest and Kanchenjunga mantled below us in autumn snow. In Lhasa, we checked into the Kyichu Hotel near the Barkhor market, where we changed money with Khampa traders, their long black hair wrapped around their heads with flaming red tassels.

Pilgrims from all parts of Tibet had converged on the pilgrims' track around the Jokhang. Bright-cheeked nomad girls, their pleated hair braided with turquoise, amber, and coral, strolled alongside leather-jacketed entrepreneurs with cell phones pressed against their ears. Others cast armfuls of crushed juniper and cedar into smoldering censers in front of the Jokhang's heavy gilded doors, sending clouds of fragrant, karma-cleansing smoke into a bright, azure sky. We joined the stream of pilgrims flowing toward the Jokhang's inner sanctum and offered prayers for the success of our journey.

As in Kathmandu, all the ordinary routines of an expedition were now self-conscious events as Bryan Harvey's high-resolution video camera infiltrated our most private moments. An energetic blond-haired surfer, Bryan rode the wave of every moment and badgered us at every opportunity for some spontaneous on-camera utterance as to what we were doing, and why.

Bryan had singled me out as the film's bridge between his American audience and the exotic world of Tibet and the Himalayas. He had filmed me in Kathmandu from the back of rickshaws and zoomed in on my face as I circled the golden Buddha at the heart of the Jokhang. Ken, Hamid, and I all shared similar concerns that National Geographic Television's character-led approach would overlook what each of us had hoped to achieve in filming the Tsangpo gorges. Our vision was not that of great white explorers penetrating the earth's last blank spot of virgin territory, but a self-effacing evocation of the hidden landscapes of mind and nature: Pemako in all its otherness.

WE SLEPT FITFULLY, due to an all-night construction team working outside on a new wing of the hotel. The Sherpas had left before dawn, and we followed soon after. The bridge leading north out of Lhasa was draped with prayer flags and framed by massive incense burners. The early rays of the sun backlit the aromatic smoke that hung across the bridge like a luminous veil.

For the first hour the road was paved and smooth, but it quickly devolved into a rutted, marginally navigable track. The "highway" east out of Lhasa had been "under improvement" for several years, but it was now unquestionably at its worst, paved with sharp rocks as a foundation for tar and asphalt. Short sections of the road had already been paved but, in between, the surface was so jarring that the tape playing in the cassette deck of our Toyota Land Cruiser jolted continuously from side A to side B, from the reveries of Van Morrison to Tuvan throat singing that Hamid had recorded on his journey into Central Asia.

When we stopped for a road crew to remove boulders that had tumbled onto the road, two dust-covered monks prostrated their way through the fallen rocks, marking the ground with the length of their bodies, their foreheads calloused and yak skin padding armoring their elbows and knees. Tibetans believe that these repeated movements combined with mantra recitation and elaborate visualizations comprise one of the fastest methods to acquire *sonam,* or spiritual merit, the elusive quality essential for escaping the endless rounds of birth and rebirth—both literal and symbolic—that characterize worldly existence. In their joyous transcendence of distinctions between pleasure and pain, these threadbare monks put our own journey into sobering perspective. They looked radiant, zealously pursuing their goal of reaching Lhasa before winter snows would make the route even more demanding. We offered them alms, with unvoiced prayers that our own hardships could be borne as lightly.

Over lunch at a primitive roadside restaurant, Bryan asked for more background on the expedition and its objectives. I had purposefully played down the waterfall in my application to the Exploration Council, but I now gave Bryan the historical perspective that he needed to shape his film.

As accurate as my account was, I felt I was falsifying my deeper intention: the search for an understanding of the paradoxical links between landscape and perception and the whole riddle of Yangsang. When the French Tibetologist Alexandra David Neel ventured into Tibet in 1923–24, she had blackened her hair with Chinese ink and disguised herself as a Tibetan mendicant. The Pundit-surveyors of the British Raj had also disguised themselves as pilgrims, as did Richard Burton when he surreptitiously circumambulated the Kaaba in Mecca. Even Bailey had perfected the art of disguise when, after his journey to the Tsangpo gorge, he served as a secret agent in Central Asia. I wondered if I hadn't inadvertantly done something similar, albeit from another direction. My interest in Pemako was less the falls than what lay beyond them, yet in my presentation to the National Geographic Society I had focused strictly on geography. If we found the legendary falls, it would no doubt be gratifying. But as a lama in Kathmandu had said of the commotion surrounding the summiting of Everest: "Why all the excitement? Isn't it just another place?"

As we resumed the bone-jarring drive, we crossed high passes and left our lumbering supply truck far behind us. Shortly before dark, we hit a wall of backed-up traffic. The Chinese equivalent of a Mack truck, called a Dong Feng, or "Eastern Wind," had broken its clutch and sunk into deep mud where the road crossed through a steep defile. At 11,000 feet, the temperature plummeted with the setting sun, and to ward off the cold we took turns helping to dig out the axle with crude spades. At 2:30 A.M. I finally retired to the Land Cruiser. I slept fitfully, too cold and exhausted to forage through the back of the supply truck to extract my down sleeping bag. The following morning, a bulldozer eventually pulled the stalled Dong Feng to the side of the road and leveled a passage sufficient to allow the remaining trucks and vehicles to continue on their way. The town of Kongpo Gyamda to which we had been headed lay less than twenty miles away, but it took us more than two and a half hours of mobile purgatory to reach it.

After chicken and cabbage soup and wok-fried greens in a Gyamda eatery, we drove four more hours on roads sporadically paved with freshly laid concrete. Road crews were still blasting away boulders with caches of dynamite, and we stopped at a roadblock beside a red Mitsubishi jeep teeming with Chinese girls of questionable repute. They hailed from Xian, they told us in broken English, and had come to Tibet as "entertainers." They invited us to a cabaret show that they would be staging that night in Bayi, our common destination.

A less pleasant fate awaited us, however. After the road reopened, we proceeded directly to Bayi's Public Security Bureau where Nima, our Tibetan guide from Wind Horse Adventure, presented our assorted permits. Tashi Choezod, our friend the chief detective, greeted us once again in his spartan office. He reminded Hamid and me that more than a year earlier we had promised to bring him a videocassette of *The Godfather.* He was visibly disappointed that we had shown up empty-handed. He then told us that he had just returned from a three-week survey tour through Pemako. After his experience, he was even more incredulous than before that we undertook these journeys for pleasure.

That year Nyingtri and Medok counties were inundated with record levels of rain, he told us, and rivers had swollen to unprecedented heights. He had counted 183 landslides on the route between the Doshung-La pass and Medok, and the passage had been extremely hazardous. An American tourist had died falling into a stream, he told us, referring, we suspected, to Doug Gordon, the kayaker on Wick Walker's expedition who had drowned on the Tsangpo somewhere below Gyala.

More distressing news followed: Tashi claimed that more than one hundred Chinese were currently camped below the Doshung-La pass with the intention of forging their way through the inner reaches of the Tsangpo gorge. A separate team would be heading in from the Po Tsangpo confluence. The Chinese had heard rumors of a ninety-eight-foot waterfall in the deepest section of the gorge, Tashi said, and had plans to "discover" it.

Only later did we learn that the Chinese had announced their plans on a BBC World Service broadcast radio report on October 23, three days before our departure from Kathmandu. The dispatch stated that: "Large sections of the Yarlung-Zangbo Grand Canyon remain completely unexplored." A team of Chinese scientists would complete "one of the most important expeditions of the century" with the express purpose of entering "for the first time" into the waterfall section, "a.k.a the Five-Mile Gap. No one has ever gone through it on foot," the announcement continued. "About forty members of the team . . . hope to be the first to walk its length, and the first human beings ever to penetrate a 100-kilometer [62-mile] section in the middle."

NEW REGULATIONS IN BAYI compelled us to sleep in the recently opened Lingchi Hotel, a colossal edifice with faulty plumbing, premised on some idle hope of mass tourism. We seemed to be its only guests.

The prospect of a multipronged Chinese expedition with the same objective as our own deeply disturbed us, and we inadvertently found ourselves poised for a race to "close the gap" and document any waterfall that might lie in its depths. The statement concerning a totally unknown one hundred kilometers was in all likelihood a misprint. But even if they had meant the ten kilometers (6.2 miles) below Rainbow Falls, we suspected that the Chinese did not know that Monpa hunters had plied animal tracks through this territory for generations. The Chinese news brief was in accord with long-standing perceptions that the Five-Mile Gap was an untouched wilderness.

If the Chinese team based near the confluence had already headed upriver, our only hope of reaching the waterfall before them lay in their attempting to travel along the Tsangpo's left bank, as we ourselves had in 1986. But if they'd done their research properly, they would know it was impossible.

As we sat in the hotel dining room over bowls of pale rice gruel, Ken invoked Pemako's fearsome protector deity. "I can't believe Dorje Traktsen would let the Chinese get away with this," he said, ignoring the fact that our own mission differed only in scale and philosophic disposition. Preparing himself for the worst, Ken said, "Whether or not that falls is over one hundred feet, it's still a natural wonder. Just to see it in its full glory will be an incredible experience."

Ken's diversions into the literature of the sublime offered a counterpoint to our geographical ambitions. As we continued our meal, Ken expounded on the Romantic poet Percy Bysshe Shelley's evocation of waterfalls in the Alps. In Shelley's alluring poem "Mont Blanc," the streams of water "flow through the mind" and represent the inseparability of human consciousness from the universe itself. In "Alastor, or the Spirit of Solitude," Shelley conjured a grander waterfall symbolizing a mystical rapture encompassing life and death. Another poet, Southey, invoked 157 varieties of descending water in the Falls of Lodore, a verbal flood far exceeding the waterfall he sought to describe.[7]

Ken also recounted his explorations of nineteenth-century landscape painting. The idealized renderings of waterfalls by the great English landscape artist William Turner (1775–1851) and the American painter Frederic Church (1826–1900) offered visions of the sublime to those who could not directly view the works of nature. Stretching the entire length of museum walls, Church's monolithic canvases of Niagara Falls drew thousands of viewers who traveled in their imagination—instead of by carriage—to the colossal waterfall on their frontier.

Niagara Falls endures as an environment in which many seek to renew their capacity for wonder. At 162 feet Niagara is far from being the world's highest waterfall, yet its three-quarters of a mile breadth and quantity of flow give it a grandeur and beauty attested to by the more than four million honeymooners and tourists who visit it each year. So important is the falls as an icon of the American nation that a joint U.S.-Canadian Fallscape committee regulates Niagara's flow to preserve its visual purity.[8] To achieve a more sublime vista and to control erosion, the falls authorities at one point turned off all the water and reshaped the dolomite rock at Niagara's crest. My great-great grandfather, Henry Martyn Baker, had visited Niagara in 1850 with his sister Henrietta and

had written in his journal that: "When I had a full view of the Falls . . . my anticipations were fully realized. . . . We [saw] more this afternoon of the grandness of nature than we had ever before witnessed."

THE FOLLOWING MORNING, October 30, we drove out of Bayi, engines straining as our Land Cruisers climbed toward the pass that would lead us down toward the Tsangpo gorge. Pilgrims en route to Lhasa were descending toward us from the 15,440-foot pass, pilgrims' staffs in hand and their possessions tied into bundles across their backs. Two monks from Kham prostrated their way along the length of the road, avoiding the shortcuts between the switchbacks, and trailed by a young novice who ferried their canvas tent and provisions in a weathered wagon.

Emerging from forests of tsuga hemlocks, towering firs, and larches turning gold in the autumn air, we reached the treeless mountain pass. As the Sherpas strung prayer flags between giant boulders, we gazed across layers of cloud toward Namcha Barwa, its upper reaches veiled by towering thunderheads. Intermittently the pyramidal summit broke free of clouds and stood illuminated by an unseen sun. We climbed back into the Land Cruisers and wound downward through dense forest into the valley of Tongyuk. Yaks and dzos foraged through the fallow fields and stacks of hay hung drying in the notches of trees. A sprawling logging camp set up by the Chinese had displaced the old shingle-roofed Tibetan village. The roadside restaurants, primitive guesthouses, and provision shops that cater to passing truckers and line the single street had been reconstructed, not in the ubiquitous timber, but in white ceramic tiles that gave the impression of an extended open air bathroom.

Twenty minutes beyond Tongyuk, we saw Western-style tents set back from the road in a rocky field. Doris and Harry Wetherbee had established a base camp there and were awaiting the arrival of Wick Walker and the remaining members of their expedition. They recounted the tragedy as far as they knew it from communications with Wick through a static-filled satellite phone. Less than seventeen miles below Gyala and upriver from where a glacier on the southern face of Gyala Pelri spills directly into the Tsangpo, Doug Gordon had failed to right himself after plunging with his kayak over an eight-foot water-fall that he and the three other paddlers had previously scouted and determined to be runnable. He'd been swept into an enormous series of rapids, and the lethal waters of the Tsangpo had closed over his head. The remaining members of the river team had searched downriver for four days without seeing a trace of either Doug or his boat.

As we drove on toward the road head, we came across the remaining mem-bers of the team who had trekked into Trulung that afternoon. Wick Walker, the expedition leader and pointman for the four-person land team, recounted how they had tried without success to travel upstream along the left bank of the Tsangpo. To reach the paddlers and help search for Doug Gordon's body, they had crossed the 13,000-foot pass that Ken Storm, Ralph Rynning, and I had climbed in 1996 and that I had told them about when we first met in McLean, Virginia. After descending to the Tsangpo, they'd traveled upriver for approximately three miles before being forced back by intractable cliffs. Mean-while, the river team had continued downstream on foot and by kayak, or as Tom McEwan put it, "boat-assisted hiking."

Wick's team had not been able to make significant headway downstream from the base of the pass and, when Tom McEwan and the other members of the river team reached them, they performed a final ceremony for Doug on the banks of the Tsangpo. Afterward, they retraced their route over what Ken had dubbed Takin Pass and trekked back to the confluence. They ate plentifully, Wick reported. Their hunter/guides had killed five takin and several goral in the swampy plains of Neythang. By Wick's estimates, they still would have been ferrying loads of dried meat back to their village. We both hoped that the res-ident herds could sustain the Monpas' sometimes immoderate predations.

FARTHER DOWN THE ROAD, a massive landslide had blocked all traffic, and we pitched in with shovels to clear a path for our Land Cruisers through the half-frozen rubble. At the small village of Dongchu (formerly Tongyuk Dzong), a half hour's drive beyond, we hired a derelict Dong Feng cargo truck to return to the site of the rockfall and to collect the Sherpas and expedition gear from our supply truck that we had been forced to abandon on the far side of the slide. They arrived after dark and we slept in a wooden shack perched above the road, not far from where Kinthup had been sold into slavery by his rogue companion.

I drifted off to sleep contemplating the strange convergence that was occurring now in the Tsangpo gorge. Wick's team had decided to return home rather than continue their journey through the Tsangpo's uncharted depths. The Chinese—as far as we knew—had already begun their siege-scale assault. Nima, our Tibetan guide from Wind Horse Adventure, informed us that Chinese Central Television was broadcasting three-minute dispatches every night documenting their progress. I could only hope they had no awareness that our small team of three Americans was headed directly for the Five-Mile Gap. The innate lure of the missing link was undeniable, but the highly publicized Chinese expedition had become something of a dark mirror in which we caught glimpses of less noble motivations.

The drive from Dongchu the next morning led through thick forests of bamboo and alder, the river we were following all the while gaining force as it dropped precipitously through the narrowing gorge. We crossed more incipient landslides, removed uprooted trees that had fallen across the track, and descended ever deeper. Late in the afternoon, we camped on the side of the road by the dissolving footbridge that we would cross the following morning to reach the Tsangpo gorge.

Four pilgrims from Kham had set up a canvas tent in the same clearing on the edges of Trulung. They sat around a campfire in thick sheepskin chubas, their long hair braided with strands of red wool. Consummate pilgrims, they were garlanded in protective amulets and had survived on alms as they made their way toward Lhasa from the far reaches of eastern Tibet. They pleaded with us for photographs of the Dalai Lama, not taking no for an answer, as if persistence itself would alter the fact that none of us had one.

As we shared the small clearing with the Khampa pilgrims, their tattered gray tent held up with a single hemlock pole, I felt a strange sense of fellowship. I could only hope that their ceaseless peregrinations, a mirror of my own spiritual restlessness, would lead them to a clear and present grace. By some interpretations Yangsang Né is simply an inner revelation, bearing only coincidental relationship with the outside world. Could it happen anywhere, this discovery of the ultimate beyul? I thought of Jesus' words in the apocryphal Gospel of Thomas: "The Kingdom of God is spread across the earth but men do not see it."

LOCAL VILLAGERS EAGER for work overran our camp and chatted up Nima and the Sherpas. Even porters who in the past had stolen from us avowed eternal friendship. According to one of our "friends" from Mondrang, the group of Chinese—forty-three by his count—had only gone as far as the confluence and then returned. If so, the way ahead would be clear for us. Trulung's headman ambled up and claimed that there never was a Chinese group encamped here at all. The Chinese had combined their forces, he said, and would be setting out together from Pe. If they could get through the gorge, they would eventually arrive here in several weeks.

Each informant offered us conflicting "facts." The Chinese expedition felt in these moments like an illusion, a projection of our worst fears. Yet unlike the pilgrims from Kham who had become adept in denying inconvenient realities, we could not will the phantom expedition into nonexistence. Still, in this strange land, where prayers are used to alter reality, a sense of enchantment enveloped us, as if the world was not so much as it appears as how we choose to envision it.

Like the Buddha led out by his carriage driver from the confines of his palace, the Tibetan road had confronted us with challenges to the spirit: from the material avarice of Tibetan pilgrims to the labyrinths of Chinese bureaucracy. In Bayi, the chief of police had dispelled all notions of an earthly paradise. When he was in Medok, he told us, one of his horses had been eaten alive by leeches, and a soldier who had broken a leg in the jungle had nearly succumbed to the same fate, his face and limbs covered in the blood-engorged freshwater worms until a band of Monpas responded to his plaintive cries.

Pemako had inspired myths and exalted ideals but the region itself harbored many harsh realities. As Chatral Rinpoche had explained: "Don't think of Pemako as a literal paradise as described in the scrolls. Pemako is a paradise for Buddhist practice, a place where all things can be encountered and brought to the path." Like the fourteenth-century Dzogchen master Longchenpa who described the greatest places of pilgrimage as those which make the mind waver, Chatral Rinpoche intimated that in places where human life is tenuous and heaven and hell converge, reality can be more intimately perceived. What would we find in the hidden depths of the Tsangpo gorge? Perhaps, in the end, it would depend as much on how we looked as what was actually there. As Tibetans say, we would have to see not just with our eyes, but with our hearts.

Down the Po Tsangpo

ON NOVEMBER 1, we awoke to the same light drizzle that had been falling continuously since late the previous evening. A Monpa hunter who had traveled with us in 1996 zipped open the door to my tent.

"Don't worry," he said, "it won't rain."

Blandly ignoring the steady drizzle, the hunter invoked our journey two years earlier when we had been blessed with uncommonly good weather. On that occasion, the hunters had convinced themselves that I was using the claw of a mythical hawk called a garuda to avert the normally pervasive rain. They'd pleaded with me at the time to give them a small piece of it, unable to believe that the compliant weather was pure coincidence.

The Monpa hunter secured a load from the Sherpas and joined the stream of porters—both men and women—flowing across the footbridge toward the fluted cliffs that line the southern bank of the Rong Chu River. We followed them across landslides and fern-draped ravines. Matted filaments of gray-green moss drifted amid the trees and the wet foliage penetrated our nostrils like a heady incense. The shrill sound of cicadas played over the hypnotic drone of the river that surged beneath us through a narrow gorge. In Tibetan meditations on the sound of water, the adept unites the fluidity within his or her own body-mind with the waters of the external environment. The same process applies to qualities of earth, fire, air, and space. If brought to completion, this form of meditation is believed to lead to a state in which the boundaries of the individual ego are replaced by a deep, transparent empathy with the phenomenal world.

Buddhist prayer flags, their colors representing the dynamic harmony of all the elements, fluttered from rocks and trees where the churning currents of the

Rong Chu joined the Po Tsangpo. The massive white water of the merging rivers reeled relentlessly toward the Tsangpo, roughly thirty miles downriver. We would follow its course to the apex of the Tsangpo's Great Bend.

A tremor on October 24 had caused numerous landslides that gouged wide swaths through the forest and, until a few days before, had blocked off the route to Tsachu. But the slopes had stabilized somewhat and, after six hours of walking, we reached Yumé, a stretch of white sand bordering the banks of the Po Tsangpo. Sulfur springs flowed from beneath enormous boulders, their warm red currents carving through rocks and sand to join with the cool waters of the Po Tsangpo. At dusk, three female Monpa porters bathed in the hot springs, coyly beckoning us, then pelting us with mud from the shallow, steaming pond. They later joined us by the fire, their wet hair shining as the moon rose above the dancing flames. Gossamer clouds gathered above the river, then vanished like phantoms. From bivouacs in wet leech-infested forests to losing our way in Adrathang—the primeval savannah from which we thought we would never emerge—past journeys in Pemako had brought us to the limits of physical and mental endurance. But now, free of leeches, gnats, and rain, Pemako was suddenly living up to the rhapsodic descriptions of the ancient scrolls.

THE FOLLOWING MORNING, November 2, we left Yumé, crossed to the opposite bank of the Po Tsangpo, and began the steep climb to the village of Tsachu. The sheer, glaciated walls of Gyala Pelri, free of their usual veil of clouds, rose above wild banana trees and towering ferns. At the outskirts of the village, I warded off predatory dogs with my bamboo staff and climbed a notched log into the home of Sonam Nima, the village headman, who had hosted Ken and me five years earlier after our first passage through the gorge. After tea and chang, Ken, Hamid, and I climbed farther up the hill with Bryan to visit Lama Topgye, in hopes of learning more about the region of the gap, and of filming for a Western audience his perspectives on the gorge.

The trail passed a small cave draped with prayer flags. An image of Dorje

Drolo, the wrathful form that Padmasambhava took on in Pemako, emerged from the rock wall.[9] Lama Topgye's wood-planked house rose above on stilts of alder wood that resists Pemako's all-pervasive dampness. We climbed up a short ladder to the door where the lama's wife beckoned us over the threshold. Lama Topgye sat in the far corner of the room in front of an altar covered with bronze and terra-cotta statues. His bell, dorje, and other ritual instruments lay on the table in front of him. We offered white khatas and told him of our intention to descend to the largest of the waterfalls and to look for the door to Yangsang. I asked if he could tell us more about the area and the nature of the portal.

No one has ever gone down all the way down to the falls, Lama Topgye told us, and he claimed to know no more than he had told us the preceding spring. He held up his hands and opened them back and forth. Somehow, he said, there is a way through the waterfall, but he offered no insight as to how to penetrate its aqueous veil. The door to Yangsang will only open when the reincarnations of three Pemako lamas come in unison, he said, looking quizzically at the pale substitutes sitting across from him on worn Tibetan carpets. I asked him to come with us, but he looked down at his admittedly frail form and said that his body was too old.

He urged us to pray to Padmasambhava and to Dorje Pagmo, the female Buddha whose citadel, he said, lies directly above the falls. This initiatress into the mysteries of earth and psyche guards the portals to Yangsang, Lama Topgye told us. Only she could lead us to our destination.

ON THE MORNING OF NOVEMBER 3, we descended from Tsachu on eroding switchbacks toward a plank bridge that crosses the Tsangpo. A group of mostly female pilgrims was climbing toward us in bright blouses and jaunty hats and, as they neared, I recognized our hostess, Tashi Tsomo, from the nights of revelry that followed our emergence from the gorge in 1993. As vivacious as before, Tashi Tsomo and her three bright-eyed companions offered to carry our packs, but they were en route to visit Lama Topgye and afterward Gompo Né, and I did not want to divert them from their pilgrimage. Tashi, Sherab, and Sangye—Auspiciousness, Penetrating Wisdom, and Buddha—resumed their climb up the ridge as we descended toward the river, a sweeping mass of white water spanned by a tenuous looking plank bridge suspended from rusted cables.

We rested on the far side of the river amid rocks and bamboo and then began a grueling four-hour climb toward the pass that would lead us to Bayu, the last village before the hunters' trails that lead into the Five-Mile Gap and the region of the waterfall.

Descending alone on the far side of the 8,000-foot pass, night fell before we reached the few scattered houses that comprise Bayu, the forest alive with the sounds and furtive movements of unseen animals. A full moon rose through scudding mist and vanished into a canopy of clouds.

The Sherpas had established themselves in a storage shed filled with baskets of maize, wheat, and barley. Hamid, Ken, and I sat in the main house with Sangye Tsering and his wife, Nima Tso, the pretty half-Khampa woman who, five years earlier and before her marriage, had infatuated Lo, our Chinese liaison officer, who had waited for us here for more than two weeks. Hunting had been good. A week earlier, Sangye Tsering and another hunter named Senge, the Lion, had returned from the ridges above Bayu with the carcasses of three bears. We sat on their skins, as Sangye Tsering urged us to buy one of their gallbladders. Not wanting to encourage the trade in animal parts, I offered instead to buy some of the crystals that he and Sangye had carried back from the slopes of the inner gorge, not because I wanted to carry rocks around with me, but because cash is a rare and needed commodity in these remote gorges.

SANGYE TSERING AND SENGE agreed to accompany us into the gap, and we headed out with them the next morning for Azadem, a cluster of five houses an hour and half beyond Bayu where we would meet Tsering Dondrup and the other hunters who had led us toward the falls the preceding spring.

We walked through rhododendron forests and across steep slopes planted with barley and maize, as well as burned-out areas of slash-and-burn cultivation where the cutting of trees had caused landslides and deep erosion. In less than an hour we were compelled to change porters when we reached an amorphous boundary between the Bayu township and that of neighboring Azadem.

To ensure a just distribution of work and income, Pemako custom dictates that porters from the preceding village must forfeit their loads (and salaries) to new porters from the next. Not only does this make for lost time and lack of continuity, but it becomes expensive as well when porters demand payment not only for the days they carry, but also for their journey home. Ironically, this unwieldy portering system originated in the tradition of *ula*, in which Tibetan government officials traveling in remote areas could enlist bearers free of charge. So as not to overburden local resources, porters would continue only as far as the next village. Delays and complications inevitably arose when villages were close together or too small to provide sufficient manpower. We faced a similar problem now and were forced to pay double wages to the few available villagers as they doubled up on loads.

Weighed down by our gear, we climbed slowly up the steep trail to Azadem that winds through a forest of rhododendrons and cascading streams. We unloaded at an empty house on the far edge of the village and set up our tents in a clearing beyond. Afterward we visited Tsering Dondrup to discuss our plans. He rallied the other hunters, and they prepared supplies for the journey into the Tsangpo's innermost gorge: sacks of chilies, dried meat, roasted tsampa, bricks of compressed tea leaves, blackened pots and kettles, thick sleeveless *goshung,* or tunics of animal skins[10] or matted wool felt, block-printed prayer flags, and freshly cleaned .22 caliber rifles.

Bryan went out with his video camera to document the proceedings while Ken, Hamid, and I sat by Tsering Dondrup's hearth, drinking tea and discussing the emerging film for National Geographic Television. Each of us had concerns about the direction the documentary seemed to be taking. Ken complained of the intrusion of Bryan's camera into every aspect of our experience and missed the unselfconscious immersion that we all valued so highly. On a somewhat different note, he commented that Bryan was focusing the film too much on me. With philosophic detachment, Hamid told him that, for coherence, a documentary film must concentrate on a single character to serve as a bridge between the subject matter and its audience. But each of us clearly felt uncomfortable that we had lost the power to direct how Pemako and our own experience would be portrayed.

We reminisced about the film on Buddhist hunters we had begun making under the auspices of the Film Study Center at Harvard University. In Hamid's and my view, the film would have invoked Pemako in all its paradox and inscrutability, with all bridges burned and "great white adventurers" deleted from the script.

"We only needed shots of the takin hunt," Hamid lamented, "otherwise it was all there."

Hamid had brought reels of film for his Bolex movie camera, but he doubted that a group as large as ours would be able to get close to any wildlife. He proposed a solution to the lost vision of the film which would also ensure that we saw as much as possible of the Five-Mile Gap. Hamid suggested that if he entered the gap from the north—near where Sangye Tsering and Senge had killed the bears—and traveled south with two or three hunters who could travel quickly with less disturbance to local wildlife, he could secure the missing footage and also look for other waterfalls that might lie hidden in the recesses of the gap. If he moved quickly, he could meet us at the waterfall that Lama Topgye had indicated as the door into Yangsang.

"It would allow us to close the gap from both sides," Hamid said, "and to make sure we cover all the ground."

Hamid's plan held strong a attraction; it would give him the chance to secure the missing footage for the film that we had begun the preceding May, far from the camera's eye. To free himself from Bryan's viewfinder, Ken considered joining Hamid in his adventure, but the waterfall held too strong a pull, and he decided to stick to the original itinerary.

I personally suspected that the waterfall that each of us had already seen from far above would fall short of 100 feet. Neither did I harbor any realistic hopes of some kind of a door behind the veil of water leading into a lost world. But the mystique of Yangsang pulled me strongly, and the prospect of reaching places with our climbing ropes that local Tibetans had not been able to go was irresistible.

We left Tsering to his preparations and climbed back up the trail to tell the Sherpas that we would be dividing into two teams so as to explore the unknown part of the gorge from both ends. Hamid enlisted one of the more experienced Sherpas, Gompo, to go with him as well as Tsering Dondrup, Sangye Tsering, and another hunter named Bu Tashi. In the morning, they would descend partway to Bayu and then climb toward a small pass called the Shati-La that leads into the gap. Tsering Dondrup said they could descend from there toward the caverns of Hugudurung, where takin would supposedly be abundant. From these caves perched above the sheer walls of the Tsangpo they would continue through the gap, keeping the river in view wherever possible.

If all went according to plan, our two parties would meet somewhere in the heart of the Five-Mile Gap, and Hamid would continue down to the falls with Tsering Dondrup on the path that we had forged. Ken and I would retrace Hamid's steps and exit the gap over the Shati-La. We imagined that we could complete the circuit in ten days or so, but the time estimates given by each of the hunters varied drastically. Were they drawing out the days to ensure additional payment? Did these places with such improbable names actually exist?

Hamid was geared for the hunt. The shaman in Tuva, the White Old Man, had given him a talismanic bear claw that he now wore around his neck. The hoary oracle had chided Hamid for his Buddhist faith. "Why put Buddha between you and nature?" he reputedly asked him. "Invoke directly the spirits of mountains and rivers; they are your true allies." Hamid later learned of a waterfall in Mongolia where the Humi masters learn their unique art of overtone singing by tuning in to the sounds that the waterfall makes at different seasons and internalizing their harmonies and rhythms.[11]

Over a dinner of egg noodles, canned tuna fish, and dehydrated miso, the conversation turned to the legendary Falls of the Tsangpo. Whatever its height, Bryan saw it increasingly as the focus to his film. He wanted to know more about the realm toward which it leads.

"If the waterfall is a doorway into Yangsang," Bryan asked, "where is Yangsang itself supposed to be? Is it a large area or relatively small?"

"Yangsang could be anywhere," Hamid answered, eager for the opportunity to provoke confusion. "According to Buddhist tradition, Yangsang does not exist separately from the mind. Even though it exists physically, its coordinates are necessarily inexact, and there are no real directions as to how to get there."

"Wasn't your trip to the mountain to get the key?" Bryan asked.

"Yes," Hamid answered, "but we didn't find it."

"You didn't?" Bryan asked.

"No. No one has."

"How do you get to Yangsang then?"

"No one ever has," Hamid replied enigmatically.

Bryan felt he was missing something and pressed Hamid to explain further.

"Knowing there's no key *is* the key," Hamid said, and went back to cleaning his Bolex.

Sensing Bryan's frustration with his cryptic replies, he offered another perspective. "To ask the meaning of Yangsang is like asking for a definition of love," Hamid said. "It can only be known through direct experience. That's why Pemako as a whole is viewed as Dorje Pagmo. To find her secret places, to enter her heart, you first have to fall in love with her. You have to give up all maps, compasses, and sense of direction. This is what the goddess demands. She is the known leading to the unknown."

Bryan still looked perplexed but later began jotting down notes in his journal.

I smiled at the exchange. As Hamid, Ken, and I all agreed—albeit from slightly different vantage points—Pemako's essential qualities could easily be missed by clinging too strongly to facts. Would Bryan's film capture Pemako's mythic coordinates or reduce our enterprise to a one-dimensional geographical adventure? Could our own sense and experience of this land—and more important the Tibetans' perception of it—ever be adequately conveyed? If our films, our writings, our lives could achieve anything, I hoped it would be only to dispel the estranged vision that has led humanity to exploit and desecrate the only outer paradise we are ever likely to know—the earth itself.

Yangsang, in the end, might simply be the recovery of that lost vision of oneness with the natural world that the first couple enjoyed in Eden, but which their own ignorance kept them from recognizing until it was irretrievably lost. As to some gateless gate leading to this lost unity, speculations were idle. Even the Tibetans had only gazed down on their sacred waterfall from the high precipices above, as if to approach too closely would temper their faith. I remembered a telling passage from Talbot Mundy's *Om: The Secret of Ahbor Valley:*

> For that which men have uncovered and explained . . . they despise. But that which they discern, although its underlying essence is concealed from them, they wonder at and worship.

Shechen-La—Pass of Great Glory

THE MORNING OF NOVEMBER 5 opened to a frenetic scene as prospective porters wrestled over our equipment and food supplies. The Sherpas had devised a sophisticated system of name tags that they handed out to stipulated porters, but the procedure collapsed as villagers ran off with partial loads and others were nearly trampled in the process.

Before the bedlam resolved itself, Hamid, Ken, Bryan, and I headed out to visit Konchok Wangpo, Tsering Dondrup's elder brother and Bayu's head lama. We had asked him to perform a ritual fire offering that morning to ensure the success of our journey, but when we arrived at his house, he told us he was indisposed and that he would do it while we were away. Bryan had hoped to capture the ceremony on film and was hardly placated when the lama produced a jug of arak, a potent home-brewed alcohol, and insisted that we imbibe liberally while he, himself, returned to his texts.

We finally set out from Azadem with a ragtag crew of porters, including the lama's nineteen-year-old daughter, Sonam Deki, who'd pleaded with her father to let her come. On the outskirts of the village, the hobbitlike old hermit whom we had seen in 1993 emerged from his house with his equally diminutive wife, both twirling enormous prayer wheels.

We crossed the stream at the north end of the village and began climbing steeply to the west through a corridor of ferns. The trail followed the edge of a narrow defile, rare sunlight streaming through towering hemlocks and an overhead tangle of moss-covered rhododendrons. After climbing steadily for four hours we reached Tsodem, a 9,000-foot-high swampy clearing covered with undulant ferns. The porters struggled in an hour later, complaining about the weight of their loads. We set up camp beneath a cloudless sky as the water by

the spring slowly transformed into a thin pane of ice. In another month, claimed one of the hunters, Tsodem would be buried neck deep in snow.

The following morning we climbed through a rock-filled defile to the 9,700-foot Tsodem-La. From the pass, Ken, Bryan, and I would descend toward the waterfall with Buluk and three other hunters while the majority of the carriers continued along the ridge with two of the Sherpas to set up a camp at Benchi Pagmo, the site of another small spring where we hoped to rejoin them five days later.

Clouds were gathering over the gorge, and our hunter-guides—Buluk, Jayang, and Drakpa—were eager to start down into the chasm. They stashed some of their food and provisions in tree branches for the return journey and slashed through undergrowth to reveal the game trail that we had followed the previous spring. Dropping quickly down a shallow stream, we stopped to eat beneath ancient hemlocks and filled up all available water containers for the push to Darup, the narrow shelf where we had bivouacked in May, waiting out three days of rain.

As we traversed across a series of landslides, the glacial spire of Gyala Pelri emerged from the clouds across the gorge. Looming up from Gyala Pelri's southern spur was the triangular citadel of naked rock that the hunters regard as the primary seat of Dorje Pagmo. Sheer 4,000-foot cliffs drop from the summit ridge and plunge into the depths of the gorge, forming an unassailable fortress.

Even the religion that conjured this uncompromising goddess defends itself against her essential nature: reality as it is. Tantric icons lead the mind beyond dualities imposed by logic and reason. Yet they also mask what Lelung Shepe Dorje had called "resplendent terror," the convergence of opposites when the mind abides in its essential nature. Carl Jung had termed it *conjunctio tremendum,* the paradoxical union of seemingly contradictory truths.

The trees cantilevered out over the abyss below us, and in several places a small misstep would have meant an unbroken fall into the depths of the gorge. We contoured across fresh landslides and clung to thin grasses that emerged from the eroding rubble. We reached Darup well before dark and sent back three of the porters to join the others at Benchi Pagmo.

In the spring, we had been stranded here for three days as a storm lashed against the sides of the gorge and unleashed rock falls on both sides of the narrow, multitiered ledge. But our campsite now proved reasonably comfortable, with boughs of hemlock and spruce forming a platform for our tents and a large fire warding off the cold autumn air.

Jayang headed out with his rifle in search of game and returned instead with a sack filled with crystals and aquamarine. He claimed we would need ropes to cross the landslide just beyond our camp. But spirits were high as we neared the crux of our journey—the descent to the waterfall.

The Shape of Falling Water

ACCORDING TO FRANK KINGDON WARD knowledge of the region below Rainbow Falls was based solely on the alleged Buddhist texts that described a series of seventy-five waterfalls in the innermost reaches of the gorge, "each presided over by a spirit—whether benevolent or malicious is not stated." The intangible guardian spirits of earth and air that Kingdon Ward had referred to are called *suma* in Tibetan, and they are customarily appeased with aromatic offerings of juniper and other incenselike plants. On the morning of November 7, Lama, the ex-monk, performed the necessary rites to ensure their benediction. Wisps of sweet-smelling, blue-gray smoke encircled the trees and curled into the sky and, as if by magic, the ominous clouds that had settled over the slopes of Namcha Barwa began to dissipate and golden sunlight bathed the eastern walls of Dorje Pagmo on the opposite side of the gorge. We strung prayer flags above the fragrant ashes with aspirations for clear weather as we began the final descent into the gorge. (Edward Abbey once wrote: "The odor of burning juniper is the sweetest fragrance on the face of the earth . . . I doubt whether all the smoking censers of Dante's paradise could equal it.")

Less than 100 yards after setting out from the ledge we crossed a landslide of shattered rock and scree, a result of the tremor ten days earlier. Buluk cut steps with a primitive adze as a cascade of small stones catapulted over the cliff below. Our heavy loads made the crossing treacherous, and a false step or displacement of shale would have sent one of us hurtling over a 100-foot cliff onto the only slightly less precipitous slope below. There were no trees or boulders large enough to use as an anchor for the rope. Our Sherpa cook, hired at the last minute and a pale substitute for Pemba, muttered prayers or curses—it was hard to tell which—as he pawed anxiously at the crumbling slope of shiny, mica-studded igneous and metamorphic rocks.

We forged on over fresh landslides as rocks continued to catapult over the precipice. The Tsangpo lay more than 2,000 feet below us, the roar of the river rising up between the walls of the gorge and drawing us into its depths. We entered a steeply tilting zone of scrub oak and ripe blueberries, until—two hours beyond Darup—Buluk suddenly indicated that we should begin the descent.

The scrub oak and rhododendrons gave way to a pathless forest interspersed with moss-laden cliffs. We slipped, clambered, and floated through interlinked ravines dense with hemlock, magnolia, and rhododendrons. Waist-high ferns obscured the ground and, in places, we broke through deceptive layers of sphagnum moss, catching ourselves in a maze of limbs and tree roots.

We soon entered an almost impenetrable tangle of rhododendrons and barberry, clinging to slopes that without vegetation would have sent us sliding down the steep ravine and over the cliffs below into the Tsangpo, still hidden from our view by the dense foliage. We angled south and, where the trees abruptly ended at a sheer 1,000-foot cliff, we arrived at the vantage point that Buluk had led me to last May with Hamid and a disconsolate Ned Johnston, eager to resume the hunt for the takin.

We secured our packs to obliging rhododendrons perched near the edge of the precipice and gazed down at Rainbow Falls that, less than half a mile away, channeled the gray-green flood of the Tsangpo into a sleek wave that poured over a rock ledge divided in the center by an outcrop of silvery granite. Beneath the falls, the Tsangpo dissolved into a sea of mist and spray and resumed its implacable flow. In less than a quarter of a mile, it crashed against the base of white cliffs that drove it suddenly due west. There, walled in by towering walls of rock and with the looming pyramid of Dorje Pagmo soaring directly above, lay the second falls that the hunters claimed was larger, although none of them had ever been closer to it than we were now.

Ravaged walls of rock and vegetated slabs tilting at impossible angles lay between us and Rainbow Falls, the waterfall that Kingdon Ward and Cawdor had seen from upstream and had named after the bands of color that arced through its spray. From his vantage point 200 feet above the river, Kingdon Ward had estimated the falls to be a maximum of thirty to forty feet high, despite having only seen its crest and the cloud of mist rising from its base. Until this point, Kingdon Ward's measurement of Rainbow Falls had never been challenged or confirmed.

Ken sighted the expedition's laser range finder on the shimmering cascade, but the falls were too far away to get an accurate reading. So was the waterfall that surged in a hidden pocket of the Tsangpo thousands of feet below us.

No discernible route led toward the river, and interlacing tree limbs formed an imposing barrier. But they also provided a means of descent: where we could not cut our way through the vertiginous terrain, we clambered down as if on a ladder. After two hours of precipitous descent, in which we lost sight of the river, we reached an exposed ledge roughly 1,000 feet above the Tsangpo. From our new vantage point, Rainbow Falls appeared as a smooth, majestic wall of wa-

ter, plumes of spray rising into the air and blending with the sinuous cascades that streamed from the steep rain-polished walls of the gorge.

Ken took out the expedition clinometer—a sextantlike instrument that calculates heights by measuring the angle of incline—and aimed it at the face of Rainbow Falls. By measuring the angle of incline from its base to its crest, our surveying instrument revealed a height of seventy-two feet, nearly twice what Kingdon Ward had estimated seventy-four years earlier. Rainbow Falls was a far more significant feature of the Tsangpo than previously suspected. More important, it raised our hopes for the waterfall below. If the hidden drop a quarter mile downstream was even higher, the legendary Falls of the Tsangpo might ultimately live up to its original billing. We plunged back into the jungle with added fervor and resumed the descent for the waterfall.

As we climbed lower, the falls disappeared again from sight, but its roar rose up through the trees ever more loudly, reverberating off the walls of the gorge. We entwined our arms around sinuous tree limbs and swung down through a hanging forest of rhododendrons and weeping pines. Much of the time we slid our way down and we often doubled back when our line of descent ended in sheer drop-offs or impenetrable thickets.

Bryan's attempts to capture our descent and the goal ahead of us reminded me of an allegorical science fiction film by Andrei Tarkovsky, *Stalker.* The film chronicles the journey of three men through a mysterious and forbidden territory in the Russian wilderness called the Zone. In the Zone nothing is what it seems and the landscape continually shifts and rearranges itself, as if an unknown intelligence were thwarting all attempts to reach a mystic sanctuary said to lie at its center and where all desires are mysteriously fulfilled. As the expedition unfolds, the protagonists' determination unravels as they question the consequences of realizing their deepest wishes.

The roar of the river increased until it filled our heads like white noise, and the forest thickened. We were soon morassed in a dense tangle of Himalayan barberry, a thorny flowering shrub that Kingdon Ward introduced to the British Isles. With Buluk and Jayang cutting a way through the thick underbrush—their inverted goral skin tunics protecting them from thorns—we slipped down the steep slope, using vegetation to keep us from plummeting into the void. At a point where the incline lessened, we peered through trees and watched the Tsangpo narrow into a roaring tide that crashed against the cliffs below us. We made our way down a series of vegetated rock ledges, overhung by jungle. Suddenly we came up against a vertical cliff that plunged below us into a green abyss.

We could find no way down and the sun had long since disappeared behind the 5,000-foot obelisk of Dorje Pagmo. It was too late in the day to bring out the climbing ropes, so, at 7,200 feet above sea level, we settled in for the night in a grove of weeping pines on a ledge overlooking Rainbow Falls. Cliffs towered above us, and plumes of white mist billowed up through the trees from the unseen waterfall still far below us.

The hunters slept around a smoldering fire of rhododendron logs, their bare feet open to the embers. For them too this was a night of mystery and anticipation.

The power of our walled sanctuary infiltrated my dreams, and I passed the night in journeys through half-submerged cities and dream-lit caverns. The words of Henry David Thoreau came to me in my sleep: "It is in vain to dream of a wildness distant from ourselves."

EARLY THE FOLLOWING MORNING, November 8, one of the Monpas appeared at my tent to tell me that they had spotted three red goral on the cliff beyond our camp. Jayang and Buluk had already headed out with their rifles. Along with giant pandas, tigers, leopards, and takin, red goral are on the list of Class I protected animals, but they are still hunted in remote parts of the Himalayas for their meat and skins. Those of us still in camp watched transfixed as Jayang and Buluk made their way across the mountainside. So far, the short-horned antelope-like creatures seemed unaware of the imminent danger. A granite slab sloping precipitously toward the Tsangpo separated them from the hunters.

From our vantage point approximately 230 yards away, we watched with dismay and fascination as Jayang took aim at the largest of the two males. The tawny beast reeled backward off the edge of the cliff and fell 600 feet down into the Tsangpo. The other male goral scampered up the slabs and was lost to view. The hunters got a clear shot at the female, who tumbled to a small ledge where several small cedars prevented her from falling over the edge.

For the next hour we watched a riveting drama as Buluk and Jayang made their way across the wet slabs and finally reached the sloping ledge where the goral had fallen. Jayang tied it across his back, and he and Buluk began their precarious traverse back across the rock face, twice slipping and nearly following the first of the gorals into the crashing waves below. When they reached the safety of the forest, Buluk shouldered the load and they soon arrived back in camp. Dropping the freshly killed goral on the matted grass as if it were a heavy stole, they sat down by the fire and, without ceremony, drank their morning tea.

Before the Monpas skinned and dismembered the dead goral, Lama performed a powa ceremony to guide its *lha*, or life spirit, to a better place. In the Buddhist worldview, enlightenment infers liberation from the tyranny of self-centered existence, including all hope for a heaven beyond the here and now. But on the way, it's believed one can incarnate in paradisiacal realms where the desired unity with cosmic forces can be more easily achieved. It's to these Elysian realms that the hunters consign their prey and banish any guilt they may harbor for breaking one of Buddhism's cardinal laws: not to willfully take another's life.

The hunters claimed that the spirit of the goral that had fallen into the Tsangpo would be carried downstream to Bodhgaya, the place of Buddha's enlightenment in northern India. At that hallowed site, they assured us, it would attain release from the cycles of suffering and pain. I thought of Doug Gordon, whose body disappeared without a trace thirty miles upriver. I could only hope that he had slipped into those same exalted currents.

Once Lama completed the soul-releasing ritual for the dead goral—and to appease any Buddhist misgivings—the hunters began an older rite and quickly skinned the carcass and stretched the red-brown hide on a frame of bent saplings. Buddhist sentiments aside, their subsistence hunting was far less harmful to the earth's ecosystem than cattle ranches in the Amazon or wheat and corn production in the United States. They would ultimately use the cured skin to make leather bags or sew two hides together to fashion one of their traditional sleeveless tunics, clothing themselves with the gifts of the forest. They sectioned the flesh and Jayang gently placed the goral's head and treasured organ meats on the open fire. When it was only lightly cooked, he handed me a piece of the liver. Whether its soul had been released or not, I felt a pang of deep remorse for the loss of so magnificent an animal that had plied these inner realms of the gorge long before the arrival of Homo sapiens. As the goral's flesh metamorphosed within my cells, I hoped to absorb something of its intimate knowledge of this older and more enduring world.

WITH THE GORAL'S HIDE stretched out on saplings by the smoking fire, we prepared for our descent to the waterfall. In historical and geographical terms, the significance of the hidden falls beneath us depended entirely on its height. Until we reached the waterfall's base and took conclusive measurements, our speculations on the matter would be no more than hopeful conjectures.

Taking only a minimum of gear, we started down the cliff at the far end of our camp, lowering ourselves down broken ledges by holding on to small saplings and to the roots of larger trees that projected from the mountainside. Below the cliff, we coursed through slanting thickets of bamboo and bracken and eventually emerged onto open rock. The walls of Dorje Pagmo loomed above, vertical displacements of the earth's crust at this fault line between prehistoric continents. A mantle of fresh snow graced her upper slopes while black cliffs cross-hatched with moss-covered ledges fell sheerly toward the Tsangpo. The falls thundered below us, still hidden from our view. We followed their sound and the column of mist that swirled against the dark walls of the gorge to the edge of a precipice and, from there, gazed down at last into the turbulent heart of the hidden waterfall.

The jade green flood of the Tsangpo funneled into a breach approximately fifty feet across and transformed into a sleek wave of what looked like polished air. Surging over the precipice and intersected by rays of sunlight, the river freed itself of all semblance of form and dissolved into incandescent foam as it crashed against an intermediary rock ledge seventy feet below and leapt forth again in arcs of light-filled spray. Filling the air with light and water, it resumed its descent until dissolving into a maelstrom of seething waves, fountaining up against the polished walls of the gorge.

"The falls!" Ken shouted in genuine rapture and then again, for the benefit of Bryan's video camera, "the glittering goal of so many explorers!" Our voices drowned in the tempest at our feet. The air buzzed with ions. The falls were colossal, a massive curtain of foam and light hurtling between sheer granite walls. To gaze into the waters was to stare into the face of impermanence, waves and particles blurring by one after the other, beyond what the mind or eye could register. In ancient Greece, Heraclitus had proclaimed, "You can't step into the same river twice," and the prospect of measuring this mass of jetting water suddenly seemed absurd to me. Yet such was our stated mission and the task now at hand.

A protruding buttress obscured the waterfall's full expanse. To view its entirety, we would have to descend the overhanging cliff directly below us. After securing two 150-foot climbing ropes to a weeping pine, I heaved them down toward the falls. I then strapped on a climbing harness, attached a Petzl descender, and launched myself out over the overhang. My feet swung in open space as I rappelled down to a large sloping ledge that we had seen from above. I had planned to tie off at the ledge to await the others, but I could not resist running out the length of the rope to see if we could reach another vantage point lower down the wall.

I rappelled another twenty feet down, buffeted by the spray of the falls, and entered a realm where there was little distinction between air and water. The wall was wet and smooth, flecked with glistening feldspar, but where the rope ended I reached a foot-wide shelf where I tied off the descending device and turned around into the face of the waterfall. The view was astounding: the mass of the Tsangpo transformed in the narrow breach into a great glittering curtain, dissolving into fractal jets and crashing into the cauldron below. Translucent spray exploded over my head and streamed down my spine. To immerse oneself in the "power, velocity, vastness, and madness [of water] affords one of the noblest lessons of nature," wrote Ruskin, the great eighteenth-century observer of natural processes. And I watched, mesmerized, breathing in the oxygen-rich waters and lost in the vast display of liquid becoming—the organic wholeness that D. H. Lawrence had once called "the wave that cannot halt!"

If there was a door through these waters into the fabled Yangsang, I imagined it to be some deep realization of the dynamic, implicit order hidden within appearances, some existential still-point in the chaos of crashing waters. "As you penetrate the flowing and not-flowing of water, the ultimate character of all things is instantly realized," states a Buddhist sutra.

Then all words and thoughts vanished in the flood. I looked up and saw Ken and Bryan far above me at the top of the cliff. They could not see the tiny shelf of rock that I was standing on, and I indicated by sign language that I would have to climb back up to the sloping ledge above me. I clamped ascenders to the wet rope, stuck my feet into slings of nylon webbing, and jumared back up to the sloping ledge. After tying into the end of the rope with a locking carabiner, I waited for Ken to descend with the measuring devices.

Bryan was not going to miss this critical moment. Although he had never rappelled before, his background as a competitive surfer gave him a certain confidence in unnerving situations. After Ken unclipped from the rope, Bryan lowered himself down to the ledge, his video camera securely looped around his neck.

Our expedition clinometer, which measured angles of incline, would be of no service until we stood at the base of the falls. Ken unstrapped the digital

range finder and focused it on the curling wave at the top of the falls and afterward on the white froth at its base.

"I can't get clear readings," Ken said. "The dial keeps bouncing."

Ken handed me the range finder and I tried to focus it on the avalanche of water at the crest of the falls and on the churning sea beneath: the differential should have given us an accurate reading of the height. But the waterfall had no fixed form or boundaries. Its clouds and spray offered only a flux of transient images, and the troughs and waves at the bottom caused the digital screen to fluctuate chaotically, as if it were measuring the waterfall's transience, its absence of abiding form.

Waterfalls are transient phenomena even from a geological point of view. Their erosive power gradually wears away the rock beneath them, until they have transformed themselves into rapids. Accordingly, existing waterfalls are relatively recent features of the earth's landscape. Niagara Falls came into existence only twelve thousand years ago, during the Pleistocene, or glacial, epoch, when the continental ice sheet melted back and exposed an escarpment of Niagaric dolomite rock, underlain by softer shales and sandstones.[12]

A similar phenomenon might have happened here on the Tsangpo, we speculated, as waterfalls typically occur where resistant, crystalline rocks overlay weaker sedimentary formations and cause what geologists refer to as differential erosion. But neither of us was qualified to speculate authoritatively on the underlying bedrock, and we renewed our efforts simply to measure the waterfall's height.

The falls were in perpetual motion, without edge or center, and unmeasurable as such by our given tools. We trained the range finder instead on the wall of rock over which the waterfall coursed. The readings were stable and yielded the necessary data. Averaging the troughs and waves, the waterfall ranged between 105 and 115 feet.

The hidden waterfall that Kingdon Ward and Lord Cawdor failed to locate may not have been the rival to Victoria Falls and Niagara that some geographers dreamed of after Kinthup's report to the Survey of India in 1884. As magnificent as it was it could hardly compare to the grandest waterfalls of the world, but it put the centuries-old question of its existence to rest.

The description of the waterfall Waddell had written in the nineteenth century based on Tibetan accounts had proved uncannily accurate. "Gathering its
waters into a narrow torrent, [the Tsangpo] precipitates itself over a cliff about
100 feet in depth, cutting and boring its way so deeply through the rocks
that . . . below these falls it is said to go quite out of sight." The president of
the Royal Geographical Society of London at that time, Sir Thomas Hungerford Holdich, had also written effusively about the undiscovered falls. He emphasized their importance as a pilgrimage site and described the "clouds of
misty spray" that rise above them, the same mysterious mists that had captivated the attention of the hunters since we first arrived at the grove of weeping
pines. The ascending column of light-filled vapors had reinforced their convictions that the place was sacred and perhaps even, as Lama Topgye had suggested, the portal to a hidden paradise.

When David Livingstone stumbled accidentally into Victoria Falls in 1865,
he likened the perpetual veil of mist for which the native tribes had named the
falls to a "flight of angels."[13] In Tibetan meditation practices performed at waterfalls, the same phenomenon is described as a dance of dakinis, referring to
the anthropomorphic expressions of the five elements that comprise phenomenal existence. Meditating on the inner essence of this dance of water droplets,
adepts could refine their spiritual awareness and enter secret spaces in the in-
terstices between their bodies and the outer landscape, using form as a doorway
to the formless.

Although our measurements of the hidden waterfall could only be reduc-
tive—even trivial from a certain point of view—they did clearly establish, after more than a hundred years of searching, that the legendary Falls of the
Tsangpo was not a myth but a reality. Moreover, the waterfall we had just measured was nearly three times as high as any other previously documented on a
major Himalayan or South Asian river.[14]

We still needed to reach the waterfall's base to compare our readings with
the range finder to those of the clinometer. There was no way down from where
we stood, so Ken slung the range finder over his shoulder and jumared back up
to the top of the cliff. When I joined him, I asked Buluk and Jayang if they had
any local name for the falls, and they told me that they refer to it simply as

Dorje Pagmo's *chinlap*, her blessings or, in literal translation, her transformative flood of power. We collectively decided to call the waterfall Pagmo Sang Bab, the Hidden Falls of Dorje Pagmo.

Before searching for a way down to the base of the falls, we stretched prayer flags between two silver-green pines with aspirations that this hidden place that had inspired dreams and speculations, lost texts, and new discoveries would remain forever inviolate, and that the guardian spirits that had kept it thus far off the map would remain ever vigilant. The multicolored banners imprinted with Buddhist mantras and images of Padmasambhava were also a message for the Chinese expedition that we half expected at our heels.

The Secret Door

NEVER HAVING ROCK CLIMBED BEFORE, Bryan had struggled with the ju-mars while ascending the overhanging cliff. He was not interested in subjecting himself to further danger or distress. "I have all the footage I need," he said confidently. "I don't need to go down to the base." He told us he planned to end the film with pans of Ken and me rappelling out over the void of the falls.

If for Bryan the film—and the expedition—were effectively over, Ken and I agreed that to complete even the outer measurements of the waterfall, we would still have to descend beneath it. Perhaps we could also resolve the question of the legendary door. From our earlier vantage point on the sloping ledge, a protruding buttress of igneous rock had concealed the waterfall's right-hand edge. We fantasized that we might find something hidden there akin to the Cave of the Winds behind Niagara or the passage through the falls in *The Last of the Mohicans*.

We threw the ropes down over the cliff on the northern side of the spur, but they only reached halfway to the level of the river. After coiling them back up, we made our way along the cliff edge looking for a break in the rock. We found a steep vegetated gully that eventually disgorged onto a moonscape of wave-polished gneiss fifty feet above the Tsangpo. We traversed out across the silvery, mica-flecked rock. The protruding buttress still hid the falls, but we were hopeful that by contouring across the slabs we would soon reach its base.

At a gap in the escarpment, I clambered down to the edge of the Tsangpo and filled my water bottle from the silt-filled waves. The water was cold and penetrating and surged before me through a flume of burnished rock. A vari-colored wall of rock swirling with gold and purple lichen rose from the waters

on the opposite bank. Two hundred yards to my right, the river cascaded over a hidden drop and disappeared into a hairpin bend. I recalled a passage from the *Tantra of the Direct Consequence of Sound* that offers instruction on meditating on waterfalls and turbulent rivers. "The dakinis' harmonies manifest in the water's thunderous roar," states the text.[15] The Dalai Lama had explained the practice in reference to wall paintings on what had once been his private meditation chamber in Tibet. One image shows a yogi meditating in front of a waterfall with a tunnel leading behind it as if into another realm. "This shows a form of meditation on the sound of the elements," His Holiness told me. "Waterfalls are the best places for this. The practitioner merges with the sound of water to open subtle energy currents within his inner yogic body. . . . When these energies are unified and circulating through the uma, the central meridian, the chakras open like petals of a lotus and previously hidden dimensions of awareness arise in one's mindstream."[16]

I climbed back out of the defile and caught up with Ken, Buluk, and Jayang, who were looking for a route across the steepening quartzite slabs. As we neared the falls, the ever-present spray had coated the rock with a slick veneer of moss. We traversed out on slimy footholds, looking for a place to anchor the

rope. We could now clearly see the waterfall as it avalanched through the cleft, but a bulge in the cliff that rose above us obscured its upper section, where we had stood only two hours before. From whatever angle we had approached, some part of the falls always remained hidden from view.

Even had we found a belay point for the rope, the ubiquitous slime and steepening angle made it impossible to proceed farther across the slabs. To get any closer to the waterfall's base, we would have had to approach from above with hundreds more feet of rope. But we could see beneath the buttress now, and no cave seemed to lead into the fall's interior. We abandoned our fantasies of anything approximating the Cave of the Winds or a passageway through this suture between ancient continents.

By taking measurements with the clinometer on the wall of rock that rose across from us and above the cauldron of foam at the waterfall's base, we were able to verify our earlier calculations. The height of any river fluctuates with the seasons and, if we had measured the falls in full flood, we might have gotten different readings. But on this day—November 8, 1998—our various measurements gave the Hidden Falls of Dorje Pagmo a height of anywhere from 105 to 115 feet. Oddly, we continued to come up with the figure 108—a sacred number in Buddhist cosmology and a figure enthusiastically endorsed by our Tibetan companions. (Coincidentally, Victoria Falls is 108 *meters* high.)

Like all data, the measurements would lead to facts, but not to the discovery of anything beyond our normal range of experience. How can one presume to measure water? I thought. From clouds, to river, to sea, where does a waterfall really begin and end? As Heraclitus had said, it all just flows away.

Po Tsangpo River
Yumé
Tsachu
Gompo-Né
Mondrong
The Confluence
Shati-La
Neygap
Five Mile Gap
Neythang
Bayu
Gyala Pelri
Hugudurung
Zadem
Azadem
Tsodem
Dorje Pagmo
Rainbow Falls
Hidden Falls
Shechen-La
Tsangpo-Brahmaputra River
Valley of the White Crystal
Pemakochung Monastery
Tselung-Chu
Secret Pass of the Dakinis
Namcha Barwa
Holmer 04

ALTHOUGH BULUK AND JAYANG had cooperated with us in our geographical mission to measure the falls from several vantage points, the waterfall's height clearly mattered very little to them. But they had looked intimately for auspicious signs and portents in the surrounding environment that might indicate a route beyond or through it. Only if the waters that flow over the falls could be temporarily stopped, like those at Niagara, would they ever be convinced that no golden road leads through the cascading water.

In the midst of my musings, Buluk asked me for the range finder. He'd been looking at the scriptlike swirls of lichen on the opposite wall, commenting that they resembled *khandro dayig*, the secret dakini ciphers that often indicate the site of a terma. The patterns faintly resembled petroglyphs or some lost runic language. The range finder doubled as binoculars, and he panned across the lithic whorls until the viewfinder came to rest at an oval-shaped opening on the rock wall across from the waterfall.

"That may be the door," he said. After minutes of gazing through the double lenses, he handed me the range finder to look for myself.

Huge waves leaped out of the Tsangpo and spilled down the smooth rock wall directly below the apparent tunnel. A perfect oval had formed in the reddish granite twenty or thirty feet above river level, and a passageway seemed to veer off diagonally into the dark heart of the mountain; how far one could only guess. Could this be the legendary portal that the correct ceremonies or rituals would cause to open? A tunnel into the heart of what once had been Gondwanaland?

The terma that Dudrul Dorje had brought forth in the sixteenth century from a lake in Powo had referred to a door in a wall of rock and a tunnel behind that one would have to follow for an entire day to reach a paradisiacal realm of healing fruits and eternal youth. According to the revealed scroll, a high pass leads even farther to an emerald palace inhabited by joyful beings in bodies of rainbow light where all desires are magically fulfilled. Were these symbolic evocations of internal meditative states, hyperbolic accounts of parallel dimensions, or simply the literary fantasies of a Buddhist sage?

The questions posed by the texts and traditional Tibetan beliefs, however diffuse and unanswerable, were ultimately as intriguing a proposition as the height of the waterfall, a fact that we quickly established with the aid of modern technology. The Falls of the Tsangpo had offered turn-of-the-century explorers a geographical quest to rival the search for the headwaters of the Nile. But the Tibetans—who knew of it already—did not view the falls as a topographical trophy but as a sacrament, a threshold between the physical universe and the world of the spirit. That Kingdon Ward and those before him never found the falls seemed strangely just, as its significance lay in qualities quite distinct from those they sought. And even when it could be seen from high above, it had been dismissed as a hydrolic event of no great consequence—its true proportions concealed by foreshortened perspective.

If the oval gateway at the base of Dorje Pagmo really was a door to some undiscovered realm, it wasn't a question of how to open it—the portal was already open wide—but how to reach it. More than 200 feet of seething white water lay between the tunnel and where we stood on the opposite side of the gorge. The waters of the Tsangpo surged up against the cliffs in a fluvial chaos that could never be crossed. Rappelling down the sheer walls of Dorje Pagmo—provided one could approach from the other side—did not look any more feasible. It would take some arcane methodology—far beyond our current means—to ever enter that mysterious passageway. And even if one did penetrate the granite veil, unless one's mind's eye was honed to an almost exquisite sensitivity, any hidden world might pass unnoticed. I felt happy that the oval passage was so thoroughly beyond reach. Some doors cannot be opened until they open first in us.

The elliptical opening in the side of the gorge was a compelling feature of the landscape, suggestive of hidden worlds and birth tunnels into new states of existence. At the same time, it was a simple geological fault and unlikely to penetrate deeply into the wall of rock, which was darkening now as shadows flooded down the sides of the gorge.

How we view the world is a strange alchemy of cultural conditioning and personal choice. One could cautiously avoid all geomorphic speculations or, like the Tibetans, allow the configurations of rock and water to guide one into more exalted thoughts and alternate ways of seeing. As the Victorian poet Robert Browning wrote: ". . . a man's reach should exceed his grasp. Or what's a heaven for?"

Poststructuralist theory holds that the meaning of words and events is forever contingent on a web of shifting contexts and points of view. The falls, the neyigs, our own conditioning all point toward a vision of the universe and ourselves that admits multiple and simultaneous perspectives, ones that free us from self-limiting opinions and open the way for true discovery—to recognize that all we see is not *the* world but *a* world, generated by a language of only half-conscious thoughts, ideas, and sensations that, as Wittgenstein observed, "could all be otherwise." Either way, we had reached a place where a Victorian dream of a legendary waterfall converged with the Tibetan quest for a paradisiacal sanctuary. Standing between the falls and the unreachable doorway, encircled by towering cliffs, the implacable drone of the Tsangpo reverberating through our cells, we shared with our Tibetan companions, each in our own way, a moment beyond time and geography.

RISING UPWARD FROM THE FOAMING CAULDRON between the waterfall and the oval door was the diaphanous fountain of mist that we had first seen from high up on the walls of the gorge. A swirling iridescence distilled from the turbulent waters of the falls, the cloud of condensed water droplets rose on vectors of air toward the heights of Dorje Pagmo. In contrast with the downward thunder of the waterfall, the mists flowed upward in etheric ease, transforming into light and air.

Carl Jung wrote of waterfalls as images of unification, alchemical symbols joining "the above to the below," the conscious mind with the vast resources of what he termed the collective unconscious. Nineteenth-century painters viewed mists rising from the base of falls as confirmation of spiritual resurrection. Livingstone wrote of a "flight of angels," and his description of the mists hovering above Victoria Falls led to the naming of a heady cocktail still offered at the Falls

Hotel. In Tibetan thanka paintings, the cycles of nature illustrate experiences in meditation. Opalescent clouds pictured above waterfalls represent *bodhichitta*, the enlightened essence inherent within all beings. Waterfalls depict its active flow and circulation through the body, mind, and universe.

When the great Terton Rigdzin Godemchen searched for the hidden-land of Dremojung in the fourteenth century, he dreamed one night that he was lost in a fog-enveloped valley. A voice guided him through the mists: "The stream of your mind is agitated by doubts and conditioned appearances. . . . Pristine consciousness—your mind's natural state—is free of conceptual thought; this is the one essential secret that cuts through every obstacle."

Godem, like other tertons, followed the meditative practices of Dzogchen, the pinnacle of the Nyingma tradition. Dzogchen's discourse makes any outward search seem futile. From the view of Dzogchen, the pristine reality symbolized by the hidden-lands is already fully present, though veiled from view just as mists can obscure the sight of surrounding mountains. "The flow of wisdom is as continuous and unstoppable as the current of a mighty river," declared Padmasambhava in a Dzogchen Tantra. "Look into your own mind to know whether or not this is true." To search for truth externally, Padmasambhava taught, is to miss its all-pervading presence.

The culmination of all Buddhist paths Dzogchen leads to lucid awareness of the mind's ultimate nature, beyond all concepts of self and other. "When you recognize the pure nature of your mind as the Buddha, looking into your own mind is resting in the [omniscient] Buddha Mind," wrote Padmasambhava.

The Tibetan translation of Buddha is *Sangye*. Etymologically, *sang* means purified of all obscurations and *gye* means vast in expansive qualities. Buddha thus refers to the great sphere of pristine wisdom in which all perceptions are viewed ultimately as reflections of mind, yet free of any reference to a self. "When truly sought even the seeker cannot be found," Padmasambhava declared, "thereupon the goal of the seeking is attained, and the end of the search. At this point there is nothing more to be sought, and no need to seek anything."

Lamas sometimes introduce the view of Dzogchen by sending their students into the mountains to look for mind. When they return not having been able to locate consciousness either in the brain, the sense organs, or external phenomena, the lama points out that not to find mind is to discover its true nature. For in that empty space—the clarity and openness between thoughts that can only be discovered experientially—lies the path to enlightenment and the realization that to search for the Buddha outside ourselves is like trying to grasp flowing water. We only come up empty-handed.

In reaching the waterfall at the bottom of the gorge, we had discovered something that was in fact no "thing" at all, but rather a dazzling display of light and waves. In Buddhist terms, its fluid dance of emptiness and appearance reflects the mind's innermost nature. Perhaps in this way, I thought, the waterfall serves as a door into the hidden realms beyond mind as we know it. In describing the quantum world beyond ordinary human perception, the physicist David Bohm wrote that: "Consciousness has to become commensurate with that different space in order to discover it. Consciousness, in fact, has to change its very state." The Buddhist termas say the same thing about reaching Yang-sang.

In Buddhism, the veil that obscures reality in its full expanse is the clinging to a sense of "I," as well as the rejecting of an "I." The key to the hidden-lands beyond those veils lies in the letting go of all hope, fear, and expectation—the subtle forms of attachment by which those luminous dimensions elude our sight. I remembered the story of the terton that Tashi Tsering had told me in Dharamsala: as the hidden treasure came closer, the terton suddenly grasped for it, and it vanished from his hands. As long as appearances are seen as separate from consciousness, the Tantras state, the essence of mind and reality remains unrealized.

Yangsang's coordinates thus lie neither outside nor inside the seeker, but in their conjunction in human consciousness. The portal opens when one realizes that one no longer needs to seek it and must simply open to that which is already fully present. In that vastness in which nothing is hidden and nothing needs to be revealed, as all is transparent, clear, and free of obscurations, the adept opens unhesitatingly to all that presents itself, without reference to the ego. And the doors, in response, open everywhere.[17]

WE HAD DESCENDED deeper into the Tsangpo gorge than any human to our knowledge had ever gone. According to the coordinates of the Pemako neyigs, we were deep in the throat of the dakini goddess Dorje Pagmo. In the Tantric presentation of the body as a system of interrelated energy centers, the throat chakra—*visuddha* in Sanskrit—means purgation and refers to the release of false concepts of reality so as to experience fully the transcendent, a world whose perfection lies in its ongoing process. Anatomically, the throat serves as a link between the head and the heart. In the hermeneutical twilight language of the Buddhist Tantras, being swallowed by the dakini—an embodiment of the divine feminine—infers initiation into mysteries beyond the reach of the rational or empirical mind: the maturing process of the psyche as it abandons false certainties and efforts to limit and control its experience and yields instead to the fecundity and flow of the world as it is. Reconnecting with full consciousness to the lost feminine unity, the adept is symbolically reborn from the dakini's secret lotus.

In our descent to the falls, we too had been swallowed by the mysteries of the gorge. In this fault line between ancient continents, we had sought something seemingly beyond reach, beyond the falls itself, and had ultimately surrendered to the incalculable reality that had enveloped us—without further thought of walls, doors, or keys. If there was any innermost secret to be revealed here in the configurations of cliffs, waters, and oval doorways, I felt no need for it: the inconceivable wonder that surrounded us was already more than enough, an intertwining world of snakes, orchids, lithe huntresses, and evanescent mist. I felt no yearning for more etheric realms, for anything akin to what Nabokov had once described as a "silent solarium for immortal souls" or Edward Abbey's "banal Heaven for the saints . . . a garden of bliss and changeless perfection." No, I preferred this wilder world of rich paradoxes, beyond the diminishments of more temperate thoughts.

I'd been drawn to these distant gorges by ancient scrolls that invoke a landscape that perhaps one was never meant to find. But the quest for Yangsang had enlivened my relationship with the earth and nature, the womb from which we all emerge. There is no paradise beyond that which is already present, even if still hidden from our view. The gates of Yangsang pervade all space, and the portals are everywhere, as numerous, say the texts, as pores on the skin or blades of grass on the earth.

The vision of Yangsang propounded in the termas foretells a form of consciousness beyond the veils of discursive thought, a space forever present for those who seek it, not in some far-off wilderness, but in our innermost hearts. When that realization dawns in the depth of one's being, the world effortlessly transforms into that which was sought. In a phrase that could as easily have come from Buddhist treasure-texts, The Book of Revelations states that: "Then I saw a new heaven and a new earth, for the first heaven and the first earth had passed away."

WITH SHADOWS LENGTHENING down the walls of the gorge and our ears brimming with the drone of the river, we climbed back over the silver-gray slabs and up the cliff above. We reached camp in near darkness, sustained by the adrenaline of our discoveries. Until now we'd had no idea what we would actually find in this forgotten corner of the Tsangpo gorge. We'd all been skeptical, yet having descended to the falls and measured its waters, we completed a journey begun more than a hundred years earlier. At the same time, we knew that discovery is not a simple process of raising a flag at spots not previously visited by outsiders or guessing at the significance of sights seen from afar.

The Hidden Falls of Dorje Pagmo, concealed in the narrowest and most precipitious section of the Tsangpo gorge, had been a perennial goal of nineteenth- and early-twentieth-century explorers. Our discovery exploded a long-standing myth concerning the waterfalls' very existence and placed it within a larger historical, geographical, and cultural context. Not least of which was the Tibetan perspective that the falls was not so much an overlooked geographical fact as a threshold to a hidden dimension or, at least, to a new way of seeing. Although such vision can't be quantified, the perspective offered by Padmasambhava's scrolls invite us to grow beyond nineteenth-century models of exploration and

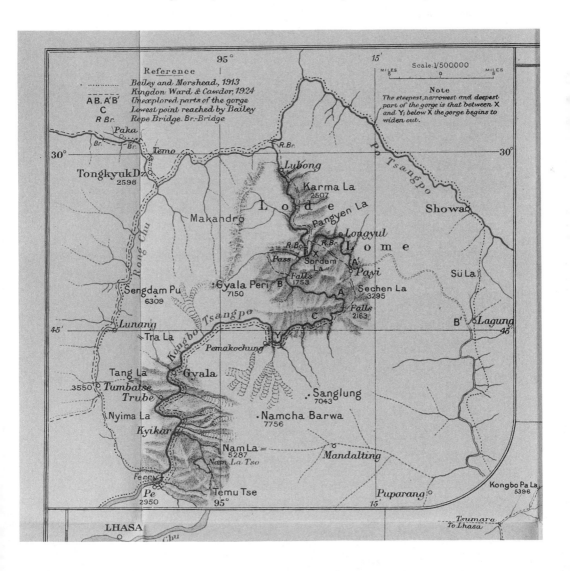

to open to the blank spaces within our own understanding—to explore not only the physical terrain but, to the best of our ability, to comprehend what the earth's wildest places mean for those who have always lived there or dreamed them into existence.

THE PORTERS SETTLED DOWN by their fires, but frost had already covered the thick grass and they had only their clothing and animal skins for bedding. I gave my heavy woolen tunic to the lama's daughter, Sonam Deki. As I sat in my tent the following morning, she came to the door with the folded tunic and her hands cupped like a chalice around a heap of freshly picked indigo-colored berries. "They're ripe," she said as she poured them into my opening palms.

The Missing Link

BESIDES LOOKING FOR WATERFALLS, our expedition's stated purpose was to explore the entirety of the Five-Mile Gap—in reality, more than ten miles of some of the most forbidding terrain on the planet. Beyond our camp at the base of the spur, the gorge transformed into a labyrinth of landslides and cliffs. The lower one traversed along the side of the chasm, the more precipitous the walls. To proceed farther into the unknown section, we would first have to climb back up to our earlier bivouac site, high on the upper slopes of the gorge. From there, we would traverse north to the next spur that would allow us to drop back toward the river.

Bryan was less than enthusiastic about the way ahead. As far as he was concerned his work was over and he was anxious to get his footage to Washington.

On November 9, we breakfasted on dried goral meat and began following our previous route up the ridge. Hoping to shorten the distance, we veered north and climbed through a series of steep gullies and cut our way through mazes of thorn-filled barberry and scrub rhododendrons. Five hours later, we finally traversed the treacherous landslides leading back to our previous bivouac site. Without water, we continued on to Darup, the small spring beneath towering hemlocks, where we carved out platforms to accommodate our tents.

In dropping temperatures and with thick clouds obscuring all views into the gorge, I spoke with Jayang and Buluk about the route ahead. I told them we needed to stay as close as possible to river level and to document the Tsangpo's course through this hidden section of the gorge. The hunters reaffirmed what was already obvious: the lower reaches of the gap are sheer cliffs, and the only way to see down into the river is to descend on intermittent spurs. Even without descending lower, they claimed, the journey through the gap involves regular ascents and descents of thousands of feet through pathless, bramble-choked ravines. There are only shifting game trails, Buluk clarified, and they're far back from the river where high cliffs seal it off to animal and man. There was clearly no set route through the zone ahead and although the distance was little more than ten miles, towering nettles, rhododendron mazes, landslides, steep ravines, and choking undergrowth made it all seem an exaggerated version of what we had already been through, a deepening journey into Dorje Pagmo's throat.

DURING THE NIGHT, the clouds that had enveloped the gorge transformed into pounding rain that, by morning, bordered on sleet and snow. Further dampening the mood, Buluk came to my tent and announced that they had nearly run out of food. According to Buluk it would be less than half a day's trek from our camp beneath the hemlocks to where our advance crew had set up a base camp at a spring called Benchi Pagmo. Buluk proposed that Jayang lead us to the forest camp while he and Drakpa, one of the other hunters, returned to Azadem to bring back fresh stores of tsampa and chilies. He insisted he would be able to meet us there by nightfall.

Following Buluk's plan, we unloaded some of our surplus climbing gear so that he could carry it down to Azadem. He and Drakpa then headed off into the mists while the rest of us packed up the sodden tents and started for Benchi Pagmo. We reached the small pass called Tsodem-La in little more than half an hour. From there, we followed a marginal path lined with sphagnum moss, spruce, and hemlocks. Banners of mist streamed through the pale trees as we followed the occasional blazes that the hunters had made in the past to mark the trail. In places, steep washouts and vertiginous landslides had erased all signs of previous passage, and fog obscured all but a narrow circumference through which we moved like wraiths. Flowing through the mists and primeval old-growth forests we finally reached a few perches that over the past five days, the two Sherpas and six Tibetans who had gone ahead of us, had carved from the 9,500-foot mountainside.

The mists briefly opened, and through the shining wetness of the forest, I looked across the gorge and saw fresh snow blanketing the heights of Dorje Pagmo. Fleetingly, I also saw a spur called Sangkami that extended below our camp into the unexplored chasms where we hoped to follow it the next morning. We spent the remainder of the afternoon huddled around the fires or escaping the drizzle under the plastic tarps that served our porters as tents.

Sonam Deki, the lama's daughter, laughed with her friend Tsering Yuden over their myriad leech bites. The two women were related through an illicit liaison that they attempted to explain to me by pointing to their fellow villagers and recounting their histories of elopement, divorce, and multiple marriages. Our entire crew of porters seemed to be made up of half brothers and sisters related to each other through their parents' complex alliances.

In the midst of these sociological digressions, Buluk and Dranak returned from Bayu with news of the Chinese expedition that in our euphoria we had nearly forgotten about. According to Buluk, a team of forty Chinese who had entered the gorge from Gyala was stranded now on the far side of the Shechen-La pass. Their porters from Pe and Gyala had apparently refused to continue and the expedition leader had sent a runner ahead to Bayu to return with a team of porters who knew the way ahead, as well as with eggs, tsampa, and any other available food to replenish their dwindling stocks. The advance scouts had returned with some food and a few porters, but we had already secured the majority of Bayu's available manpower. Buluk smiled when he recounted how disappointed the Chinese leader had been to hear that a team of Americans had already descended to the falls and was now continuing deeper into the gap.

More worrisome to us, Buluk reported that the dzongpon, or governor, of Tibet's Nyingtri county was accompanying the team. Although our permits were perfectly in order, we knew this meant very little if the issue of national pride came into play. Also, there was the fact that we had employed the majority of Bayu's and Azadem's potential porters. We wouldn't reach Azadem again for another five days, but from there we planned to head out immediately for Tsachu with the same crew of porters. In a strange twist of fate, the unintended race for the waterfall had led to the possibility that the Chinese would be stranded in the gorge without porters or guides.

Bryan was more eager now than ever to pack up and leave. He had brought a Magellan satellite phone—the size of a small laptop computer—and he wanted to phone in a report to National Geographic concerning the discovery of the waterfall before the Chinese got there. He hadn't been able to get any reception whatsoever in the gap—all satellite signals seemed to be blocked by the walls of the gorge—but he was hopeful he'd be able to phone in from Azadem. He was also anxious to get his film out of Tibet as quickly as possible in case we ran into any resistance.

HEAVY MISTS HUNG OVER OUR CAMP the following morning, November 11. We could hear the Tsangpo droning through unseen chasms 3,000 feet below us, but visibility was restricted to the towering hemlocks that surrounded our tents. Despite our concerns about the Chinese, we had committed to fully exploring this unknown section of the gorge. The first major spur descends from Benchi Pagmo and, in hopes that the fog would soon burn off, we began making preparations to follow it as far as possible, and, we hoped, gain views into the tight hairpin bend below the Hidden Falls.

We arranged for the Sherpas and the porters to proceed higher up on the face of the gorge and to set up a camp in a small glen known to the hunters as Zadem. Ken, Bryan, and I would head down the spur with Buluk and Jayang. Once we were in sight of the river, if conditions allowed, we would try to traverse north and reach Zadem from below. Across the gorge, the peak of Dorje Pagmo lay garlanded in mist; like a harem dancer made more beguiling by what she hid from view.

Fifteen minutes from camp we came upon a recent landslide, worse than anything we had yet encountered. The drop was perilous and, though the rocks seemed relatively stable, Bryan didn't want to risk a crossing that wasn't absolutely necessary. He opted to wait behind at a large boulder emerging from the side of the mountain. Ken and I continued on with the two hunters, the mists clearing as we descended a spine of rock beyond the slide. Gyala Pelri emerged from the clouds; Dorje Pagmo cast off her diaphanous veils. But the Tsangpo itself remained hidden beneath the cliffs that steepened as they approached the level of the river.

As the cloud banks dissolved, a spherical rainbow suddenly appeared in front of us and hovered over the abyss. A second circle of rainbow-colored light manifested around the first one, forming a double nimbus. Reflections of our bodies suddenly appeared within the circle of fog and sunlight. Buluk and Jayang kept muttering: "Beyul. Beyul." Eventually the vision dissipated and the gorge lay revealed below, free of clouds.[18]

We continued down the ridge to where it briefly leveled, but we still could not see the Tsangpo. It lay beneath us, lost in the layered corrugations of the gorge. We angled south and descended a precipitous ravine. Neither of the two hunters had ever ventured into this unknown section of the gap, but they had caught the fever and seemed as eager we were to see every corner of the river and to locate the third, smaller waterfall that Lama Topgye had spoken about.

As we descended lower, the terrain progressively steepened and became more hazardous. Where we could no longer proceed, we cleared branches and peered out over the cliffs. We saw the Tsangpo as it flowed northwest from the Hidden Falls and, half a mile or so later, entered a torturous **U**-bend where it careened into the base of the spur and then almost immediately doubled back on itself and surged due south as a mass of foaming water. A quarter mile beyond, it crashed against the lower walls of Dorje Pagmo and disappeared from sight where it flowed northwest again at the base of the Sangkami spur. Through the range finder we could see innumerable cascades and lesser waterfalls, but nothing as distinctive as the jetting falls that Lama Topgye had described to us in Tsachu.

Although we could see and photograph the full length of the Tsangpo from the Hidden Falls to the base of the Sangkami spur, a rocky promontory blocked our view of the easternmost corner of the **U**-bend. Having come this far, we were determined to see down into the hidden pocket. In hopes of gaining a sight line beneath the intervening protuberance, we scrambled downward for another hour until a sheer cliff dropping down into the Tsangpo barred all further progress. The innermost corner of the **U**-bend remained resolutely hidden, and we resigned ourselves to starting back up the spur.

While descending, we had kept an eye out for possible ways to traverse north and reach Zadem without having to climb back up to Benchi Pagmo. But

steep cliffs lined the northern side of the spur, and we could find no way through. Besides, Bryan had waited behind above the landslide, and we needed to return to Benchi Pagmo to fill our water bottles at the spring and retrieve some of our gear.

By 4 P.M. we had recrossed the landslide and reached the point where we had left Bryan. But despite having made visual contact with him two hours earlier from lower on the ridge, he was nowhere in sight and made no response to our calls. We could only hope that he had returned to wait at our previous night's camp.

Quickening our steps, we reached Benchi Pagmo a half hour later and found Bryan desparately trying to kick-start the fire. He had misread our hand signals and imagined that we had contoured around the ridge and abandoned him above the landslide. Unwilling to cross the unstable slope of mud and talus and catch up with us, he had returned to Benchi Pagmo and looked for the route to Zadem that the porters had forged that morning. He'd found only incipient game trails that petered out into jungle. Admittedly in a state of panic, he had decided to try to make his way back to Azadem if he couldn't resurrect the fire. If he could keep it going, at least he knew he wouldn't freeze to death.

By the time we were all back on track, it was close to 5 P.M. and we had only two hours of daylight left. Buluk claimed that it would take us four hours to reach Zadem, but we were traveling light and were determined to keep as quick a pace as possible. We had three working flashlights between the five of us and enough battery power to illumine the final two hours if it truly took as long as Buluk claimed.

We climbed steeply to a small pass. As the sun set over the rim of the gorge, we descended into a lush forest carpeted in ferns and moss. Moving as quickly as possible, we followed a rocky stream bed and emerged after another hour into a haunting stand of weeping pines. In fading light, we made our way through the forest until, rounding a house-sized boulder, we heard voices ahead and imagined that some of the Sherpas had come back to look for us.

As the figures approached, we suddenly recognized Tsering Dondrup, and behind him the hunter Sangye Tsering with his characteristic swashbuckling grin. We then saw Hamid, his face and arms inflamed with insect bites. Our own appearance was in all likelihood equally fearsome and, despite our joy at our sudden reunion, we kept our distance. Hamid and the hunters had been tracking an elusive boar lower down the valley and, as it was almost dark, had been looking for the trail that would lead them back to Zadem where they had camped under an overhanging boulder.

As we stumbled on through the forest, Hamid excitedly recounted his adventures in the gap. "It's a gnat-infested hell," he claimed with obvious relish, and went on to describe the route that he and the hunters had taken from Bayu.

They had descended into the gorge from a pass below Shati Pemayangdzong, a fluted pinnacle that looms over the northern end of the Tsangpo's Great Bend and which local tradition reveres as the repository of still-undiscovered termas, concealed there by Padmasambhava 1,200 years ago.

From a point roughly opposite from where Kingdon Ward and Lord Cawdor had reentered the gorge in 1924, they forged upstream through dense jungle and across avalanche chutes. Two days into their journey, they came across a herd of approximately twenty takin. The hunters pursued them through the dense forest, and Sangye Tsering shot a large male that tumbled down a cliff and landed near Hamid's feet—providing him with critical footage to complete the film that we had begun with Ned Johnston the previous spring.

They continued on toward the cave sanctuary of Hugudurung where large numbers of takin reputedly shelter during the winter. The animals had not yet arrived, so Hamid and the others continued on through an unending maze of spiny shoulder-high stinging nettles. One of Sangye Tsering's hunting dogs became so filled with vegetal toxins, Hamid said, that he died before they emerged. Red ants and small unidentifiable insects had plagued their steps as they labored under the weight of the freshly slaughtered takin.

The following afternoon, Sangye Tsering shot a large Assamese macaque, a short-tailed monkey known as one of the most resilient and adaptable of all primates. Despite four bullet holes through its chest, it fought furiously with Sangye Tsering's dogs, slashing one of them across the throat before it finally collapsed. Hamid had filmed the macaque's final gambit but suffered a similar wound across his left arm. The hunters skinned the tawny monkey but left its body in the notch of a tree. They already had more meat than they could carry.

Over the next two days they'd forged through what Hamid called a "savage Eden." Where conditions allowed, they'd dropped their loads and followed steep spurs that jutted down toward the Tsangpo. But like our own investigations in the U-bend below the Hidden Falls, they'd seen no waterfalls higher than fifteen or twenty feet.

After reaching camp, the hunters made smoke offerings of juniper and cinnamon bark to aid the transit of the animals that they had killed while Ken, Hamid, and I discussed our strategy for the days ahead.

Originally, Ken, Bryan, and I had intended to retrace Hamid's passage through the northern part of the gap while Hamid had planned on following the path that we had forged to the Hidden Falls. But to duplicate each other's routes did not seem the best use of our resources, especially in such unforgiving terrain. Hamid's journey had clearly verified that this area that for so long had been considered terra incognita was well known to these Buddhist hunters. Hamid observed that they had names for each stretch of forest and significant feature of the landscape. He had already followed whatever spurs he could and photographed these previously hidden sections of the Tsangpo.

One major spur remained, however: the right fork of the one that we had followed the day before, the one that had been inaccessible from Benchi Pagmo due to intervening cliffs. If we could reach it from Zadem, it would lead us below the U-bend and allow us to see into a section of the Tsangpo that neither party had yet seen. Ken and I decided that documenting this last unknown stretch of river and looking for the mysterious third falls were more important to us than retracing Hamid's steps through the part of the gap that we hadn't seen.

Hamid had already passed through the gauntlet and decided to head back directly to Azadem and Bayu. The hunters had full loads of fresh meat and they were eager to take it home. Hamid wanted to film the continuity of their hunting foray and to document their return to the village. The falls would have been a lengthy diversion, adding days to their journey.

For Hamid, the hunters epitomized the rich paradoxes central to life in Pemako. "These hunters have traveled more deeply than anyone else into these remote gorges," Hamid observed. "They face death almost on a daily basis, both in the lives that they take and their own lives that they risk. It makes their Buddhist faith more poignant and real. They eat and dress in the skins of the animals they kill. They have great reverence for life, but they have deep convictions about what lies beyond that threshold. Is this life of the hunter—dwelling at the heart of life and death—not as pregnant with meaning as the monk or yogi sitting in a cave and meditating upon those things that he has abandoned?" Hamid imagined a film that would focus on Tsering Dondrup's ambiguous identity as both hunter and Buddhist practitioner.

While Hamid conjured scenes of a possible docudrama in which Tsering would eventually offer his gun to the village lama, giving up his quest for game for an inner search for illumination, Ken and I determined that we would head out the following morning to investigate a possible route down the final spur.

It wasn't a clear mission, however: Tsering Dondrup reiterated that the third waterfall that Lama Topgye had spoken about was not a true falls but a place where the entire Tsangpo funnels through a narrow flume, jetting out horizontally before crashing again into a mass of white water. According to Tsering Dondrup, this jetting waterfall did not lie concealed in the hidden pocket of the U-bend, as we had initially imagined, but beyond the end of the Sangkami spur. When we pressed him on where to look as we descended toward the river, he became more vague and admitted that he hadn't actually seen it. Another older hunter named Choeden claimed to have seen it long ago but couldn't remember where it was or how to get there. We knew what spur we would have to follow to get anywhere close to the Tsangpo, but the location and even the very existence of the third falls was now in question. We resigned ourselves to the possibility of spending our last day in the gap scrambling through a trackless wilderness in search of a chimera.

AT DAWN ON NOVEMBER 12, Hamid and his crew of hunters began the climb back toward Azadem. Ken, Bryan, and I left camp when the first rays of the sun permeated our hidden meadow and began melting the ice that had formed overnight in the cooking pots that we had used to store water. Together with Buluk, Jayang, and Choeden, we followed twisting game trails to the southern edge of the forest plateau where the right fork of the Sangkami ridge rose above us as a line of heavily vegetated 200-foot cliffs. From a large vine-strung boulder that we used as a landmark to ensure our return, we headed southwest along the base of the cliffs and dropped down a steep ravine, following a track left by migrating takin. After an hour of bushwhacking through briars and across steep slopes of bamboo, the vague trail began to climb toward the Sangkami spur. Amazed at the navigational skills of the takin, we followed their tracks up a series of broken, moss-covered ledges that eventually led us to the crest of the right fork of the Sangkami spur.

We were now firmly in the deep throat of the gorge and choking on the underbrush. From the outset, Bryan had been less than enthusiastic about this last foray, and the prospect of forging onward through the tangle of briars and precipitous ledges held no appeal. He had had enough shots of brambles, cliffs, and landslides, he said, enough of traipsing through the wilderness, following Ken and me on our quixotic quest for the third falls. The route ahead was entangled with thick vines, and the track of the takin that had led us onto the spur had vanished without a trace. With little hope that the forest would open and allow him to get shots down into the Tsangpo, Bryan announced that he would return the way we had come and meet us back in camp.

Ken and I continued with the hunters through a maze of vertiginous ridges, the river hidden below us by a screen of thick moss-brimming trees. We made repeated descents and ascents through the steep jungle until we came to the edge of a promontory where the trees ended abruptly at the top of a vertical cliff. We lowered ourselves to a precarious vantage point where Jayang cut through a tangle of tree boughs and we could gaze down between our feet to the Tsangpo, swirling beneath us in a series of cataracts and minor waterfalls. With the range finder, we panned across the white water from where the river rounded the corner out of the U-bend and surged downstream toward Hurgudurung and Neygyap. We saw a litany of lesser waterfalls that seemed to accord with the seventy-five listed in the lost scrolls, but nothing that stood out as the mysterious jetting fountain. Convinced that it must exist somewhere, Choeden determined that it must lie on other side of the ridge, in the narrow corner of the U-bend that we had been unable to see during our descent from Benchi Pagmo. We were below the line of the cliffs that had obscured our view the day before, and we decided to traverse southeast and see if we could reach a lower point on the left branch of the Sangkami spur.

An hour of hazardous bushwhacking brought us to the edge of a precipice

where we could finally get a clear view into the hidden corner of the U-bend. There was no sign of any horizontal jet of water, just a seething maelstrom as the Tsangpo pounded against its eastern boundary and like liquified jade turned back on itself to flow along the tectonic fault line. It felt right, in the end, to leave behind us the lingering mystery of the third falls. But we also felt a certain sense of completion; not unlike Lord Cawdor who, on December 16, 1924, had written in his journal: "We have exhausted all the possible methods of getting a sight of that part of the Tsangpo which we have missed, and have left hardly any room for any more falls than those we have seen."

As we retraced our steps toward Zadem, we felt a sense of closure, but, as on all past expeditions into Pemako, a sense too that we were on the edge of mysteries that we would never fully fathom. Historically, the Five-Mile Gap had come to represent the discrepancy between dreams and their fulfillment. Although we had penetrated this final refuge of the unknown, a larger mystery had opened around us. The Buddhist word for paradise is *shingkam*, or pure field, that by definition has no boundaries or divisions. All walls are in the beholder—the *marig ki drib yol*, the curtains of ignorance, that obscure perception of a synergistic, interpenetrating reality at the heart of all experience. The Tsangpo gorges had led us into a different way of thinking, into a world in which mind and nature, texts and landscape, interfuse and enrich each other. I thought of Marlowe's words in *Heart of Darkness*: "Going up that river was like traveling back to the beginning of the world."

That night, Ken and Bryan hardly slept. They reported in the morning that enchanting singing had awakened them near midnight and continued through-out the night. It reminded Ken of the melodious recitations of the Gesar Epics that he had heard in Ladakh. Bryan wondered if the porters were celebrating our impending return. I had heard nothing, although I had slept fitfully.

The Pemakopas and the Sherpas had slept near the fire but when I asked them about the singing, they claimed to have slept early after their customary mantra recitations and prayers. They'd heard nothing like what Ken and Bryan reported. Maybe they were only dreaming, I said. But Choeden, the older hunter who had joined us on our last foray, said that it was an auspicious sign.

"We often hear such singing when we hunt in the gorge," he told me, "par-ticularly if we have made many prayers to Dorje Pagmo and Padmasambhava. We hear voices, but never see anyone and, although we can hear the words, we can't understand the meaning."

Choeden told me that they often hear duets sung between a male and a fe-male. Sometimes they hear voices calling their names, but there's never anyone to be seen.

"The singing comes as a blessing of Dorje Pagmo," Choeden asserted. "Your friends are lucky."

Encouraged by Choeden's revelations, Jayang acknowledged that on past so-journs in the gap he had heard the jingling ankle bells of dakinis. He had wit-nessed strange lights and apparitions and been entranced by their songs.[19]

Perhaps that's paradise after all, I mused, when all boundaries between outer and inner experience have broken down. Or perhaps, on the other hand, it's no more than delectable madness.[20]

The Way Out

QUANTUM PHYSICISTS HAVE LONG RECOGNIZED that we see only a portion of the world around us. The most intellectually rigorous and accurate model of the physical universe produced by Western science, quantum physics offers a paradoxical world of shifting perspectives and possible probabilities and—like Buddhism—fully acknowledges the role of consciousness in shaping reality.

In quantum physics, the very act of observation alters the supposedly objective reality that is being observed. As Neils Bohr and Albert Einstein asserted in their Copenhagen Interpretation, the observer fundamentally creates reality by observing it, and *how* we look determines the phenomena that we perceive. "Until an observer sees an atom, the atom occupies an infinite number of possible positions simultaneously," wrote a noted physicist. "Upon observation, all of these possibilities collapse into a single reality."[21]

The famous uncertainty principle formulated in the 1930s by Werner Heisenberg observed that subatomic particles such as electrons can't be definitively located in space but can only be said to occupy probable, estimated locations. The spatial location of a particle remains inherently ambiguous until the observer's intent, or method of inquiry, causes it to manifest in a particular time and space.

In Buddhist Tantra the world is perceived as a luminous web of energies and possibilities. Just as the physicist's intent influences where, when, and how electrons manifest from the vast field of probability, Tantric practitioners apply a similar principle to alter and expand their view of reality, to free it from the reference point of an observing subject and still more from the oxymoron of an objective object wholly distinct from human consciousness. By altering states of consciousness through ritual and meditation, adepts manifest latent, simultaneous realities, beyond the bounds of conventional perception. Yangsang lies in this interworld between mind and nature and, like the particles sought by quantum physicists, where the terton seeks that hidden dimension influences where it will be found. Intention transforms latent possibilities into actual events, and just as subatomic particles appear in the world in response to our method of inquiry, potential realities are realized by first imagining their possibility.

THE TEAM OF CHINESE SCIENTISTS currently stranded below Pemakochung was also searching for a waterfall whose possibility had been imagined more than a century earlier. Bailey's book, *No Passport to Tibet,* had been translated into Chinese and had helped alert the nation to the historical quest. The Chinese Academy of Sciences had recruited top geologists, botanists, reporters, and media personnel to form "one of the most important expeditions of the century."

National prestige played a large part in how the Chinese expedition presented itself. Before we had reached the road head at Trulung, Tibetans recounted that they had seen nightly clips on Chinese television documenting the team's progress. They told us that they had prayed to Padmasambhava that the

veils of their promised land would remain firmly drawn, and that the Chinese would not be able to penetrate their last sanctuary as they had their homeland, forty years before.

We had beaten the Chinese Academy of Sciences to the falls, but were we any more entitled to be here? Bryan was poised to send his news release to National Geographic, and Ken and I pondered all the implications. Whatever we could say about this place would only veil its true proportions, or still worse, turn it into the latest ecotourism hotspot—the world's deepest gorge, the last great waterfall, the real Shangri-La. But the die was cast, and if we refrained from reporting the discovery of the falls the Chinese version of events would prevail. We could only try as best we could to convey the meaning of the falls for those who dwell in these remote gorges and who draw both their livelihood and inspiration from its waters, animals, and plants. Pemako had revealed itself as a landscape of the heart, a realm of unbounded possibilities where those who venture here dream themselves into a larger existence. But we knew better than to try to convey such ideas through international media.

If the Chinese had coerced their porters to proceed, they could show up at any moment. To avoid any unpleasant encounters, we decided to return to Azadem as quickly as possible. Bryan buried his exposed film cassettes at the bottom of his pack in case we were challenged, and we left Zadem on the morning of November 13.

As we contoured along the sides of the gorge, Gyala Pelri soared into the sky much as an early explorer had described it: "A perfect jewel; one might have fancied it to be the immaculate abode of some radiant god, feeding on pure light." We crossed the tree-covered Tsodem-La and descended quickly through wet ferns and gnarled rhododendrons. The Tibetans were eager to get home and we covered the distance to Azadem before the sun had disappeared over the horizon.

The village buzzed with unaccustomed activity. Hamid had been filming the hunters as they offered the blackish head of the takin to Lama Konchok Wangpo. He performed the requisite rites, sending its spirit to greener pastures on the curling clouds of blue-gray smoke.

Several men from Tsachu were camped on the lama's porch. Over bowls of chang, Tsachu's headman, Sonam Nima, told me that more than fifty Chinese were based at their village above the confluence. As few porters were available in Bayu or Azadem, the expedition leader in Tsachu dispatched Sonam Nima with twenty men to carry food supplies to the Chinese team stranded behind the Shechen-La. According to Sonam, the Chinese hadn't gotten farther than Shekarlungpa. Only when an advance party arrived in Azadem would he and his men head into the gorge to relieve them. "There are lots of plants that they can eat there in the meantime," Sonam Nima said with a grin.

It seemed like more than coincidence that within a matter of days our two expeditions with no prior knowledge of each other had nearly collided in the Tsangpo gorge. Difficulties with their porters had apparently prevented the Chinese from proceeding more quickly, and we felt admitted gratification at having beaten them to the falls.

Later in the evening, Bryan finally got a signal on the Magellan satellite phone. He came into the house and said that his supervisor at National Geographic Television, Maryanne Culpepper, wanted to speak to me.

"They *are* nice falls, aren't they? I've always hoped someone would discover them."

"Congratulations," said the voice, traveling through thousands of miles of space. "You found the falls. Why do you think you succeeded while others did not?"

I felt a strange foreboding. Her question framed our discovery in the context of who got where first, not on what the falls—to our minds at least—actually represented. I thought back to a cartoon from *The New Yorker* that the librarian of the Explorers Club had once pinned to the club's bulletin board. The drawing showed a great white explorer in a pith helmet standing beside his native guide as they gaze up at a curtain of falling water. The caption reads: "They *are* nice falls, aren't they? I've al-ways hoped someone would discover them," a droll reminder of the relative na-ture of all discovery.

"The Tibetans knew of this waterfall long ago," I finally said. "They kept it secret because of its importance in their own religious beliefs. A Chinese Acad-emy of Sciences expedition is headed there now and may view it very differ-ently. We were simply the first to reach it and document its height. Our role now is to help explain what the falls signifies in the Tibetan Buddhist world-view, as well as in terms of nineteenth- and early-twentieth-century notions of exploration."

Whatever I said, the focus on the other side of the planet remained on our expeditionary coup, and I could sense its importance to the National Geo-graphic Society in counteracting the negative publicity that it had received for sponsoring the ill-fated kayaking expedition. I went back inside and sat by the fire wondering at the drama in which we had inadvertently involved ourselves.

"The word *discovery* carries a lot of ambiguity," Ken offered. "Is it the first person to see something who gets credit for discovering it? Or is it the first per-son to reach it and place it in historical and geographical perspective?"[22]

"Similarly pointless debates have raged about who set foot on the summit of Everest first—Sir Edmund Hillary or Tenzing Norgay Sherpa," Hamid quipped, somewhat disgruntled that he was unlikely to appear in Bryan's film as he was not present at the waterfall during Bryan's defining shots. Bryan had ig-nored Hamid's solo passage through the gap because he could not see how to integrate it into his film.

OUR DEPARTURE FROM AZADEM on November 15 was plagued by a surfeit of prospective porters. We had drawn up a name list and placed all of the loads in a back room, all to no avail. Some villagers tried to climb in through the win-dows and one even appeared at the smoke hole on the roof. Even once the loads were distributed, they changed hands through some form of inside trading. Cash was hard to come by in these remote gorges.

Once the porters had headed out on the trail, we resigned ourselves to further rites of departure. At the bottom of the hill below Azadem, we were compelled to drink arak and chang at the home of Buluk's father-in-law, while his wife, Tsering Yuden, breast-fed her two young babies before heading out with us toward the trailhead. Another mile down the trail we drank more chang at Buluk's house, where he showed us a trove of quartz crystals, aquamarine, and other stones that he had harvested from the gap. I traded some for our climbing ropes and tarps, as well as two pairs of unwashed Patagonia socks.

We were apprehended again farther up the hill, at the house of one of the hunters who traveled with Hamid through the gap. Along with the requisite farewell chang, Senge tried unsuccessfully to get him to buy the dried gallbladder of a bear that he had killed a month earlier. Clearly the people of Pemako needed an alternative source of income.

By midday, we regrouped with our similarly inebriated porters and began the grueling climb to the pass that would take us to the bridge below the confluence. Beams of sunlight filtered through the mossy forest and cast magenta light on the fluted walls of Shati Pemayangdzong, which rose behind us over the apex of the gorge.

The Chinese had taken over Tsachu, and I had told the Sherpas to try to set up camp near the bridge across the Tsangpo. With the steady flow of chang, communications had been less than optimal and by the time we reached the bridge, half of the porters had already gone ahead, following a faint trail through the jungle that they said would lead to Ganglam, a small village high on a ridge above the confluence. It was nearly dark and the trail was marginal and the drop below often precipitous. With only three flashlights for the more than twelve of us in the rear guard, we proceeded very slowly. Eventually, however, the gradient lessened, and we entered the outskirts of the village, a collection of no more than five or six houses scattered along the ridge, 2,000 feet above the river.

We finally located the house that the Sherpas had commandeered for the night. They had woken up the residents, restored the fire, and begun preparing a meal. The matriarch of the household looked on mournfully as we used up the supply of water she'd stored in a great iron cauldron. It's an hour's journey just to collect water, she said. Nonetheless, we enjoyed a simple meal and dried ourselves by the fire. The chaos of our presence delighted the young children of the household, but the old woman was visibly put out. She showed me a gangrenous left arm—the aftereffects of a viper bite—and asked if we had any medicine that could restore its use. I helped her as best I could.

As elsewhere, only the old, the infirm, and the very young were left in the villages; all others had been recruited by the Chinese as porters for their multipronged siege on the Tsangpo gorge. We retired to tents that the Sherpas had set up on a flagstone threshing ground a short distance above the house.

THE FOLLOWING MORNING, November 16, Ken, Bryan, and I descended with Jayang, Buluk, and Tsering Yudon to the pilgrimage site of Gompo Né, an hour's climb below Ganglam. Hamid had gone down earlier so he could film independently of Bryan, who was eager to document this Jurassic realm of limestone caverns that I had last visited with Ani Rigsang. Buddhist pilgrims traditionally visit the site to pass through an archetypal landscape that forms a microcosm of the journey ahead, or the one through which they have already passed. In a circuit through cave tunnels, ravines, and jungle, they inscribe a symbolic passage from birth to death to resurrection.

Our journey began by choosing *lhashing*, or life sticks, from the surrounding forest. We cut notches in the saplings for every year of our lives and placed them upright, along with countless others, against an enormous boulder, thus establishing the auspicious circumstances for our spirits to ascend after death to the paradise of Padmasambhava, a realm often linked to the innermost heart of Pemako.

We proceeded next through a symbolic birth channel, signifying emergence from the womb. After squeezing headfirst down the narrow passage, we had to suckle a limestone protuberance that represents the teat of Padmasambhava's consort Yeshe Tsogyal, Lake of Primordial Wisdom, who concealed the Pemako neyigs. Nurtured by the life milk of this revered emanation of Dorje Pagmo, we continued through a jungle exploding into green light and drank from dark pools with leaves of bamboo to remove obscurations of vision. We then passed through a narrow tunnel that allegedly closes in upon one if one entertains doubts or falls into mundane thoughts.

The pilgrimage circuit continued through limestone passageways that purify past karma and ended on a ledge where we lay down like corpses to enact a symbolic death. Rising from this *shi-sa*, or dying ground, we found ourselves at the edge of the Tsangpo, gazing across the river at the fluted walls of Shati Pemayangdzong where Padmasambhava supposedly concealed important teachings that will be revealed when humankind is ready.

As we sat amid these fertile mysteries by the banks of the Tsangpo, Tsering Yuden led the others in a pilgrimage song that they later told me had been composed long ago by Orgyen Dorje Dranak, a master of the lineage of the Immortal Heart Drop.

Ah ho! The secret land of Pemako
A Pure Realm for the Buddhas
of past, present, and future
Just thinking of this place I become joyful . . .

Crystal glaciers adorn the sky
Rain falls like nectar from the gods . . .
And rainbows fill the valleys . . .

Walled round by snow peaks, cliffs, and jungle,
This hidden-land of Padmasambhava is
A place where fortunate beings can find enlightenment

With rocks like molten iron and
Trees like the hair of demons
Pemako appears like a realm of fearsome Rakshas . . .
Those without pure perception will have no chance here

With caves for meditation,
Healing waters and medicinal plants
This is a place for yogis and Vidyadharas

Rainbow-colored birds spread their wings,
Their songs like melodious mantras . . .

This great land of Pemako is a pure realm of the Buddhas
Thinking of this place I became joyful
And with pure devotion,
Make offerings of this song.

Our passage through Gompo Né marked the end of our journey through the sacred land of Pemako. We climbed back to Ganglam and, after retrieving our packs, continued on up the ridge to Tsachu where we discovered that a drunken official from a village above Yumé had waylaid the majority of our porters, insisting that they relinquish their loads to men from Tsachu. The fact that Tsachu's headman, Sonam Nima, had already agreed to let us take our porters from Bayu all the way to the trailhead at Trulung because the Chinese had already enlisted all of the locally available manpower had no bearing on his thinking. Matters were further complicated by the fact that the Chinese were paying their Tsachu porters only 45 yuan a day, and several wanted to defect and take advantage of our inadvertently higher pay scale.

After heated discussion, the drunken-eyed official finally allowed our original porters to proceed. We started down the trail ahead of them in the fading light, circumventing an agitated bull and crossing landslides and narrow trails carved out of the granite cliffs above the Po Tsangpo. Only after we had reached the sulfer-carved sands of Yumé did we discover that three of our meekest porters had eventually succumbed to pressure by a trio from Tsachu, who appeared with our loads late in the evening.

At Yumé, we were not alone: a subdivision of the Chinese Academy of Sciences expedition had left Tsachu earlier that day and had encamped there en route to Trulung. A female journalist from Beijing named Linzi spoke passable English and, as we sat on logs around a communal bonfire made from driftwood, she told us that the 1998 China Tenyen Yarlung Tsangpo Biggest Scientific Expedition was being sponsored by a prominent Guanjou-based manufacturer of "health clothing." Along with top Chinese scientists, they had sent journalists, news reporters, and TV personnel to report on the expedition's progress and discoveries.

Three different teams, with specialties in fields such as atmospheric science, botany, zoology, and geology, were focusing on different parts of the gorge, Linzi told us. One group had begun near Gyala and was following the Tsangpo as far as they could, always keeping the river in sight, if not actually traveling on its banks. They'd enlisted a Tibetan mountaineer named Rochen to help them reach the waterfall. "He has never been in this area before," Linzi told us, "but he has climbed Everest eight times."

Another division of more than fifty had crossed the Doshung-La and spent more than a week in Medok, studying plants and wildlife. They were now following the river north toward Tsachu, Linzi said, where all the groups would converge. She was leaving before the onslaught made conditions there unbearable.

Linzi also told us that the scientists in Tsachu were investigating the feasibility of building a hydroelectric dam that would flood the inner gorges of the Tsangpo—much like Glen Canyon in the southwestern United States—and divert the water northward to fuel China's ever-expanding industrial growth.[23] They had dispatched a side expedition to Neythang where a Chinese television crew had filmed the Monpas hunting takin. Two Mondrong villagers were standing near us by the fire and, shifting into Tibetan, I asked them whether this was true. The Chinese had paid them to kill almost an entire herd of takin, they told me. Because of this, the Monpas said, the weather had been steadily getting worse.

Their stories only amplified what we already knew. The Chinese expedition had little concern for the environment; the formerly pristine campground at Yumé had been trashed with cast-off tin cans and plastic wrappings of instant Chinese noodles. Despite their massive numbers—more than five hundred including their porters—the Chinese had no toilet tents, our journalist friend confided. Linzi had spent ten days in Tsachu and had quite obviously had enough. She asked if we had room in our Land Cruiser to drive her back to Lhasa.

IRONICALLY, THE EARLIEST KNOWN literary account of a bucolic paradise in the remote mountains of Asia appears not in Tibetan literature, but in a Chinese poem called "Peach Blossom Spring" written by Tao Qian, who lived between 365 and 427 C.E. The poem describes a fisherman who follows a stream of peach blossoms into a tunnel through a mountain and arrives in a hidden-land where hermits have attained extreme longevity and flowers scent the air; in essence, Shangri-La. The fisherman leaves to tell others about the hidden paradise, but like Conway in *Lost Horizon,* he cannot find his way back. The poem had an enormous influence on Chinese culture and landscape painting and would have been known to any Tibetan familiar with China's literary and artistic heritage.

Throughout Chinese history, artists and writers made reference both directly and indirectly to the peach blossom paradise, conveying through their art a perennial longing to escape the travails of worldly life for the peace and serenity of distant mountains—whether literally, or through art and imagination. After the Manchu invasion, many Chinese artists and dispossessed Ming dynasty officials expressed their resistance to foreign occupation in poetry and paintings of idealized realms.[24] One spare, monochromatic painting by a disenchanted government official from this period shows a small, solitary figure on a path leading to a tunnel through the mountains. "Maybe this is the opening," states the calligraphic inscription, a reference to the long dreamed-of peach blossom sanctuary.

An earlier Chinese hanging scroll from 1658–60 is called *Listening to the Waterfall*. Composed by a poet-artist named Zhang Feng who renounced government service to become a Buddhist monk, the painting shows a lone figure sitting above a cascading waterfall amid fantastic cliffs. Mists rising from the depths of the chasm and the repeated contours of the mountain walls echo the falling water as it reverberates off the cliffs, and through the mind of the beholder. Using delicate brush strokes, the artist reinforced the merging of sight and sound in a poem that appears in the upper left-hand corner of the scroll:

> *Looking up I see rocky cliffs;*
> > *bending down I hear rushing water.*
> *The mountain trees are tall and distinct;*
> *The valley flowers burst forth brightly*
> *The call of a yellow bird [pierces]*
> > *the myriad layers of gray mist.*
> *Those with tranquil hearts can walk on undaunted;*
> > *[And having passed, they can] enjoy this place forever.*

In 1687, the artist Dai Benxio (1621–93) created a haunting, visually complex scroll entitled *The Pines of Mount Tiantai,* a mountain retreat favored by Buddhist sages and where a tantalizing stone arch points toward the paradise of the Immortals. In strong brushwork, Dai Benxio painted on the scroll: ". . . I have heard that most of these strange pines have met the sad fate of extinction. It seems that once the natural wonders of the sky, earth, mountains, and rivers are exposed to the intimate scrutiny of this dusty world, they do not last long. This indeed is cause for lament."[25] Cause for lament indeed: Linzi told us that in order to build what would be the world's largest hydroelectric project, the Chinese government was thinking to use nuclear power to blast a tunnel through the heart of Pemako. It recalled the words of Henry Miller: "Every Utopia confers upon us a new hell. The chasm widens and deepens. The isolation becomes more intense."

TWENTY-FOUR HOURS LATER, on the night of November 17, we rolled into the Nyingtri Hotel in Bayi. China Central Television was broadcasting the progress of the Chinese expedition on the television set in the hotel lobby. Set to synthesized music, the digitalized images of the gorge, rare plants, and staged Monpa dances revealed a last great place to be claimed for the Chinese Motherland, a synth-pop Shangri-La. I worried what our own National Geographic Television film would convey to audiences in America and realized that if we actually had found Yangsang we would have had to cover our tracks, confuse and elude at all costs. Or else, like the world's most magical places, it would soon be desecrated with a road or hotel, like the one we were now in. (Two days later in Lhasa, a Tibetan friend told me how her elderly mother had watched the daily dispatches on their small black-and-white TV and, fingering her rosary, prayed that rockfalls and avalanches would bar their progress, anything to keep the Chinese from entering this last bastion of Tibetan hope.)

The dream of an earthly paradise hidden in the deepest heart of Pemako, of a realm which cannot be measured or fixed on any map, had inspired generations of Tibetans and many in the West as well. That dream was now in danger of vanishing as what had previously been hidden became fodder for TV audiences and, quite possibly, for the turbines of the world's most ambitious hydroelectric plant. The dream of Shangri-La, whatever its local expression, is a defense against crass materialism, and although the vision can lead to escapist fantasies, I was saddened to watch the mysteries of the Tsangpo gorge slip away across the screen.

Beyond the specter of commercial logging and—so far—hydroelectric exploitation, the Tsangpo gorges may be technologically undeveloped, but the inalienable unity between nature and humankind promoted by its peoples offers a vital counterpoint to unmitigated dreams of material progress that, were the

Chinese to endorse it, would contribute to a wiser, more resplendent world. For behind the paradisiacal ideal of the beyul lies the recognition that by changing the way we view the world—and acting on that vision—the world itself transforms. Yet as the ancient Capuchin, Father Perrault, had observed at Shangri-La, the nations of the world seemed to be "strengthening, not in wisdom, but in vulgar passions and the will to destroy."

Weighted down by these thoughts, I climbed to my appointed room on the third floor of the empty hotel. I navigated the square-cut porcelain tiles and poured cement of the staircase, passing shadowy chambermaids wearing white surgical masks that obscured all but their eyes.

The hotel's archaic plumbing eventually yielded a tub full of hot water and, with water streaming from the rusted pipes, I immersed myself in my first bath in more than month. In *Lost Horizon*, Conway had told his host at Shangri-La that modern plumbing was, to his mind, "the only certain boon . . . that the East can take from the West." At the Nyingtri Hotel that blessing had yet to be fully realized, but the steaming waters did offer a welcome sanctuary away from Bryan's video camera as well as from my persistent thoughts.

Ever since we crossed the bridge at Trulung and met with our Chinese drivers, I'd felt as if I'd crossed a threshold into profane space. Pemako's cloud forests and hidden waterfalls seemed suddenly distant memories. As to Yangsang, I thought of the prescient words that Voltaire had written in 1770: "Si Dieu n'existait pas, il faudrait l'inventer." ("If God did not exist, it would be necessary to invent him.") Losing myself in these reflections, I opened the taps to let in more steaming water. The pipes clanked as it streamed through the rusted spout, the hot, healing balm dissolving the legion of wounds and insect bites that I had amassed over weeks in the gorges. I listened as the water poured from the pipes, its sounds enveloping me as I lay back in the porcelain tub. Molecules of hydrogen and oxygen flooded my brain and nerves as the room filled with evanescent steam and water spilled through crevices in the floor. The water's sound filled all available space, connecting to the waters within my cells and the rivers flowing through my veins. Soon there was only the water and its myriad convolutions; its eddies, whorls, waves, and bubbles.

Flowing through my pores and over the edges of the tub, the water swelled across the cracked and grimy floor until the bathroom walls dissolved in mist and with them, all thoughts of hidden scrolls and rediscovered waterfalls. As the Buddha pointed out, waterfalls are in essence no thing at all, just shimmering displays of water, light, and air, their very features—like ourselves—an optical illusion of the senses. The water submerged my ears and my breath came as if from beneath a rising sea. Where did this water ultimately come from? Where was it going when it disappeared into the drains of this remote hotel?

I recalled the words of Marcel Proust: "The real journey of discovery consists not in seeking new landscapes, but in having new eyes." Would we learn to bring forth what is hidden, to rescue into consciousness the endangered worlds and ideas that enlarge our sympathies and our senses and connect us to a greater whole, beyond the perennial tides of ignorance, greed, and aggression? With the chrome taps opened wide, and the wild thundering of the waterfall still within me, I could only hope those radiant waters, hidden in our deepest collective being, would never be dammed or diverted but—like the dream of unknown places—carry us beyond all divisions into the currents of the unbound heart.

We shall not cease from exploration
And the end of all our exploring
Will be to arrive where we started
And know the place for the first time.
Through the unknown, remembered gate
When the last of earth left to discover
Is that which was the beginning;
At the source of the longest river
The voice of the hidden waterfall . . .

—T. S. ELIOT, "Little Gidding," *The Four Quartets*

We are surrounded and embraced by her; powerless to separate ourselves from her, and powerless to penetrate beyond her . . . We live in her midst and know her not. She is incessantly speaking to us, but betrays not her secret.

JOHANN WOLFGANG VON GOETHE[1]

All poetic language is the language of exploration . . . I dare say it is meaningless until one has drifted into a certain vein of thought.

EZRA POUND

If we have not found heaven within, it is a certainty we will not find it without.

HENRY MILLER

Epilogue:
The Veils of Paradise

ON JANUARY 6, 1999, the National Geographic Society issued a press release stating that the discovery of the Hidden Falls of Dorje Pagmo had resolved a mystery that "had been the source of myth and speculation for more than a century." The director of National Geographic's Expeditions Council told a reporter from the *Chicago Tribune*, "If there is a Shangri-La, this is it!" Newspapers around the world subsequently ran headlines such as SHANGRI-LA DISCOVERED and HIDDEN PARADISE UNMASKED, often on the same page as news of calls for President Clinton's impeachment over his affair with Monica Lewinsky.

The National Geographic Society immediately commissioned me to organize a return expedition to the Tsangpo gorges to document their natural history. Our team reached no farther than Lhasa, where the Chinese authorities revoked our permits and informed us that the Yarlung Tsangpo Great Canyon had been closed until further notice. I silently rejoiced that Dorje Pagmo had let fall her veils.

When Beijing's policies changed and Pemako reopened, the elements—some would say Dorje Traktsen—took over the role of barring entry. In June 2000, a glacial dam on the Yigrong River burst its walls and a cataclysmic flood of mud and water swept away bridges across the Po Tsangpo and the lower Tsangpo gorge. Water levels rose more than 600 feet above the normal high water mark, unleashing landslides and transforming the lush jungles that grew along the canyon walls into a moonscape of barren rock.[2] The Hidden Falls of Dorje Pagmo—upriver from the confluence—had remained unaffected, but access to the region was entirely cut off.

By January 2002, seven world-class kayakers took up the challenge of continuing beyond where Wick Walker's team had pulled out of the Tsangpo's upper gorge. Walker had acknowledged that "defining success on a first river descent is a subjective and elusive task," but the expedition led by Scott Lindgren and sponsored, in part, by Chevrolet's Chevy Avalanche reached within a mile of the beginning of the Great Bend, albeit with extensive portages.[3] Ken Storm had headed the expedition's land support team and guided the kayakers out of the gorge with their boats on their backs well before they neared the Five-Mile Gap.

In Tsachu, the Chinese had erected a concrete and bronze memorial to their expedition in the fall of 1998, displacing a row of prayer flags that had once traced the movements of the winds. Lama Topgye had passed away in 2001 and the Chinese had begun relocating the local populace to Bayi; those who remained spoke alternately about an ecological preserve[4] and an impending dam, the construction of which would submerge the Tsangpo's inner gorge and obliterate the Falls of Dorje Pagmo.

BRYAN HARVEY'S FILM, *Secrets of the Tsangpo Gorge*, had debuted at Telluride's MountainFilm Festival and ended with the exploding waves of the hidden waterfall. Hamid Sardar had edited his footage from his journey through the gap, but the plan to combine it with Ned Johnston's never materialized. The needed reels remained sealed in the vaults of the Film Study Center at Harvard University. After completing his doctorate, Hamid redirected his energies toward central Asia, where he made a film about a tribe of nomadic reindeer herders who seek guidance in their migrations from a ninety-three-year-old female shaman.

Discouraged by China's plans for developing the Tsangpo gorges into a new ecotourism hotspot (he'd even heard talk of a planned cable car to the falls), Ken turned elsewhere in his quest for pristine wilderness, purchasing an island in northern Lake Superior inhabited only by a herd of deer and a roaming bear. "It's my own private Pemako," he said from his office in Minneapolis.

Between trips to Tibet, I'd stayed in Kathmandu, seeking to give voice to the mystery of the hidden waterfall and the lure of unchartable terrain. As I immersed myself in writing, Nepal's streets erupted in riots after the crown prince gunned down the majority of the royal family.

As the book neared completion, I sublet my house in Nepal and took up temporary residence in an eighteenth-century mill house near New York where a waterfall pours over a stone ledge. I wrote at a large oak table overlooking the falls and a pond where a female trumpeter swan plied the waters or stood luxuriantly, her right leg tucked beneath her, where the waters gather and stream over a fifteen-foot wall of rock.

Fall came, and the trees around the pond turned bright gold, red, and ochre, and leaves spilled into the waters like crumpled scrolls and swept over the lip of the falls. With the brush of her wings, the swan traced patterns across the amber surface of the lake, and I thought of the goddess Dorje Pagmo who, in the guise of a snowy vulture, had guided the treasure-revealer Lhatsun Jikme into the heart of the beyul.

Hidden-lands open everywhere; they are as much modes of perception as actual places. In his "Essay on American Scenery," written in 1836, painter Thomas Cole pleaded that "we are still in Eden; the wall that shuts us out of the garden is our own ignorance and folly." At Walden Pond, Henry David Thoreau wrote passionately in defense of nature, "if only to suggest that the earth has higher uses than we put her to." Following Emerson's dictum that "the whole of nature is a metaphor for the human mind," Thoreau envisioned wilderness as an image of unexplored capacities. He advocated "uncivilized free and wild thinking" as an antidote to civilization's excesses and urged his readers to explore their "own higher latitudes."

The scrolls describing beyul are as "wildly natural and primitive, mysterious and marvelous, ambrosial and fertile"[5] as the works of literature that Thoreau praised as nourishing humankind's identification with outer and inner nature. In its original sense, wilderness conveys both awe and threat, alluring mystery and a sublimity that reconnects us to our source. The hidden-lands of the Tsangpo gorges embody its essence. Yet so too does every moment when the veils drop and we see into the heart of things.

The pond took the shape of an interdependent living whole, transforming and metamorphosing before my eyes. Perhaps I had found Yangsang after all, I felt, a shining world where a swan could transfigure into an embodiment of the muse and give testament to Wallace Stevens's maxim that "realism is a corruption of reality." Can we ever peer behind the veils that enrich our vision of nature, or are they perhaps as Goethe wrote in *Faust*, a necessary protection against some blinding truth? As Emily Dickinson wrote: "A charm invests a face/ Imperfectly beheld—The lady dare not lift her veil."

We feed on mystery, whether the enticements of unknown lands or a masked dancer revealed more perfectly by what she hides. The scrolls describing the beyul lead us similarly into wonder, for they are accounts of processes in the mind as much as in the external world. There is no real separation or boundary between our selves and the world around us, and an ever-present wildness and radiance lies at the heart of our tamest vistas.[6]

As the final words of the book flash across my computer screen, the swan eyes me through the open windows as leaves like yellow parchment swirl around her legs and flow over the edge of the falls. With her webbed feet rooted at the top of the waterfall, she spreads her wings rapturously as water spills from her feathers and her breast rises toward the sky. Forming the arc of an unbounded circle, she lets out a piercing cry—or laugh—and vanishes into unutterable space.

Glossary

ABHISEKA (T: *dbang skur*) Annointment, empowerment, or initiation. A ceremony in which a student is ritually entered into the mandala of a particular Tantric deity, thus empowering him or her to practice the meditative rites associated with that specific expression of enlightenment.

ABOR (*Adi*) Assamese word, no longer current, meaning savage or "one who does not submit" in reference to tribes such as the Minyong and Gallong Adis who live in present day Arunachal Pradesh.

AFFLICITVE EMOTIONS (*nyon mongs kyi sgrib pa*; Skt: *klesavarana*) The disturbing emotions and mental states that obscure the nature of reality and fuel the processes of rebirth in cyclic existence, or *samsara*. These obstructing mental states are generally referred to as the five poisons of desire, anger, delusion, pride, and envy.

AMRITA *See* Nectar.

APPEARANCE (*snang ba*) A sense impression or mental occurrence; anything that is experienced by a conscious mind. In Buddhist philosophy appearances are viewed as mental events, empty of inherent existence and beyond constructs such as arising, dwelling, and ceasing.

AWARENESS (*rig pa*; Skt: *vidya*) In the context of Dzogchen awareness refers to consciousness devoid of ignorance and dualistic fixation.

BARDO (*bar do*) Intermediate state; commonly refers to the state of consciousness and lapse of time between death and the next rebirth, but can also indicate other transitionary phases such as meditation, dream, death, or even the gap between two thoughts.

BEYUL (*sbas yul*) Secret or hidden land; paradisiacal realms in remote parts of Tibet and the Himalayas described by Padmasambhava in hidden scrolls. Beyul have outer, inner, secret, and ultimately secret (*yangsang*) dimensions, corresponding to levels of initiation in the Buddhist Tantras.

BINDU (*thig le*) 1. The red and white essences within the body. 2. Spheres or circles of light. *See also* Tigle.

BLESSINGS (*byin rlabs*; Skt: *adhisthana*) Wave of splendor, conveying the grace and heightened receptivity which descend upon the devout practitioner from the gurus of the lineage, awakening a sense of greater reality.

BLISS (*bde ba*; Skt: *sukha*) Bliss, clarity, and non-thought (*bde gsal mi rtog pa*). Three temporary experiences that arise in meditation. Fixation on them plants the seeds for rebirth in the three realms of samsara. Without fixation, they are adornments of the awakened state. *See also* Great Bliss.

BODHICHITTA (*byang sems, byang chub kyi sems*) Bodhi mind; awakened state of mind. The aspiration to attain enlightenment for the sake of all beings. In the context of Dzogchen, the mind's innate wakefulness synonymous with *rigpa*, or pristine awareness. Absolute bodhichitta is often described as emptiness indivisible from compassion—radiant, unshakable, and impossible to formulate by concepts. In Tantra, bodhichitta also refers to the subtle red and white essences normally located in the body at the level of the navel and the crown chakra, and which converge at the heart during the death process and in deep meditation.

BODHISATTVA (*byang chub sems dpa'*) Someone who has developed bodhichitta, the aspiration to attain enlightenment in order to benefit all sentient beings. A being who has realized the empty nature of phenomena and the non-existence of individual self and who is free from the *klesas*, or ordinary emotions.

BUDDHA (*sangs rgyas*) Literally, "awakened"; the Enlightened One; a perfected Bodhisattva who attains complete, perfect enlightenment in a human form. Although numerous Buddhas are said to have manifested in past ages to show the way to enlightenment, historically, the Buddha refers to Sakyamuni Buddha, who was born Prince Siddhartha in Lumbini in southern Nepal in the sixth century B.C.E.

BUDDHA FIELD (*sangs rgyas zhing khams*) Pure realm or Buddhist paradise inhabited by bodhisattvas. Refers also to a "field" of experience in which one's true nature becomes vividly apparent. As stated in a Buddhist scripture: "They arise from one's own mind and have infinite form."

BUDDHAHOOD (*sangs rgyas*) Perfect and complete enlightenment, in which one dwells neither in samsara nor nirvana; the state of having eradicated all obscurations and being endowed with the wisdom of seeing the nature of things as they are and with the wisdom of perceiving all that exists.

BUDDHA-NATURE (*bde gshegs snying po*; Skt: *tathagatagarbha*) The potential for enlightenment or enlightened nature that is inherently present in each sentient being; the essence of mind—distinct from discursive thought—within which all thoughts arise.

CENTRAL CHANNEL (*kun 'dar ma, dbu ma*; Skt: *Avadhūti*) The principal channel of subtle energy which runs from the base of the spine to the crown of the head. When psychic energy or wind (*rlung*; Skt: *prana*) circulates through the central channel, the yogi recognizes the mind's fundamental nature of clear light.

CHAKRA (*'khor*; Skt: *cakra*) Wheel or junction of subtle energy channels within the body often referred to poetically as "lotuses." The five principal chakras are located at the crown of the head, the throat, the heart, the navel, and the perineum.

CHANG Intoxicating beverage made from fermented barley or other grain.

CHANNELS (*rtsa*) Winds and essences (*rtsa, rlung, thig le*) are the components of the subtle vajra body. The body's vital forces (*thig le*) circulate through three principal energy channels which, in the deluded state, are related to the three poisons: attachment, hatred, and ignorance; in the wisdom state they are related to the three kayas, or dimensions of light, energy, and form. *See also* Nadi.

CHARNEL GROUND (*dur khrod*) A site where bodies are left to decompose or to be eaten by wild animals. Frequented by ghosts and spirits, a charnel ground is considered an optimal environment for advanced practitioners to develop their realization.

CHULEN (*bcud len*; Skt: *rasayana*) Literally, "essence-extract." An advanced practice based on sustaining the body with essences of medicinal plants, minerals, and elemental energy in order to purify the body, heighten concentration, and remove dependency on ordinary, material food.

CIRQUE A bowl-shaped depression in the headwaters of drainage areas formed by the accumulation of ice and its erosive action on the underlying bedrock.

CLEAR LIGHT (*'od gsal*; Skt: *prabhasvara*) The essential nature of mind which is undefinable yet characterized as being of the nature of emptiness and luminosity. It appears when the body's vital energies have been brought into the central channel and may be related to photons emitted by DNA. Recalling what Wordsworth called "internal brightness," the mind's fundamental nature of clear light is the subtle basis for all other mental activity.

COMPASSION (*snying rje, thugs rje*; Skt: *karuna*) A key principle of Mahayana Buddhism, describing the motivation and action of a bodhisattva. In the context of Dzogchen, one of the three aspects: essence, nature, and compassion. Compassion here has a much deeper meaning than selfless kindness and the wish to alleviate the suffering of others. It is the natural expression of the indivisibility of emptiness and luminosity.

CONSCIOUSNESS In a Buddhist context, consciousness refers to luminous (*gsal ba*) awareness (*rig pa*) which, free of any intrinsic content, knows or apprehends the objects appearing to it.

CYCLIC EXISTENCE (Skt: *samsara*) The cycle of death and rebirth characterized by suffering and dissatisfaction arising from ignorance of the true nature of reality.

DAKA (*dpa 'bo*) Male counterpart of dakinis; enlightened male practitioner of Tantric Buddhism.

DAKINI (*mkha' 'gro ma*) Literally, "one who goes in the sky." Spiritual beings who fulfill enlightened activities and intentions; female Tantric deities who protect and serve the Buddhist doctrine and practitioners. Also refers to enlightened female practitioners of Tantric Buddhism as well as nodal energies within the subtle channels. Representing the fertile open space out of which the play of samsara and nirvana arises, dakinis are tricky and playful. They inspire the union of skillful means and penetrating awareness and represent the inspirational impulses of consciousness that lead to understanding and wisdom.

DALAI LAMA A title signifying ocean of wisdom, given to a line of incarnations beginning with the Tibetan master dGe 'dun grub in the fourteenth century. The Dalai Lamas are regarded as earthly incarnations of Avalokiteshvara, the Bodhisattva of Great Compassion.

DANANG (*dag snang*) Pure perception, or literally "seeing inside"; denotes a sacred outlook arising from the experience of the phenomenal world as a pure expanse of emptiness and luminosity; often associated with the vision of landscape by Tantric lamas during dream, meditation, or other altered states of consciousness; from a Buddhist standpoint, seeing things as they actually are.

DEITY (*yidam*) In Tibetan Buddhism, deities represent the true nature of one's own mind. On a relative level they embody varying expressions of wisdom and compassion through which the practitioner attains liberation.

DELUSION (Skt: *klesha*) The three principal delusions are ignorance, aversion, and attachment. The destruction of these and their instincts bestows nirvana.

DHARMA (*chos*) The teaching of the Buddha; the true nature of phenomena and mental events.

DHARMAKAYA (*chos sku*) The realm of truth; the mental or unmanifest aspect of the three kayas, devoid of constructs. The body of enlightened qualities.

DORJE (Skt: *vajra*) Literally, "diamond" or "thunderbolt," but generally refers to a ritual implement used in Tantric rites to symbolize compassion and skillful means as well as the indestructible adamantine nature of enlightened mind.

DORJE PAGMO (Skt: *Vajravārāhi*) Literally, "Adamantine Sow." Female Tantric deity embodying the practitioner's enlightened nature. Her sow head ornament represents the transformation of ignorance into pristine awareness. "Queen" of all dakinis.

DUALISTIC VISION (*gnyis 'dzin*) Experience structured as perceiver and object perceived.

DZO A yak-cow hybrid, bred for their greater milk production. The female is known as a dzomo.

DZOGCHEN (Skt: *Mahasandhi* or *Atiyoga*) Literally, "the Great Perfection." The third of the three inner tantras in the Nyingma tradition of Tibetan Buddhism, Dzogchen emphasizes direct insight into the primordial purity of all phenomena and the spontaneous presence of the Buddha's qualities in all beings.

ECOTOURISM A branch of the tourism industry that strives to minimize ecological or other damage to areas visited for their natural or cultural interest.

EIGHTFOLD PATH Virtuous practices conducive to the annihilation of ignorance and craving. The Buddha's Noble Truth of the Way to the Termination of Suffering, namely: Right View, Right Resolve, Right Speech, Right Conduct, Right Livelihood, Right Effort, Right Awareness, and Right Meditation.

EMPTINESS (*stong pa nyid;* Skt: *sunyata*) The fact that phenomena and the ego are empty of, or lack, any unchanging, intrinsic essence or existence. Although things are *ultimately* empty, they nevertheless are said to exist *conventionally* in dependence on causes and conditions. *See* Sunyata.

ENLIGHTENMENT (*byang chub;* Skt: *bodhi*) Awakening to Buddhahood from the sleep of ignorance; perfect knowledge.

FIVE BUDDHA FAMILIES The five families (*rigs lnga*) of buddha, vajra, ratna, padma, and karma correspond ultimately with the purified aspects of the five psychophysical aggregates of consciousness, recognition, feeling, mental formation, and form. The five Buddha consorts are the pure form of the five elements. Earth: Mamaki, consort of Ratnasambhava. Water: Buddha Locana, consort of Akshobhya. Fire: Pandara Vasini, consort of Amitabha. Air: Samaya Tara, consort of Amoghasiddhi. Space: Akasha Datishvari, consort of Vairochana.

GANACHAKRA (*tshog kyi 'khor lo*) A Tantric feast offering in which desire and sense perceptions are made part of the path, and phenomenal existence is celebrated in its intrinsic purity.

GARUDA (T: *khyung*) Mythical bird that preys on nagas and which is said to be able to travel from one end of the universe to the other with a single movement of its wings.

GELUG (*dge lugs*) A later school of Tibetan Buddhism founded by Je Tsongkhapa as a reformation of the Kadam tradition of Atisha Dipamkara. The present head is His Holiness the fourteenth Dalai Lama.

GNOSIS A term used by heterodox Christians to refer to a subjective and immediate experience of truth. Gnostics advocated dwelling in an internal "effortlessness" suffused with the energy and power of the Divine Source. "Whoever has not known himself has known nothing," states the gnostic Book of Thomas the Contender, "but he who has known himself has at the same time already achieved knowledge about the depth of all things."

GREAT BLISS (*bde ba chen po;* Skt: *mahasukha*) Joy transcending pleasure, pain, hope, and fear and inferring total existential freedom in the wisdom of bliss and emptiness beyond conceptual thought. The uncompounded quality of changelessness. Great bliss of the lower gate (*'og sgo bde chen*) refers to the union with another's body (*gzhan lus snyoms 'jug*).

GREAT GAME The term given by the novelist Rudyard Kipling to the often deadly struggle between the British and Russian empires for political ascendancy in Tibet and central Asia. Between the 1830s and 1890s, Russians and Britons, assisted by native agents, penetrated the unknown and forbidden cities of this romantic and wild region, often incognito. Played out by soldiers, spies, explorers, archaeologists and cartographers, many perished in the attempt.

HEART CENTER Depending on the context, refers either to the heart chakra or to the center of the heart chakra where the body's subtlemost winds (*rlung*) and vital energies are said to reside as a five-colored luminous sphere.

HERUKA (*he ru ka, khrag 'thung*) A wrathful manifestation of Tantric energy; activation of the positive qualities of the mind; the masculine principle of energy and skillful means that makes situations powerful and creative. The Tibetan word means blood drinker, that which drinks the blood of ego-clinging, doubt, and dualistic confusion.

HEVAJRA TANTRA (*kye rdo rje'i rgyud*) A Tantra based on the semiwrathful heruka, Hevajra. He is an exclamation of joy. Hevajra transforms sense pleasures and form into joy through realizing the identity of form and emptiness. Hevajra is depicted in four-, six-, and twelve-armed forms, dancing in union with his consort, Nairatmya, the embodiment of pure selflessness.

HIGHEST YOGA TANTRA (*bla na med pa'irnyal 'byor;* Skt: *anuttarayogatantra*) The highest system of Tantric theory and practice according to the Gelug and other later traditions of Tibetan Buddhism. It includes advanced techniques for controlling and manipulating the body's vital energies, making enlightenment possible in a single lifetime.

IGNORANCE (*ma rig pa;* Skt: *avidya*) The root of cyclic existence, not knowing the way in which things actually exist.

KANGLING Ritual trumpet fashioned from a human thigh bone and used to invoke spirits and cut through conceptual thought.

KARMA (*las*) Literally, "action." A willed action of body, speech, and mind, and the impression or seed this leaves on one's personal continuum, which must eventually ripen and produce a result; the causal connections between actions and their consequences.

KHAMPA A Tibetan from the eastern province of Kham, a region known both for its fierce warriors and enlightened sages.

KHATA A silk offering scarf often inscribed with auspicious symbols and signifying purity and goodwill in all transactions.

KORA (Skt: *parikrama*) Ritual circumambulation around a holy object or shrine, an action believed to confer merit and align one with spiritual forces.

KORDE RUSHEN Literally, "separating samsara and nirvana." Introductory Dzogchen practices involving psychodrama, physical yoga, visualization, and mantra to reveal the nature of mind by dynamically cultivating altered states of awareness.

KUKRI A curved machetelike knife widely used throughout Nepal for everything from chopping firewood to sacrificing animals.

LIBERATION (*thar pa*) Freedom from all compulsive karmic patterns, mental obscurations, delusion, and discontent. Emancipation from samsaric existence.

LOPA Tibetan word for primitive forest-dwelling tribal peoples inhabiting the southern slopes of the eastern Himalayas, including Mishmis, Adis, Daflas, and other groups in India's northeastern frontier.

LUMINOSITY (*'od gsal*) Literally, "free from the darkness of unknowing and endowed with the ability to cognize." The two aspects are empty luminosity, like a clear open sky, which is the cognizant quality of the nature of mind; and manifest luminosity, such as five-colored lights, images, and so forth. Luminosity is the uncompounded nature present throughout all of samsara and nirvana, as well as an experience arising through meditation, possibly associated with DNA's inherent bioluminescence.

MANDALA (*dkyil 'khor*) Literally, "concentric circle"; a mandala is a symbolic, graphic representation of a Tantric deity's realm of existence and, more generally, a symbol of the infinitely pure sphere of consciousness and perfection of being; an integral dimension purified of all dualistic concepts. The Tibetan word *dkyil 'khor* means center and periphery. It is the unification of many vast elements into one, through the experience of meditation. Seeming complexity and chaos are simplified into a pattern and natural hierarchy. The outer world, one's body and state of mind, and the totality can all be seen as mandala. The constructed form of a mandala has as its basic structure a palace with a center and four gates in the cardinal directions.

MANTRA (*sngags*) Mystic syllables, usually Sanskrit, recited in conjunction with the visualization of a particular tantric deity; a means of transforming energy through sound.

MERIT (*bsod nams*) The positive karmic result of virtuous action.

MILAREPA (*mi la ras pa*) 1040–1123. A famous Tibetan yogi renowned for his mystic poetry and mastery of the Tantric yogas. "Repa" means cotton-clad and designates yogins proficient in *tummo* who, as a result of raising their body temperature, wore only a single cotton cloth despite Tibet's cold winters.

MONPA Non-Tibetan forest-dwelling people generally inhabiting the southern slopes of the Himalayas, parts of southeastern Tibet, and northern Myanmar.

NADI (*rtsa*) The channels of vital energy in the subtle body. In Highest Yoga Tantra, the practitioner meditates on the nadis, prana, and bindu (*rtsa, rlung, thig-le*) to realize the fundamental mind of Clear Light. In this context prana is likened to a horse, mind-consciousness to the rider, and nadis to the pathways.

NAGA (*klu*) Powerful long-lived serpentlike beings who inhabit bodies of water and often guard great treasure. They belong half to the animal realm and half to the god realm. They generally live in the form of snakes, but many can change into human form and they are often depicted as human from the waist up with a serpent's tail below. They are said to control the weather, especially rain, and are associated with fertility.

NÉ (*gnas*) Sacred site, power place, or place of pilgrimage. Lamas distinguished between two types of nés: *rangjung-ki-ney* and *chinlap-ki-ney*, self-manifested natural power places as well as ones that result from the blessing power of highly realized masters.

NECTAR (*bdûd rtsi*; Skt: *amrita*). Literally, "deathless." Nectar of immortality, ambrosia (conferring immortality or other powers). Blessed liquor, used in Vajrayana rites and meditation practices. More generally, spiritual intoxication. Can also refer to internal glandular secretions resulting from the practice of Tantric yoga.

NEYIG (*gnas yig*) Guide, or description of a Buddhist holy place, often in the form of a revealed text.

NGAKPA (*sngags pa*; Skt: *tantrika*) A lay Tantric practitioner often distinguishable by his or her red and white robes, long hair, and bone or conch shell earrings.

NIRVANA (*mya ngan* [*las*] *'das* [*pa*]) The cessation of everything samsaric such as ignorance and suffering, the liberation of an Arhat or a Buddha. Freedom from compulsions, including the innate tendency of the mind to grasp at inherent existence. Ultimately refers to a radical freedom from suffering and its underlying causes. The freedom from all negative mental states, afflictive emotions, and ignorance of the true nature of reality.

NYINGMA (*rnying ma*) "Ancient Ones": one of the four major schools of Tibetan Buddhism. The Nyingmas adhere to the original form of Tantric Buddhism brought to Tibet in the eighth century by Padmasambhava and others. The special teachings of the Nyingma are known as Dzogchen, or the Great Perfection.

OBSCURATIONS (*sgrib pa*) The veils that obscure the direct perception of the nature of mind and phenomena and attributed to the effects of karma, disturbing emotions, habitual tendencies, and dualistic knowledge.

PADMASAMBHAVA (*pad ma 'byung gnas*) Literally, "originated from a lotus." The eighth-century Tantric master—also known as guru Rinpoche, the precious teacher—who helped establish Buddhism in Tibet, the alleged author of the hidden scrolls describing beyul.

PRANA (*rlung*; Skt: *prana*). The winds or energy currents that pervade the psychophysical organism. In Tantra, mastery of this vital energy can transform the mind at its most subtle level. *See also* bindu, nadi.

RAINBOW BODY (*'ja' lus*) The transformation of the bodily substance into multihued light. At the time of death of a practitioner who has reached the exhaustion of all grasping and fixation through the Dzogchen practice of togal, the five gross elements which form the physical body dissolve back into their essences—five-colored light. Sometimes only the hair and the nails are left behind.

RENUNCIATION The attitude of complete detachment from the experiences of samsara.

RIGDZIN (*rig 'dzin*; Skt: *vidyadhara*) Literally, "wisdom holder." Realized master in the Tantric tradition.

RINPOCHE Literally, "precious." A title used for highly learned or reincarnate lamas.

SAMANTABHADRA (*Kun tu bzang po*) Literally, "the All-Good, Ever-Excellent One"; the all-pervasive primordially enlightened Buddha, blue in color and naked, often depicted in union with Samantabhadri, who is white in color. This Buddha principle is considered the ultimate source of all the Tantras of Vajrayana Buddhism.

SAMSARA (*srid pa'i 'khor ba*; Skt: *samsara*) Cyclic existence, vicious circle, or round of birth and death and rebirth within the six realms of existence, characterized by suffering, impermanence, and ignorance. The state of ordinary sentient beings fettered by ignorance and dualistic perception, karma, and disturbing emotions.

The unenlightened state, characterized by a sense of incompletion and recurring frustration.

SANG (*sangs*) Ritual offering of aromatic plants and wood such as cedar and juniper that are moistened to create a purifying smoke said to be pleasing to local deities and to clear obscurations.

SHAMAN Term deriving from the Tungusic word saman referring to those individuals who cross into the supernatural world at will and deal with the forces that influence and determine ordinary life.

SHINJE CHOGYAL (*gshin rje chogyal*; Skt: *yama*) Buddhist Lord of Death who, on a popular level, confers judgment on the deceased and determines their future incarnation. As a support for meditation, Shinje embodies the energy of impermanence, the law of karma, and one's inevitable mortality.

SIDDHA (*grub thob*) "Accomplished One." A term for enlightened masters in the Tantric tradition. Siddha has the connotation of one who, besides being realized on the absolute level, has mastery over the phenomenal world; Tantric master who attains direct realization outside the conventional course of study.

SIDDHI (*dngos grub*) Literally, "success," "complete attainment"; there are eight common siddhis arising from the practice of yoga. Among these are clairvoyance, clairaudiance, the ability to fly through the air, the ability to read thoughts, and control of the body and external world, enabling one to transform both at will. The supreme siddhi is enlightenment.

STUPA (*mchod rten*) A dome-shaped monument containing relics of the Buddha or Buddhist saints and built according to universal principles of harmony and order. Stupas are believed to radiate healing energy throughout all existence.

SUBLIME According to the eighteenth-century philosopher Edmund Burke, "Whatever is fitted in any sort to excite the ideas of pain, and danger, that is to say whatever is in any sort terrible . . . is a source of the sublime; that is, it is productive of the strongest emotion which the mind is capable of feeling."

SUBTLE BODY The network of subtle nerves and energy channels which serves as a basis for realizing the fundamental mind of clear light.

SUNYATA (*stong pa nyid*) Emptiness; a doctrine emphasized in Mahayana, which stresses that all conceptual frameworks are empty of any abiding reality. In Tantra, sunyata is equated with the feminine principle—the spacelike continuum of unconditioned potentiality.

SUTRA (*mdo* [*sde*]) Discourse or teaching by the Buddha; all esoteric teachings of Buddhism belonging to Hinayana and Mahayana, the causal teachings that regard the path as the cause of enlightenment, as opposed to the esoteric, Tantric teachings.

TAKIN From the Mishmi. A blue-eyed horned ruminant of the eastern Himalayas distantly related to the Arctic musk ox, but closer in appearance to the African gnu.

TANTRA (*rgyud*) Literally, in Sanskrit, "the continuum or thread of innate wisdom permeating all experience." Tantra refers to esoteric Buddhist scriptures and oral teachings which offer specific methods and yogic practices for liberating the mind from samsaric existence.

TERMA (*gterma*) Concealed scrolls and related dharma treasures hidden by Padmasambhava and his consort Yeshe Tsogyal that inspire the quest for enlightenment. Terma can also refer to revelations that occur within the minds of highly realized adepts.

TERTON (*gter ston*) A revealer of hidden dharma treasures, the location of which is often indicated by a dakini.

THANGKA A Tibetan painted scroll depicting one or more Buddhist deities or mandalas.

TIGLE (Skt: *bindu*) The essential fluids or drops which flow through the central channel, and sometimes appear as spheres of light.

TSALUNG (*rtsa-rlung-thig-le*) Meditation and yogic practices involving breath control and visualization of the body's network of psychic energy channels, leading to the experience of Great Bliss. *See also* tummo, channels.

TSAMPA Roasted barley flour which, mixed with butter and tea, is the staple of the Tibetan diet.

TULKU (*sprul sku*) Literally, "apparitional body." The incarnation of a previously enlightened teacher who forestalls final liberation to continue to work for the benefit of sentient beings. In some cases, multiple incarnations are recognized representing the body, speech, mind, qualities, and activities of the previous teacher.

TUMMO (*gtum mo*; Skt: *chandali*) A form of Tantric yoga which uses breath control and visualization to cultivate an inner psychic heat which burns through conceptual thought and reveals the clear light of the awakened mind.

VAJRA (*dorje*) "Diamond scepter"; Ritual implement representing bodhichitta, the indestructible mind of enlightenment, and the means by which to attain it. *See* Dorje.

VAJRA BODY (*khams drug ldan pa'i rdo rje'i lus*) Vajra body endowed with the six elements. The six outer elements are the five elements and the element of mental objects (*chos khams*). The six inner elements are flesh, blood, warmth, breath, vacuities, and the all-ground consciousness. The six secret elements are the nadis as the stable earth element, the syllable HANG at the crown of the head as the liquid water element, the AH-stroke at the navel center as the warm fire element, the life-prana (*srog gi rlung*) as the moving wind element, the avadhuti central channel as the void space element, and the all-ground wisdom as the cognizant wisdom element.

VAJRASATTVA (*rdo rje sems dpa'*) A Sambhogakaya Buddha associated with the purification of mental obscurations who embodies the enlightened qualities of all five Buddha families and the direct intuitive apprehension of ultimate truth.

VAJRAYANA (*rdo rje theg pa*) Diamondlike, indestructible vehicle. A form of Buddhism associated with ritual practices and secret oral instructions based on the inner Tantras and believed to offer an accelerated path to enlightenment.

YANGSANG (*yang gsang*) An abbreviation of Chimé Yangsang Né, literally, "the innermost secret place of immortality"; a paradisiacal realm said to lie at the heart of Pemako and reachable only by those with faith and vision.

YOGA (*rnal 'byor*) True path; the integration of learning into personal experience. In Sanskrit, yoga literally means union. Yoga thus refers to methods for achieving union with the state of enlightenment with emphasis on personal training as opposed to scholarly learning.

YOGI/YOGINI (*rnal 'byor pa*) Tantric practitioner; usually connoting someone who has already attained some level of realization of the natural state of mind. One who follows yoga, or a true spiritual path.

Notes

EPIGRAPH

1. F. M. Bailey, *No Passport to Tibet* (London: Rupert Hart-Davis, 1957).

PREFACE

1. John Whitehead, *Far Frontiers: People and Events in North-Eastern India 1857–1947* (London: British Association for Cemeteries in South Asia, 1989), pp. 149–75.

PART ONE: THE CALL OF HIDDEN-LANDS

1. Rigdzin Godemchen (*rig'dzin rgod kyi ldem phrucan*), "Knowledge Holder Endowed with Vulture Feathers" (1337–1408), spent months deciphering the symbolic texts and afterward embarked on a perilous journey for one of the paradisiacal valleys described in the scrolls. Guided by visions and prophetic dreams, he wandered for years through the jungles and ravines of what is now Sikkim in search of the inner reaches of Beyul Dremojung, the Hidden Land of Rice. Lacking conventional means, he tied letters to the necks of compliant vultures and dispatched them across the Himalayas with news of his progress. He kept a meticulous journal of his dreams and visions and was guided on his quest by a dakini, a female embodiment of enlightened vision. In one dream, she gathered up clouds as if they were strands of silk and revealed a tantalizing glimpse of his long-sought sanctuary, a lush valley encircled by sheer and shimmering peaks. But what he'd seen in his visions continued to elude him on the ground. He eventually returned to Tibet, having located the outer and inner reaches of the beyul, but not its coveted secret and innermost secret realms.

For further details of Godemchen's dream see Hamid Sardar-Afkhami, *The Buddha's Secret Gardens: End Times and Hidden-Lands in Tibetan Imagination* (Dissertation, Harvard University, Department of Sanskrit and Indian Studies, 2001), pp. 109–127.

2. For more details regarding Lhatsun Namkha Jikme's further opening of Sikkim see the manuscript *History of Sikkim* written in 1908 by their Highnesses the Maharajah of Sikkim, Sir Thutob Namgyal, 9th Chogyal of Sikkim, and Maharani Yeshe Dolma. Copies of the manuscript may be found in the Oriental and Indian Office Collection, London, under reference MSS Eur E 78, and in the manuscript department library of the School of Oriental and African Studies (London University), ref: MS 380072.

3. Five hundred years later a lama named Tulku Shakya Zangpo (1475–1530) followed the directives revealed by Rigdzin Godemchen and opened Yolmo's outer nés, or sacred places. The hidden scrolls had indicated the hazards he would face on the way:

> A wall of snow. Below, hidden under thick forests that are difficult to cross, lies a rugged valley. The gods, demons, and protector spirits of this place are fierce. . . . The rock cliffs rise sheerly towards the sky, and the wild *tsen* deities are wrathful; there are numerous female poisoners, witches, and yetis with the faces of birds. . . . Carefully examine the cliffs, rivers, and forests. Place path markers in the dense forest. Bring axes and chisels to clear the way. When you are unable to proceed because of rain or mist; pray to Padmasambhava and invoke the protector deities. . . . (Quoted in Sardar-Afkhami, *The Buddha's Secret Gardens*)

Yolmo was further opened in 1723 by a lama named Sorya Senge who was granted title to the land after curing a minister's wife of plague and performing death-repelling rituals in the court of Bhaktapur in the Kathmandu valley.

4. Chatral Rinpoche later explained three types of né, in terms of the three aspects of reality elucidated in Mahayana Buddhism: A Nirmanakaya né refers to a power place that is physically manifest within the landscape. Sambhogakaya nés such as the paradises of Padmasambhava or Amitabha lie in parallel visionary dimensions, while the Dharmakaya né—also known as *chokyishingkam*—is reality itself as perceived by a Buddha, or awakened being. *Yangsang né* is the self-secret dimension within the Nirmanakaya né—the inseparable union of its materiality and innate emptiness.

5. Adapted from "Milarepa and the Pigeon," in *The Hundred Thousand Songs of Milarepa, Volume One,* translated by Garma C. C. Chang, pp. 88–9. Further accounts of Milarepa's experience in Yolmo are evoked in his poem "Song of the Yogi's Joy."

6. Dakinis (T: *Khandroma*) are female spirits, apparitional manifestations of bliss and emptiness who remove obstacles on the spiritual path and provide insight into the nature of mind and reality. Dakinis represent the hidden essence of the phenomenal world as well as the practitioner's own yogic body of subtle energies. Ultimately, they appear within a practitioner's mindstream as empty, radiant awareness but dakinis can also appear as humans, adopting a variety of forms from crone to virgin to sexual consort. In their absolute form dakinis represent the unconstrained energies of enlightened mind, manifesting both internally and externally to guide practitioners to their goal. They are akin to Rainer Maria Rilke's angels who "break you open, out of who you are."

7. Chatral Rinpoche had described the valley in a poem:

> The mountains rise like spiked weapons towards the sun.
> The mountains that lie in shadow spread like flames. . . .
> In this snow-encircled, broad sandy plain, Padmasambhava and
> An assembly of realized beings,
> Thinking of those in later generations,
> Hid innumerable profound Dharma treasures . . .

> All around and in every place, fragrances fill the air
> Plantains and other edible plants
> Bloom in abundance without being sown,
> Amiable birds, water fowl and wood pigeons. . . .
> Empty the mind of its weariness . . .
> Inner understanding and virtues naturally increase,
> Benefiting the activity of path, view, and meditation.

> For the practitioners of rushen and nyen sachöd
> There is no better place than this!
> This strife-free hidden-land of Padmasambhava,
> Is no different than the eight great charnel grounds of India.
> Surrounded by moats of water and walls of earth and rock,
> Graced perpetually by clouds, mist, and rain,
> [the valley] is naturally sealed [from the outer world] . . .

> If from among hundreds there are a few
> Endeavoring to practice Dharma from their hearts,
> I say, "Come to this place for the attainment of Buddahood in this life!"
> Practitioners of the inner yogas remove obstructing conditions here . . .
> May there be spontaneous and auspicious benefit for oneself and others.

8. The essence of these preliminary practices was described in a seventeenth-century work entitled *Flight of the Garuda:* "With the conviction that Samsara and Nirvana are of one taste . . . walk, sit, run and jump, talk and laugh, cry and sing. Alternately subdued and agitated, act like a madman. Finally abide in a state of peace and contentedness. . . . Practicing in this way . . . your realization [of mind] becomes as vast as the sky, your meditation naturally radiant and . . . without reference points, prejudice or attachment, your actions become spontaneous . . . and saintly, making no distinction between self and others. Detached from whatever you say, your speech becomes a melodious echo. Without desire for anything at all you are like a garuda soaring through space or like a fearless, intrepid lion . . . free from the beginning, like bright clouds in the sky. . . . See Keith Dowman, translator, *The Flight of the Garruda.* (Boston: Wisdom Publications, 1994).

9. Dudrul Dorje discovered a scroll that Padmasambhava's consort was said to have concealed in a cave on the northern bank of a tributary of the Po Tsangpo River. The terma, or revealed treasure-text, was entitled *Self-Liberation through Hearing of the Great Blissful Land of Pemako*. In it, Padmasambhava announced the conditions for opening the hidden-land:

> In a future age, armies will invade Tibet from
> east and west.
> In order to benefit the suffering Tibetans, I,
> Padmasambhava have prepared the hidden-
> lands.
> Of the many hidden valleys, the most extraordi-
> nary is the great blissful Buddha Realm of
> Pemako.
> Just by recalling it for only a moment opens the
> path to Buddhahood,
> There is no need to mention the benefit of
> actually going there . . .
> Many kinds of samadhi will arise spontaneously
> in one's mind . . .
> The wisdom channels will open . . . .
> I, Padmasambhava, and an ocean of siddhas and
> dakinis as well as peaceful and wrathful
> deities can all be directly seen . . .
>
> A miraculous "power grass" grows there; who-
> ever finds and eats this plant, even old men,
> will become like sixteen-year-old youths . . .
> There is a grass called *tsakhakun*; whoever eats this
> grass can have visions of various celestial
> realms and underworlds.
> There are hundreds of edible fruits
> And numerous grains growing spontaneously.

10. The most extensive descriptions of beyul were unearthed in 1366 by the itinerant lama Rigdzin Godemchen during a period of anarchy and civil war preceding the collapse of the Mongol Dynasty in 1368. His revealed yellow scroll called the *Outer Pass-Key to the Hidden-Lands* contains route descriptions to remote sanctuaries such as Beyul Dremojong in present-day Sikkim. Like a literary treasure map, the texts also gave directions to hidden troves of gold and precious gems specifically designated to finance the expeditions.

In a style common to most neyigs, Godem-chen's texts begin with apocalyptic prophecies of wars and devastation, invoking a time when Tibet will be surrounded on four sides by armies "pressing in like mountains," and "the minds of Tibetans will be lost in enmity and discord, like small birds carried off by hawks." The texts then shift into eulogies for the hidden sanctuaries concealed on the edges of the Tibetan plateau. Some are described as being so inaccessible that they will never be found, but for several, the scrolls offer precise directions. The way is never easy. As Padmasambhava writes: "Without concern for rain, fog, or the venomous vapors of the earth . . . head fear-lessly into the gorges where valleys and forests merge!" (See Sardar-Afkhami, *The Buddha's Secret Gardens* for full translation of Godemchen's text.)

11. In 1717 Mongol hordes again invaded central Tibet, burning and looting monasteries and killing monks and civilians alike. The carnage ultimately led to a great persecution of the Nyingmapas, the followers of Padmasambhava's lineage, by the ascendant Gelugpa, or reformed sect supported by Tibet's Mongol overlords.

The depredations of invading armies coupled with the sectarianism within Tibetan Buddhism itself led many lamas of the old school to believe that the dark age predicted by Padmasambhava had finally come. An Italian Jesuit, Hippolyte Desideri, who lived in Lhasa from 1712 to 1727 studying Tibetan Buddhist texts, shared a similar view. Astounded by the accuracy of the prophecies that Padmasambhava had made concerning the future Mongol and Chinese invasions that had occurred during his residency, he wrote: "These are facts. Let everyone explain so abstruse a mystery according to his own feelings."

12. L. A. Waddell, *Lhasa and Its Mysteries* (New Delhi: Gaurav Publishing House, 1978; Originally published New York: Dutton & Co. 1905), p. 453.

13. Waddell, *Among the Himalayas* (Westminster: Archibald Constable & Co., 1899), p. 66

14. As early as 1854 Major Jenkins, commissioner of Assam, dispatched a traveling mendicant up the lower reaches of the Tsangpo, "but the poor fellow was speared on the frontier by

savages." (See Bailey, *China-Tibet-Assam,* London: Jonathan Cape, 1945, p. 7).

15. See L. A. Waddell, "The Falls of the Tsangpo (San-pu), and the Identity of that River with the Brahmaputra," *The Geographical Journal,* vol. V, no. 3 (London: Edward Stanton, 1895), p. 254:

> As regards the still unsettled question of the identity of the Tibetan Tsang-po with the Brahmaputra, I have seen no reference, in the bulky publications on the subject, to the evidence afforded by etymology. Now, it is interesting to note that the Tibetan word *Ts'ang-pu* is the literal equivalent of the Sanskrit *Brahmaputra,* and means "the son of Brahma." And a curious Tibetan legend associates Brahmaputra with the Tsang-po river near Lhasa. The legend relates how the son of Khri-srong-deu-tsan, who reigned about 750 A.D., was drowned in the river, and the king ordered that the river at that spot should receive a certain number of lashes daily, as a punishment for its crime. After a time the spirit of the river, unable to endure any longer such an unjust punishment, appeared before the king *in the form of Brahmaputra,* and besought the king to cast a piece of wood into the river. On this being done, the wood was immediately carried off downstream. In this way the river-spirit showed that the water which drowned the prince had long since passed on, and that the water at the spot was wholly innocent of the offence for which it was being whipped.
>
> But as Hindu mythological names, such as Brahma, were unknown to the Tibetans before the reign of Srong-tsan-gam-po in the seventh century, A.D., it is practically certain that this interpretation of the Tibetan word, as synonymous with the Indian god Brahma, is of much more modern date, and is, I think, due to the Lamas, like the Brahmans in regard to many of the vernacular river-names of India, having twisted the native name so as to give it a mythological meaning.
>
> For the common Tibetan name for the river is Tsang-po, not Ts'ang-pu, and it means "the pure one," which is a common title of rivers in general, and evidently denoting the well-known character of all great rivers to purify themselves quickly from organic contamination. And this river, as the largest river of central Tibet, is called *"The* Tsang-po" *par excellence;* just as the Ganges and many other great rivers are known to the natives simply as *"the river"* . . .
>
> Still, it is remarkable to find that the etymology of this river is so near to that of Brahmaputra, and that its root is certainly cognate with that of Brahma. And in an indigenous work on the geography of Tibet, [bsTon-pahi-sbyin-bdag-byung-ts'ub, by gLong-rdol Lama, an author who is identified by some with . . . Ngag-wang Lo-zang Gyat'so—the fifth of the so-called Grand Lamas of Lhasa] written about two hundred years ago, the author writes that "the rivers of U-Tsang (i.e. Central and Western Tibet), on uniting, discharge into the Lohita . . ." The *Lohita* is, of course, a classic Indian name for the Brahmaputra river.

16. *Report on the Explorations of Explorer K-P 1880–89 in Sikkim, Bhutan, and Tibet* (Dehra Dun: Office of the Trigonometrical Branch, Survey of India, 1889), p. 15.

17. John Whitehead, *Far Frontiers: People and Events in North-Eastern India 1857–1947* (London: British Association for Cemeteries in South Asia, 1989), p. 146.

18. Sir Thomas Holdich, *Tibet, The Mysterious* (New Delhi: M.C. Mittal Inter-India Publications, 1983; first published London: Alston Rivers, Ltd., 1906), p. 219.

19. In 1898, Lieutenant Colonel Waddell summed up the British government's interest in Tibet:

> This mysterious land has at the present time a very special interest for us. . . . Its gold-mines, which are probably the richest in the world, should alone make it of commercial importance. . . . Much of the country, however, is habitable and has many promising resources undeveloped. And with an English protectorate over Tibet, replacing the shadowy Chinese suzerainty over that country . . . and secured within the English "sphere of interest," England would not only prevent a possible Russian wedge being imposed between her

Indian, Burmese and Chinese possessions, but she would consolidate her position from the Indian ocean to the Northern Pacific, and gain thereby the paramount position throughout Asia.

20. Holdich, *Tibet, the Mysterious*, p. 336. Holdich also recognized the obstacles presented by the hostile tribes on the Tibetan frontier:

These tribes who bar the way are neither Tibetan nor Assamese; their origin and ethnographical extraction is conjectural, and they are in social ethics, in manners and customs, amongst the most irreclaimable savages in the world. We have no influence with Abors and Mishmis; Tibetan priesthood does not touch them, or affect them in any way. The Christian missionary cannot reach them. They are but half-clothed aborigines of those jungles which they infest, and which they are determined to keep to themselves. Above all they are profoundly impressed with the notion that we are afraid of them . . . these savages dance their war dances on their own wild hills and proclaim to the mountains that we dare not cross their frontier. Such action on their part is, of itself, no reason for our interference, but there may be other reasons of which they know nothing which may finally make it imperative that we should move freely through their country. . . . Possibly it will not be long before such action is recognized as essential to the progress of Indian trade.

21. Whitehead, *Far Frontiers*, p. 165.
22. Quoted in Charles Allen, *A Mountain in Tibet*, p. 169.
23. A. Bentnick, "The Abor Expedition: Geographical Results," *Geographical Journal* 41 (1913): 97–114. Quoted in Ken Storm, "The Exploration of the Tsangpo Gorges: The Quest for a Waterfall," in Frank Kingdon Ward, *Riddle of the Tsangpo Gorges* (reprint) (Woodbridge: Antique Collectors' Club, 2001), p. 40.
24. Originally known simply as Peak XV, the mountain which Tibetans knew as Jomolungma, Goddess, Mother of the World, lay beyond British jurisdiction and was trigonometrically measured in 1852 from a ridge above Darjeeling (more than 100 miles away). In 1856 the mountain was renamed after Sir Colonel George Everest, the former Surveyor-General of the Great Trigonometrical Survey of India.

25. At its greatest geographical extent in the years following World War I maps of the British Empire were often centered 40 degrees west of Greenwich, allowing the colony of Australia to be shown twice. The Mercator projections made Canada look far larger than the United States and in many maps only British parts of Antarctica were shown. British territories were shown in red and the popular saying "The sun never sets on the British Empire" implied immortality.

26. Holdich, *Tibet, The Mysterious*, p. 219.
27. Bailey, *No Passport to Tibet*, pp. 25–6.
28. *Clear Light: A Guide to the Hidden-Land of Pemako* from *Three Roots Wish-Fulfilling Jewel* offered spells and incantations to overcome obstructions as well as practical advice for dealing with snakes and insect bites and rituals for appeasing the local guardian spirits. To locate Pemako's innermost secret center was not a matter of crashing through the wilderness. Following the directives of the scrolls, pilgrims painted mantras on their ritual hand-drums as well as on green prayer flags to pacify the nearly incessant rain and snow. As the terma stipulated: "Search for the hidden places like a worm, moving slowly and steadily along the earth. Then stalk them like a wild beast—a leopard or a tiger—without any fear."

29. Bailey learned more about local history and the prophecies that had led pilgrims to settle in this "promised land." In the early 1800s, Monpas from eastern Bhutan and the region of Monyul, in what is now Arunachal Pradesh, had followed mystical texts similar to those that had urged Jedrung and his fellow Khampas into the territory of the Chulikata Mishmis. Pemako's innermost sanctuary was not located on any map and the descriptions in the neyigs were often ambiguous and contradictory. Each lama who opened the way was ultimately guided by visions that illuminated the guidebooks' cryptic accounts. While Jedrung and his fellow Khampas had looked

southeast for the lost paradise, only to be turned back by hostile tribes, the Monpas had headed north up the Tsangpo River toward its innermost gorges, driving the original Lopa inhabitants southward into the jungles of Assam. Despite extraordinary efforts the coveted paradise failed to materialize for any of its seekers. Doubting only their own merit, the Monpas, Khampas, and Pobas who had converged in these wild valleys determined that the time had not yet come for the door to open. Following injunctions outlined in the prophecies, they built temples in the jungles and performed elaborate offertory rites to local spirit-protectors, waiting in this verdant world in hopes that the route would one day be revealed.

The rajah of Powo had assisted the Monpas in their war against Pemako's tribal inhabitants. Once the area was settled, the Pobas lay claim to the entire region and extracted taxes both from the new arrivals as well as from the remaining Lopas. Over time, the Lopas assimilated many aspects of Monpa and Tibetan culture, often adopting their style of dress, language, and Buddhist beliefs. The Lopas who had been pushed across the border into Assam continued to mount raids on the new settlers. As Bailey noted on page 3 of his *Report on an Exploration on the North-East Frontier in 1913* (Simla: Government Monotype Press, 1914):

> For many years the southern border between the Poba territory and that of the independent Abors or Lopas remained undefined and, as is usual with these people, the frontier villages remained in a perpetual state of war. About the year 1905 the Abors raided up the valley and burned the village of Hangjo below Rinchenpung and penetrated as far as Giling. Up to this time the Pobas had allowed the frontier villages to settle their accounts with the Abors as best they could, but they now became alarmed and sent troops into Pemako to help their subjects on the frontier. The Pobas defeated the Abors and forced them to recognize a frontier line. They built a *dzong*, or fort, near Jido which they called Kala Yong Dzong and posted an official there.

Although the colony in Mipi paid no tax to Po Me (Powo), the latter considered them as their subjects and paid the Mishmis for the land on which the Tibetans had settled. The price was twenty-five swords, twenty-five ax handles, two loads of salt, four rolls of woolen cloth, and two Tibetan chubas, or woolen coats.

30. Two years earlier, in 1911, Chinese forces had burned Showa to the ground and decapitated all but the two queens and a fourteen-year-old princess.

31. Sir Richard Burton. *Life*, I, p. 258. Quoted in Fawn M. Brodie, *The Devil Drives: A Life of Sir Richard Burton*. (Eyre and Spottiswoode, 1967), p. 141.

32. Henry Morton Stanley, *African Notebook of 1876* (quoted in Brodie, *The Devil Drives*).

33. George Seaver, *David Livingstone: His Life and Letters* (New York: Harper, 1957), pp. 583, 594.

34. Patrick French, *Younghusband: The Last Great Imperial Adventurer* (London: HarperCollins, 1994), p. 362. Younghusband later reflected humorously on his civilization's mania for appropriation. On a journey to Italy to see the pope he wrote to his daughter Eileen that he had "discovered a brand new lake between Rome and Florence which no European had ever seen before—because no one ever looks out of the window. . . . It was a great find. I could not find out what the natives call it. I shall call it Lake Eileeno."

35. Following his return from Tibet, Bailey headed a British delegation to Tashkent in central Asia, where he served undercover as a secret agent. In these closing years of World War I, Bailey perfected the Pundits' penchant for disguise. So complete was his cover that Bolshevik revolutionaries eventually recruited him to search for an elusive British spy who was no other than Bailey himself.

36. The text had been revealed by Jatsun Nyingpo (1585–1656) and was entitled *Sadhana for Clearing the Obstacles for Entering the Hidden Land of Pemako*. It prescribed ritual smoke offerings made with the flesh of snakes, fish, and birds to clear obstacles on the path. One recipe involved mixing plant resin, sulfur, and white mustard seeds with the meat of a raven or an owl.

37. In the early Buddhist Tantras, pilgrim-

age centered on *shaktipithas,* or places of power associated with the initiate's mystical anatomy. Based on the Tantric vision that the body is a microcosm of the entire universe, the external pithas associated with the chakras and body parts of a cosmic goddess were held to correspond to vital points in the practitioner's own subtle physiology. By practicing at these sites, adepts sought to free the currents of vital energy called *lung* that flow through the body's subtle meridians, or *tsa,* thus aligning themselves with universal energy currents and progressing toward enlightenment.

The locations of the pithas were the antithesis of common ideas of paradise. Charnel grounds and wild jungles frequented by predatory beasts and flesh-eating dakinis offered a more potent context for retrieving repressed contents of the psyche and overcoming the bonds of fear and attachment.

38. Herbert Guenther, *The Life and Teachings of Naropa* (London: Oxford University Press, 1963), p. 26.

39. Ibid., pp. 42, 77.

PART TWO: THE GORGE

1. According to Chinese satellite calculations, the "Yarlung Zangbo Grand Canyon" is 17,800 feet deep and 310.2 miles long with extensive rapids where water flows at up to 53 miles an hour.

2. The malevolent demoness known as the Srinmo was seen as encompassing the entirety of Tibet, a devouring female representing the disowned energies of a warrior culture. With the Jokhang representing a stake through her heart, twelve additional temples were constructed at the corners of three concentric squares spreading out across the Tibetan landscape. The first four immobilized her shoulders and hips, while the next square pinned down her elbows and knees. Four others temples in Tibet's outermost frontiers held down her feet and hands. The monastery at Puchu Serkyi Lhakhang in Kongpo, which Kingdon Ward visited in 1924, secures her right elbow.

3. Research begun in 1994 by the Swiss Federal Institute of Technology in collaboration with earth scientists at the Chengdu Institute of Geology and Mineral Resources

confirm that the Tsangpo's average gradient between Gyala and Medok is nearly 160 feet per mile.

4. Frank Kingdon Ward, *Riddle of the Tsangpo Gorges* (London: Edward Arnold & Co., 1926), p. 205.

5. Following Kingdon Ward's epic quest for the Falls of the Brahmaputra, two other plant collectors—George Ludlow and Colonel Henry Elliot—traveled several days below Gyala in May of 1946, collecting seeds of more than forty species of rhododendrons. Since then, with the emerging threat of a Chinese invasion, no foreign expeditions were admitted into the Tsangpo gorge region until 1991 when a joint Chinese-Japanese team made the first attempt to climb Namcha Barwa—until that time the world's highest unclimbed peak. As Kingdon Ward had written before his death: "Our knowledge of Tibetan geography would be greatly increased by an ascent of Namcha Barwa, and of Gyala Pelri, those twin peaks which stand on either side of the Tsangpo at the gateway to the gorges."

6. Khamtrul Jamyang Dondrup Rinpoche, *The Lama's Heart Advice Which Dispels all Obstacles: A Concise Guidebook to the Hidden Land of Pemako.* Unpublished manuscript, translated by Brian Gregor, 2002.

7. Even Padmasambhava, who first spoke of Pemako as an Elysian haven, narrowly escaped this fate. Toward the end of his sojourn in Tibet, self-serving ministers threatened by his growing influence counseled the king to have him drowned in the Tsangpo:

> This sorcerer and master of various illusions, a savage from the barbaric borderlands . . . adept in evil spells, has deceived Your Majesty's mind . . . He should be thrown in the Tsangpo river before the very eyes of . . . the king, ministers, queens, and everyone else in the country.

8. In the cult of the sublime, "the beautiful elements in nature are the enduring expression of God's loving benevolence, while the vast and disordered in nature express his infinity, power, and wrath, and so evoke a paradoxical union of delight and terror, pleasure and awe." Edmund Burke, the eighteenth-century philosopher in

his greatly influential *Philosophical Enquiry into Our Ideas of the Sublime and Beautiful*, bases the sense of beauty on the passion of love and associates it with pleasure, while "whatever is fitted in any sort to excite the ideas of pain, and danger, that is to say, whatever is in any sort terrible . . . is a source of the *sublime;* that is, it is productive of the strongest emotion which the mind is capable of feeling." M. M. Abrams, *Natural Supernaturalism: Tradition and Revolution in Romantic Literature* (New York: W.W. Norton, 1973), p. 102.

9. Kingdon Ward, *The Riddle of the Tsangpo Gorges*, p. 130.

10. The suture between the colliding continents is further identified by serpentinites, soft green rocks quarried by the local populace to fashion cooking pots.

11. Sometime between 1365 and 1372 the terton Sangye Lingpa revealed a treasure-text from behind the falls called *Shinje Tsedak* (Yamantaka, Lord of Life), in which the dark blue god holds out his hand in the mudra of assurance and in the other holds a blazing jewel. Khamtrul Rinpoche explained that the deity behind the waterfall refers not to actual death but to the momentary transcience of all phenomena, the nature of which is both suffering and liberation. Geographical sites such as the Falls of Shinje Chogyal, Khamtrul said, support what Tibetans call *danang*, or sacred vision, in which perceptions of the environment are transformed and exalted. During his own journey through the gorges Khamtrul had written: "In this supreme of sacred lands, those who exert themselves in spiritual vision will be uplifted by the Buddhas of the ten directions. . . . Whoever travels through this land on pilgrimage . . . will be utterly victorious over the darkness of anger, ignorance, and attachment."

12. In the fourteenth century the terton Sangye Lingpa extracted hidden scrolls from the slopes of Namcha Barwa as did Dudrul Dorje nearly three centuries later. These texts had opened routes into Pemako and the sanctuary said to lie at its heart. Following the directives of the scrolls, the eighteenth-century lama Choeje Lingpa had searched for Pemako's sequestered paradise but died in the jungles before finding it. His lineage of revealed treasures—The Immortal Heart Drop—prospered in the Great Bend region of the Tsangpo gorge, furthered by his reincarnation, Choling Garwang Chimé Dorje. Born into a local Monpa family in 1763, Chimé Dorje ventured deeply into the Tsangpo's innermost gorges in search of the mysterious portal to the lost sanctuary. He was joined in his efforts by two contemporary lamas; Rigdzin Dorje Thokme (1746–97), Limitless Vajra, and Gampopa Orgyen Drodul Lingpa (b. 1757), both of whom enjoyed the patronage of Powo's hereditary king, the Kanam Gyalpo. The three lamas became known collectively as Beyul Rigdzin Namsum, the Three Emanational Awareness Holders Who Opened the Hidden-Land (of Pemako). Protected from invading forces by its extreme topography and ascribed with powerful spiritual energies, Pemako's renown spread throughout the Land of Snows. Choeje Lingpa's revealed terma *Wishfulfilling Light Rays: Opening the Door to the Hidden Land* described it as follows:

The sacred land of Dechen Pemako—
The Lotus of Great Bliss!
Glaciers cover the surrounding mountains,
Below them are walls of rock . . .
Lower down lie forests.
Fruits and medicinal herbs fill the valleys.
The mountains and trees appear like dakas and
    dakinis dancing.
Vast jungles are like demonesses with their manes
    swept back,
And rocky spires rise like piercing weapons.
The rivers roar due to the high passes and
    precipices that seal the boundaries.
There is no danger of invasion from outer forces.
Those who dwell here enjoy the fruits of this
    blissful realm.
The sounds of the elements resound like mantras
    of . . . peaceful and wrathful deities.
The birds that live here have beautiful colors of
    white, yellow, green, red, and blue; their songs
    are the happy sounds of Dharma.
The waters have eight qualities.
And there are hundreds of edible plants . . . and
    varieties of fruits and crops,
Incense-bearing trees, and powerful medicinal
    herbs.
Samaya!

13. The neyigs refer to Dorje Pagmo Ludrolma, "Vajra-varahi in her form of subduing serpents." Lying on her back, her left arm wields a snake and extends into the region of Powo. Her right arm shapes the valley of lower Kongpo and holds a scorpion whose generative organ is held to be located at Gyala. Pemako's most important monastery rises from Dorje Pagmo's navel chakra in the lower Tsangpo valley. Farther south, concealed in vast and luxurient jungles, lies her secret center, the area associated with Yangsang Né, Pemako's still undiscovered paradise.

As a support for meditating on the mind's innermost reality, Dorje Pagmo's sow head ornament and glistening third eye represent the transmutation of ignorance into luminous awareness. Her right hand holds a curved blade that severs all dualistic conceptions of self and other. Her tiara of skulls, bone ornaments, and wild disheveled hair convey freedom from all fears and attachments, while life-enhancing nectar overflows from her human skull bowl. Tibetan texts maintain that Dorje Pagmo's wisdom mind of emptiness and bliss pervades all beings, although they are largely ignorant of it.

14. George Patterson, *Patterson of Tibet.* (San Diego, CA: ProMotion Publishing, 1998), p. 58.

15. Although each of Dorje Pagmo's chakras corresponds to specific topographical features or areas within Pemako, the neyigs differ in their designation, discrepancies based on the differing visionary experiences of individual tertons. While most texts refer to the mountain Gyala Pelri as Dorje Pagmo's crown chakra, the identification of the throat and heart centers varies considerably. More elusive still is the geographical referent for Yangsang Né that some texts say lies in her heart chakra and others in the secret lotus center of her genitalia. Some of the discrepancy is attributable to Tantric practice by which the heart chakra only opens once the lower centers have been activated, their energies blazing upward to illuminate the heart, throat, and crown. Generally, Dorje Pagmo's five principle chakras refer to areas in Pemako encompassing several pilgrimage sites. For example, in the Powo history the five chakras are listed as follows: Crown chakra—Gyala Pelri; throat chakra—Gompo Né to Drakpodrukpuk; heart chakra—Polungpa; navel chakra—Rinchenpung; secret chakra—Ksipa Yudzong. Shepe Dorje, on the other hand, locates the heart center at Rinchenpung and the navel chakra farther south at Drakar Tashi Dzong.

16. The neyigs refer to Pemako as the greatest of all charnel grounds. In this context the charnel ground signifies the world in its most elemental form and the transcendence of fear through Tantric rites. In one practice, yogins and yoginis visualize themselves being ritually dismembered in a charnel ground by a dark emanation of Dorje Pagmo. More elemental still was Padmasambhava's initiation in the charnel ground of Sitavana (Cool Grove) when he was swallowed by a dakini and traveled through her chakras to her secret lotus, the ultimate charnel ground of all. This sense of being devoured and transformed recurs throughout Tantric literature. See Khamtrul Rinpoche's experience of a visionary journey to a paradisical realm as recorded by Edwin Bernbaum in *The Way to Shambala.*

17. Notable discoveries and introductions from the Tsangpo gorges included: *Rhododendron cinnabarinum* spp. *xanthocodon* Concatenans Group ("Orange Bill"), *R. lanatoides, R. venator, R. montroseanum, R. parmulatum, R. leucaspis, Primula florindae, P. cawdoriana, Cotoneaster conspicuous,* and *Berberis calleantha.* These and other species of rhododendrons were planted throughout the British Isles in the first decades of the twentieth century when new introductions and the works of writers such as William Robinson inspired a revolution in gardening tastes. As Ken Cox wrote in a recent (2001) reprint of *Riddle of the Tsangpo Gorges:* "The scale of introductions during this period [1910–50] were [sic] unprecedented both in the number of species and the volume of seed. . . . A number of wealthy landowners such as J. C. Williams, Lionel de Rothschild, Lord Aberconway and others sponsored plant hunting expeditions . . . landscaping their expanding woodland gardens in a 'natural' style, with ponds, streams, ravines and meandering paths, into which they planted the exciting new Magnolias, Rhododendrons, Azaleas, Camellias, and Meconopsis." As Cox

further observed: "They founded the Rhododendrons Society where they competed
amongst each other for ribbons. There was a
neverending stream of spectacular new species
of rhododendrons coming in and they planted
them in the thousands."

Several species of rhododendrons are
indigenous to Europe, six from Western
Europe, and several more from the Turkish-
Russian frontier. Now that *Ledum* are considered part of the genus *Rhododendron,* an
additional two European species can be considered. The "wild" *Rhododendron ponticum* has
flourished in the United Kingdom for at least
300 to 400 years and may have existed there
from before the last Ice Age. The deciduous
azaleas from the eastern parts of the United
States were introduced in the seventeeth and
eighteenth centuries by William Bartram and
other pioneer explorers. One or two Asiatic
species were introduced in the eighteenth
century, includuding *Arboreum.* The tropical
varieties were introduced from the 1750s onward
from Borneo and other parts of southeast Asia.
From 1848 to 1853 Joseph Hooker introduced
many species from Sikkim. All of the species of
rhododendrons brought back by Kingdon Ward
still flourish in British gardens.

18. A year earlier, in 1728, Shepe Dorje had
acted as mediator between the recently installed
7th Dalai Lama and a minister who had ascended to power after bringing to an end a
period of civil war and brutal Manchu oppression. The opening of hidden-lands, like the
construction of stupas and performance of
Tantric rites, was believed by Tibetans to repel
negativity, including the armies still gathered on
Tibet's frontiers.

Although Tibet had been repeatedly invaded
by Mongol armies, the first decades of the
eighteenth century were a period of great
political instability and power struggles between
the Dzungkar Mongols and China's Qing
Dynasty that had asserted hegemony over Tibet.
The 6th Dalai Lama was murdered in 1706 and,
before his successor could be enthroned, armed
Gelugpa monks supported by Mongolian
mercenaries terrorized any Tibetan factions that
opposed the temporal authority of the Dalai
Lama and his regents. An edict put forward by

a scheming Tibetan minister and supported by
the Qing emperor led to severe persecution of
the Nyingmapa sect, which followed the teachings of Padmasambhava. An independent Jesuit
priest resident in Lhasa at that time referred to
the Gelugpas as "deceitful wolves. . . . From
the first of December 1717 until the end of
October 1720 they ill treated and murdered the
monks of [the Nyingma order] and all who
had dealings with them. Many of their monasteries were sacked and destroyed, the richest and
most honoured Lamas were killed, while others
fled deprived of everything and sought refuge
in caverns."

In 1726, when Lelung Shepe Dorje was
twenty-eight years old, he met with Miwang
Sonam Topgyal, a Tibetan minister known also
as Polaney, who over the following two years
was instrumental in ending Tibet's civil war and
mitigating the persecution of the Nyingmapas.
Polaney had received teachings from Jetsun
Migyur Palgyi Dronma (1699–1769), the
daughter of Terdak Lingpa, who was one of the
foremost Nyingma masters of that time. He
also received empowerments and transmissions
from Shepe Dorje who, while nominally Gelugpa, had deep affinity for the more free-roving
style of the Nyingmapas. Despite the renewed
stability following Polaney's rise to power, Tibet
was still threatened by Dzungkar Mongol
troops that had withdrawn to the borderlands.
During this time of political and social turmoil
the hidden-lands of Padmasambhava promised
both refuge and spiritual redemption.

Shepe Dorje's account of his journey,
"Delightful True Stories of the Supreme Land
of Pemako," reveals the spiritual as well as
political forces that underlay the opening of
hidden-lands. A contemporary of the treasure-
revealer Choeje Lingpa who recognized him as
a master of his lineage, Shepe Dorje was sponsored in part by Miwang Sonam Topgyal who
later became Tibet's de facto ruler. Before
departing from Lhasa, Shepe Dorje performed
fire rituals and other rites to remove obstacles
to his impending pilgrimage. He advanced the
political prospects of his primary sponsor by
making feast offerings to the Miwang's principal protector deity. He was instructed in visions
to "meditate on supreme emptiness and gener-

ate great bliss through the union of skillful means and primordial wisdom." By thus building the foundations of meditative absorption, he was told, "the auspicious circumstances will coalesce to open the hidden places of Pemako."

On the second day of the second month of the Female Earth Bird Year (1729) Shepe Dorje began his journey with two spirit mediums—one male and one female—whose trances would later indicate the route they should follow toward their destination, the Secret Forest of the Dakinis in Pemako's innermost center. A protector deity named Mentsun Chenmo spoke through the male spirit medium: "Kyi! I was sent by Padmasambhava to assist the knowledge holders in opening the sacred places of Pemako. I will not deviate from protecting your task. When you and your retinue return safely to your place of origin make offerings to appease me." Nearing the entrance to the Tsangpo gorge, Shepe Dorje performed a ceremony to Dorje Lakpa, the protector of Pemako's western gate, whose "palace" lay amid the ice of Namcha Barwa. Unlike most Buddhist rites, they offered the blood of a black goat and other substances that had been indicated in Shepe Dorje's visions. As the lama wrote:

> It is important here to honor the eight classes of spirits with blood and meat, and each morning to make ritual offerings of fragrant incense and other pleasing substances to the protector deities so as to pass without hindrance.... Write the wishfulfilling prayer of 13 secrets on a red flag and erect it on high ground while reciting mantras. Perform sacred dances and ... play instruments unceasingly. Visualize Padmasambhava on the crown of your head and his attendants at your sides. Invoke the fearsome *mamos* to guide you on the path. If danger approaches, generate the pride of the ferocious mantra protector Lokitriyi and perform the rites of expelling and combustion. Otherwise, visualize ... that Avalokiteshvara [the bodhisattva of supreme compassion] sends forth light rays to eliminate all obstacles. Recite the three sacred syllables and the deity's heart mantra. Imagine that the diseases and magical disturbances caused

by the elements and local spirits all are pacified.

Before departing from Gyala, Shepe Dorje performed Tantric feast offerings to accumulate merit and appease the deities. He followed the directives of the prophecy and enlisted a young girl born in the monkey year to walk ahead of his group bearing the trident of a wrathful protector spirit. Besides a male and a female *kudanpa*, or spirit medium, his party included three yogis, a *siddha* named Sangye Lhundrup, a "woman of good lineage" named Pema Roltso and her attendant, as well as a cook named Dorje Lhunpo, Indestructible Spontaneity. Shepe Dorje wrote that a local guardian spirit entered into one of the mediums and declared: "I have used both peaceful and wrathful methods to impart the blessings and siddhis [of this sacred land] ... To enter through Pemako's western gate recite the wishfulfilling verses of this hidden-land and enter while dancing and singing."

They set out into the gorge playing flutes, drums, and kangling, accompanied initially by an entourage of monks, patrons, and local villagers. "When we passed the gate," Shepe Dorje wrote, "I began to dance and spontaneously sang the following verse: 'Rainbows paint the high blue sky. There lies the spontaneously formed palace of Padmasambhava and his dakini consorts. Please grant common and supreme accomplishments to those fortunate enough to have gathered here ...'" Shepe Dorje then turned into the dense forest and began climbing toward the first pass. "Our continuous dancing, singing, fervent prayers, and sounds of ritual instruments increased our meditative awareness," he wrote. "Our vision expanded without limit and we effortlessly made the difficult ascent."

19. Wordsworth's thought extended themes in *Paradise Lost*, one of the most influential works in English literature. Both Wordsworth and Milton presented life as a pilgrimage from the innocence of undifferentiated consciousness to loss and ultimate reintegration of all that had been divided. This integrative journey necessitates not only the ascent to heaven but an equally vital descent into what Wordsworth

called the "dim uncertain ways" of hell, a sentiment which pilgrims in Pemako would necessarily share.

On his approach to the Tsangpo gorge, Lord Cawdor read a critique of Milton's *Paradise Lost* that had been published in London's *Spectator* in March 1712. (Cawdor's other reading included the Bible—"more because it is such good reading than for any religious reason"—and Boswell's *Life of Johnson* and *Travels in the Hebrides*.) Joseph Addison's critique of *Paradise Lost* and subsequent essays on "The Pleasures of the Imagination" contributed much to the Romantic cult of the sublime and its influence on orthodox religious thought. Addison wrote how "The beauty and grandeur of nature do not exist independently of the human mind but only through interaction between them" and the extent to which the imagination, faced "with the extraordinary degrees of grandeur or minuteness" revealed by concepts of the sublime [largely forwarded by Thomas Burnett's *Sacred Theory of the Earth* (1680)] is "swallowed up in the immensity of the void that surrounds it."

Addison's essay in the *Spectator* on June 23, 1712, prefigures the Victorian fascination with waterfalls and the continued quest for the Falls of the Tsangpo: "There is nothing that more enlivens a prospect than rivers, jettcus [jets of water,] or falls of water," Addison wrote, "where the scene is perpetually shifting . . . and sliding away from beneath the eye of the beholder." Addison's writings suggest clues as to how the Falls of the Tsangpo had grown larger in imagination the more efforts failed to locate it geographically. Writing in 1712 of the poet's prerogative to embellish nature, Addison maintained that, "he can as easily throw his cascades from a precipice of half a mile high as from one of twenty yards . . . in a word, he has the modeling of Nature in his own hands, and may give her what charms he pleases. . . . The understanding, indeed, opens an infinite space on every side of us."

20. The gardens at Auchindoune were laid out in the late 1920s by Jack Cawdor's uncle, Ian Campbell. The young lord had entrusted him with the precious seedlings he had brought back from the Tsangpo gorges as Cawdor's head gardener—who was nicknamed "Deathray"—was notorious for bringing plants to a premature end.

21. Despite the fact that the lotus does not grow in Tibet's mountainous environment, its symbolism was retained as a metaphor for the awakening mind. Buddhist deities are invariably shown seated on lotus flowers symbolizing the mind of enlightenment. These flowers are not simply graphic representations of psychic processes. As a 1996 issue of *Nature* points out, the lotus has the "remarkable ability to regulate the temperature of its blossoms to within a narrow range, just as mammals do. Only two other species of plants have been found to be able to regulate their temperature, both in the eaurum-lily family: the skunk cabbage and a philodendron known as elephant ear. Just how the lotus does it is unknown, but it begins heating up as its flowers start to bloom. Then as the night cools its petals, the flower takes in more oxygen and gives off more carbon dioxide, converting more carbohydrates to energy. As the sun rises, heat production wanes. A single lotus flower can put out one watt of energy. That means that forty lotus blossms can put out the same amount of heat as one living room lightbulb, and seventy flowers can produce the heat of a human being at rest. It is believed that lotus flowers may act to lure in pollinators, most likely beetles. Beetles trapped in a closed blossom all night were found to be very active while inside, spending the night mating and feeding, and emerged covered in pollen and ready to complete their work as pollinators." However potent the metaphor, the lotus itself was unknown in Tibet, as the climate could not support such tropical flora, except perhaps in Pemako. Yet here it was no ordinary lotus that pilgrims sought, but the thousand-petaled lotus symbolizing enlightened awareness.

A Chinese artist once related a story from the Tang dynasty about a man who would sleep at night at the bottom of his wooden skiff, drifting on a lake full of blossoming lotus flowers. The purpose, he related, was not to experience his own dreams, but to dream the dreams of the lotus.

22. Khamtrul Rinpoche offered vivid accounts of these plants in his manuscript, *The Lama's Heart Advice which Dispels All Obstacles:*

The magical herb that increases happiness is white in color and tinged with red. Its five flowering buds smell like elephant bile. Its petals are small and curled like an infant child.

The magical herb that bestows immortality resembles a red lotus flower tinged with black. Its camphor-like aroma spreads in the wind. It has eight leaves and is shaped like a crimson toad.

The magical herb that grants all supreme and mundane siddhis, is a golden flower tinged with red. It exudes a scent of nutmeg. The tips of its six petals are slightly curled; its blue leaves hang upside down like a cuckoo.

The magical herb that empowers one to fly through the sky like the wisdom dakini Dorje Pagmo is a blossoming flower like red coral that has been polished with oil. It has an aroma of aloe wood and the pungent taste of cumin. Its three petals resemble the shape of a garuda [a celestial hawk] soaring in the heavens. Its leaves are formed like a peacock with breasts of lapis lazuli.

The magical herb that reveals intrinsic realization is a blue flower shaped like a bell. A single whiff intoxicates the mind with its scent of white sandalwood. Its petals are contoured like a bulbous and shiny seed in the shape of a vajra. Its leaves resemble the plumes of a small light green rooster.

This describes the five supreme magical herbs that are found in the Hidden-Land of Pemako. During the day they emit a shower of rainbow light while at night they burn like fire, quavering in dancing light. These herbs contain magical power. They are sacred to this holy land and extremely difficult to find.

On the sacramental occasions of the 10th and 25th days of the lunar cycle, pray one-pointedly to Padmasambhava to fulfill . . . the stages of approach and accomplishment of one's yidam [tutelary deity]. In preparing the tantric substances for appeasing the hosts of assembled dakinis, bind the dharma protectors and eight classes of gods and demons through oaths and commands. Throughout all times, encourage them to persevere in their entrusted tasks. Thereafter, by receiving their blessings and power, one will come to behold these five types of supreme medicinal herbs.

Their rays of rainbow-colored light expand over the landscape like a stealthily creeping mouse. Whatever the direction of the wind, these medicinal herbs sway and bend like sharp swords. As they move, their dewlike nectar is flung outward and . . . their secretions can be collected in an oblong spoon like drops of precious jewels. As one ingests their inner essences, the plants' innate blessing power is actualized and one experiences the co-emergence of bliss and emptiness. Physically, one begins to transform into the body of a youthful deva [divinity] and attains immortal life. . . . Pray that all sublime siddhis, both supreme and mundane, be instantly attained—like the sky-delighting dakinis who encircle the world . . .

23. See Herbert Guenther, *The Life and Teachings of Naropa* (London: Oxford University Press, 1963), p. 53: "When [Naropa] was waist-deep in the water, he slipped and went under. Since the water had been disturbed, leeches and other vermin came in swarms and bored into his body. The loss of blood gave him the sensation of being dissolved, and the water flowing into this emptiness made him feel frozen. Tilopa asked: 'Naropa, what is wrong with you?' And Naropa answered: 'I dissolve, I freeze, through the bites of leeches, I am not master of myself and so I suffer.'"

24. The takin has always been a semi-mystical beast in Tibetan belief, and its origins are attributed to the divine workings of a Himalayan saint named Drukpa Kunleg. Villagers in Bhutan wanted proof of the lama's powers, and he asked for a cow, consuming the entire carcass. This was not enough, however, and he then asked for a goat. "This proves only your gluttony," the distressed villagers cried. But then in a Tantric twist, he took the head of the goat and fixed it to the body of the cow, slapped it on its back and sent it bounding off into the mountains.

The takin's taxonomy is equally improbable, its closest relative being the arctic musk ox. Its habitat is confined to the eastern Himalayas. Bailey refered to the takin as "perhaps one of the rarest game animals in the world," not because it was on edge of extinction but because "it happens that its habitat is almost unapproachable." His comments reveal a perception of the natural world conditioned by his own imperial sensibilities in which physical objects were valuable in direct proportion to the degree that they could be possessed.

25. In Tantric Buddhism, hunters also represent the notion of transformation and the deceit of common perception. In one parable, the mahasiddha Naropa encounters a mystic hunter with a pack of hounds who states the following (quoted in Guenther, *The Life and Teachings of Naropa*):

> A hunter, I have drawn the arrow
> Of the phantom body which is free from
>   preferences
> In the bow of radiant light, the essence
> I kill the fleeing deer of this and that,
> On the mountain of the body believing in an I
> Tomorrow I go fishing in the lake.

Hunting even had its Tantric Buddhist proponents. The mahasiddha Maitripa traveled to the jungles in the Himalayan foothills, where he was initiated by a hermit-sage named Savaripa and his two huntress consorts. When he recoiled at their taking of life, one of the reed-clad women replied with this allegorical song:

> In the forests of cyclic existence runs the boar of
>   ignorance
> Releasing the arrow of peneterating wisdom
> I slay the boar of primordial unknowing
> Will you partake of this flesh of non-duality?
> Enjoy the corpse—the Great Bliss!

26. Shepe Dorje's narrative helps illuminate this perspective. "When travelling to these sacred places, fear naturally transforms into great splendour and one remains perfectly at ease. A new spiritual awareness flares up in one's stream of consciousness: a conception-free unity of bliss and emptiness.

"Peculiar sounds are heard from assemblies of female deities, dakinis, and demi-gods (asuras). One hears the sounds of singing, dancing, and hidden instruments. Amidst it all are the spontaneous reverberations of secret mantras and the aroma of sweet smelling fragrances. The shared experience of these occurrences in the minds of different people is sufficient in itself to make these places objects of trust and veneration!"

27. The well-known Tibetan lama Chogyam Trungpa Rinpoche had traveled through Pemako in 1959 while escaping the Chinese invasion. He and his companions had run out of food, but did not realize that they could eat the oddly shaped fruit that dangled above their heads. "Our journey now took us through yet stranger country," Trungpa wrote in his memoirs; "there were all sorts of trees forming a dense jungle with no level spaces; a tangle of mountains with continual rain and mist. For the first time we saw banana trees, but did not know that the fruit was edible and dared not experiment." They resorted instead to boiling and eating their yak-leather bags. Chogyam Trungpa, *Born in Tibet* (London: George Alan & Unwin, 1966), p. 238.

The fruit of the plantain, or cooking banana, is not only edible but its Latin name, *Musa paradisiaca*, denotes a time when it was considered to be the fruit of the tree of good and evil in the Garden of Eden. According to Islamic myth, Adam and Eve concealed their nakedness after the Fall, not with fig leaves, but with the more accommodating leaves of *Musa paradisiaca*. The notion that the fruit of the tree of knowledge was an apple came much later, possibly because, in Roman times, apples were highly regarded and eventually became the standard fruit of Western Europe. The paintings of Adam and Eve that show the first couple beneath an apple tree are all European; other cultures favored different candidates for the forbidden fruit, including the hallucinogenic mushroom *Amanita muscaria*.

28. A news brief in *Outside* magazine later that year (December 1993) stated: "In a world where uncharted territory is increasingly rare, this is the kind of competitive spirit that's come to haunt the exploration of the Tsangpo Gorge."

29. The Puchu Serkyi Lhakhang immobilizes the Srinmo's right elbow. Early in the seventeenth century, the terton Jatsun Nyingpo, Rainbow Heart, had discovered treasure-texts concerning Pemako inside the temple's central

pillar as did the treasure-revealer Rigdzin Chogyur Lingpa a century later.

PART THREE: THE MOUNTAIN

1. Kanjur Rinpoche followed a text entitled *The Bright Torch Guide to the Path to the Secret Land of Pemako* that had been written on sixteen sheaves of birch bark by Jedrung Jhampa Yungney in 1911–12. He followed the milk-white river to its source where he confronted a great waterfall. After days of prayer and meditation, the waterfall stopped of its own accord and revealed a deep cavern leading into the depths of the mountain. With a single attendant, Kanjur Rinpoche entered the cave and followed a passageway that led them to a numinous valley surrounded by glacier-covered peaks and rich in wild fruit and medicinal herbs. They spent three weeks inside the heart-shaped valley, although to them, it had seemed a single day.

2. Bhakha Tulku was born in 1944, three years before the Communist revolution. His Holiness the 16th Karmapa and His Holiness Dudjom Rinpoche had both recognized him at a young age, not only as the tenth incarnation in the Bhakha Tulku lineage, but also as a tulku of the fifteenth-century treasure-revealer Pema Lingpa. At the age of nine, he began a three-year solitary meditation retreat in Powo under the tutelage of a lama named Pulung Sangye Dorje. One month after completing his retreat, he embarked on a six-month pilgrimage through Pemako. Pema Lingpa's teachings had spread throughout Pemako in the 1700s, and as the principal emanation of this revered terton, Bhaka Tulku was responsible for the spiritual welfare of the many temples in Pemako dedicated to the Pema Lingpa lineage. His uncle had traveled through China with Jedrung Trakpa Gyalsten—the reincarnation of Jedrung Jhampa Yungney—and witnessed the beginnings of a major cultural upheaval. Upon his return he urged his extended family members to resettle in the secluded valleys of lower Pemako.

Together with a tutor, two monk attendants, his mother, two younger brothers, and three other families and their servants, Bhakha Tulku crossed the Dashing-La pass from Powo. His father was away on a trading expedition in Kham and his older brother had gone to study in Beijing, as was the custom among noble families.

When Bhakha Tulku and his family members reached Chimdro, they stayed for a month as guests of Jedrung the second. Afterward, he traveled to Kundu Dorsempotrang and, over the next several months, to Rinchenpung and the lower Tsangpo valley, looking for a place where they might settle. In Medok, plans changed abruptly when Bhakha Tulku received news from Dudjom Rinpoche that he was to begin a rigorous course of study at Mindroling, the great Nyingma center of learning a day's journey south of Lhasa. Three years later, after the Communist invasion, Bhakha Tulku fled to India where, in 1969, he married the daughter of the second Jedrung, Thinley Jhampa Yungney, who had settled in Tezu in Arunachal Pradesh.

3. Current statistics from the Lohit district of Arunachal Pradesh (lower Pemako) show an annual rainfall of nearly 40 feet per square meter (12,000 mm). In their September 2000 "Ecological Survey of the Medog Area in the Yarlung Tsangpo Great Canyon National Reserve," George Schaller, Lu Zhi, and Endi Zhang include a graph showing an annual rainfall in Medok of 3,000 mm, or only 10 feet. By comparison, the Amazon receives approximately 9 feet of rain per year, the Pacific Northwest, 7.

4. According to Bhakha Tulku, Powo may have been one of the first places in Tibet to be inhabited. The origin myth of the Tibetan race traces its line of descent to a monkey and rock ogress in the Yarlung valley. As Yarlung is high and arid, there are no monkeys there and Bhakha Tulku believes it more likely that this myth was borrowed from the almost subtropical valley of Powo.

Bailey and Morshead had reached Powo in 1913. A decade later the intrepid French adventurer Alexandra David Neal traveled through the same territory disguised as a Tibetan beggar.

Waddell recounts that in 1793 a detachment of five hundred Chinese soldiers en route from Szechuan to the borders of Nepal lost its way in Lower Po and were so captivated by "the beauty and fertility of the country that the men decided to go no further and to make it their home. They married women of the country and greatly prospered, and their descendants still occupy the land. . . . While Po-tö (or 'Upper Po') is under the rule of Lhasa, Po-Ma is independent in fact, it being under the nominal control of a high Manchu officer stationed at Lhasa who is known as 'Envoy to the Savage Tribes' or 'Third Amban.' Po-Ma is visited by Lao-Shan and Yunnanese traders, and it carries on a large trade with Derge, Jyade, and Lhasa. The horses of Po-Ma are famous throughout Tibet, and its leatherwork, ironwork, and jewelry, as well as the products of its looms, are celebrated and in great demand. The products of the soil are varied and of excellent quality, and altogether this country would seem to be the most fertile spot of Tibet." (Quoted in Waddell, *Lhasa and Its Mysteries*, p. 502.)

5. Bhakha Tulku had explained the origins of the monastery's location. In the seventh century, Tibet's reigning emporer, Songtsen-gampo, had sent his most trusted minister to escort his Chinese bride from the Tang dynasty court. They fell in love, and the minister conspired to take the most circuitous route back to Lhasa as possible. As they entered the Powo valley, the princess gave birth to their stillborn child and consulted geomantic texts to determine the most auspicious burial site. Centuries later, Bhakha (Burial Ground) monastery was built at the site of the grave.

6. Adapted from Lobsang Lhalungpa, translator, *Mahamudra: The Quintessence of Mind and Meditation* by Tagpo Tashi Namgyal (Boston: Shambala Publications 1986), p. 333

7. On the slopes of the Gawalung-La, Terton Taksham Nuden Dorje revealed the terma cycle of Yidam Gongdu and its enumeration of Pemako's twelve outer territories, forty inner ravines, and sixteen secret territories.

8. As described in Padmasambhava's *Luminous Web: Seven Profound Teachings which Open the Gate of the Hidden-land*:

> In the center of Pemako there are five nectar-bestowing plants. Whoever consumes "the excellent plant of miracles" will remain free of all disease and attain miraculous powers. One's body will become youthful and capable

of flying through the sky. Without abandoning the physical body, one can attain celestial realms. . . . Whoever eats the "plant of increasing bliss" experiences the inexhaustible union of joy and emptiness. . . . Whoever partakes of "the plant of purification" dissolves all karmic obscurations and the eighty forms of habitual thought. They will recall countless previous lives. Whoever eats "the plant which severs disturbing emotions," will never think of food or drink . . . and samadhi will arise spontaneously. These are the supreme plants of the realized adepts (siddhas). Whoever eats them will release all blockages of the inner energy channels and directly perceive the realms of the Buddhas.

Lest one imagine that collecting these botanical wonders is an easy task, the text clearly identifies the obstacles:

> This excellent plant . . . will appear instantly to fortunate persons of strong devotion. Those less fortunate whose thought is defiled and those who break their spiritual commitments, for these beings it is invisible!

Nonetheless, the text offers specific instructions for harvesting the mind-altering flora:

> You should approach it slowly like a cat stalking. When you first cut into it, the watery sap should be dropped on the ground. Then comes a milky liquid like a drop of melted butter. This you should consume.

Although research suggests that the Soma preparations of the ancient Aryans included *Nelumbo nucifera*, India's sacred lotus, as well as the hallucinogenic mushroom *Amanita muscaria*, which induces sensations of flight, little mention is made in Tibetan literature of the pharmacopoeia of enlightenment. A well-documented article by Scott Hajicek-Dobberstein in volume 48 (1995) of the American *Journal of Ethnopharmacology* reports the use of the distinctive scarlet and white-flecked *Amanita muscaria*, or fly agaric mushroom, by several Siberian tribes, as well as Nagarjuna, Aryadeva, and other early Tantric Buddhist siddha-alchemists. A section of the eleven-volume *Nyingtik Yabtsi*—a collection of esoteric practices allegedly dating back to the eighth century—clearly describes a vision-inducing preparation made from the tropane alkaloids of Himalayan datura, an eerie plant with spiked leaves and soft white trumpet-shaped flowers that blossom only in darkness.

The exalted accounts of Pemako's magical plants ascribed to Padmasambhava recall the *tangatse* berries ingested by the "lamas" of Shangri-La in Hilton's novel, part of the key to their extreme longevity, along with yogic breathing practices and listening to Mozart played on the piano by bewitching, if hundred-year-old, Chinese nymphs.

9. Official records from 1995 reveal that tigers killed 140 head of cattle and 27 horses. In subsequent years the rate of predation declined. In 1998 only 60 head of cattle and 4 horses were killed. On September 28, 2001, Beijing's state media reported that Chinese scientists planned to spend five million yuan to develop pig farms "in order to feed a rare group of Bengal tigers that have preyed on Tibetan yak herds." The official Xinhua news agency reported that: "at least 20 Bengal tigers live in Tibet at altitudes of more than 4,000 meters on the southern slopes of the Himalayas where they feed on domesticated yak herds in remote Medog county and other areas of southeastern Tibet. . . . The county will ban hunting and encourage local herders to drive the tigers into higher mountains, where the government will provide food from the pig farms, Wang Wei of the State Forestry Bureau told the agency."

10. When the predations of the Mishmi tribes in Mipi proved unrelenting, Jedrung Rinpoche returned to Chimdro with many of his followers and established a temple called Tashi Choeling, Auspicious Place of the Dharma. Jedrung Rinpoche had not stayed long there, nor had he been able to resettle at his monastery in Riwoche in Kham. Conflicts had developed between Jedrung and his main attendant, Garra Lama, who had collaborated with the Chinese. The scheming attendant escaped reprisal but the central Tibetan authorities had arrested Jedrung in his stead. He was placed under house arrest at Talung

monastery north of Lhasa and died ten years later.

In 1919, Jedrung Rinpoche's reincarnation was discovered in Riwoche and, through rigorous tests, another tulku, or incarnation, was found in the Tibetan district of Zayul. Both of the young tulkus were installed at the monastery in Riwoche. At the age of twenty, the incarnation from Zayul, Jedrung Trakpa Gyalsten, married a local woman and settled in Chimdro to head the temple of Tashi Choeling. Peko (short for Pemako) Jedrung, as he came to be known, began sponsoring the construction of shelters along the pilgrims' trail to Kundu, paying local Monpas in mithun cattle for their work. In 1911–12—during his period of confinement—his previous incarnation, the first Jedrung Rinpoche, had composed a guidebook to Pemako's long-sought sanctuary. Written on sixteen sheaves of birch bark, *The Bright Torch Guide to the Secret Land of Pemako* prophesized some forty years before the event, that in the Dragon Year (1951), foreign armies would invade Tibet and wars, famine, and epidemics would follow. Those who did not leave within five years of the Horse Year (1958) would be "chained by the lassoes of the devils." In 1959, when Communist forces overran Tibet, Peko Jedrung fled from Chimdro with his family and nineteen others in the hope of establishing better relations with the Chulikata Mishmis in Mipi. They brought goods to trade, and guns and swords in case negotiations broke down. But obstructions came now not only from the Lopas but from the commander of an Indian border patrol who forced Peko Jedrung and his retinue to settle at a refugee camp in Tezu in Arunachal Pradesh.

11. We weren't the first Westerners to arrive in Chimdro. Bailey and Morshead had come in 1913 on their way from Mipi, and in 1935, an explorer named Ronald Kaulback had ventured through Shingke en route from Burma to the upper Salween River. "Shingke is a meeting-place for Khampas, Pobas, Zayulis, and Mishmis and Abors from the unadministered border territories of Assam," Kaulback wrote. "There Tibetans and Lopa (savages) face each other on the verge of their lands with veiled hostility. The Tibetans call all the jungle tribes Lopa who live in the no-man's land between south-

eastern Tibet and India. The Abors and the Mishmis are the largest tribes, and of these the Abors are still the most bloodthirsty. Tibetans rarely venture through Abor country, which lies to the south and south-west of Poyu. But occasionally, if sufficient numbers can be found, a party of traders or pilgrims will make the journey. Sometimes they get through to India, sometimes they don't." John Hanbury-Tracy, *Black River of Tibet* (London: Frederick Mullen, Ltd., 1938), p. 156.

12. Jean Delumeau, *History of Paradise: The Garden of Eden in Myth and Tradition* (New York: Continuum Publishing Company, 1995), p. 16.

13. Ibid., p. 18. Like early Christian accounts of Eden, Buddhist scriptures described the Buddhist Pure Lands as literal heavens and simultaneously as emanations of states of consciousness. Later Mahayana Buddhist scriptures professed an infinite number of Buddhas, as well as an infinite number of Buddha Fields (*Buddha-Ksetras*): "transcendent universes, created by the merits or the thoughts of the Buddhas" and as "innumerable as grains of sand or pores on the skin." Once the doors of perception are cleansed, the sutras state, the Pure Lands "rise from one's own mind and have infinite form." Edward Conze, *Buddhism: Its Essence and Development* (New York: Philosophical Library, 1951), p. 154.

14. Delumeau, *History of Paradise*, p. 17. The first Buddhist Pure Lands were described in the fourth century C.E. in the *Abhidharmakosa*, a systematic analysis of mind and universe that includes accounts of transitional realms where Buddhas abide before taking earthly incarnations. These richly conjured heavens were elaborated upon in later Buddhist texts and appeared in murals on monastery walls as idealized realms where adepts could aspire to be reborn on their journey toward total liberation. Free of strife and graced with "rows of palms, strings of bells, lotus lakes with jewels, gold, beryl, crystal, red pearls, diamonds and coral," the Buddhist Pure Lands promised postmortem heavens for the faithful, while their earthly manifestations in remote, often inaccessible regions of the Himalayas and beyond offered perennial goals for devout pilgrims. Although not Nirvana, the immortal inhabitants of these

earthly paradises enjoyed unending grace, and ultimate deliverance was ensured for all who gained access.

15. Quoted in Delumeau, *History of Paradise*, p. 48.

16. Ibid., p. 52. The original wording may be found in John Noble Wilford's "The Topography of Myth and Dogma" on page 47 of his book *The Mapmakers* (New York: Vintage, 2001): "Many great lordes have essayed many times to go by those rivers [Ganges, Nile, Tigris, and Euphrates] to Paradise, but they might not spede in theyr way, for some dyed for werynesse . . . some waxt blynde and some defe for noise of the waters, so no man may passe there but through speciall grace of God."

17. In the orthodox Christian view, Adam and Eve's partaking of the forbidden fruit symbolizes man's rejection of God's will and the subsequent loss of the primal unity with the divine represented by Eden. Christian Gnostics, who flourished in the first and second centuries of the Christian era, on the other hand, depicted the story of Paradise as an allegory for deeper truths about human nature.

Like the the Tibetan treasure-texts, the Gnostic scriptures were lost for more than 1,600 years until archaeologists discovered a trove of more than fifty papyrus texts in an earthen jar on a cliff in the Egyptian desert near Nag Hammadi in December 1945, and two years later, the famed Dead Sea Scrolls in desert caves in Israel. Many of the revealed gospels are attributed to Jesus and his disciples, just as the Tibetan termas are ascribed to Padmasambhava.

Unlike their orthodox Christian counterparts, the rediscovered Gnostic texts portray the serpent in the story of Paradise as a teacher of divine wisdom, revealing to Adam and Eve the duplicity of a god who would cast them out of Eden for fear of their eating of the Tree of Life. "What kind of god is this?" wrote the Christian author of the *Testimony of Truth*. In this esoteric reading of Genesis, the forbidden knowledge is less the fruit than the serpent that offers it, the molting snake whose shedding skin suggests mysteries of renewal and transformation. In another Gnostic text, Eve represents perfect primal intelligence and manifests as the serpent to lead humanity to spiritual illumination. Urging the fruit upon the first couple, the snake states: "When you eat of it, your eyes shall open and you shall come to be like gods, recognizing evil and good." Elaine Pagels, *Adam, Eve and the Serpent* (New York: Random House, 1998), p. 67.

Other Gnostics read the story of Adam and Eve as an allegory of the soul's (Adam) discovery of the authentic spiritual self (Eve). A second-century poem called "Thunder: Perfect Mind" presents her—like Dorje Pagmo—as the energy pervading all existence, human and divine.

> I am the first and the last.
> I am the honored one and the scorned one.
> I am the whore and the holy one.
> I am the wife and the virgin.
> I am the bride and the bridegroom,
>   and it is my husband who begot me.
> I am knowledge and ignorance . . .
> I am foolish and I am wise . . .
> I am the one whom they call Life [Eve]
>   and you have called Death . . .

18. Quoted in Michael Tobias, *After Eden: History, Ecology and Conscience* (San Diego: Avant Books, 1985), p. 60.

19. Quoted in Delumeau, *History of Paradise*, p. 110.

20. D. H. Lawrence, *Studies in Classic American Literature* (Garden City, New York: Doubleday & Company, Inc., 1953), p. 152.

21. Research by the mycologist Terence McKenna (see especially *Food of the Gods: The Search for the Original Tree of Knowledge*) suggests that the principal ingredient of soma—the ritual intoxicant of the Vedas—was not *Amanita*, but the more psychoactive and benign psilocybin-containing *Stropharia cubensis*. McKenna also makes a case for *Peganum harmala*, Syrian rue, which occurs widely along the ancient caravan and trade routes of Asia. (A flowering specimen of *Peganum nigellatrum kunge* was collected by one G.M.B or F.M.B [F. M. Bailey?] in the Tsangpo valley on August 21, 1924 at an altitude of 11,500 feet.) Rich in the beta-carboline harmaline, a less toxic and more psychoactive alkaloid than its near relative harmine, which occurs in the

South American ayahuasca plant (*Banisteriopsis caapi*), Syrian rue was first identified with soma in 1794. See *Haoma and Harmaline* by David Flattery and Martin Schwartz (Berkeley, University of California Press, 1989). McKenna speculates that the plant may have been used in synergistic combination with psilocybin-containing mushrooms and possibly influenced the iconography of early Tibetan art. See Terence McKenna's *True Hallucinations* (San Francisco: HarperSanFrancisco, 1993 Cambridge, U.K., Cambridge University Press, 1997). German scientists who first isolated harmaline named it telepathine because of its ability to induce telepathy and clairvoyance.

In *The Plant Book* (Cambridge, U.K.: Cambridge University Press, 1997), D. J. Mabberley writes that *Peganum harmala* was used as a "truth drug" by the Nazis and as an intoxicant in central Asia. Images seen during visions, Mabberly claims, were reflected in Persian art styles and gave rise to the concept of "flying carpets" (cf. flying broomsticks in Europe, perhaps due to Black Henbane, *Hyoscyamus niger* L.). Its oil was used as a dye (Turkish red) for carpets and the brimless felt hats known as tarbooshes.

22. Waddell, *Lhasa and Its Mysteries*, p. 439.

23. John Allegro, *The Sacred Mushroom and the Cross* (London: Hodder & Stoughton, 1970), p. 105.

24. According to a Chinese publication entitled "Economic Macrofungi of Tibet" *Psilocybe coprophila, P. cubenis,* and *P. merdaria* can all be found in Tibet.

25. These recipes include other other exotic ingredients such as madder root, *acacia catechu,* human bone marrow, black hens' eggs, chang, fish brains, owls' eyes, parrots' tails, porcupine blood, jaw bones of tigers, white lotus flowers, peacocks' hearts, red and white sandalwood resin, hyssop, Tibetan tuberose, juniper seeds, barberry, turmeric, eyes of Tibetan antelopes, white goats' milk, gold and turquoise powder, arura (*myrobalan arjuna*), and *piper longum.*

26. As lama Shepe Dorje had proclaimed on his journey through Pemako in 1729: "Identifying with Dorje Pagmo's throat center, or Sambhogakaya chakra, is to abide in the playful union of the cognizance and emptiness of mind itself. At the Nirmanakaya chakra at the

navel one abides in the consciousness that gives rise to appearances. Entering the Dharmakaya chakra at the heart which is empty yet cognizant and which cannot be grasped, is to abide in the primordial purity of enlightened mind."

27. Adapted from *Mother of Knowledge: The Enlightenment of Yeshe Tsogyal* (Namkhai Nyingpo, translated by Tarthang Tulku. Edit. Jane Wilhelm, Dharma Publishing, Berkeley, 1983).

28. Lama Chonam and Sangye Khandro, *The Life and Liberation of Princess Mandarava: Indian Consort of Padmasambhava* (Boston: Wisdom Publications, 1998), pg. 144.

29. Some neyigs—in conformity with other visions—locate Rinchenpung within Dorje Pagmo's heart.

30. Medok once was the seat of a Nyingma monastery called Tambo Gompa. Bhakha Tulku spent three months there during his pilgrimage through Pemako in 1956. The local Monpas had urged him to remain and offered his family rice fields and mithun cattle. With a premonition of what would soon befall Tibet, Bhakha Tulku pressed to stay in Pemako, telling his mother, "If we leave this place we will never meet again." At his tutor's insistence, they left Pemako over the Doshung-La pass. Bhakha Tulku's father met them on the far side of the pass with horses and mules for the onward journey to Lhasa. After Bhakha Tulku entered Mindroling, his mother and father returned to Powo. Fighting with the Chinese broke out in 1958. His father headed the local Powo resistance and commanded a militia of seven hundred men. In 1959, as the Communist forces invaded Lhasa, Bhakha Tulku fled over the Himalayas to Bhutan with his tutor. His mother, father, and other family members had all died during the predations of the Chinese Liberation Army.

36. At the heart of the curriculum was Dudjom Lingpa's treasure-text—*Lamp for Dispelling the Darkness of Ignorance*—that he had unearthed from the Cave of the Great Moon in eastern Tibet. In hermeneutical prose, the terma directs its readers through "the five outer, inner, and secret chakras" and guides them "into valleys shaped like dancing dakinis." The terma states that in the innermost valley, "a river streams from the right eye of Chenrezig [the

Lord of Compassion]." To reach these depths that the terma likens to *Sukhavati*—the Buddha field of Perfect Bliss—the scrolls stipulate that the terton should take the company of a consort born in the year of the bird, horse, mouse, or ox and proceed in "the non-dual state . . . in which emptiness and appearance are one vast expanse." To fulfill the prophecy, a lama from Nangchen named Terton Nangé Orgyen Dorje Dranak offered his daughter to Dudjom Rinpoche, but the synchronicity required to open the door to Yangsang broke when Dudjom Rinpoche's attendant fell in love with the hapless girl.

PART FOUR: THE WATERFALL

1. William Archer's critically acclaimed play, *The Green Goddess*, was first performed in January 1921. It dramatizes the story of two Englishmen and an Englishwoman who crash-land in a fictional Himalayan kingdom lorded over by a highly cultivated, if barbarous, rajah who keeps them as virtual prisoners while lavishing them with every possible comfort. The play dramatizes the imperialist prejudices of the English in India during the height of the British Raj. The play was made into a silent film in 1923 and an early talkie in 1930.

2. Twelve hundred years ago, Padmasambhava came to Terdom with his consort, Yeshe Tsogyal, to escape from Tibet's scheming ministers. They sought refuge in a cave perched more than 17,000 feet above sea level on one of Terdrom's towering limestone escarpments. Yeshe Tsogyal allegedly reached enlightenment there and the cave and the hot springs became focal points for a thriving retreat center for female Tibetan adepts. Several of them, such as Ani Rigsang, spent years in solitary meditation and were widely believed to have attained high levels of realization.

3. See Michael J. Harner, "The Sound of Rushing Water," in Michael J. Harner, ed., *Hallucinogens and Shamanism* (London: Oxford University Press, 1973), and Michael J. Harner, *The Jívaro: People of the Sacred Waterfalls* (New York: Doubleday/Natural History Press 1972).

4. Wade Davis, *Light at the Edge of the World: A Journey Through the Realm of Vanishing Cultures* (Washington, D.C.: National Geographic), p. 86.

5. Michael Tobias, *Environmental Meditation* (Freedom, CA: The Crossing Press, 1993), p. 188, and Melvin Konner, *The Tangled Wing: Biological Constraints in the Human Spirit* (New York: Holt, Rinehart & Winston, 1982).

6. The prospectus for Walker's "Riddle of the Tsangpo Gorges Expedition" began as follows:

> In 1924, Captain F. Kingdon Ward trekked through most of the 200-mile Tsangpo Gorge, accompanied by The Earl Cawdor, eight female Tibetan porters, and a guru named Walrus. His description of the part he could not reach, between the 24,000 foot peaks of Gyala Pelri and Namcha Barwa, reads in part: "There is a legend current amongst the Tibetans, and said to be recorded in certain sacred books kept in the monastery at Pemakochung, that between the Rainbow Fall and the confluence, there are no less than seventy-five of these falls, each presided over by a spirit—whether benevolent or malicious is not stated. Supposing that to be more or less true, and supposing each fall or rapid to be only twenty-feet high, the difference of height is easily accounted for."
>
> This account lays to rest the rumor of a huge waterfall deep within the mountains, and only about five miles of the river's route remain untraveled . . . A small highly skilled and highly mobile team of white-water kayakers and canoeists propose to complete Captain Ward's interrupted traverse.

7. In China, the Taoist master Li Bai (701–61), active during China's golden age of poetry in the Tang Dynasty, produced two highly influential poems about waterfalls. The poems describe standing beneath the waterfalls on Mount Lu and listening to their sounds and observing their textures. These two poems became icons for waterfalls throughout east Asia, influencing art and poetry in Korea and Japan and signifying places of mental and spiritual escape where one could go, at least temporarily, before reentering civic life.

In Japan, poetry and literature invoked indigenous scenic and religious sites as in the twelfth-century novel *Tale of Ise*, which describes a journey to a series of waterfalls and established a pilgrimage ideal of going to sites previously visited by monks, hermits, poets, and artists in order to re-create their original experiences.

8. In a treaty signed jointly by the United States and Canada in 1950, the two nations agreed to reserve sufficient amounts of water for flow over Niagara Falls to preserve their scenic value. The agreement provided for a minimum daytime flow during tourist season of 100,000 cubic feet per second and a minimum of 50,000 at all other times. All water in excess of these amounts, estimated to average about 13,000 cubic feet per second, was made available for diversion for power generation, to be divided equally between the United States and Canada.

9. Riding on the back of a pregnant tigress representing the volatility and potential of every moment and wielding a vajra in one hand and a deadly scorpion in the other, Dorje Drolo is invoked in situations where reason and logic hold no sway over obstructive elements. Padmasambhava is said to have manifested in this radical form to tame the Tibetan borderlands and to transform religious practices based on fear and superstition into ones dedicated to cultivating wisdom and compassion.

10. Women sometimes use bear skins for their traditional goshung; children typically wear ones fashioned from the skin of monkeys. Men usually wear ones made from the hides of the red goral, a small short-horned antelope.

11. See also G.I. Gurdjieff's *Beelzebub's Tales to His Grandson* (New York: Arkana, 1992) and David Hykes's *Harmonic Humi Masters.*

12. The earth's oldest waterfalls originated far earlier, during the late Tertiary period (65,000,000 to 2,500,000 years ago), when episodes of uplift raised the great plateaus and escarpments of Africa and South America. Tisisat Falls at the headwaters of the Blue Nile on the Ethiopian Plateau and Angel Falls in Venezuela both formed as a result of this pre-Pleistocene upward movement of the earth's crust.

13. More than twice as wide and twice as deep as Niagara Falls, Victoria Falls on the

Zambezi River on the Zambia-Zimbabwe border plunges over a sheer precipice to a maximum depth of 355 feet with a mean discharge of 38,000 cubic feet feet per second. A characteristic veil of mist overhangs the falls, for which local tribes named it Mosi-oa-Tunya, the Smoke that Thunders.

The waters at its base churn and foam in a deep pool known as the Boiling Pot, 420 feet beneath the Falls Bridge that was constructed in 1905 as part of the projected Cape to Cairo Railway line that was intended to traverse the entirety of British-held territory on the African continent. At the time the British explorer David Livingstone became the first white man to see the falls on November 16, 1855, several river islands near the brink of the falls were being used by local chieftains to offer libations and other sacrifices to the gods below. Livingstone noted several additional sites at the falls where the Tonga people perfomed sacred rites. He himself likened the rising mists to a flight of angels. Livingstone named the falls after Queen Victoria of the United Kingdom, and his discovery opened the area to European hunters, missionaries, and sportsmen. In 1900, with the signing of a treaty with the local chieftain by the British South Africa Company, European settlers began arriving from the south and a railway line was brought to the falls by 1904, the year of Younghusband's mission to Lhasa. The Falls Bridge was completed in 1905 and a township established that was duly named Livingstone.

14. In Henry Morshead's *Report on an Exploration on the North East Frontier 1913* (Dehra Dun: Office of the Trigonometrical Survey, 1914), he wrote that: "It is noteworthy that the falls of 30 feet on the Tsangpo at Pemakochung are higher than anything hitherto recorded on the big rivers of Tibet and the Himalaya; indeed the only other known instance on a large Himalayan river is the 20 feet fall on the Indus near Bunji." After Kingdon Ward and Lord Cawdor's journey in 1924, the highest documented drop on any major Himalayan river was the 30- to 40-foot falls at Neygyap, ten miles downriver from Rainbow Falls. For comparison it is worth noting that the Hidden Falls of Dorje Pagmo is roughly 50 feet lower than

Niagara (162 feet), but neither are anywhere close to being the world's highest. The highest is Angel Falls on the Rio Caroní in Venezuela which falls 3,212 feet. Second is Yosemite Falls in California, which drops 2,425 feet. Third highest is Marsdalsfossen in Eikesdal, Norway, with a 1,696–foot drop, 974 feet of it uninterrupted. Of all countries, Norway has the greatest number of high waterfalls, including Kile Foss at 1,841 feet and Vettis Foss in Mørkedola at 1,218 feet. The next highest European waterfall is Reichenbach Falls in Switzerland, with a drop of 623 feet.

15. The text further states: "The mind's innate indwelling luminosity is vividly clear without distinctions between nighttime and daytime. . . . The *tigle*, the luminous nuclei (residing in the body) manifest spontaneously without exertion. This is the measure indicating experiential mastery (of this practice)."

16. His Holiness explained that practitioners of the Yoga of the Five Elements meditate successively on the natural sounds of water, earth, fire, wind, and space, allowing them to permeate their consciousness and guide them toward an experience of what he called the Subtle Mind of Clear Light. By cultivating subtler levels of sensory awareness, the practitioner recognizes in the flowing sounds of the elements the nature of mind itself—an unbroken flow of empty radiance. By contemplating Buddha Nature in the roar of falling water, His Holiness asserted, the mind no longer grasps at phenomena, but allows them to pass through consciousness without obstruction—like water flowing over the edge of a falls.

Above the waterfall on the Lukhang mural, a yogi lies on his knees and places his head against the earth. His Holiness referred to a Tantra called *The Illuminating Lamp* that instructs the adept to crouch down above a turbulent waterfall and, with "the gaze of an elephant," direct awareness into the heart of the water. "When you listen continuously to the sound of water," the Tantra states, "the supreme unborn essence will fully emerge. . . . You will come to understand the flow of the mind in future, present and past." Quoted in full in David Germano's "The Elements, Insanity, and Lettered Subjectivity," in Donald S. Lopez, Jr., ed., *Religions of Tibet in Practice* (Princeton, NJ: Princeton University Press, 1997), pp. 328–31.

"These are not outdated practices," His Holiness stated. "They can help the mind to disengage from obscuring emotions and cognitive processes and to develop an inner condition of joy and compassion. The destructive emotions of fear, anger, and greed and the subtle grasping that stems from not recognizing our true nature veils reality itself and leads to great problems throughout the world. These practices pictured on the Lukhang walls are just different methods that Dzogchen has developed to use the circumstances of one's life to overcome disturbing mental tendencies and develop spiritually. It's not that you have to go to a waterfall, but if you're near one it can be very useful."

17. During an audience with the Dalai Lama I asked him why the mind fails to recognize this fundamental unity. "Disturbing emotions have always been part of the human condition," His Holiness answered, "but it is not our essence. When the world is too preoccupied by the external, these impulses grow. They can poison the mind and lead to hatred and oppression. But that destructiveness is not beyond our control. If we reflect on the origin of these destructive feelings, we see that much of the sorrow and helpless anger in our lives is caused not by external events but by the arising of disturbing emotions. The best antidote is to develop mindfulness and awareness of how these impulses arise."

A search for an understanding of human existence beyond the parameters of science and reason had led me into the world of Tibetan Buddhism. But for the past fifteen years, the Dalai Lama had also found inspiration in the work of neuroscientists, cosmologists, and quantum physicists, who explore reality through experimentation, measurement, and logical deduction. These scientists, in turn, had often discovered new ways of approaching their own disciplines through Buddhism's insights into cognition, consciousness, and intention. His Holiness steered our discourse toward what he had learned in this interface between Buddhism and Western science.

"Buddhist teachings stress the importance of understanding reality; they are not based on inflexible beliefs. For 2,500 years Buddhists have investigated the workings of the mind and carried out what could be called 'experiments' to overcome our tendencies toward destructive emotions and to cultivate positive ones. The Buddhist practices for cultivating compassion, equanimity, and mindfulness have deepened our understanding of consciousness and emotions. Beyond any kind of religious faith, they can help one achieve greater peace and equanimity, the foundation for any deeper spiritual development."

His Holiness went on to describe how scientists he had met used imaging devices to show what actually takes place inside the brain. Neuroscientists had revealed that meditation strengthens the neurological circuits that calm the portion of the brain that triggers fear and aggression, His Holiness asserted. Other experiments had used electroencephalographs to measure the brain waves of meditating monks and shown that they had increased activity in those centers of the brain associated with positive emotions such as love and joy.

"You don't have to become a Buddhist or adopt any particular religious faith to develop these qualities," His Holiness said. "Everybody has the potential to lead a peaceful, meaningful life. The key point is mindfulness, a state of alertness in which the mind does not get caught up in thoughts or sensations, but lets them come and go, like watching the flow of a river.

"If we only search outwardly and materially for fulfillment," his Holiness continued, "the world will be filled with frustration and discontent. If we look inside and outside simultaneously . . . without walls or divisions of any kind, our eyes may open to a world such as we have not yet imagined."

He pointed to another image from the Lukhang wall—a painting of one of Padmasambhava's disciples from the eighth century who incarnated 1,000 years later as Dudrul Dorje, the great Pemako Terton. Kyuchung Lotsawa's mastery of yogic powers had enabled him to speak the language of birds, His Holiness asserted. The image showed a beaming monk soaring through the sky, holding on to the tail feathers of two luminously painted birds.

18. Similar apparitions occur regularly at other sacred sites such as Mount Ermei Shan in China's Szechuan province, where devout pilgrims have actually thrown themselves from the summit in hopes of merging with the Buddha-essence. The same phenomena also occurs in the Alps, where the luminous spheres were previously associated with heavenly angels.

19. As catalysts of illumination, dakinis penetrate reified parts of the psyche, areas that have remained dark and hidden, and offer new life in the full, unbounded flow of existence. When Lelung Shepe Dorje traveled through the Tsangpo gorges in 1729, he too experienced the dakinis' nocturnal songs. He also wrote of hearing the spontaneous sounds of musical instruments and of a "sweet smelling fragrance that spreads all around." He also described the "resplendent terror" brought about by Pemako's hazardous terrain: a condition in which one is perfectly at ease amid perilous circumstances and in which "the experience of simultaneous bliss and emptiness ignites one's stream of consciousness."

The Buddhist Tantras assert that dakinis dwell equally in the outer phenomenal world as well as in the subtle energy channels of the adept's body. When duly acknowledged, they sever the cords of positivist thinking that constrain perception and open doors to realms of scintillating interdependence, beyond the boundaries of self-limiting desires. Milton had suggested as much at the end of *Paradise Lost* when he wrote of our mythic progenitors. Having lost their cherished dream of a confined garden, "the *whole* earth now lay before them."

The dream songs of the dakinis—half heard, half imagined, totally unverifiable—had opened us to the ungraspable mysteries of the gap, the innermost landscapes of the heart that open when we abandon efforts to edit experience and flow fearlessly into the mysterious heart of things. There are no doors because there is, in essence, no inside or outside, only what quantum physicists describes as an all-pervading wholeness in flowing movement.

20. In the early nineteenth century, Keats had described something similar as the key to all achievement in art and life: ". . . when man is capable of being in uncertainties, Mysteries, doubts, without any irritable reaching after fact & reason."

21. Fred Allan Wolf, quoted in Richard Leviton's, "Through the Shaman's Doorway" (*Yoga Journal*, July/August 1992).

22. A month after our return from the falls the National Geographic Society issued a press release that acknowledged that "for hundreds of years the Monpa hunters who inhabit the lower Tsangpo gorge have guarded the area [of the falls] from outsiders. For them it is both a place of pilgrimage and a sacred hunting ground. . . . Monpa hunters guided the team into the innermost gorge in pursuit of an answer to the century-old riddle of the falls' existence."

Certainly, the Hidden Falls of Dorje Pagmo was not a true discovery in the outer sense. Just as Arab slave and ivory traders had reached the sources of the Nile long before Sir Richard Francis Burton, John Hanning Speke, or Samuel Baker, there was nothing new in our discovery except the waterfall's height and its subsequent position in the annals of Western exploration.

Controversies that emerged on our return revealed the darker currents of exploration: the ego-driven agendas, jealousies, and competition in the effort to put oneself—as opposed to new landscapes—on the map. (For more on this subject, see Michael McRae's *The Siege of Shangri-La: The Quest for Tibet's Secret Hidden Paradise* [New York: Broadway Books, 2002].) By appropriating remote geographies, explorers brought knowledge of distant lands to their own societies and paved the way for trade in goods and ideas. But even at its best, exploration has often been no more than a veiled attempt to conquer and control.

The accounts of our expedition in the international press prompted a response in the *China Daily* on January 29, 2000. The headline CHINESE EXPLORERS GET TO THE FALLS FIRST brought attention to a previously unreported account of a Chinese military helicopter that had flown over the gorge in 1987 and photographed the area of the hidden falls. But the report acknowledged that no Chinese ever reached the "core section" of the gorge on foot until late 1998—after our expedition. As the *China Daily* article stated:

Although Chinese scientists are surely not short of bravery, rigour and a desire for perfection, they sometimes may be slow to communicate their findings. . . . Although the report on the Society-funded expedition was certainly newsworthy, the area has been no mystery to Chinese explorers. "The four Americans might be the first group of Westerners to catch sight of the waterfall," Yang Yi-chou, a geologist with the Chinese Academy of Sciences (CAS) and one of the four organizers of the expedition, told China Daily in an interview. "But we Chinese were the first to make the actual discovery of the waterfall," Yang said. . . . According to Yang, Che Fu, a Chinese photographer with the People's Liberation Army (PLA) Pictorial, was the first person from outside Tibet to find and record the waterfall on film. . . . While flying across the canyon in an army helicopter, he caught a bird's-eye view of two waterfalls on the Yarlung Zangbo River, which roars through the canyon and becomes the Brahmaputra River after crossing into India.

He took some pictures and showed them to Professor Yang after returning to Beijing. It was the first time Yang obtained concrete evidence of the existence of waterfalls on the main part of the river. "One of the two waterfalls is what the American adventurers call 'Hidden Waterfall,'" Yang said. "We named it No. 1 Zangbo Badong Falls."

In the following years, Yang, along with professors Gao Dengyi, Li Bosheng and Guan Zhihua, also with CAS, trekked into parts of the canyon several times on scientific surveys. It was Yang, Gao and Li who determined in 1994 that the canyon is the deepest of the world, being 5,000 meters deep on average and 496.3 kilometres long. . . . They were not able to explore the core section of the canyon until last October. . . . They found not only the two waterfalls, No. 1 and No. 2 Zangbo Badong Falls, but also two other groups of multilevel waterfalls which were unknown to the world. They were named Rongzha Falls and Quigu Dulong Falls . . .

In actuality, "Rongzha Falls" is the same waterfall that Frank Kingdon Ward and Lord Cawdor reached in 1924 and described in the "Falls of the Brahmaputra" chapter of Riddle of the Tsangpo Gorges. Ken Storm, Ralph Rynning, and I revisited the site in 1996, accompanied by the grandson of Kingdon Ward's 1924 guide.

The China Daily article contains a further misconception when it states that the famous "Rainbow Falls" discovered by Kingdon Ward no longer exists: "During last year's expedition, the Chinese explorers arrived at the site where Kingdon Ward described where he found the falls, but failed to find it. 'We think it was destroyed by an earthquake of magnitude 8.5 (on the Richter Scale) that took place on August 15, 1950,' Yang said."

As Ken Storm wrote in a supplementary chapter of a 2001 reprint of Kingdon Ward's Riddle of the Tsangpo Gorges: "The Chinese speculation that Frank Kingdon Ward's Rainbow Falls may have been destroyed in the Assam Earthquake of 1950 is, of course, incorrect. What they call 'No. 1 Zangbo Badong Falls' is undoubtedly Rainbow Falls although the height given, 33 meters, is too high. 'No. 2 Zangbo Badong Falls' is almost certainly our 'Hidden Falls of Dorje Pagmo.' Their measured height of 35 meters corresponds closely to our own results."

23. On October 22, 2000, The Telegraph reported from Beijing that: "Chinese leaders are drawing up plans to use nuclear explosions, in breach of the international test-ban treaty, to blast a tunnel through the Himalayas for the world's biggest hydroelectric plant. The proposed power station is forecast to produce more than twice as much electricity as the controversial Three Gorges Dam being built on the Yangtze river. The project, which also involves diverting Tibetan water to arid regions, is due to begin as soon as construction of the Three Gorges Dam is completed in 2009." China's official Xinhua news agency reported that the China Water Conservancy and Hydropower Planning and Designing Institute would begin a feasibility study for the proposed hydropower plant in the Great Bend of the Tsangpo in October 2003. "The river drops by 2,755 meters in the 500 kilometer-long U section," the release stated, "leading to a water energy reserve of

about 68 million kilowatts, or one tenth of the national total."

The proposed storage dam would form part of a national strategy to divert water from rivers in the south and west (i.e. Tibet) to more than 600 cities in northern China that suffer from chronic water shortages, Xinhua reported. A 38 million kilowatt power station situated at Medok "would harness the force of a 9,840 ft drop in terrain over only a few miles." From a vast reservoir at the base of the tunnel, the water would be redirected across more than 500 miles of the Tibetan plateau to arid regions of China's Xinjiang and Gansu provinces. The capacity of the station would make it the world's largest power generation facility—more than double the 18 million kilowatt output of the controversial plant at the Three Gorges, which will submerge towns and historical sites and displace more than 1.2 million people. The astronomical cost of blasting the tunnel through Namcha Barwa had not yet been announced, but *The Telegraph* stated that it "appears likely to surpass £10 billion." The *Telegraph* further stated that: "International opposition may bar Beijing from World Bank loans for the project and prevent it from listing bonds and shares on world markets to fund the scheme. If, as its experts believe, China has to use nuclear materials in order to blast the proposed 10–mile tunnel, the country will attract international opprobrium for breaching the Comprehensive Test Ban Treaty."

If the Chinese do proceed with the proposed dam, they will face fierce opposition in India and Bangladesh, where the lives and livelihoods of millions of people along the Brahmaputra would be at the mercy of Chinese dam officials. (Just as thirteen dams that the Chinese have planned along the Salween and others along the Mekhong and Irrawaddy will jeopardize agriculture and increase flood risks in Cambodia, Laos, and Vietnam.) During the dry season, dam officials could withhold water crucial for irrigating Assam's agricultural areas. During the monsoon flood season, they would be compelled to release the swelling reservoirs, with potentially catastrophic consequences downriver. Statements in the Indian press have been alarmist. In New Delhi, the *Daily Times*

reported: "China's move not only threatens the environment but also national security. If Beijing goes ahead with the Brahmaputra project, it would practically mean a declaration of war against India." China's proposed diversion of the Tsangpo would also cripple a highly controversial plan on the part of the Indian government to interlink thirty of its own rivers by 2012.

Tibetans living in exile in India have also voiced strong objections to the proposed dam. A report released in July 2003 by the Tibetan government-in-exile emphasizes that the Tibetan plateau is Asia's principal watershed and the source of its ten major rivers, including the Tsangpo-Brahmaputra, the Indus, the Mekong, the Salween, and the Irrawaddy. Based on findings of the United Nations Development Program, the Asian Development Bank, the World Bank, the International Centre for Integrated Mountain Development (ICIMOD), and other studies, the thirty-page "Tibet 2003: State of the Environment" maintains that gross mismanagement of Tibet's environment during the fifty years of Chinese occupation has resulted in biodiversity loss, grassland degradation and devastating floods in the downstream regions of south and southeast Asia. The report claims that potentially destructive development projects that exploit Tibet's natural resources will in the long run prove disastrous for Tibetans, China, and neighboring countries that depend on the life-sustaining river waters of the Tibetan Plateau. It urges China to "reconsider these big projects and replace them with small-scale development projects that materially benefit the Tibetan people and which do not undermine the integrity of Tibet's ecosystem."

Over the past thirty years, China has built more dams than the rest of the world combined, and thirty-one large hydroelectric projects are currently planned along the Yangtze and its tributaries, the Mekong, the Salween, and the Tsangpo. Yet the nation's push toward rampant industrialization is not without internal criticism. The proposal to dam and divert the Yarlung Tsangpo has drawn fire from several Chinese scientists. Yang Yong, a geologist connected with the 1998 Tenyen Expedition, said the dam could become an economic disaster amid growing signs that the volume of water flowing in the Tsangpo—like that of the Yangtze and Yellow River—is lessening every year. "Environmental conditions in the upper reaches of the Tsangpo continue to deteriorate," he said, "with glaciers receding and tributaries and lakes going dry."

In *Riddle of the Tsangpo Gorges*, Kingdon Ward recounted a prophecy made by Padmasambhava that the waters of the Tsangpo would one day be diverted and flow over the Doshung-La pass. The Chinese seem intent on fulfilling this vision, although in their version, the waters will pass beneath it. Beijing's Chinese Academy of Engineering Physics has recommended that the gargantuan task be accomplished with nuclear explosives. The gorge's seismological instability is well documented. The greatest earthquake ever recorded had its epicenter in the lower Tsangpo gorge in the year of the Chinese invasion, and the Great Assam earthquake of 1897 was possibly even larger. But even if an earthquake-proof dam could actually be constructed, the Tsangpo gorge's unique ecosystem would be destroyed and waterfalls and forests would vanish beneath the rising waters of the artificial reservoir. Where negatively charged ions once ensured one of the purest air qualities on the planet, vegetation rotting in the stagnant waters would give rise to greenhouse emissions. Yet in China's commitment to rapid economic development, what use is an Eden, or nature itself, if it doesn't generate cash? As Chinese vice premier Wen Jiabao stated in a press release: "In the 21st century, the construction of large dams will play a key role in exploiting China's water resources . . . and pushing the national economy and the country's modernization forward."

Communism promised the peoples of China and Tibet a sociological earthly paradise. Yet railways, oil and gas pipelines, petrochemical complexes, hydroelectric dams, airports, highways, military bases, and new cities for migrants from Mainland China have negatively impacted much of Tibet's environment and culture. A dam in the Great Bend of the Tsangpo would destroy one of the earth's most pristine environments, and submerge forever the Hidden Falls of Dorje Pagmo and the regions toward which it leads.

24. Traditional Chinese landscape paintings were called "images of the mind," as painters went to the mountains for inspiration but created the scrolls in their studios. No attempt was made to represent the landscape realistically, nor to trick the mind into a three-dimensional perspective. The paintings distilled the essence of natural scenery and created new, idealized realms that viewers could visit in their imaginations.

25. The Chinese response to nature was not always so positive and, judging by early historical accounts, the wilderness offered neither solace nor delight. In 303 B.C., a banished court official named Chu Yuan wandered through the region of Tung-t'ing lake in northern Ho-nan province, where he found only "dark and interminable forests, the habitation of apes and monkeys. And mountains, wet with rain and mists, so high that the sun was hidden." Quoted in Yi-Fu Tuan. *Topophilia: A Study of Environmental Perception, Attitudes, and Values.* (New York: Columbia University Press, 1974), p. 103.

EPILOGUE: THE VEILS OF PARADISE

1. Quoted in *Nature* (1869), vol. 1, p. 9.

2. On April 9, 2000, a massive landslide—the largest ever recorded in Asia and the third largest in the world—formed a 1.6-mile long barrage of mud and rock on the Yigrong Tsangpo River, a northern tributary of the Po Tsangpo. The river had backed up steadily behind the rubble, creating a lake 10.5 miles long, 2 miles wide, and nearly 200 feet deep behind the earthen barrier. With the onset of summer rains, the water was rising more than six feet per day.

The Chinese Government never reported the landslide, either in state media or the international press. Recognizing the risk of a potentially devastating flash flood, the Chinese People's Liberation Army quietly warned local people in the canyons downstream to evacuate their homes, and a team of soldiers began digging trenches to divert the waters that were building up behind the 200-foot-high wall of mud and rock. By early June, they could not keep pace with the rising water and ordered that the road be closed between Kongpo and

Powo. On the night of June 10, the drainage ditches widened in heavy rain and the dam eventually burst, releasing a tidal wave of mud and water and sweeping away bridges across the Po Tsangpo and Tsangpo rivers.

Authorities in Beijing had not warned the Indian Government of the impending disaster. The flood surged through Pemako without any reported casualties, but it unleashed havoc across the border, destroying more than twenty bridges and submerging fifty-five villages in Arunachal Pradesh and Assam. More than 50,000 people were left homeless, and hundreds were rescued from treetops and rooftops by Indian air force helicopters. A month later, more than one hundred people were still missing, and at least thirty had died, some from what the Indian press called "timber fishing" as villagers sought to harvest precious teak, bamboo, and other varieties of logs that the swirling floodwaters had unearthed from the jungles.

Indian newspapers initially reported that the dam had been an artificial one in the Great Bend of the Tsangpo River and implied that the breach may have been caused by "water mismanagement" on the part of the Chinese. Quoting an anonymous Indian official, the Associated Foreign Press in Arunachal Pradesh's capital, Itanagar, reported on July 10 that, "Preliminary findings suggest the floods in Arunachal Pradesh were due to the breach of a dam on the Tsangpo, as the river makes a turn to enter India." The widely read *Indian Express* quoted Arunachal's state minister of information and public relations, Takam Sanjay: "We strongly believe there could be artificial reasons for the river Siang [the name of the Tsangpo as it flows through Arunachal Pradesh] to flood the hills."

3. Scott Lindgren and other team members filmed the expedition for *Outside* Television Productions. The hour-long documentary, *Into the Tsangpo Gorge*, aired on NBC Sports on May 26, 2002. *Outside Magazine* ran a cover story in July 2002.

4. In 1999, the Tibetan Forestry Bureau mapped out a 3,540 square mile area encompassing Namcha Barwa and Medok and declared it an "ecological reserve." Within months, Beijing upgraded it to national status

and designated the area as the "Yarlung Tsangpo Great Canyon National Reserve."

Ranging in altitude from less than 3,000 feet along the line of control with India to the 25,530-foot-high massif of Namcha Barwa to the west, the reserve is bounded to the north and east by the Kangri Karpo range—a subbranch of the Himalayas with peaks rising to more than 19,000 feet. A northwestern extension continues up the Yigrong River—a tributary of the Po Tsangpo—into the area where the devastating flash flood in June 2000 wreaked havoc in the lower Tsangpo gorge.

The Yarlung Tsangpo Great Canyon National Reserve contains Tibet's last remaining tigers, as well as other rare mammals such as black muntjac and capped leaf monkeys. The project's focus on wildlife and forest conservation has also sought to develop alternative income sources for the reserve's 114 villages and estimated 14,745 residents, many of whom hunt and engage in other ecologically destructive practices such as slash and burn agriculture.

Renowned field biologist and wildlife conservationist George Schaller conducted initial studies of the region's biodiversity in collaboration with the Tibet Forestry Department, but he remained skeptical that the designated reserve would stop the poaching of wildlife or protect the environment unless the government actively prepares and implements a management plan for the reserve.

In Bayi, Ken Storm had learned that the Chinese had grandiose hopes for the region and were actively planning for a major influx of mainland Chinese and foreign tourists. "Holiday villas" were underway to facilitate access to the world's deepest gorge. The remote village of Bayu would become an educational and cultural center where tourists could buy locally produced trinkets and handicrafts.

5. Thoreau, *Journal*, 2.

6. Our minds have no real or absolute boundaries; on the contrary, we are part of an infinite field of intelligence that extends beyond space and time into realities we have yet to comprehend. The beyul and their dakini emissaries are traces of the original world, inviting us to open to the abiding mystery at the heart of all experience, the inseparability that infuses every action, thought, and intention.

Bibliography

Abrams, M. H. *Natural Supernaturalism: Tradition and Revolution in Romantic Literature*. New York and London: W.W. Norton, 1973.

Allegro, John. *The Sacred Mushroom and the Cross*. London: Hodder and Stoughton, 1970

Allen, Charles. *A Mountain in Tibet*. London: André Deutsch Limited, 1982.

Archer, William. "The Green Goddess," 1921.

Aris, Michael. *Hidden Treasures and Secret Lives: A Study of Pema Lingpa and the Sixth Dalai Lama*. New Delhi: Indian Institute of Advanced Study in association with Motilal Banarsidass, 1988.

———. "Report on the University of California Expedition to Kutang and Nubri in Northern Nepal in Autumn 1973." *Contributions to Nepalese Studies*, vol. 2, 1975, pp. 45–87.

Aziz, Barbara Nimri and Matthew Kapstein. *Soundings in Tibetan Civilization: Proceedings of the 1982 Seminar of the International Association for Tibetan Studies Held at Columbia University*. New Delhi: Manohar Publications, 1985.

Bacot, Jacques. *Le Tibet Revolte: Vers Népemako la Terre Promise de Tibetaines*, Paris: 1912.

Bailey, F. M. *China, Tibet, Assam: A Journey, 1911*. London: Jonathan Cape, 1945.

———. "Exploration on the Tsangpo or Upper Brahmaputra." *Scottish Goeographical Magazine*, vol. 30, Feb. 1914.

———. *No Passport to Tibet*. London: Rupert Hart-Davis, 1957.

———. "Report on an Exploration of the North-East Frontier 1913." Simla: Government Monotype Press, 1914.

———. "The Story of Kinthup," *Geographical Magazine* 15 (1943): 426–31.

Bentnick, A. "The Arbor Expedition: Geographical Results." *Geographical Journal* 41 (1913): 97–114.

Bernbaum, Edwin. *The Way to Shambhala.* New York: Anchor Books, 1980.

Bishop, Peter. *The Myth of Shangri-La.* Berkeley and Los Angeles: University of California Press, 1989.

Blondeau, Anne-Marie. "Analysis of the Biographies of Padmasambhava According to Tibetan Tradition: Classification of Sources," in *Tibetan Studies in Honour of Hugh Richardson,* edited by Michael Aris and Aung san Suu Kyi. Warminster, U.K.: Oxbow Books, 1980, pp. 45–52.

Bokenkamp, Stephen R. "The Peach Flower Font and the Grotto Passage," *Journal of Asian and Oriental Studies,* vol. 106, no. 1, 1986, pp. 65–77.

Brauen-Dolma, Martin. "Millenarianism in Tibetan Religion," in *Soundings in Tibetan Civilization,* Proceedings of the 1982 Seminar of the International Association for Tibetan Studies held at Columbia University. Edited by Barbara Aziz and Matthew Kapstein. Delhi, 1985.

Brodie, Fawn McKay. *The Devil Drives: A Life of Sir Richard Burton.* London: Eland, 1986.

Burton, Richard Francis. *Life,* I.

Chang, Garma C.C. *The Hundred Thousand Songs of Milarepa.* Boston and London: Shambhala, 1977.

Chonam, Lama and Sangye Khandro, translators. *The Life and Liberation of Princess Mandarava: The Indian Consort of Padmasambhava.* Boston: Wisdom Publications, 1998.

Clark, Graham. "A Helambu History." *Journal of the Nepal Research Center,* vol. 4, 1980, pp. 1–38.

Cocker, Mary. *Loneliness and Time: The Story of British Travel Writing.* 1992.

Conze, Edward, I. B. Horner, David Snellgrove, and Arthur Waley. *Buddhist Texts Through the Ages.* Boston and Shaftesbury: Shambhala, 1990.

Cox, Kenneth, ed. "Frank Kingdon Ward's *Riddle of the Tsangpo Gorges:* Retracing the Epic Journey of 1924–25" in *South-East Tibet.* Original text by Frank Kingdon Ward, ed. Kenneth Cox. Additional material by Kenneth Cox, Kenneth Storm, Jr. and Ian Baker. Woodbridge, UK: Antique Collector's Club, 2001.

David-Neal, Alexandra. *My Journey to Lhasa.* Boston: Beacon Press, 1986.

Davis, Wade. *Light at the Edge of the World: A Journey Through the Realm of Vanishing Cultures.* Washington, D.C.: National Geographic, 2001.

Delumeau, Jean. *History of Paradise: The Garden of Eden in Myth and Tradition.* New York: Continuum Publishing Company, 1995.

Dhondup, K. *The Water-Horse and Other Years: A History of 17th and 18th Century Tibet.* Dharamsala: Library of Tibetan Works and Archives, 1984.

Diamond, Stanley. *In Search of the Primitive: A Critique of Civilization.* London: Transaction Publishers, 1974.

Diemberger, Hildegard Gemma Maria. "Beyul Khenbalung, the Hidden Valley of Artemesia: On Himalayan Communities and their Sacred Landscape," in *Mandala and Landscape.* Edited by A.W. MacDonald. New Delhi: D.K. Printworld, 1997, pp. 287–334.

———. *The Hidden Valley of Artemisia: Tibetan Sacred Geography as Seen Within the Framework of Representations of Nature, Society, and Cosmos.* Dissertation zur Erlangung des Doktorgrades der

Philosophie an der Grund—und Integrativwissenschaftlichen Fakultat der Universitat Wien, 1992.

Dorji, Tseten. "A Collection of Prophecies of Things to Come and Accounts of Padma-bkod from the Library of Ri-bo-che Rje-drun of Padma-bkod" (*Sbas yul padma bkod kyi lam yig ma 'ongs lung bstan sna tshogs phyogs gcig tu bsdus pa'i Gsung pod*). Tezu, Arunachal Pradesh: published by Tseten Dorji, Tibetan Nyingmapa Monastery, 1974.

Dowman, Keith. *The Flight of the Garuda*. Boston: Wisdom Publications, 1994.

———. *The Power Places of Central Tibet*, London: Routledge Kegan Paul, 1988.

Dudjom Rinpoche, Jikdrel Yeshe Dorje. *The Nyingma School of Tibetan Buddhism: Its Fundamentals and History*. Translated by Gyurme Dorje and Matthew Kapstein. Boston: Wisdom Publications, 1991.

Eisenberg, Evan. *The Ecology of Eden: An Inquiry into the Dream of Paradise and a New Vision of Our Role in Nature*. New York: Vintage Books, 1999.

Elsner, Jas and Joan-Pau Rubiés. *Voyages and Visions: Towards a Cultural History of Travel*. London: Reakton Books, 1999.

Erhard, Franz-Karl. "A Hidden Land in the Tibetan-Nepalese Borderlands," in *Mandala and Landscape*. Edited by A. W. Macdonald. New Delhi: D. K. Printworld, 1977, pp. 335–64.

———. "Political and Ritual Aspects of the Search for Himalayan Sacred Lands," in *Sacred Places and Powerful Places in Tibetan Culture*. Edited by Toni Huber. Dharamsala: Library of Tibetan Works and Archives, 1996.

———. "The Role of 'Treasure Discoverers' and Their Writings in the Search for the Himalayan Sacred Lands." *Tibet Journal*, vol. 19, no. 3, 1994, pp. 3–20.

Ferrari, Alfonsa. *Mk'yen Brtse's Guide to the Holy Places of Central Tibet*. Serie Orientale Roma, XVI. Rome, 1958.

Fletcher, Harold, ed. *A Quest for Flowers*. Edinburgh: Edinburgh University Press, 1975.

French, Patrick. *Younghusband: The Last Great Imperial Adventurer*. London: HarperCollins, 1994.

Germano, David Francis. "The Elements, Insanity, and Lettered Subjectivity," in *Religions of Tibet in Practice*. Edited by Donald S. Lopez, Jr. Princeton, NJ: Princeton University Press, 1997, pp. 328–31.

———. *Poetic Thought, the Intelligent Universe, and the Mystery of Self: The Tantric Synthesis of rDzogs Chen in Fourteenth Century Tibet*. Ann Arbor, MI: UMI Dissertation Information Service, 1992.

George, James. "Searching for Shambala" in *Search: Journey on the Inner Path*, edited by Jean Sulzberger. New York: Harper & Row, 1979.

Guenther, Herbert V. *The Life and Teachings of Naropa*. London: Oxford University Press, 1963.

Hajicek-Dobberstein, Scott. "Soma Siddhas and Alchemical Enlightenment: Psychedelic Mushrooms in Buddhist Tradition." *Journal of Ethnopharmacology* 48 (1995), p. 99–118.

Hamilton, Angus. *In Abor Jungles*. London: Eveleigh Nash, 1912.

Hanbury-Tracy, John. *Black River of Tibet*. London: Frederick Muller, Ltd., 1938.

Harner, Michael J. *The Jívaro: People of the Sacred Waterfalls*. New York: Doubleday/Natural History Press, 1972.

———. "The Sound of Rushing Water" in *Hallucinogens and Shamanism*. Edited by Michael J. Harner. London: Oxford University Press, 1973.

Hilton, James. *Lost Horizon.* New York: William Morrow & Co., 1933.

Holdich, Sir Thomas. *Tibet, the Mysterious.* New Delhi: M.C. Mittal Inter-India Publications, 1983. (First published London: Alston Rivers, Ltd., 1906.)

Huber, Toni. "A Pilgrimage to La-phyi: The Sacred and Historical Geography of a Holy Place in South-Western Tibet," in *Mandala and Landscapes.* Edited by A. W. Macdonald. New Delhi: D.K. Printworld, 1997.

———. "What Exactly are Caritra, Devikota and Himavat? A Sacred Geography Controversy and the Development of a Cult of Tantric Buddhist Pilgrimage Sites." *Kailash: A Journal of Himalayan Studies,* vol. 16, 1990.

Jackson, David. *A History of Tibetan Painting.* Vienna: Osterreichische Akademie der Wissenschaften, 1996.

Kapstein, Matthew. "The Purificatory Gem and Its Cleansing: A Late Tibetan Polemical Discussion of the Apocryphal Texts." *History of Religions,* vol. 28, no. 3, 1989, pp. 217–44.

Karmay, Samten Gyaltsen. *The Arrow and the Spindle: Studies in History, Myths, Rituals and Beliefs in Tibet.* Kathmandu: Mandala Book Point, 1998.

———. *The Great Perfection: A Philosophical and Meditative Teaching of Tibetan Buddhism.* Leiden: E.J. Brill, 1988.

Khamtrul Rinpoche, Jamyang Dondrup. *The Lama's Heart Advice Which Dispels All Obstacles: A Concise Guidebook to the Hidden-Land of Pemako.* Translated by Brian Gregor, 2002.

Kingdon Ward, Frank. "Explorations in South-Eastern Tibet." *Geographical Journal,* February 1926.

———. *Pilgrimage for Plants.* London: George G. Harrap & Co. Ltd., 1960.

———. *A Plant Hunter in Tibet.* London: Jonathan Cape, 1934.

———. *Plant Hunting at the Edge of the World.* London: Victor Gollancz, Ltd., 1930.

———. *Plant Hunting in the Wilds.* London: Adelphi, 1931.

———. *Riddle of the Tsangpo Gorges.* London: Edward Arnold & Co., 1926.

———. "Through the Gorge of the Tsangpo." Manuscript archived at the Royal Geographical Society, London, 1925.

Konner, Melvin. *The Tangled Wing: Biological Constraints in the Human Spirit.* New York: Holt, Rinehart & Winston, 1982.

Lane, Belden C. *The Solace of Fierce Landscapes: Exploring Desert and Mountain Spirituality.* New York: Oxford University Press, 1998.

Lawrence, D.H. *Studies in Classic American Literature.* New York: Doubleday & Co., 1923.

Leviton, Richard. "Through the Shamans Doorway." *Yoga Journal* July/August 1992.

Lhalungpa, Lobsang. *Mahamudra: The Quintessence of Mind and Meditation by Tagpo Tashi Namgyal.* Boston: Shambala Publications,

Lingpa, Jigme. *The Dzogchen: Innermost Essence Preliminary Practice.* Dharamsala: Library of Tibetan Works and Archives, 1998.

Lopez, Donald S. *Prisoners of Shangri-La: Tibetan Buddhism and the West.* Chicago: University of Chicago Press, 1998.

Lyte, Charles. *Frank Kingdon-Ward: The Last of the Great Plant Collectors.* London: John Murray, 1989.

MacDonald, A.W., ed. *Mandala and Landscape*. New Delhi: D.K. Printworld, 1997.

MacDonald, Alexander. "A Nepalese Copper Plate from the Time of Prithvinarayan Shah's Father." *Kailash*, vol. 1, no. 1, 1973, pp. 6–7.

McGregor, John. *Tibet: A Chronicle of Exploration*. London: Routledge & Kegan Paul, Ltd., 1970.

McKay, Alex, ed. *Pilgrimage in Tibet*. U.K.: Curzon, 1998.

Meyer, Karl E., and Shareen B. Brysac, *Tournament of Shadows: The Great Game and the Race for Empire and Central Asia*. Washington, D.C.: Counterpoint, 1999.

Morshead, H. T. *Report on an Exploration on the North East Frontier 1913*. Dehra Dun: Office of the Trigonometrical Survey, 1914.

Mundy, Talbot, *Om: The Secret of Ahbor Valley*. San Diego: Point Loma Publications, 1924.

Namgyal, Maharaja Sir Thutob K.C.I.E and Maharani Yeshay Dolma of Sikkim. *History of Sikkim* (1908), bearing the seal of the India Office Library, dated April 24, 1930.

Norbu, Chogyal Namkhai. *Drung, Deu and Bon: Narrations, Symbolic Languages and the Bon Tradition in Ancient Tibet*. Dharamsala: Library of Tibetan Works and Archives, 1995.

Nyingpo, Namkhai. *Mother of Knowledge: The Enlightenment of Yeshe Tsogyal* translated by Tarthang Tulku. Berkeley: Dharma Publishing, 1983.

Office of the Trigonometrical Branch, Survey of India. *Report on the Explorations of Explorer K-P 1880–84 in Sikkim, Bhutan, and Tibet*. Dehra Dun, 1889.

Official Account of the Abor Expedition 1911–1912, General Staff India, Simla, 1913.

Orofini, Giacomelli. "The Tibetan Myth of the Hidden Valley in the Visionary Geography of Nepal." *East and West*, vol. 41, 1991, pp. 239–71.

Padmasambhava. *Advice from the Lotus Born: A Collection of Padmasambhava's Advice to the Dakini Yeshe Tsogyal*. Kathmandu: Rangjung Yeshe Publications, 1994.

———. *The Light of Wisdom*. *Lamrim Yeshe Nyingpo* with commentary by Jamgon Kongtrul the Great. Boston and London: Shambhala, 1995.

———. *Natural Liberation: Padmasambhava's Teachings on the Six Bardos*. Commentary by Gyatrul Rinpoche. Translated by B. Alan Wallace. Boston: Wisdom Publications, 1998.

Pagels, Elaine. *Adam, Eve, and the Serpent*. New York: Random House, 1988.

Patterson, George. *Patterson of Tibet*. San Diego, CA: ProMotion Publishing, 1998.

Petech, Luciano. *Central Tibet and the Mongols: The Yuan-Sa skya Period of Tibetan History*. Rome: Serie Orientale Roma 64, 1990.

Prats, R. "Some Preliminary Considerations Arising from a Biographical Study of the Early Gter-ston," in *Tibetan Studies in the Honor of Hugh Richardson*. Oxford, 1979, pp. 256–60.

Qui, M. "Tiger-Human Conflict in South-eastern Tibet." *Cat News*, 24:7 (1996).

Qui, M., Zhang, M. and W. Liu, "A Preliminary Study on the Bengal Tiger (*Panthera tigris tigris*) in Namcha Barwa, Southeastern Tibet." *Acta Theriologica Sinica* (in Chinese), 1997, 17(1), 1–7.

Rangdrol, Tsele Natsok. *The Circle of the Sun*. Translated by Erik Pema Kunsang. Kathmandu: Rangjung Yeshe Publications, 1990.

———. *Empowerment and the Path of Liberation*. Kathmandu: Rangjung Yeshe Publications, 1993.

Reid, Sir Robert. *History of the Frontier Areas Bordering on Assam from 1883–1941.* Shillong, 1942.

Reinhard, Johan. "Khembalung: the Hidden-Valley," in *Kailash,* vol. 6. (1978), pp. 5–37.

Rhie, Marilyn M. and Robert A. F. Thurman. *The Sacred Art of Tibet.* London: Thames and Hudson, 1996.

Romm, James S. *The Edges of the Earth in Ancient Thought: Geography, Exploration, and Fiction.* Princeton, NJ: Princeton University Press, 1992.

Sardar-Afkhami, Hamid. *The Buddha's Secret Gardens: End Times and Hidden-Lands in Tibetan Imagination* Dissertation. Cambridge: Harvard University, Department of Sanskrit and Indian Studies, 2001.

Schaller, George B., Endi Zhang, and Lu Zhi. *An Ecological Survey of the Medog Area in the Yarlung Tsangpo Great Canyon National Reserve, Tibet.* Report No. 5 of the John D. and Catherine T. MacArthur Foundation Grant "Biodiversity Conservation in the Himalaya of the Southeast Tibet Autonomous Region," September 2000.

Schama, Simon. *Landscape and Memory.* London: Fontana Press, 1995.

Schell, Orville, *Virtual Tibet.* New York: Metropolitan Books, 2000.

Schweinfurth, Ulrich. "F. Kingdon Ward and His Impact on Western Knowledge of the River Gorge Country of Southeastern Tibet." Heidelberg University, South Asian Institute, Department of Geography, 1974.

Seaver, George. *David Livingstone: His Life and Letters.* New York: Harper, 1957.

Shabkar, Lama and Jatang Tsogdruk Rangdrol. *Flight of the Garuda.* Translated by Erik Pema Kunsang. Hong Kong and Kathmandu: Rangjung Yeshe Publications, 1986.

Shepe Dorje, Lelung. *Delightful True Stories of the Supreme Land of Pemako.* Translated by Lama Ugyen and Ian Baker, 2001. Archived at the Nyingma Institute of Higher Tibetan Studies, Gangtok, Sikkim.

Simmer-Brown, Judith. *Dakini's Warm Breath: The Feminine Principle in Tibetan Buddhism.* Boston and London: Shambhala, 2001.

Snellgrove, David. *Himalayan Pilgrimage,* Boulder, 1981.

———. *Indo-Tibetan Buddhism: Indian Buddhists and Their Tibetan Successors.* Boston: Shambhala, 1987.

Stein, R. A. *Tibetan Civilization.* Stanford: Stanford University Press, 1972.

Storm, Ken Jr. "The Exploration of the Tsangpo Gorges: The Quest for a Waterfall," in *Riddle of the Tsangpo Gorges* (reprint) edited by Kenneth Cox. Woodbridge, UK: Antique Collectors' Club, 2001.

Swinson, Arthur, *Beyond the Frontiers.* London: Hutchinson & Co., 1971.

Tarthang Tulku. "Masters of the Nyingma Lineage," in *Crystal Mirror,* vol.11. Berkeley: Dharma Publishing, 1995.

Thondrup, Tulku. *Hidden Teachings of Tibet: An Explanation of the Terma Tradition of the Nyingma School of Buddhism.* London: Wisdom Publications, 1986.

Thrangu, Rinpoche. *Illusion's Game: The Life and Teachings of Naropa.* Boston and London: Shambhala, 1994.

———. *Songs of Naropa.* Kathmandu: Rangjung Yeshe Publications, 1997.

Tobias, Michael. *After Eden: History, Ecology and Conscience.* San Diego: Avant Books, 1985.

————. *Environmental Meditation.* Freedom, CA: The Crossing Press, 1993.

Trungpa, Chogyam. *Born in Tibet.* London: George Allen & Unwin, 1966.

Tsarong, Tsewang J. *Tibetan Medical Plants.* Kalimpong, India: Tibetan Medical Publications, 1994.

Tsogyal, Yeshe. *The Lotus Born: The Life Story of Padmasambhava.* Boston: Shambhala, 1993.

Tuan, Yi-Fu. *Topophilia: A Study of Environmental Perception, Attitudes, and Values.* New York: Columbia University Press, 1974.

Waddell, L. Austine. *Among the Himalayas.* Westminister: Archibald Constable & Co., 1899.

————. "The Falls of the Tsangpo (San-pu), and the Identity of that River with the Brahmaputra," in *The Geographical Journal*, vol. 5, no. 3. London: Edward Stanton, 1895.

————. *Lhasa and Its Mysteries*; with a Record of the Expedition of 1903–1904. New Delhi: Gaurav Publishing House, 1978. (Originally published, New York, Dutton & Co. 1905.)

Walker, Wickliffe, W. *Courting the Diamond Sow: A Whitewater Expedition on Tibet's Forbidden River.* Washington D.C.: National Geographic Adventure Press, 2000.

Waller, Derek. *The Pundits, British Exploration of Tibet and Central Asia.* Lexington: The University Press of Kentucky, 1990.

Whitehead, John. *Far Frontiers: People and Events in North-Eastern India 1857–1947.* London: British Association for Cemeteries in South Asia, 1989.

Wilford, John Noble. *The Mapmakers.* New York: Vintage Books, 2001.

Wordsworth, William. *The Prelude; or Growth of a Poet's Mind.* London: Oxford University Press, 1960 (Originally published 1805).

Wylie, Turell. *The Geography of Tibet According to the 'Dzam-gling-rgyasbshad.* Serie Orientale Roma, XXV. Instituto Italiano per il Medio ed- Estremo Oriente, Roma, 1962.

————. "The Tibetan Tradition of Geography." *Bulletin of Tibetology*, vol. 2, no. 1, pp. 17–25.

Zangpo, Ngawang. *Sacred Ground: Jamgon Kongtul on "Pilgrimage and Sacred Geography."* Ithaca, NY: Snow Lion Publications, 2001.

TIBETAN TREASURE-TEXTS (TERMA) QUOTED OR REFERRED TO IN THE TEXT

The Bright Torch Guide to the Secret Land of Pemako. A mind-treasure of Jedrung Jhampa Yungney (Jedrung Pung).

"Clear Light: A Guide to the Hidden-Land of Pemako," from the text *The Three Roots Wish-fulfilling Jewel.* Discovered by Rinchen Riwoche Jedrung Pung.

"Clear Mirror for Identifying the Five Miraculous Plants," from a subsection of Padmasambhava's *The Luminous Web: Seven Profound Teachings which Open the Gates of the Hidden-Land.* Revealed by Dorje Thokma.

The Concise Sadhana to Pacify Obstacles and Enter the Hidden-Land. Revealed by Terton Jatsun Nyingpo.

The Delightful True Stories of the Supreme Land of Pemako. Lelung Shepe Dorje, 1729.

"Dispelling Clouds and Increasing Faith: A Guide to Pemako," an excerpt from the *Kathang Treasures.* Discovered by Terton Dudrul Dorje (1615–1672).

Guide to the Heart Center: The All-Gathering Palace of Vajrasattva that Liberates Upon Seeing. Revealed by Pawo Orgyen Chongon.

A Guide to the Hidden Land of Pemako. Discovered by Jatsun Nyingpo (1585–1656).

The Lama's Heart Advice which Dispels All Obstacles: A Concise Guidebook to the Hidden-Land of Pemako. A mind-treasure revealed by Jamyang Dondrup Rinpoche.

A Lamp for Dispelling the Darkness of Ignorance: A Guide to the Most Secret Land of Pemashri. Revealed by Dudjom Lingpa ant Manthang.

Ode to the Sacred Land of Pemako. Composed by Terton Orgyen Dorje Dranak.

Relieving the Darkness of the Heart. Revealed by Terton Dorje Thokme.

Rituals and Rites for Pemako's Protector Spirits, in Accordance with the Blazing Wish-fulfilling Mind that Opens the Gates to the Hidden-Land. Revealed by Terton Dorje Thokme.

Self-Liberation Through Hearing of the Great Blissful Land of Pemako. Discovered by Terton Dudrul Dorje.

Wish-fulfilling Light Rays: Opening the Door to the Hidden-Land and Removing the Heart's Darkness. Discovered by Terton Orgyen Dorje Thokme (1746–1797).

Index

List of Illustrations

I have journeyed to sacred places in utter joy,

Like a swan landing on a lotus lake

And the vase of my heart is filled to the brim with the

Nectar of their sublime qualities.

NGAWANG KUNGA TENDZIN
The 3rd Khamtrul Rinpoche (1680–1728)